Praise for *Remain in Love*

'Frantz has done an effective job of rebalancing the Talking Heads story, offering an angle on the band that fans will relish' *Sunday Times*

'I commend *Remain in Love* to discerning rock fans everywhere' *Observer*

'A memoir as sharp and sometimes caustic as the music they made'
Daily Express

'Amidst the bad blood, Frantz offers charming detail of the band's early years' *Uncut*

'A book by a man who is giving the best impression of someone having all the fun' *The Herald*

'A love letter to both Talking Heads and his wife, the band's bassist Tina Weymouth . . . The book captures 1970s New York, with cameos from Andy Warhol, Brian Eno and James Brown, and makes being in a band sound the most exciting job ever' *Daily Mirror*

'Electrifying. *Remain in Love* is possibly the most uxorious rock 'n' roll memoir ever written' *Wall Street Journal*

'While [*Remain in Love*] does offer a vivid backstage glimpse of New York's downtown scene in the '70s and beyond, what sweetens the read is that even after all these years, the torch Frantz carries for his spouse could still burn down the house' *O, The Oprah Magazine*

'A romance as much as a mer self – is
here for a good time' *Pitchfork*

'[*Remain in Love*] has great stor entures
that Chris and I have shared i say: I'm
gobsmacked. I devoured this and all the love
Chris has for Tina . . . One of the most potent examples of living the dream'
Debbie Harry, musician and author of *Face It*

'Crackling with verve, comedy, calamity, crisp detail, forward motion, and abiding affection, speckled with an all-star cast of punk legends and pop idols . . . a rock music memoir like none other – a candy kiss with a kick to it'
James Wolcott, author of *Lucking Out*

'This swift-paced, well-written book has the upbeat tone of dreams coming true . . . I dare any drummer to write a better book!'
Duncan Hannah, author of *20th Century Boy*

'Heads and drums and funk and roll: herewith Chris Frantz outs himself as a Writing Head and Raconteur First Class'
Charles Shaar Murray, author of *Crosstown Traffic: Jimi Hendrix and Post-War Pop*

REMAIN IN LOVE

TALKING HEADS, TOM TOM CLUB, TINA

CHRIS FRANTZ

WHITE
RABBIT

First published in the United States in 2020 by St. Martin's Press,
an imprint of St. Martin's Publishing Group

First published in Great Britain in 2020 by White Rabbit
This paperback edition published in 2021 by White Rabbit
an imprint of The Orion Publishing Group Ltd
Carmelite House, 50 Victoria Embankment
London EC4Y 0DZ

An Hachette UK Company

1 3 5 7 9 10 8 6 4 2

A CIP catalogue record for this book is
available from the British Library.

ISBN (Mass Market Paperback) 978 1 4746 1514 3
ISBN (eBook) 978 1 4746 1515 0
ISBN (Audio) 978 1 4746 1516 7

Typeset by Born Group
Printed and bound in Great Britain by Clays Ltd, Elcograf S.p.A.

MIX
Paper from
responsible sources
FSC® C104740

www.whiterabbitbooks.co.uk
www.orionbooks.co.uk

For Tina

CONTENTS

ACKNOWLEDGMENTS

Very special thanks to the good people who helped me throughout the writing of this book. Your kindness is greatly appreciated: Elizabeth Beier, Lee Brackstone, Tomas Cookman, Sloan Harris, Daniel Kirschen, Megan Wilson, Rob Filomena, Frank Gallagher, Ira Lippy, Paul Wexler, Wally Badarou, Dolette McDonald, Steve Scales, Ednah Holt, Frederic Serfati, J. R. Rost, Jeff Jones, Duncan Hannah, Marc Kehoe, David Hansen, Lloyd Stamy, Gareth Murphy, Ed Bicknell, Damita Pearson, Lynn Nora, Nicola Mcquaid, Hannah Phillips, Jennifer Sarkissian, and Mia Bohling.

PREFACE

I had the great fortune to not only be a founding member of one of the most unique and exciting rock bands of all time, but to do so alongside the love of my life, Tina Weymouth. Together with David Byrne, and later Jerry Harrison, we created a new paradigm we called "Thinking Man's Dance Music." The name of the band was Talking Heads. We found inspiration in the bands we loved—the Velvet Underground, David Bowie, James Brown, Al Green, Otis Redding, Booker T and the MGs, Kool & the Gang, the Stooges, and the psychedelic garage bands of the sixties—but we didn't sound like anyone else. We didn't copy anyone's style. And no one could copy ours.

I met Tina in painting class at the Rhode Island School of Design and we became young lovers. Tina supported me in my dream to be in a different sort of rock band and, with my encouragement, she eventually became a crucial member of that band and an iconic pioneer for women in music.

We moved to New York City with a plan to make our mark on the history of music and art. We found that we were not alone in this dream. Television, Patti Smith, Blondie, and the Ramones were already there, and seeing them perform at a funky dive bar on the Bowery was all we needed to further inspire us to create new original songs in a style of our own.

You could say that Tina and I were the team who made David Byrne famous. We were very good at shining the spotlight on him. We created

a band that was post-punk before there was Post-Punk, new wave before there was New Wave, and alternative before there was Alternative. We had some hits along the way, too. With "Psycho Killer," "Take Me to the River," "Life During Wartime," "Once in a Lifetime" "This Must Be the Place," "Burning Down the House," and "Road to Nowhere," we enjoyed artistic, critical, and commercial success, a rare combination. We toured with the Ramones, XTC, Dire Straits, B-52s, Pretenders, Eurythmics, Black Uhuru, Simple Minds, the Police, Psychedelic Furs, and Devo, to name a few.

We played on *Dick Clark's American Bandstand*, *Saturday Night Live*, *Late Night with David Letterman*, and *The Old Grey Whistle Test*. We were there for the advent of MTV with our video for "Once in a Lifetime."

Then, during a break from Talking Heads, we did it again with our new band called Tom Tom Club, which sounded completely different from Talking Heads and gave Tina and me our first worldwide hit songs and gold records with "Wordy Rappinghood" and "Genius of Love." Tom Tom Club performed live on *Soul Train* one morning in Hollywood before going over to the Pantages Theater to shoot *Stop Making Sense* with Jonathan Demme directing us as Talking Heads.

Anyone who has been playing music professionally for over forty years has lived a life with many twists and turns. In this book, I will tell you all about them, from our art-school days to our induction into the Rock and Roll Hall of Fame. A number of books have been written about us, but most of them are not very good and none of them have given the reader the true inside story. With *Remain in Love*, I will do just that.

REMAIN IN LOVE

1

THE BEST SEAT IN THE HOUSE

On December 17, 1980, at the Palasport—aka PalaEUR Arena—in Rome, Italy, at 21:00, Talking Heads took the stage. The support band, a well-known Two-Tone ska band called the Selecter, had warmed up the audience to a maniacal point and when I ran up the huge metal ramp to the stage and took my seat on the drum riser behind my Mojave Red Rogers drum kit and looked out at the many thousands of fans, I knew I had the best seat in the house. In the cold gray light of the arena, the mass of mostly young Italian men was swaying, pulsating, and screaming like one huge wild beast. The air was warm and damp and thick with cigarette smoke. This crowd was so overwhelmingly loud that we in the band were taken aback. We'd been touring the world to packed houses everywhere, but no audience compared to this one for its sheer animal intensity. It was almost frightening, like a modern version of the mob in the ancient times of the Colosseum.

From my drummer's throne—that's what they call it—I waited for Tina Weymouth, Jerry Harrison, and David Byrne to strap on their guitars and signal each other that we were ready to rock. Our friend, guitar hero Adrian Belew, was joining us as well. Tina, looking exceptionally fine in a dress she had made herself, a strapless white sheath with a slit on the side all the way up to the top of her thigh, gave her shiny blonde hair a toss and played *boom, boom, boom, boom, boom, boom, boom-boom-boom*. Her familiar introduction to

"Psycho Killer" set off a roar from the audience so loud that I had to ask the monitor man to turn up my monitor so I could hear the band. This was the next-to-last show of the Remain in Light European tour and it was going to be a doozy.

One by one we were joined onstage by the phenomenal Steve Scales on percussion, the wonderful keyboard wizard Bernie Worrell, the gorgeously soulful Dolette McDonald on vocals, and the body-rocking additional bass of Busta "Cherry" Jones. Our energy level was a good match for the audience's. This is the set that we played:

"Psycho Killer"
"Warning Sign"
"Stay Hungry"
"Cities"
"I Zimbra"
"Drugs"
"Once in a Lifetime"
"Animals"
"Houses in Motion"
"Born Under Punches (The Heat Goes On)"

"Crosseyed and Painless"
"Life During Wartime"

ENCORE 1
"Take Me to the River"

ENCORE 2
"The Great Curve"

I was the timekeeper, the groove master, the foundation on which this divinely sexy and artistically compelling music was built. When I think of all the drummers I have heard over the years, the ones I love most are not the ones who play the most technically complex, fast, or difficult parts. I love the drummers who make you want to dance and feel good about yourself. I think of playing the drums the way I think about making love: You should not be frantic. You should not be a show-off. You should not aim to impress. What you should do is be sensitive to the song, the tempo, and the melody. You should serve both the song and the band while occasionally surprising them in a good way. You should be powerful, yet supportive. You should spread the love.

On this December night in Rome, I was feeling my love for our band and especially my love for Tina. Everyone onstage that night was a star, but I was captivated all over again by Tina. She shimmied and bopped and played with a master's authority. I was proud of her and the way we locked together musically. We were playing in what rhythm and blues players call "the pocket." The rest of the band was soaring on top of that. The overall feel transported every soul in the arena to a heavenly climax. On the final encore, as we played "The Great Curve," Tina stepped to the side of the stage and mounted the giant PA speaker tower without missing a beat on her Hofner Club bass until she was standing high atop of us all. The crowd, already ecstatic, had no idea how hard she and the band had worked to reach this moment in time, but I knew. For me, it was a dream come true. Sometimes people ask me if it is hard to play music and tour with my wife. I tell them that I've never known any other way and I love it. I really do. It takes kindness, patience, and a good sense of humor. But most of all, it takes a willingness to accept love and return love. Every man should be so lucky.

2

HOW DID I GET HERE?

When people ask me where I'm from I say Kentucky. I was born on May 8, 1951, in the Army Hospital at Fort Campbell, Kentucky. My father was a tall, good-looking, bright young Army officer named Robert Lewis Frantz and my mother was a real knockout, a Southern belle whose maiden name was Suzanne Holton Allen. They had been introduced by a classmate of my father's at West Point, my mother's brother, my uncle Jim. My mother and her parents had come up to West Point on the train from Kentucky to spend the Christmas holiday with Jim. Cadets were not allowed to leave West Point for holidays, so there were parties and dances for the cadets and their families. It was in this very formal atmosphere that my parents met. There must have been a pretty good spark between them because, out of all the young cadets my mother danced with that Christmas, it was my father that she began a long-distance romantic correspondence with. Letters were posted back and forth from New York to Kentucky every week. After graduating from West Point, in 1946, my father's first post was at Fort Knox, where he did his basic training and could see my mother, who was studying at the University of Kentucky. He was delighted to be able to drive his new Buick, a graduation gift from his father, to court my mother at her parents' home in nearby Louisville. My mother's parents, realizing that his intentions were good, approved of Bob, and soon he and Sue announced their engagement.

They were married in Louisville in a big church wedding on November 20, 1948.

My dad took his new bride on a honeymoon to The Cloister at Sea Island, Georgia, and, following that, they took up residence at Fort Buchanan, just outside of San Juan, Puerto Rico, where he served in the 18th Cavalry. They had a ball in Puerto Rico, swimming in the sea, drinking Don Q rum, and dancing to the latest calypso and mambo records with the other young officers and their wives. The enlisted men gave them a black-and-white cocker

spaniel puppy as a wedding present. My parents named her Missy because that's what all the local ladies called my mother.

I like to think that I was conceived in Puerto Rico. I believe that I was. It sounds so romantic! I must be an island guy in my soul. In late 1950, my father was transferred to Fort Campbell, Kentucky, which is right on the Tennessee border near Clarksville. This was an 18th Cavalry post, meaning lots of trucks, jeeps, and tanks. My father told me a story about a friend of his, hungover from the wild night before at country music star Roy Acuff's Dunbar Cave, sitting on top of a tank turret during some maneuvers, who moved a bit too slowly to get out of the way and got his leg shot by one of his own men. "My God, I've been shot!" he said, calmly looking down at the blood gushing out of his leg. Fort Campbell also became the home of the 101st Airborne Division. The command was comprised of Army pilots and paratroopers and there was much craziness during their activities both on duty and off. Jimi Hendrix was a paratrooper at Fort Campbell in the early '60s. Can you imagine?

My father was a captain by the time I was born. I have no doubt that

my parents were deeply in love and both sides of my family welcomed my arrival. I was named after my father's dad, Charton Christopher Frantz. My grandmother, Ruth Allen, came down on the train from Louisville to help my mother with the baby. I was taught to call her "Mammy" and I developed and held a special bond with her. As far back as I can remember, Mammy told me that I came from a fine family and I didn't have to kowtow to anybody.

Not long after I was born, my father was asked if he would like to study law at Harvard Law School at the Army's expense. They didn't have to ask him twice. My parents packed up their belongings and shipped them to Cambridge, Massachusetts. While my father drove the family station wagon north, my mother and I flew up to Boston. My parents found a nice house to rent in Arlington; it was the setting for my earliest memories.

I remember my mother pleading with me to be quiet as my father studied law in his basement office. I remember standing on the stairs and playing my ten-inch 78-rpm records of "Teddy Bears on Parade" by Jack Arthur and "Rudolph the Red-Nosed Reindeer" by Gene Autry on my wind-up record player. I remember riding on the Swan Boats in Boston Common. I remember the children's Christmas parties at Harvard Law School. I remember being bundled in a snowsuit and my father hoisting me up to sit on his shoulder as we went outside to build a snowman. I remember sitting in my high chair and my mother feeding me delicious things she'd had delivered from S.S. Pierce—that is, until my father found out how expensive delivery from S.S. Pierce was. I remember getting two baby chicks on Easter Sunday and chasing them all over the yard. I remember tasting Indian food for the first time when my mother's friend, Jeri Irani, made dinner for us. I had a little friend named Candy Chimples whose father was also studying at the law school. Our parents became very good friends. Years later, her brother John would handle the projections for the *Stop Making Sense* tour and film. This was a happy time for all of us and, when my father graduated, I know my parents were sorry to go. My mother especially would miss the other law school wives she had made friends with and the quaint ambiance of Cambridge in the 1950s.

The Army assigned my father to the Pentagon and we moved to Fairfax, Virginia. The best memory I have from this time is the birth of my brother Roddy. He was born in the hospital at Fort Belvoir in January of 1955. While my mother was in the hospital, I had a young brown-skinned

babysitter who was sweet as could be and let me watch all the TV I wanted. I was three-and-a-half years old so my viewing was mostly *Captain Kangaroo*, *Mighty Mouse*, and *Howdy Doody*. We also listened to the radio. My favorite songs were "Rock Around the Clock" by Bill Haley and His Comets, "Tutti Frutti" by Little Richard, and "The Ballad of Davy Crockett" by Bill Hayes. When my mother brought Roddy home from the hospital, we had to tone the party down a little bit, but not too much. My parents gave me a Davy Crockett coonskin cap with a tail that I wore for years.

Not long after Roddy was born, my father received orders to go to Korea. He was an Army lawyer now and, following the Korean War, there was much legal work to be done. Most of the fighting was over, but the clean-up operation, both legal and physical, was immense. My mother, Roddy, and I moved in with my grandparents while my father was overseas. They had moved across the river from Kentucky to Indianapolis, Indiana. My grandfather, who we called "Pappy," had become a federal arbitrator, and my grandmother, Mammy, was a buyer of women's lingerie for the L.S. Ayres department store chain. Mammy loved making buying trips to New York City and I enjoyed visiting her at her office, where we would sometimes join her for lunch. In the dining room of the department store there was a huge treasure chest and, after lunch, I was allowed to take some treasure. The little trinkets I retrieved were terribly exciting to a four-year-old with a vivid imagination.

My mother enrolled me in the Peter Pan Nursery School run by two very kind sisters, spinsters who both answered to the name of Miss Walters. They both had hunchbacks. We learned music and art and geography. They taught us how to draw and how to sing. When we had mastered the words and melody to "La Marseillaise," we paraded around the schoolhouse, carrying and waving the French flag. We learned about French food and how to properly pronounce "café" and "croissant." The next week we would learn about Italy or Spain. It was a wonderful nursery school education and I attended both years my father was overseas.

After school I would try to convert my Radio Flyer wagon into an airplane, using the driveway as a runway. When my wagon failed to fly, I remember asking Pappy to help me lift my wagon up a ladder to the roof of the house so that I could take off from there. Instead of saying no, he told me I would need to get a pilot's license first.

On the day my father came home from Korea, there was a big celebration. He brought us all gifts. Mine was a big wooden battery-operated battleship that would remain on my bedroom dresser until I went off to college.

My father announced that his next post would be at the Judge Advocate General's School at the University of Virginia in Charlottesville. We would be moving there in a couple of weeks.

Charlottesville was a sleepy Southern university town back then. My parents bought their first home, a little pale yellow, frame ranch-style house on a half acre of land on Bennington Road in a new development called Hessian Hills. My father put up a really great swing set with a baby swing for my brother Roddy and built a little treehouse for me and my friends.

The backyard abutted a large, shady, ancient forest where I could explore to my heart's content. There was wildlife galore. I remember rabbits and raccoons and deer, but I particularly remember box turtles. I could catch them easily and bring them home. I made a small pen out of chicken wire and fed them little balls of raw hamburger and leaves of farm-fresh lettuce. I also remember poisonous copperhead snakes that lived in and around the

forests and streams. My father warned me about them and taught me how to avoid them. I had recurring nightmares about wading across streams teeming with deadly copperheads and coral snakes.

I had a transistor radio and discovered Elvis Presley. He wasn't known as "The King" yet. He was known as "Elvis the Pelvis" and he rocked the airwaves. "Hound Dog" was his massive hit of the moment and the radio would faithfully play it every hour both day and night. I really loved "Hound Dog," but my mother would roll her eyes and tell me, "Oh, Chris! He is so common!"

I started kindergarten at Belfield School that fall. It was a brand-new small private school built on farmland. It was not unusual to see cows grazing right next to our playground. The classes were small and I made some new friends. I carpooled with my neighbors. One girl and her brother would come over to my house after school to play. She was a year older than I was and, if it was raining, we would go down to the basement to play. We would crawl under my father's homemade desk and she would pull up her blouse and ask me to nurse from her nipples. She would ask me if I was getting any milk and I would stop and say, "No, not yet." Then she would ask me to keep trying. This was her favorite game to play with me, but never with her brother. She told me that would be wrong.

I had a little bike with training wheels that I learned to ride. One day one of the neighborhood kids asked me if I would like to try his big boy's bike. I should have asked him how the brakes worked before I started riding down the steep hill that we lived on. I remember panicking when I realized that I couldn't stop. I just kept riding faster and faster until, finally, I sailed across busy Barracks Road at the foot of the hill, narrowly missing a farm truck, and crash-landed into an electrified, barbed-wire fence. I was pretty cut up from the barbed wire, and the front fender of the bike was all scratched and twisted. Cars whizzed by, but I bravely marched the bike back up the long hill, where the boy was waiting in front of our house with my mother. Relieved to see me still alive, she treated my cuts and scratches with Mercurochrome and Band-Aids. We got the boy's bike fixed, but I still have a scar on one of my eyelids from that episode.

My mother made friends quickly in Charlottesville. Even though she was busy raising two young boys, she volunteered to work at Monticello, the home of Thomas Jefferson. The restoration of Monticello was an ongoing

process and a very meticulous one. Still, there were over 200,000 visitors in 1957. I felt very happy as a six-year-old to be able to roam the grounds and surrounding forest unsupervised. There were all kinds of things to explore, like building sites, archaeological digs, and winding hillside trails. My mother told me, with great pride, that Thomas Jefferson was a distant cousin of ours and that made the dreamy summer afternoons we spent there all the more meaningful to me.

On the weekends that autumn my father would pick up a little extra cash as a high school football referee. He would put on his black-and-white striped shirt, hang a whistle around his neck, and off we would go in the Ford station wagon to schools like Woodberry Forest, Randolph-Macon Academy, and Staunton Military Academy. It was exciting for me to see my father, who always stayed in good shape, running up and down the field. He was a good referee. On the way home we would get a bite to eat somewhere. My father was always good about spending quality time with his children. His own father, Charton, had been just the opposite and, although they were married, had never actually lived with my grandmother, Gladys. Instead, Charton chose to live at the posh Pittsburgh Athletic Club. He owned a bakery and also a whiskey distillery in Berlin, Pennsylvania, called Old Man Frantz Whiskey. When my father was born in Pittsburgh, my grandmother took the baby and moved in with her parents. Her father, John Lewis, had come to Pittsburgh from Newfoundland, where his family had moved from the Isle of Jersey five generations before. They were Grand Banks fishermen who eventually migrated south to Pennsylvania, where the winters were not so long. I never heard my father say a bad word about his father, but he did tell me that his grandfather, John Lewis, was the one who raised him and gave him love and guidance.

Knowing my fondness for animals of all types, my parents gave me a gift of a white rabbit with pink eyes. I called him Pinky. My father built a fine rabbit hutch in the backyard that could be moved inside when the weather got cold. How I loved that creature! I would feed him rabbit food and give him water. We played together in the backyard every day until the day our neighbor's Doberman pinscher, who was normally on a leash, swooped down, grabbed Pinky by the throat, and shook him 'til he was dead. There was much blood and violence and I blamed myself for not protecting the poor bunny. But I was only six years old and the Doberman was only doing

what he had been bred to do. Not long after that I found a wild baby rabbit in my mother's periwinkle beds. When there was no sign of a mother to save him, my own mother allowed me to keep him. He was a cottontail and lived with us for a good long while.

When my father completed his service at the JAG School, he retired from active duty in the Army, but remained an officer in the Army Reserve. He joined a law firm as a junior partner in his hometown of Pittsburgh, where he had many potential clients. We moved there at the end of my first-grade school year. While my mother was pleased about my father's new job, she was not crazy about the idea of moving to Pittsburgh. She loved her life in Charlottesville and all of her friends there. It was a world redolent of history, society, antique dealers, writers, and Southern gentlemen and ladies. It was also a small town full of wild and interesting characters. William Faulkner was the artist-in-residence. When Faulkner's fans would stop to stare at his home, hoping to catch a glimpse of the great man, he was known to come out of the front door, unzip his pants, and pee onto his lawn from the front porch. Teddy Kennedy was at the University of Virginia Law School. His admission to the law school was controversial because he had been expelled from Harvard for cheating. My mother was scandalized to hear that he had abandoned one of his dates on a dark country road late at night when she refused to have sex with him.

We all hated to leave Charlottesville. The last night we were there, after the moving men had packed up all of our belongings, we spent the night with my mother's friend, Smitty, a real estate agent, who sent me out to the stream in her backyard to gather watercress for sandwiches. Being so young, I was not aware of how heavily she was drinking. She just seemed very happy to me. Later that night, after we had all gone to bed, we were awakened by bloodcurdling screams and the sound of footsteps running up and down the halls. My mother and father told me to stay in bed while they went to help Smitty, who was suffering full-blown delirium tremens. This was terrifying to Roddy and me, but my mother kept coming back to tell us that everything was going to be okay. Smitty's son came to her rescue and took her to the hospital. The next day, on the long drive to Pittsburgh, I noticed that my mother was crying, but trying not to let us know.

Our first home in Pittsburgh was a little two-bedroom town house in a suburban development called McKnight Village in the North Hills, where a

lot of young families lived. There were loads of kids my age and we did have fun together. We rode our bicycles for miles. We scaled massive granite walls. We climbed tall trees and sometimes fell out of them, knocking the wind out of our chests.

Musically, it was the heyday of the novelty song. Sheb Wooley's "The Purple People Eater" and Brian Hyland's "Itsy Bitsy Teenie Weenie Yellow Polka Dot Bikini" ruled the airwaves, but no song had greater impact than Chubby Checker's "The Twist." Everyone was twisting. There were Twist parties and Twist contests.

For a long time I was very happy listening to my parents' collection of 78s. They had the Mighty Sparrow, Harry Belafonte, Blind Blake, and lots of other great Calypso artists' records in boxes down in the basement. They had given me a portable record player that would play 78-, 45-, and 33-rpm records. They also gave me a little red plastic transistor radio that I would tune into rock and roll radio stations, like KQV, and the R&B station, WAMO. Like many other kids my age, I listened to the radio in bed at night, imagining that one day I would have a band with a song on the radio.

In 1961, when I was ten years old, I had a young friend who really loved to sing. He had a great voice, deep for a child, but he was shy about singing in front of people. So he would take a long garden hose and sing into one end from behind some bushes while my friends and I would stretch out the hose and listen to his voice through the other end. The kid could really sing like a pro and was willing to sing a song over and over until we got tired of it. One day he sang us a song called "Big Bad John." It was a spoken-word song, sort of a tall tale, about a big, powerful coal-mining hero. There were a lot of coal mines in Pennsylvania and the song seemed very real to us kids. My friend had memorized every word and I liked his a cappella version a lot. Later that same day, I heard the record on my little radio and the DJ said the song was recorded by Jimmy Dean. The backing track was coolly syncopated and reminiscent of Calypso with the sound of a chisel striking a rock in a mineshaft providing the accents. I rode my three-speed bike to Gimbels Department Store and asked for the 45 single version of "Big Bad John." The lady who sold it to me said it was the number one record in the country. It was the first record I ever bought.

My mother and dad decided to build a house of their own in O'Hara Township. Kerrwood Farms was another new development with lots of kids

my age. I was enrolled at Kerr School, which was walking distance from our new house. I remember this period of time so well. I was eleven years old and I was walking to school on a chilly, wet morning in Pittsburgh, Pennsylvania. The sky was gray and flat looking. There was sleet coming down. I was wearing my white Safety Patrol strap and I was supposed to make sure that the other kids didn't get hit by a car. It only took me about ten minutes to walk to school and all the other kids must have been running early or late because I didn't see a soul. Music—"Walk Like a Man" by the Four Seasons—was looping around in my head. I was not feeling very cool at all since my mom made me wear galoshes that morning. I felt, *I may not be cool today but one day I will be cool! I will be an artist, maybe even play in a band!* I felt that *One day, I will be respected and have something important and interesting to say. Girls will pay attention to me! I will go away from here and travel far and, when I come back, the girls will be in awe of my accomplishments and want to talk to me! They will think I am cool and they will want to sit next to me!*

But, sadly, for now, I am only cool to the little kids who look up to me because I am a Safety Patrol who tells them when it is okay to cross the street. Then, as I turn the corner, I see Christine and Benedicte on their way to school. As I watch them walking together, I think they are the prettiest girls in the neighborhood. Then I see Dave, my best friend at the time. Dave waits for me to catch up. I notice that his mom has made him wear galoshes, too, so now I don't feel so bad. We are both a little nerdy in our flannel-lined corduroy trousers and boxy, brown winter coats. Under our knit caps, we have crew cuts. Dave wears braces on his teeth and I wear a retainer. Dave is good at math and science, while I'm not sure I'm very good at anything yet. When we catch up with Christine and Benedicte, we say, "Hi," and I notice that *they* do not have to wear galoshes. I also notice that their penny loafers are really wet and cold looking and have cinders stuck to them. In those days, the cinders from the steel mill furnaces were spread on the icy roads as traction to prevent cars from slipping and sliding. Anyway, Christine and Benedicte don't care. They are giggling and cheerful and say hello to each of us by name. Christine is very tall, blonde, and willowy. She already has the beginnings of a woman's figure. She also has a fantastic sense of humor. Benedicte has moved to our neighborhood from France. She is a slender, petite brunette with a kind of beatnik attitude. She wears a lot of black, unusual for a child in those days, and she seems to be aware of things the

other kids were not aware of yet. Benedicte is cool and Christine is hot! I have a crush on both of them. As we reached the doors of Kerr School, the girls turn to us and say, "See you in band practice!"

There was more than one reason I loved band practice, and I did love it. We would have a couple of group lessons per week during regular classroom hours, and then we would practice all together as a band in the auditorium after school. When I arrived at Kerr, I had been trying to play the trumpet, but it wasn't happening for me. It wasn't for lack of trying. I put in the practice hours, but I wasn't getting anywhere with my horn.

I was very fortunate to have a great band teacher named Jean Wilmouth. He was a mallet instrument guy himself, who played marimba, xylophone, and vibes. When I mentioned to him that I was getting nowhere on my trumpet, he said he thought I had a very good sense of rhythm, so why not try the drums? I just wanted to play music, so I said yes right away, and he gave me a pair of sticks and a practice drum pad, which was a rubber pad mounted on a piece of wood. Then he gave me a quick run through of drum rudiments and a beginner's book and told me to start practicing. I did practice and I practiced hard. You begin with a single stroke roll, then you learn a double stroke roll, then a five stroke, then a seven stroke. I got good at these before I moved on to paradiddles and ratamacues. What, you may ask, is a paradiddle? It's when you hit the drum one time with your left stick and again with your right stick and then twice with your left again. Then you hit it once with your right stick, once with your left, and twice again with your right. LRLL, RLRR, you repeat the pattern while slowly increasing the tempo, preferably with a metronome, until you have a smooth, repetitive pattern. The ratamacue is a single-stroke roll with a "drag" at the top of the pattern. It makes for a good basic drum fill. LRLR, RLRL. I got good at these, too. After a couple of months, I had a seat with the drum section of the school band. Boy, was I happy! Now, we are not talking drum kits or even rock and roll. We are talking one single snare drum on a stand. They always had the biggest guy play the bass drum, so that was not for me, although I did get to crash the cymbals from time to time. We learned to play songs by George Gershwin, Aaron Copland, and Scott Joplin. Particular favorites of mine were "Stranger in Paradise" by Alexander Borodin and "Begin the Beguine" by Cole Porter. We also performed a song that was at the top of the charts at the time called "Java." It was recorded by New Or-

leans trumpeter Al Hirt and composed by the great Allen Toussaint. On that tune I played only the ride cymbal, but this was my introduction to the feel of syncopation, which was a real ear-opener for me. Now I could imagine beats that had rhythmic surprises that make people want to swing their hips and dance.

When I was twelve years old my little sister, Ruthie, was born. It was Sunday, May 26, and I had been an acolyte at church that morning. When my father pulled in the driveway, my grandfather Pappy came flying down the backyard stairs to tell us it was time to take my mother to the hospital. I had never seen him move so quickly. Roddy and I were so excited that we were actually jumping up and down. Later that evening, we got a call from our father telling us with great pride, "Chris and Roddy, you have a baby sister!" Ruthie, who got beauty *and* the brains! She would grow into a bright and beautiful woman with a good head for business who never fails to be kind, helpful, and understanding.

One Sunday evening in 1964, after dinner, my family was watching the *Ed Sullivan Show* as we did almost every Sunday. When Ed Sullivan introduced the Beatles to America in a theater of frenzied, screaming young girls, like many other young people I had an epiphany. This band made everyone feel that each song spoke directly to them. I sat there on the family couch watching them on our portable black-and-white television set with its rabbit-ear antenna and I was immediately transported to a better place. I felt warm and positively optimistic. Even my mother loved the Beatles, causing my father to tease, "Oh, Suzanne, you are such an Anglophile!" On the school bus the next morning, the girls were already singing Beatles songs in unison. The advent of the Beatles and "the British Invasion" that followed was, and still is, one of the most culturally important events of my lifetime.

In 1964, at Aspinwall Junior High School, my band teacher Mr. Springman believed that band class was just as important, if not more so, as any other academic subject and he ran a tight ship. If you weren't with the program, he kicked you out. I was thrilled when he asked me to create a marching cadence for the band's appearance in the Memorial Day parade. I still remember it, too.

I joined a group of friends from the school band to play some rock and roll and impress the girls. Lloyd Stamy was and still is a real go-getter. Together with some other school bandmates, he created the first rock and

Family Portrait, 1963.

roll band I was a part of. Lloyd was the lead singer and also played trumpet. Ernie Maynard played trombone. Ray Bayer, who played clarinet in the school band, was on electric guitar. Herbie Purcell played a bass guitar. At some point Tom Kleeb joined us on guitar, too. We mostly just practiced a lot, learning a repertoire of Beatles, Beach Boys, Dave Clark Five, and Ventures tunes, as well as the Kingsmen's "Louie Louie" and Johnny Rivers's "Secret Agent Man." Because we had horns, we could also play hits by Herb Alpert and the Tijuana Brass.

The band was called the Lost Chords, which I still think is a very cool name. One Sunday summer afternoon, we were rehearsing at my house with the windows open. Nobody had air-conditioning back then. We were playing our thirteen-year-old hearts out when a police car rolled up to our house. The officer said we'd have to stop because he'd had complaints from a neighbor. My mother took control of the situation and told the officer, "You should be ashamed of yourself. These are good boys playing good music. Nobody should be bothered by that on a summer afternoon. Don't you

have anything more important to do?" The chagrined cop said, "Well, don't play too much longer," and left. I can only remember playing one show with the Lost Chords. It was a Youth Fellowship Dance at the Fox Chapel Presbyterian Church. How clean cut can you get? Still, the experience of playing rock and roll with those guys sparked a lifetime love of playing live music and for that I'm very grateful.

On a trip with my mother to Kaufman's Department Store in downtown Pittsburgh, while she was doing some other shopping, I headed for the record department. They had a huge selection, but I already knew what I wanted. It was the Beach Boys' *Surfin' USA* with a colorful picture of a surfer riding a gigantic wave on the cover. I had been listening to the track "Surfin' USA" for months already on my radio and the DJ said it was from their second album, which had been released in 1963. So, that's the one I got. To this day, I have never really surfed, although I did try once. But the idea and the theme of surfing had an enormous appeal to me then and still does. There's just something about sets of curling waves and freedom and girls in bikinis and the music that goes with it that will never go out of style, even if Jimi Hendrix declared that it should.

My other album purchase at Kaufman's that day was the soundtrack to the film *Goldfinger*. I hadn't even seen the movie but the combination of the picture of the nude gold-painted girl on the cover and the amazing title track by Shirley Bassey was enough to entice me to buy it with my hard-earned lawn-mowing money.

Later in life, I had the great pleasure to meet Brian Wilson at a club in Ibiza, of all places, when Tom Tom Club was also on the bill. His *Smile* concert at Carnegie Hall gave me chills and brought tears of joy to my eyes. In Talking Heads and Tom Tom Club, we worked for years with Jeff Hooper, Shirley Bassey's favorite Welsh soundman, the only soundman she'll work with.

3

IT'S GOT TO HAVE SOUL

In 1965, when I was about to enter the ninth grade at age fourteen, I left my home in Pittsburgh and traveled to the Northern Neck of Virginia, where I attended Christchurch School on the banks of the Rappahannock River near the Chesapeake Bay. Christchurch was an Episcopal boys' boarding school where we wore coats and ties every day and observed very traditional Southern values and lifestyle. I liked most aspects of the school and quickly made some good friends. We listened to a lot of popular music in the dormitory. Many of us had portable record players in our rooms, which were more like cubicles without doors. Even the bathroom stalls did not have doors, which took some getting used to. You learned to avert your eyes and, if possible, your nose.

Since I was a drummer without any drums, I really got into my record collection and was excited to share my thoughts and opinions about music with the other guys. I was mainly a Beatles, Rolling Stones, and Beach Boys fan. Some people preferred the Beatles because they were cute and some preferred the Stones because they were the bad boys. I enjoyed both bands and loved the Beach Boys for their positive teenage reinforcement. I was one of the few students at the school from north of the Mason-Dixon line and I guess my record collection reflected this, too, because one of my friends came into my room and said, "Goddamn, man! the Beatles and the

Me at age fourteen.

Stones are queers! You need to hear some James Brown, Sam and Dave, Otis Redding and the Tams!" Then he added the Four Tops, the Temptations, and Jr. Walker & the All Stars. He was so adamant that I needed to be educated that he brought a stack of those very records into my room and proceeded to play *James Brown: Live at the Apollo* for me. Even over my tiny speakers, the band and the singer were undeniably immense. I got the message right away: it was a no-brainer. My friend then cued up a Stax record, *Otis Blue: Otis Redding Sings Soul*. I was amazed to hear "Respect" and "I've Been Loving You Too Long," and especially Otis's version of the Rolling Stones' "Satisfaction." Then he played some Motown Hits for me: "The Way You Do the Things You Do" by the Temptations, and "Shotgun" by Jr. Walker & the All Stars. These Motown hits were pretty pervasive at the time so I had heard them on the radio, but somehow, in my tiny dormitory room, on my little portable record player, they took on a new, more important meaning. I may have been looking for acceptance by my new Southern peer group, but I had no doubt that this black music was beautiful and sexy,

and I was hooked. I came to realize that no white man could say "Hunnh!" like James Brown and I was a believer in the awesome power of what had come to be called Soul Music.

Something else was happening, too. A folk singer called Bob Dylan was writing big hits like "Blowin' in the Wind" for Peter, Paul and Mary and "Mr. Tambourine Man" for the Byrds. He was a freaky-looking dude with a whiny singing voice that drove some people nuts. His defenders argued that he elevated the content of the popular song to real poetry. I was in the second group. The breakthrough for me was "Like a Rolling Stone." When I heard it for the first time, I loved it from start to finish (and it was long, too). My friend and classmate Robert Murphy learned that Dylan was playing The Mosque, in Richmond, Virginia, and bought some tickets. Robert invited me home to the Berkeley Plantation in Charles City for the weekend. Located on the James River, it had been the home of President William Henry Harrison. Robert's family lived in the guesthouse. His parents drove us to the show along with his neighbor, the adorable Betty Bagby from nearby Westover Plantation.

We had nosebleed seats, but that didn't matter to us. Betty sat between Robert and me. I think all three of us were terribly horny. Dylan teetered out onstage all dressed in black, wearing pointy Beatle boots and sunglasses. A single spotlight followed him to the center of the stage, where he sat on a tall stool and played a set of his famous folk songs. His music was direct, moving, and for the most part very serious. After playing his original version of "Mr. Tambourine Man," he teetered back off the stage for an intermission.

When Dylan returned, it was with his full electric band, including Robbie Robertson and some other members of the band. You have probably heard that Dylan was booed and vilified for making his move to electric music at the Newport Folk Festival, but that did not happen the night we saw him. The audience greeted each new song with cheers, and by the time Dylan counted off the intro to "Like a Rolling Stone," the crowd, ourselves included, were in love with this guy. We were fans forever.

Years later, in 1990, after Roy Orbison died, Roy's widow, Barbara, asked us to play a fund-raiser at the Universal Amphitheater, in Burbank, California, to help build a homeless shelter in Roy's name. Tina, Jerry, and I accepted her invitation with pleasure and performed "Sweet Dream Baby" as

Shrunken Heads. The headliner was Bob Dylan with the original reunited Byrds. While we were watching their set from the green room on a video monitor, Bob's big security men came in and said, "Everybody out! Bob's coming in and doesn't want to see anybody!" Emmylou Harris, Bonnie Raitt, Wendy & Lisa, Iggy Pop, Patrick Swayze, and a host of other great musicians, including Tina and Jerry, got up and left the room. I decided to stay. I wanted to meet Bob. Because I was wearing a blue blazer, I think Bob's people thought I worked there and didn't shoo me out. When Bob strolled in, he asked me casually, "Hey, man! Where did everybody go?" I told him his people had kicked everybody out and Bob said, "Oh, shit. Even Emmylou?" "Yes," I said. "Even Emmylou."

4

BACK TO PITTSBURGH

After two years at Christchurch School in Virginia, I felt like going home to my family. I had learned valuable lessons about how to be a person of honor who tells the truth, how to be a gentleman, and to not always believe other boys' tall tales of sexual conquests. Still, I needed to expand my intellectual and artistic horizons. I enrolled as a day student in a boys' preparatory school called Shady Side Academy in the Pittsburgh suburbs. It had a reputation for creating community leaders and sending its graduates to the better colleges and universities. By this time, I had my driver's license and my parents bought me a sea-foam-green used Ford Mustang so I could commute back and forth to school. Having my own car was certainly a thrill. This was the autumn of 1967, following the Summer of Love. Culturally, things were heating up, even in Pittsburgh, which had long been conservatively provincial in outlook. Businessmen and professionals still wore gray flannel suits and fedoras to work. Even young married women dressed in matronly outfits. The "swinging sixties" never really reached the adults of Pittsburgh, but there was an awakening among the kids. On any given night, and especially on weekends, the hippest young people would flock to Walnut Street to see and be seen. For those old enough to drink, there was the Fox Café and the Encore Club. For the rest of us, there was Village Pizza and a coffeehouse called the Loaves and Fishes sponsored by the Calvary

Episcopal Church. The Loaves and Fishes had open-mike nights and poetry readings that really appealed to me. It was also a center for anti–Vietnam War activism. You could have an espresso or a glass of cider and hang out all night listening to young poets and folk singers. Some nights were truly electrifying. I never read any of my own poetry there, but I tried to look the part wearing my denim jeans and work shirt.

At school I was happy to have some excellent and challenging teachers. Several come to mind, like David Britton, a graduate of Middlebury College, who skied, rode a motorcycle, and taught English, including a course called Adolescent Rebellion. The latter was of great interest to me. We read Aldous Huxley, Ken Kesey, James Baldwin, Tom Wolfe, Allen Ginsberg, John Knowles, J. D. Salinger, Eldridge Cleaver, and Malcolm X. My parents were mystified by some of these selections, especially by a book called *Summerhill: A Radical Approach to Child Rearing* by A. S. Neill, about a progressive "free" school. But they were pleased with my enthusiasm.

I had a very interesting French teacher named Antoine Cordahi, an Egyptian Jew who had fled Nasser's regime to come to the USA. Mr. Cordahi was something of a dandy who wore black silk suits with purple shirts and Beatle boots. He also taught Music Appreciation, which I loved. This was the first time I heard Debussy, Satie, Herbie Hancock, and the first rock opera, *Tommy* by the Who. The course was a real turn-on.

In September of 1968, I signed up for classes in Studio Art. My teacher was a young painter named David Miller. It's no exaggeration to say that this man changed my life. He taught drawing, painting, and collage. But more importantly, he instilled an appreciation of contemporary art in me. Dada, Abstract Expressionism, Pop Art, Minimalism—he was passionate about all styles of art and his passion was contagious. He was and still is a very humble, friendly, and unpretentious person. He had studied at the Chicago Art Institute and then earned a Master of Fine Arts degree from the University of Wisconsin at Madison. By the time we met, he was already a very accomplished painter.

When I first walked into Miller's class, which was held in a big studio in the basement of one of the dormitories, he asked me, "Are you the son of Colonel Frantz?" I told him I was and he smiled and said, "Colonel Frantz is a good man." He told me he was in the Army Reserve and served as an aide to one of my dad's fellow officers. This was during the height of the

Vietnam War. Most of my friends shunned and even disdained the military, so this was a very welcome and bonding connection to make.

Mr. Miller opened my eyes to the idea that anyone can be an artist. He taught us that, if you want to, you can call anything art. Marcel Duchamp's *Fountain* was, in fact, a urinal. Robert Rauschenberg's *Erased de Kooning Drawing* was just that, a drawing by de Kooning that Rauschenberg spent painstaking days carefully erasing. Then there were Andy Warhol's soup-can paintings. A single painting of a Campbell's soup can is one thing, but a wall of thirty such paintings becomes a major statement that art is to be found in our everyday lives. This was a revelation and another great turn-on for me.

Around this time, I read W. Somerset Maugham's *The Moon and Sixpence*. The book is very loosely based on the life of painter Paul Gauguin. It's the story of a London banker who decides to abandon his humdrum existence in business, and also his wife and children, to become a painter, first in Paris and, eventually, in Tahiti. I had been thinking a lot during this time about how to escape the existence that young men in my position were expected to lead. We were being trained to be leaders in business or law or medicine. Neither we nor our parents ever expected that we would lead the life of a full-time artist. As much as I loved rock and roll and playing music, I was not convinced that I had what it takes to be a great rock and roller. Those guys came from London or Liverpool, Memphis or California. I was from Pittsburgh. I did not feel cool at all. But wait, maybe I could be a painter! Andy Warhol was from Pittsburgh and he had become the most famous, coolest artist alive!

So, under David Miller's immensely talented influence, I became an artist. It was as if a switch flipped in my brain. I would study art and I would live in the art world. No banks or business for me. I would create my own future and damn the consequences! I still remember the day I had this epiphany. I was seventeen years old.

In addition to the theory and philosophy of contemporary art, David Miller taught us basic studio skills, like how to stretch and prime a canvas and how to mix paint so that it doesn't end up looking like mud. "Never use a color straight out of the tube or jar. Always add a little bit of white or another color to make it your own," he said. Then he said, "Don't hesitate to mix media. Like Rauschenberg, make transfers from color maga-

J. Allon Photo

CHRIS FRANTZ
Arts Festival Student Coordinator

zine images by wetting the paper with turpentine, laying it on the canvas, and rubbing the back of the paper with a blunt stick until that photo of Brigitte Bardot or JFK is transferred onto your canvas, then paint around or on top of that. Have music playing while you work. It will inspire you."

One assignment Mr. Miller gave us was to copy a famous painter's masterpiece. Probably because I was a horny teenager, I chose one of Renoir's voluptuous nudes. I did my best to copy the painting faithfully in oil and spent days working on it. The pinks and yellows and flesh tones were sexy to me, but the image itself was stiff and had none of the breath and life of the original. I expressed my disappointment to Mr. Miller and he came over to my easel, took a look and asked, "Do you mind if I try something?" I told him to please go ahead, and he took my brush and painted two big squiggles across her face. Suddenly, the painting was better and much more interesting. I loved this!

In my junior year, when it was time to apply to colleges, Mr. Miller floated the idea that I should go to a good art school, or a university with a good art department. This made complete sense to me. But when I told my parents, they spoke to Mr. Miller and begged him, "Please don't suggest to Chris that he should go to art school. How will he ever support himself?" It was a fair enough question, but Mr. Miller was very persuasive. He told them, "Well, you know, I'm going to recommend that Chris apply to the Rhode Island School of Design. It's not just any art school. It's the Harvard of art schools." Because my father had graduated from Harvard Law School, and because of Harvard's elite reputation, my parents suddenly thought, "Oh, the Harvard of art schools? Well, that sounds interesting." That

autumn, I visited RISD with my father. I had applied to the early decision review. When it was time for my interview with the director of admissions, a charming baby-faced guy by the name of Bruce Helander, he asked me how I was doing. I told him I loved the school, but that I was a little nervous about whether I would be accepted or not. He looked at me with a big smile, laughed, and said, "Don't worry, Chris. You're going to get in." I later found out that he called Mr. Miller and said, "We've accepted more of your students over the past few years than any other school in the country. Not only that, when they arrive here, they are really well prepared. I don't know how you do it, but you're doing something right."

When the letter of acceptance arrived, I felt like I had hit the lottery. When you think about it, in many ways, I had.

I made some great friends at Shady Side Academy. Fritz Shiring was an excellent guitarist and a fun guy who drove a boss red GTO. His father, a doctor, had passed away at a young age and his mother welcomed us kids to hang out at their house listening to records and playing music. John Dixon played bass guitar and styled himself like the *White Album*–period John Lennon. Together, he and Fritz had a band called the Villagers that I would watch with fascination as they rehearsed in Fritz's basement. They played early psychedelic hits from bands like Cream, the Jimi Hendrix Experience, and the Rascals. Jake Turner was an aspiring actor, a skier, and a surfer during his summers at Beach Haven, New Jersey. Martin Walrath and I bonded over a mutual love of the blues, which was enjoying a renaissance thanks to British bands like the Rolling Stones and the Animals reintroducing us to the form. I clearly remember listening to James Brown's "Cold Sweat" for the first time on Martin's home stereo. Dan Arnheim was a cheeky yet brilliant writer and actor, and Bill Oppenheimer, from Mobile, Alabama, regaled us with stories from the Deep South. Doug Day was a bright and awesomely talented folk singer who never lacked enthusiasm for any form of artistic expression. Pat Hannah was a friend who gave the best parties and possessed a vast secret knowledge of Pittsburgh society. Pat was just beginning what would become a fabulous vintage-car collection.

While Shady Side was an all-boys' school back then, we did have some really smart and fabulous female friends. Some went to private school and

some went to public school. They were mostly brilliant, too. Ellen Dwyer, who died much too young, would go on to study history of art at Yale, then followed up with more study of the decorative arts at the Winterthur Museum, and, finally, the Carnegie Museum, before landing in New York City as a leader in estate sales at Cartier. I first met Ellen in a special coed poetry class our schools had arranged. I wish she had taken better care of herself. Sandy Hazlett was also a poet. Her father was one of the founders of the International Poetry Forum, where she and I heard and met Robert Lowell, Claire Bloom, Anne Sexton, James Dickey, Mark Van Doren, and Judy Collins. Today, Sandy is a published poet herself. Susie Finesman was a fashion-forward young woman who moved to New York, got a great gig at HBO, and later started her own literary agency in Los Angeles. Marina Posvar, whose mother was a Metropolitan Opera star, moved to Pittsburgh when her father, a classmate of my father's at West Point, became the chancellor of the University of Pittsburgh. Marina became a very fine actress who now does work on behalf of cancer patients and is a two-time survivor herself. Rebecca Litman—whose father, Lenny, was a film and culture critic for the Pittsburgh Press—went to art school in San Francisco and then moved to New York, where she became part of the downtown music scene, and is a longtime right-hand person to composer Phillip Glass. Lisa Dodds was a person that every guy I knew had his eye on. Her own mother told me, "I told her, if you've got it, flaunt it!" Lisa was a total rock and roll fan and was the first person to play me a Led Zeppelin album as she danced around the room in hip-hugger jeans. She studied at RISD for a while, too. I don't mean to imply that they were girlfriends of mine—my girlfriend lived in Kentucky—but they were all good friends who were both interesting and beautiful.

Did I forget to mention drugs? This was the sixties, after all. While I was truly frightened of heroin and downers from what I had heard about them, I had no fear of marijuana, hashish, LSD, mescaline, and speed. I had one friend whose father was a physician and came to school one day with a bag of what he called black beauties. He said he had swiped them from his father's doctor's bag. These capsules brought on euphoria and what felt like boundless energy that lasted at least twelve hours. Then came the crash, which was no fun at all. We learned that a couple of Rolling Rock beers would take the edge off of that crash pretty well. Marijuana seemed like a

harmless giggle compared to black beauties and sometimes we would try both at the same time. Acid was the king, though.

After reading Aldous Huxley's *The Doors of Perception* and various accounts in *Life* magazine, I couldn't wait to try LSD. One of the first times I tried it was with a friend who was visiting from out of town. We were enjoying the new feelings we were experiencing and laughing uncontrollably when I realized that it was time for the family dinner. *Thanksgiving* dinner! My friend and I gathered at the table with my parents, brother, and sister, doing our best to maintain our composure, but when my father began to carve the turkey we both dissolved into giggles. This was not a bad trip—it was a wacky trip! I remember my father looking at us with real curiosity as if to say, "What the hell is so damned funny?" My mother knew something was up, too, but what? We forced ourselves to eat to avoid detection. By the time the pumpkin pie was served, we were fully hallucinating and loving the texture of the pie.

I had a friend who would drive a hundred miles to Kent State University to score the best acid and bring it back to us. Why did we, who had every advantage in life, feel the need to take LSD or any other drug? In my case, it was simply a desire for new and exciting experiences. In spite of my good fortune in life, at the age of seventeen I felt like I was missing out on something—something intangible. I didn't just want to get high, I wanted to experience the deeper feelings and connections made by the great artists and musicians, and hoped that psychedelics would open my eyes to a secret, more enlightened world. I believe that they did.

Not long before my graduation from Shady Side, I went to a party at an older friend's apartment in a blue-collar neighborhood called Bloomfield. There were maybe twenty high school kids of both sexes there. We were smoking grass and listening to the new Jimi Hendrix album, *Band of Gypsys*, when suddenly a team of plainclothes cops crashed the party. They made all of us line up while they proceeded to search our friend's apartment from top to bottom. I think they patted down and searched every guy there except me. I don't know why they didn't search me, but it was a good thing because I had a big lump of hash in my pocket. The cops expressed their disappointment to one another that they didn't find any "hard stuff." Then they marched us outside, where two paddy wagons were waiting: one for the boys and one for the girls. We were taken to jail, to individual holding

cells. After stewing for a while, we were each allowed one phone call. I called my father and woke him up to tell him the situation. Everyone else's parents came to get them right away, but my dad said he was going back to sleep and would come and get me sometime the next day. I tried to sleep on the cold steel platform that served as a bed, but I was terrified and sleep did not come. One of the cops said if my father didn't come soon they would move me to the big jail, put me in a uniform, and shave my head. I also imagined that I would be expelled from school just before graduation. It was a bad night.

The next day, which was Sunday, my father came downtown to get me after church. On the ride home he said that I was lucky that there would be no charges against me but that my friends who hosted the party would be charged with "operating a disorderly house." This was a charge that was normally issued against houses of prostitution, but had been expanded to include teenage pot parties. If my school ever found out about this, they didn't say so. My friends and I all graduated as planned. I received an award as the most improved student. The joy and relief I felt standing in my blue blazer and white duck trousers on graduation day was immense. Now came the real test: Could I make it as an artist or would I have to pursue some more traditional profession? I was the first member of my family to make this leap, but I would not be the last.

5

KENTUCKY LOVE

I have always loved Kentucky. All of my mother's family lived there and I especially enjoyed visiting my grandparents in Mason County. We would visit them often because my mother remained very close to her parents. They were very sweet and kind to us children. I can remember one Christmas when my grandfather, Pappy, who was the mayor of his tiny hometown of Washington, dressed up as Santa Claus and rode the town's brand-new fire engine down Main Street in the snow with the siren blaring, before handing out presents to all the little children at the Volunteer Fire Department.

The summers were even better. I helped Pappy by doing house painting on his own house and also on some rental houses he owned. There are few things hotter than painting a tin roof in Kentucky in July except for cutting and housing tobacco and baling hay in August. I did that, too, out at my friend Kippy Parker's family farm in Mays Lick.

Kentucky people really knew how to live. There was always some kind of party or picnic to go to and there were so many pretty girls. Before I got my driver's license, my cousin Holton Cartmell would pick me up in his Ford Model A to take me on double dates. We would take our dates to Bisotti's, the drive-in hamburger joint with curbside service across the river in Ohio. People cruised around and around Bisotti's until it was time to see the movie at the Drive-In Theater. This is where I learned what "making

out" was all about. After a few dates, I thought I knew it all until a cute girl visiting from out of town stuck her tongue in my ear. I hadn't expected that but I liked it!

Sometimes Holton would pick me up in a different car, take me out onto Route 68, and ask, "You want to catch a quick hundred?" Then he would stomp on the accelerator with all the windows down, and watch the speedometer until we hit a hundred miles per hour. Then he would gradually slow down to the speed limit and light a cigarette.

The first girl I dated in Kentucky was called Annie. She was really pretty and popular and would invite me to go with her to parties and sock hops; the latter took place in the high school gym, and you had to take your shoes off so you wouldn't scuff up the basketball court. Annie had two sisters, a very sexy older one named Sissy and an adorable younger one called Whoopsie. Whoopsie was an early fan of Cher and wore stylish bell-bottoms just like Cher did. I think she sewed them herself. There were also dances for teenagers at the country club, where we'd get dressed up and do "The Alligator" or "The Dog" after drinking a few illicit beers or shots of bourbon. A band called The Torquays from Lexington performed. They wore uniforms similar to Paul Revere & the Raiders, and they really knew how to put on a show.

Another fun thing we did was to go to the Germantown Fair, where they had a horse show, a mule show, a baby show, and all kinds of livestock on display. There were tractor pulls, pie-eating contests, and freak shows. There was a big tent full of hoochie-coochie girls who would stand in front of the tent and give you a little preview before the show. This was a real honest-to-goodness country fair, not the tamed-down version you're likely to see today.

The highlight of the fair came just after sunset when "Dick Clark's Cavalcade of Stars" hit the stage. The band I remember best was called The Yellow Payges.

They were a stylish, long-haired, Beatle-esque rock band. They were excellent, but I wondered what they thought about playing at this little country fair in Germantown, Kentucky. Whatever they thought, they didn't let it affect their performance. The girls in the audience were wild for them.

When I went back to boarding school, Annie and I wrote letters to each other every week, but eventually she got interested in another guy who lived in the same town. Who could blame her? Long-distance relationships are hard, especially when you're only fifteen. I was sad but not devastated.

The next time I visited Kentucky, I was introduced to a very petite, stylish, and good-looking girl named Sandi. We hit it off—and I mean really hit it off—right away. We'd go on double dates with my friend Sam Dryden, who'd pick us up in one of his muscle cars. My cousin Holton had enlisted and gone to Vietnam, but his brother David became a good friend. We cruised the drive-in restaurant, went skinny-dipping in ponds and swimming pools, and talked about what we wanted to do with our lives. Sandi introduced me to Lex Browning. Lex played guitar and dug a lot of the same bands that I did. We'd go to his place and play records and smoke joints of wild marijuana we found growing in forgotten corners of farmers' fields. It wasn't very strong, but it was plentiful and if you smoked enough of it you felt really nice. Almost everybody smoked cigarettes, too. Kentucky was tobacco country. I remember bumper stickers that said "Smoking Is Good for You!" You could buy a pack of cigarettes at the drive-through window of the Working Man's Friend Tavern for nineteen cents. They would also sell you a six-pack of beer if you were old enough to drive.

By the time I turned sixteen and got my driver's license, I would drive from Pittsburgh to Kentucky, a distance of three hundred miles, to visit my grandparents and see Sandi and my other friends. I had the idea to apply for a summer job working at Browning Manufacturing, which was owned by Lex's family. They were the largest employer in the town of Maysville. Sandi's father was an executive there, too. Browning's made electrical transmission parts. I made an appointment with Sandi's dad for an interview. He gave me an application to fill out and next thing I knew I was working in the factory. There were three eight-hour shifts; I started on the one that began at 7:00 A.M. My grandmother would get up early, make me a hearty breakfast of bacon, eggs, and toasted salt-rising bread, and send me off with a tomato and pimento cheese sandwich in a brown paper bag.

Factory work was like nothing I'd experienced before. It was my first real job. For starters, I'd never heard people use the f-word in every single sentence before. I'd never operated machinery before, either. On this job I

was making electrical transmission parts on a huge lathe from iron castings of different dimensions. Some were only a few inches in diameter and some were a couple of feet in diameter and all sizes in between. The lathe would cut and form the casting into something resembling a pulley called a sheave. As the iron casting was cut, the metal was cooled by a stream of water that created a lot of steam. It was like an industrial steambath on the factory floor. After eight hours of this, I would punch the time clock and go home, take a bath, and go visit Sandi and make out. It wasn't an easy job, in fact it was very hard work, but the pay was good and some of the other workers took a liking to me. They were patient with me, even though I wasn't able to make as many pieces a day as I was expected to. It's fair to say that these older guys were amused by me trying to keep up with them.

One weekend, Lex and I drove out to the Blue Licks State Park, where the last battle of the American Revolution was fought, and took some acid. The weather was perfect. We read all of the plaques around the park describing the battle. The battle was fought on August 19, 1782, long after General Cornwallis had surrendered at Yorktown; the news of the British surrender had not reached Kentucky yet. Daniel Boone was among the pioneers fighting the British there; his son Israel was killed along with sixty-five other revolutionaries. As our trip started to peak, we wandered through the ancient forest of tall trees and sparkling streams and fossil-covered limestone boulders. We followed the trails worn down by immense herds of buffalo that traveled here for the natural salt licks. We spent a good deal of time laughing our heads off until our sides hurt. By the time the sun set, we were finally okay to drive home, listening to "Proud Mary," "Honky Tonk Women," and "In-A-Gadda-Da-Vida" on the FM radio.

My summers in Kentucky were wonderfully free. My grandparents were happy to look after me and pleased to see that I was making friends and having a good time.

They allowed me to come and go as I pleased. On Sundays, I went with them to the Presbyterian Church next door. Who knew that Tina and I would later be married there?

After church, we would drive out to the Thoroughbred Grill in Mays Lick, where my grandparents would catch up with their friends. It seemed like everybody knew each other. We'd order fried chicken, fresh tomato

salad, corn pudding, and tall glasses of sweet tea with a sprig of mint. For dessert we'd have transparent puddings, a local dessert tart made of baked sugar, butter, egg whites, and a little vanilla.

I brought Tina down to Washington to meet my grandmother in the summer of 1973. When we arrived and I introduced Tina to Mammy, I could tell they immediately liked each other. When I gave Mammy a hug and a kiss on the cheek, she said in her lilting Southern accent, "Why Chris, you're hot as fire! Come on in and have an iced tea and let's us talk." Tina loved the sound of her voice and has often reminded me of this and of her first visit to Kentucky. It's the kind of place you want to come back to, and we did.

6

RISD

I was very happy and excited to arrive at the Rhode Island School of Design. I was ready for action. Art! Girls! Parties! Fun! As far as I was concerned, RISD had it all. My parents drove me from Pittsburgh to Providence. After I checked in and registered, my mother and father helped me unpack my clothes and my stereo system from their Ford Country Squire station wagon with the faux wood paneling on the side, and carry them up the stairs to my assigned room in Nickerson Hall. It was a fairly new building, a simple contemporary redbrick design that fit well with the existing historic colonial architecture of what was known as College Hill in Providence. My room was on the fourth floor in the back with a little balcony overlooking a small green tree-lined field. I immediately felt at home and picked one bed for myself on the right-hand side of the room. My roommate, a guy named Hugh Roberts from Pottstown, Pennsylvania, outside of Philadelphia, had not arrived yet.

After we lugged all my things up four flights of stairs, and my mother kindly unpacked my clothes and put them neatly in the dresser and closet, there came that emotional moment when you have to say goodbye to your parents who are so proud of you—and who are footing the bill for everything. I hugged and kissed them and was going to say goodbye right there, but then decided to walk them back to the car and see them off on the long

drive back to Pittsburgh. My father handed me enough cash to open a small bank account and they were off.

That night, after dinner in the refectory, I did a little exploring with some of the guys who lived on the same floor of the dorm. Chris Morse, from Rockland, Maine, was tall, lanky, and hilarious. He smoked a briar pipe, wore a tweed jacket, and had a beard and ponytail. His wisdom teeth had just been removed and his cheeks were still puffy. Geoff Stevens, from Chicago was skinny as a beanpole with wire-rimmed glasses, and Rico Eastman, from Maryland was small in stature but big of heart. We wandered all over College Hill and marveled at the street names: Benefit Street. Angell Street. Hope Street. It was a balmy evening and somebody passed a joint around. We were just rambling and getting to know each other. Chris Morse turned us on to the humor of the comedy duo Bert & I. He knew all their routines by heart in that crazy downeast Maine accent of theirs. *Ayuh*. When we got back to the dorm that first night, my roommate had still not arrived. It had been a long day and I fell asleep thinking about a very petite and pretty girl I had seen that afternoon while we were checking in. I heard her say her name was Andi.

In the morning, after breakfast, we walked down the hill to Memorial Hall to have our photo ID picture taken. The photographer was an androgynous creature named Karen Achenbach. She was very tall, slim, unusually attractive, and dressed in a red satin cowboy shirt, jeans, and cowboy boots. When she looked at me, she winked and told me to look at the camera lens, not at her. The photo she took would be used not only for my student ID but also in printed form for what was called the RISD Facebook. The facebook was distributed to faculty members so that they could match a face to a name if necessary, but also fell into the hands of a few curious students. There were a lot of beautiful young people at RISD, so it was very interesting.

The rest of the day was filled with orientation meetings and such. Every freshman at RISD was enrolled in a group of courses called Freshman Foundation. This included Life Drawing, 2D Design, 3D Design, and Art History. There were no exceptions. You had to know the basics.

Outside the refectory before dinner that night, there were some cool upperclassmen checking out all the new talent. I don't think predatory is the correct way to describe them, but they were definitely curious and horny. You could feel them checking you out and sizing you up and wondering

if you were straight or gay. Any gay freshmen were likely to still be in the closet. It usually wasn't until sophomore year that they came out.

Like any other school, RISD had its cliques and Karen Achenbach and her clique were hanging out that night at the refectory. I walked up to her and said hello. Her roommate, Kenny Goodman, was with her. Kenny always wore shades, was skinny and chic in tight-fitting black clothes, and gave me the impression he wished he were someplace else. He was a man of few words—at least with me—had a dark mystique, and seemed capable of dirty deeds. Donald Munroe was another member of this clique. Don had long, straight, blond hair and was as friendly and light as Kenny was serious and dark. He had a way of acting that some people would call swish. In his denim jacket and tight flared jeans, he was very good-looking. Don had a wonderfully acerbic sense of humor and would snap his fingers to punctuate his killing jokes. David Frasier was another member of this gang. He was very tall and thin with a huge head of Pre-Raphaelite curls, like a huge blond Afro. He was super calm, observing all around him. Finally, there was Andrea Kovacs, a brilliantly articulate young artist from Kew Gardens, Queens, New York. Andrea dressed in beatnik-black from head to toe with jet-black hair, heavy black mascara, and eyeliner. She was capable of very cutting remarks and fired barbs off as fast as she pleased. She could also be completely adorable if she liked you. I was relieved that she seemed to like me.

I soon realized that this clique was probably emulating Andy Warhol's Factory crowd. Just the year before, Warhol had come up to the RISD Museum with his entourage for a show he called *Raid the Icebox*, where he went through the museum's basement storage and selected his favorite pieces to put on exhibit upstairs. Andy's presence caused a lot of excitement at the school, which he enjoyed up to a point. He drew the line when an anti–Vietnam War activist began shouting and protesting. Andy just got up and walked straight out of the museum to the chartered tour bus that would convey him and his entourage back to the Factory in New York City.

During dinner that night, I saw Andi—the girl I'd spotted my first day at RISD—across the room. She was sitting with some friends talking excitedly and laughing a lot. I took the plunge, walked over, and said, "This looks like a fun table. Mind if I join you?" Andi looked and me and asked, "What's your name?" I told her and she said, "Mine's Andi. Actually, it's Andrea but everyone calls me Andi. Andi Shapiro." Andi and I became very

close very quickly. We were both interested in drawing and painting. I suspected she was very good and I soon found out she was. Andi was very petite and beautifully proportioned. With long, dark, naturally wavy hair and bright blue eyes, she was absolutely beautiful. She had a smattering of freckles across her cheeks and long dark eyelashes. Her personal style was somewhere between Katharine Hepburn's and Diane Keaton in *Annie Hall*. She had a keen wit, and still does, but was also capable of great seriousness. Once, while I was in a moment of reverie, she said to me, "Oh, Chris! You're not happy. You're just stoned!" She was sometimes critical of me. Andi was a very smart and cultured person. She was from Chappaqua, New York, and invited me to visit her family there. Her parents took us into the city to see Anthony Hopkins in *Equus* on Broadway, still my favorite Broadway play.

My roommate, Hugh Roberts, finally showed up with a great excuse for his lateness: He had broken his leg and wore a plaster cast from his knee down to his toes. He said his friends called him Huey. He was well over six feet tall with a shag haircut. I helped him with his luggage and stuff. It turned out that we had some similarities in our background. We were WASPs and we'd both attended prep school for boys. Both of our fathers were lawyers. We liked to make art and get high, and we were hoping to break the mold we felt we had been expected to fill. We loved James Brown yet we also dug the Velvet Underground, Captain Beefheart, Terry Riley, and Moondog. I could tell we were going to get along just fine.

Later that night, in our room after a joint and a few glasses of red Almaden wine, Huey told me about a terrible thing that had recently happened to him. His mother had committed suicide. She'd been missing for some time when investigators found bits of charred bone and the steel shanks of her high heels in the old basement incinerator. They said she had opened the little door and crawled into the flames fully clothed. Foul play was not suspected. Had she left a note? I didn't ask. I remember feeling how strange and heavy this must be for any young guy and I felt bad about this, but Huey seemed emotionally strong and resilient.

When classes began, I was relieved to find out that I was not completely out of my league. I had imagined that all the best artists from all the best schools had come to RISD and wondered if I could possibly compete. It turned out that many of my classmates had the same fears, but most of us did just fine.

I especially enjoyed my life-drawing class, taught by George Pappas. We

drew from nude models. Drawing a nude person can be a little awkward at first, but you get used to it. You have to learn how to really look deeply at the model, and to see how the shapes are connected and how the body flows, even at rest. Mr. Pappas pointed to different parts of the model's body to stress the importance of understanding the skeletal system underneath. We had a number of models of all ages and sizes, but there was one young woman who was ravishingly beautiful. She was a tall, full-figured brunette with the look of an exotic dancer. She was escorted to the class each morning by a tall, dark, muscular guy with hair down to his waist. He must have been her boyfriend. She would undress behind a curtain and then walk to the center of the class in a silk kimono. We students were ready, perched on our drawing benches with large pads of newsprint paper, pencils, charcoal sticks, and Conté crayons. She stood on a platform—a sort of mini stage—and then she would drop the kimono to the floor to reveal her amazing physique. She had the figure and facial features of the young Sophia Loren. Mr. Pappas asked her to turn around and said, "Look at her back. The scapula are like little wings. See how delicate and beautiful the bones of her back are." He was right; we were learning to train our eyes to really observe the human figure. You learned to see what muscles and bones were doing under the skin to hold the body together. I don't think I was the only student in the room who became sexually aroused while drawing this particular model. She was powerfully sexy. If she wanted to, she would look you right in the eye and hold that gaze until you broke it. She never said a word to anyone. I believe she only modeled for Mr. Pappas's class. I never saw her in any other classes. At the end of the class, her boyfriend would arrive to walk her home.

RISD did not have any fraternities or sororities or sports teams, thank God, but we did have some great parties and dances. For the first dance of that year, the band was Flo and Eddie of the Turtles with members of Frank Zappa's band, including the great Aynsley Dunbar on drums. Soon he would be working with David Bowie and Lou Reed, but not yet. Flo and Eddie were great singers and highly entertaining. Andi and I danced together that night for the first time. We had a ball and spent much of the evening dancing alongside Donald Munroe and Andrea Kovacs. I had become friends with them and looked up to them as artists and personalities. To me, they were among the stars of the school.

The following weekend there was an even wilder dance. This time the

band was made up of some hilarious habitués of RISD itself. Some had already graduated and some were still in school. Their band was called the Fabulous Motels. Charlie Rocket was the front man. Tall, slim, good-looking, and dressed in a silly superhero costume, he sang and rocked a boss electric accordion complete with distortion and feedback. On vocals and clarinet was a husky guy in a pink tutu and ballet shoes called Rudy Cheeks. They had a really great singing drummer named Sport Fisher. A painter named Dan Gosch, also dressed in a superhero costume, played a nutty gnome on a toy drum kit and xylophone. The guitarist was a guy called John Scherff and the bass player called himself Domino Floater. The scantily clad background singers and dancers were called the Tampoons and they were Barbara Conway, Bonita Flanders, and tiny, petite Mary Clarke. The Fabulous Motels were not just a great parody of rock and roll, they were a parody of show business itself. They had very funny and cool original songs, but also rewrote hit songs of the day. For example, "Sweet Soul Music" became "Men" with lyrics like, "Do you like big men, y'all? Big strong men, y'all? Spotlight on John Wayne, now. Spotlight on Ernest Borgnine!" They made playful references to kinky sex in a song called "I Wanna Be on Top This Time (and Use My Riding Crop This Time.)" We loved the Motels and always looked forward to their RISD shows. Not only were they loads of fun, they were a good example of how music and art went hand in hand. They were Dada itself.

On the weekends, Andi and I visited the RISD farm outside of town on Narragansett Bay to draw outdoors on the beach. Then we would hitchhike to Newport to eat oysters and clams and drink Narragansett beer at the Black Pearl on the harbor. We didn't have a lot of spending money, but this new life was utterly romantic and the feeling of independence was fantastic.

Huey and I did some wild things together. We would set our alarm clocks for 5:00 A.M., wake up and take some acid, then go back to sleep. Then we would wake up tripping and go to classes. A big part of the trip was to be able to maintain your composure so that no one was the wiser. This was a real challenge. Looking back, I don't know how I did it. I don't believe LSD ever improved my artwork, but it certainly loosened me up so that I was ever more mindful of the beauty of my surroundings and the people in my life.

7

MARTINA

Let me tell you about the first time I saw Tina Weymouth. It was at the very beginning of the school year in September of '71. I was relaxing on the grass of the "RISD Beach" at the corner of Benefit and Angell Streets. The "RISD Beach" was a little grassy park featuring a large bronze abstract sculpture called *Daybreak* by artist Gil Franklin. This was a place where the art students hung out between classes to chat, gossip, exchange ideas, or maybe just catch some rays. It was late afternoon, sunny and warm, a perfect New England day. I was sitting with Charlie the Model. Everyone at RISD knew Charlie. He was an artist's model for life-drawing and figure-painting classes. He was a big guy—well over six feet tall—barrel chested, physically fit, with a kind and sweet disposition. When he saw you coming he would say, "Hi, friend!" Some people said he had been shell-shocked. I don't know. There was something different about Charlie, but then a lot of people in the RISD community were different. So, Charlie and I were sitting on the grass exchanging pleasantries and watching people go by. I was feeling mellow, but still noticing things.

Suddenly, as in a scene from a Truffaut movie, I saw a girl pedaling down Benefit Street in our direction on an old yellow three-speed bicycle. She wore a blue-and-white-striped French sailor's shirt and very short shorts. She was slender, fit, and her legs were fabulous. As she pedaled by, her blonde

shag haircut tossed in the breeze. She was watching the traffic, so she didn't look in our direction, but I could see her face was lightly freckled and extremely pretty. Her eyes were set wide apart and seemed to reflect a keen intelligence. She was smiling to herself about something. I had never seen her before, so I thought she must be one of the new kids. As she rode off, I said to Charlie, "Wow! Did you see her?" Charlie smiled at me and said, "That's my friend Martina." Even though this was the first time I'd seen her, I felt some kind of familiarity or maybe even kinship. I had to meet Martina.

The following day, my afternoon class was Figure Painting, taught by Richard Merkin. I knew Richard a little bit but this was my first class with him. Painting is a hard thing to teach—in fact, some people say it can't be done—but Richard was a great teacher. He was a true dandy, always dressed with tremendous flair. This day, his black hair was slicked straight back. He had a full mustache. He wore a voluminous, puffy white shirt open at the neck, with a red ascot, baggy khaki trousers, and black ballet pumps. His glasses were wire-rimmed and he was smoking English Ovals with a short cigarette holder. He was a trip!

One of my friends, an effete and smart young guy named Gregor, and I were setting up our easels at one end of the studio when I realized Martina, who was wearing a khaki navy flyer's jumpsuit, was setting up at the other end of the room, closer to the female model. The model was sitting in a tableau of brightly colored fabrics and café furniture, bottles, and glasses that Merkin had set up for us to paint. As our teacher prowled the room offering advice and encouragement, I didn't want to stare, but all I could think about was this new girl. How should I introduce myself? What could I possibly say to her? Should I play it cool or come on strong? I didn't know what to do. But then an opportunity presented itself.

At the end of the class, Gregor sauntered over to her, took one look at the painting she was working on, and said, "Obviously, you have no idea what you're doing." I don't know what he was thinking or why he would say such a thing, but she looked crestfallen. Here was my chance. I walked over to this beautiful girl and said, "I'm sorry about my friend's bad manners. Obviously, *he* has no idea what he's doing." She smiled at me with a sense of relief and laughed. "I like this class," she said. I told her I did, too. I said, "My name is Chris. It's really good to meet you." As she cleaned up her painter's palette

and packed up her paints, she turned to me, looked at me with her bright blue eyes, and said, "It's nice to meet you, too. My name is Tina."

Later that evening, I spied Tina in the Refectory and asked her to join our table. I introduced her to the others at the table, including my girlfriend, Andi. During the conversation, we found out that Tina had transferred to RISD from Barnard College in New York City at the recommendation of her art history professor. When he saw her portfolio of drawings he told her, "If I could draw like that, I'd be going to RISD." So, here she was! She

Tina when I met her.

had entered the summer Foundation program and felt much happier here than at Barnard. During the summer, she had made good friends with some other transfer students, including her boyfriend, architecture student Peter Coan. I had expected there would be a boyfriend. I mean, how could there not be? Peter was not with her tonight, however, and we had a long getting-to-know-you conversation. Tina said that she had two brothers and five sisters and they had moved around a lot because her father, Ralph, was a U.S. Navy officer and her mother, Laure, was from France. I told her, what a coincidence—my father was a U.S. Army officer. Further conversation revealed that her father was an admiral who had attended the Naval Academy. I told her that my father was a general and had attended West Point. During this period of time, because of the Vietnam War, there was a pretty strong antimilitary feeling among college students and young people in general. I think Tina and I felt a sense of camaraderie because we both knew that, despite the war in Vietnam, there were a lot of fine people in the military. We knew what it was like to be an officer's kid.

One thing about artists and art students is that we love to sit around talking and smoking. Another thing we had in common was that Tina and I both smoked Camels. So we talked and talked and smoked and smoked. I quickly realized that Tina had the gift of gab and could really hold forth in a conversation. She claimed to be a shy person, but once she came out of her shell there was no stopping her. I was fascinated, Andi was less so. After dinner we said good night to Tina and Andi turned to me and said, "I'll bet she's not even a real blonde."

8

WORDS IN PAPERS, WORDS IN BOOKS

Andi and I were happy together. We'd been dating for a year and we confided in each other and had some very good times together. She had a lot of seriously deep thoughts that she expressed very clearly and I was a good listener. She needed a good listener. I found out later that her parents were breaking up during this time and, naturally, this took its toll on her. She became judgmental of the other art school kids and she started pointing out my personal flaws. One time we were lying in the grass in front of her dormitory, enjoying the warm October sun, when she suddenly started enumerating all of my failings. She didn't like it that I got high as often as I did. She thought I was an underachiever and should work harder and be more serious. I told her that I was painfully aware of my own inadequacies, but I was doing my best to be a good boyfriend to her and a good guy in general. She apologized, but it was obvious that something was really bothering her. I think we both had roving eyes at this point, but I still found her to be a beautiful and fascinating person. Stephen Sprouse, a younger guy we both knew casually, sat down beside us. He was dressed smartly in rust-colored corduroy Levi's and a burgundy cashmere sweater over an oxford cloth shirt. Stephen was probably the most clean-cut guy in the whole school. He came from Indiana. He had only been at the school for a couple of months and intended to major in fashion design.

He said, "I want to ask your advice. Halston wants me to come to New York and work for him. Do you think I should do it?" Halston was super popular at the time and had been recently featured on the cover of *Time* magazine. I imagined that, because Stephen was such a sweet kid, he might get chewed up and spit out by the fashion world. Still, it was a very tempting offer. A RISD degree is no guarantee of employment. Au contraire. I told him to go for it. Go visit with Halston and get the lay of the land first before leaving RISD. Andi completely agreed and that was the last I saw of Stephen until I met him again in 1976 when he was living in the same building as Debbie Harry and Chris Stein on the Bowery. He had become a protégé of Andy Warhol and was doing sensational work of his own. Debbie was his muse and he dressed her in a unique and edgy, glamorous style. He used a lot of bright red camouflage and and backward calligraphy in bright Day-Glo colors in his fabrics.

I was out of the dormitory now and had moved into my own apartment at 161 Benefit Street upstairs from the fabulous Joe's sandwich shop. Joe's served deli-style sandwiches named after vintage movie stars, funky musicians, and local celebrities. They had a big wooden barrel of home-made pickles and the smell of them wafted upstairs throughout the entire building. It was a fun place to hang out. The wisecracking owner, Dewey Dufresne, was married to a lovely woman named Polly from Pittsburgh. Her parents were friends with my parents, so Dewey was always very nice to me and teased me a bit less than his other customers. Their son, who was a tiny baby named Wiley when I lived above his dad's sandwich shop, would become a famous young chef in New York's Lower East Side with his restaurant, wd~50, on Clinton Street.

161 Benefit Street was just a few steps away from the RISD campus. A friend of Donald Munroe's named Fred Lutz needed a roommate to share the rent and I was pleased to accept his offer. This was the same building that Donald and his roommate, Joan Schwartz, lived in, as well as Kenny Goodman and Karen Achenbach. It was a pretty cool scene—at least I thought it was until someone crawled in the back window and ripped off my stereo and all my records. That hurt.

My little bedroom was very dark and sad so I bought a gallon of cantaloupe-colored paint to brighten the walls. I adjusted the lighting and that made the room seem much warmer and happier. That was the extent of my redecorating. I didn't really spend much time in the apartment except to

sleep, and I still took my meals in the Refectory with Andi and other friends, so I never used the kitchen except to make some coffee in the morning.

My roommate, Fred, soon decided to move to a big old loft on Pine Street in downtown Providence. This was 1971 and artist's lofts were a new idea in Providence. I had no trouble finding a new roommate. He was a Deadhead from Greenwich, Connecticut, named Chris Lushington. Chris looked like a hippie with waist-length hair, but he also had a serious, puzzled Clint Eastwood vibe. He said he liked music that was played tight like the Grateful Dead and I would correct him: "The James Brown band is tight. The Grateful Dead are loose!" One time I went with Chris and some other friends to see the Dead in a giant Quonset hut outside of Providence. We all marveled at the band's humongous sound system—it was the biggest we had ever seen, pretty crazy looking, and boy, it was loud. The Dead jammed on and on. It seemed like forever. Chris was thrilled. I was wondering how much longer it could go on. I also realized that I missed playing music and wondered how I could get my drums up to Providence from my parents' basement in Pittsburgh.

One day Charlie the Model told me that his dog had puppies and he wanted me to have one. He was looking for a good home for each puppy. I asked him what kind they were and Charlie said, "The mother is an Afghan Hound and the father is a German shepherd." I told him I would have to think about it and Charlie said, "Why don't you come out to see them and see if you like them?" So, I got into Charlie's car with him and drove to his home in the country. Sure enough, the puppies were supercute and friendly, very happy little creatures. Charlie said, "They've already had their shots and they're healthy and smart." There was one in particular, a blonde, that caught my eye. In a moment of sweetness, I said I would take her. Charlie drove us back to RISD. On the way back to town we stopped at a pet store, where I bought her a red collar, a red leash, and some dog food. That night she slept on my bed with me. I named her Lucy. The next morning she gobbled down a big lump of hashish that was sitting on my bedside table and slept for two days! I was very concerned, but when she finally woke up she was hungry, thirsty, and more playful than ever.

About the same time, Tina was shopping in the RISD bookstore, when a tall, well-dressed Asian man approached her with a little black sheepdog in his arms. He asked Tina if she would look after his dog for a couple of

weeks. Tina didn't even know the guy but the little dog was so cute and Tina loved animals so she said yes, she would take care of her. The guy said, "She's a Puli, an Hungarian sheepdog. Her name is Natasha."

It turns out the guy was breaking up with his wife and had no intention of taking Natasha back, but that was fine because Tina quickly became attached to her. Natasha had a bold personality and became Tina's little dreadlocked bodyguard. Tina put a red bandana around Tasha's neck and took her everywhere, even to painting classes. One day, after a few weeks, when Tina was walking on Benefit Street, Tasha, excitedly barking and jumping, ran up to a young mother and her newborn baby. This was the wife of the man who had left Tasha with Tina. She told Tina that she was happy that Tasha had found a good home and she hoped that Tina would keep her. Tina assured her that she would, knowing that the woman had enough responsibilities with a newborn child already.

Lucy and Tasha were sometimes playmates. Tina still seemed to be in love with her boyfriend, Peter, and I was still seeing Andi. Andi and I were very close, but I was not exactly sure of where I stood with her. I could see that she was strongly attracted to a couple of older guys, but our romance kind of sputtered along. I was very fond of Andi. She was adorable, but I could tell that she was struggling with her emotions. She was going through a difficult time.

One night I screwed up my courage and knocked on Tina's door. Her apartment was only a block away from mine, so I made up the excuse that I needed some dog food. Tina was sweet and kindly offered me some. I said thanks and good night. When Tina closed the door, I stood there with Lucy, wondering how to say what I had really wanted to say. I knocked again. When Tina opened the door, I confessed, "I didn't really come here for dog food. I came here tonight because I want to sleep with you." Tina looked at me with big blue eyes, smiled, and said, "Chris, I like you, too, but you know I already have a boyfriend whom I love very much. I couldn't do that!" I paused and finally said, "Well, I'm a very patient guy. If for any reason that doesn't work out for you, I'll be waiting." Tina said, "We'll see," smiled again, and closed the door.

Whew. I had never been what you'd call a smooth operator with the ladies, and now my heart was pounding. As I walked back to my place with Lucy, I felt a great sense of relief having made my real feelings known to Tina. She had not completely shot me down. There was hope.

9

ARTISTIC DAYS GO BY

After a summer working as a welder, cutting and welding caisson pipes for a company called Universal Welding outside of Pittsburgh, I was thrilled to return to RISD. Intense labor and hanging out with the some pretty tough characters were great incentives to stay in college.

I had spent many of my evenings in my parents' basement playing drums along with my favorite records and I wished I were in a real band. I still dreamed of being a musician even though the painting thing was going fine. I've always maintained that the urge to play music and be a performer is the same impulse that drives you to create a painting. Music and art go hand in hand. Feeling as I did, I asked my father to drive me and my drum set up to Providence. My parents had always encouraged my interest in music. I remember so vividly the Pittsburgh Youth Symphony concerts my mother took me to. I loved all styles of music, but I felt most passionate about rock and roll and rhythm and blues.

There had been a new draft lottery. College deferments were out and my lottery number was terrible. I was number 21, which meant, unless something happened, I was going to Vietnam. My father, who was a general by then, told me that if I was drafted he would see to it that I got a post with the Army band. Fortunately for me, President Nixon abolished the draft in 1973 and I was allowed to finish school. I know he was a bad guy, but I'll always be grateful that Nixon did that.

When my father and I arrived at RISD that fall, I moved my drums into my apartment. I soon found out that a better apartment upstairs, the one Karen Achenbach and Kenny Goodman had recently vacated, was available. The landlord said I could have it. It was two rooms with a kitchen in the middle and a single bathroom. I took the front corner room, which had a view up Benefit Street to the RISD campus. The apartment was funky but had plenty of windows and high ceilings. There was a working fireplace with a marble mantelpiece in my room.

In a different lottery, Andi and I got a prime painting studio in the turret of the Carr House building. We were still together and we shared a deep love of drawing and painting. The studio was big enough for two people to work and had abundant natural light. The curved windows overlooked the "RISD Beach" and I could see my new apartment down Benefit Street. Tina was not so lucky and got a studio in a room full of cubicles with fluorescent lighting that she had to share with a girl named Candy who never stopped chatting. After the first day, Tina found the situation intolerable and decided to work in her apartment instead.

Tina and I did have one class together. It was a figure-painting class taught by a guy who was probably the worst teacher I have ever had. I overheard him say to Tina when she asked him a question about her work, "Oh, what does it matter? You're just going to get married and make babies anyway."

Between the bad teacher and the bad studio situation, I admired Tina for having the gumption to stick it out.

In January of '72, a guy I knew named Juan Evereteze asked me if I wanted to join a soul band he was putting together called the Brotherhood. Right away I told him yes. Juan was a soul brother from Boston with a huge Afro who played trumpet. He told me the rest of the band would come down from Boston on Saturdays to rehearse, work up a set, and eventually perform at the RISD spring dance. I told him I was down for that. Meanwhile, we needed a place to rehearse. I got in touch with Fred Lutz, who had a big old loft downtown. I said I would pay him a portion of the rent if I could keep my drums there and rehearse on the weekends. Fred was sharing the loft with a clever electronics enthusiast named Floyd Luton. Floyd had installed all kinds of electronic locks and security in the loft, which was a good thing. They agreed to let me use the place for music part time. The guys in the Brotherhood were serious players.

Some of them had studied at Berklee School of Music, which later became the Berklee College of Music. I was definitely the weak link but the other guys were very patient with me and kept good senses of humor. By playing with them, I got better. The hardest thing for me was to get the feel right on the slow ballads. I had never played a song as slow as those R&B ballads in my life. Eventually, I almost got it right. We played covers of soul classics and current soul hits: "Express Yourself," by Charles Wright & the Watts 103rd Street Rhythm Band; "I Want To Take You Higher," by Sly and the Family Stone; "Rock Steady," by Aretha Franklin; "Cowboys to Girls," by the Intruders. Stuff like that. By the time the spring dance came along, we would be smoking hot.

I needed spending money to buy herb and pay for my share of the Pine Street loft, so I got a part-time job washing dishes at a cool little bistro called David's Pot Belly on Hope Street. The owner, David Levine, had sold his restaurant by the same name on Christopher Street in New York and moved to Providence after his wife had been sexually assaulted. He wanted to give her a new start in a safer environment. David was a brash New Yorker, but he knew his business. He had been in charge of catering at The Woodstock Music and Art Festival before everyone got overwhelmed by the thousands of hippies and kids that descended there. The restaurant served omelets and fancy hamburgers, salads and over-the-top desserts. They did a very brisk lunch business and a more mellow dinner seating. There must have been a cuteness rule because the waitresses were all extremely fetching, especially one young woman called Anki, but I was in the back with the cooks in a tiny little kitchen with no air-conditioning. The cooks were hip young guys. Billy Paden and a black guy known only as Jimmy made the omelets with all kinds of delicious fillings. Chip Young and Josh Miller operated the broiler and cooked the burgers, which also had tasty fillings—you know, a burger with cheese on the inside.

I learned the importance of working fast and moving carefully around the tiny kitchen so as not to bump the cooks. I enjoyed the job and learned how to crack three dozen eggs into a bowl with one hand. I made salads by the ton with each leaf torn by hand. David Levine took a liking to me and I worked his restaurant until I graduated from RISD.

* * *

One chilly Friday night, I was walking down Benefit Street smoking an un-filtered Camel cigarette, when I heard the desperate sobbing and crying of a young girl coming from the bushes in front of the Colonial Apartments, where a lot of RISD kids lived. I had to find out what was wrong, so I climbed a short flight of stairs, and peered behind the shrubbery, and lying there in a weeping heap was Tina. I asked her if she was okay and she said, "No. I feel awful!" She had broken up with her boyfriend, Peter. A so-called friend had then immediately moved in with him without even telling her. On top of it all, she had caught a cold and the twelve-hour cold medicine she had taken did not mix well with the blackberry brandy she was drinking.

I asked if she would like to go to my place and she nodded yes, still sob-bing. Tina was strong but petite and the combination of brandy and cold medicine on an empty stomach had completely overpowered her. Breaking up with her boyfriend, even though it was her idea, had caused her great sadness. She was grieving. I picked her up and carried her down the street to my building, up four flights of stairs, and into my apartment. I laid her on my bed and propped her head up with two pillows and covered her with a warm blanket. I put a bucket on the floor beside her just in case. She was already asleep and breathing evenly. Keeping my clothes on, I lay down on the other side of the bed and closed my eyes.

In the morning, I made us breakfast. Using the skills I learned at David's Pot Belly, I made an omelette filled with peaches and cream cheese. Tina loved that. I turned on my little black-and-white portable TV and tuned in to *Soul Train*. The featured artist that morning was Al Green with a live band, singing "Love and Happiness." I loved watching the kids dance their fresh new angular dance moves. Tina loved it, too! We watched James Brown, Marvin Gaye, the Spinners, and Kool & the Gang. This would become our Saturday morning ritual, omelettes and *Soul Train*. Of course we loved the music, but the dancing was a revelation. The kids on *Soul Train* were invent-ing new dance moves with every show. During the Soul Train Line, the dancers would groove through a gauntlet of hand clapping and foot stomp-ing. It was so cool and sexy to see. I could never dance that radically, but I admired anyone who could. The performances by Marvin Gaye, Al Green, the Delfonics, Hamilton Bohannon, and James Brown made me rush to the record store to buy their latest albums.

From this time on, while not really making public displays of affection,

Tina and I became closer and closer until we were spending a great deal of time together. I had a bounce in my stride and Tina had a twinkle in her eye. We had been good friends for over a year and now we were falling in love.

One class we enjoyed together was a study of Conceptual Art taught by Alan Sondheim. Alan's was an appreciation class and he schooled us about all the great new conceptual artists like Vito Acconci, Dennis Oppenheim, Robert Smithson, filmmaker Michael Snow, and musicians Steve Reich, La Monte Young, and Philip Glass. Alan arranged for La Monte Young to do a performance at RISD. La Monte started off by saying there would be no smoking allowed and then proceeded to do his Hindustani drone thing with slide projections of giant mandalas on a screen behind him. The performance lasted for hours with all of us smokers twitching from withdrawal.

The performance artist James Lee Byars came to our class to read his avant-garde poetry while dressed in a bunny costume. He was very gentle and sweet.

Not so gentle and sweet was the writer and performance artist Kathy Acker. She called herself the Black Tarantula at the time and her poetry was a little bit beat and a whole lot pre-punk. Her reading was totally X-rated and nasty. She was making a strong statement about what a woman could be in contrast to what they were expected to be. Alan had asked me if Acker could use my apartment because the school was not providing a hotel room for her that night. I said yes, of course. I could stay with Tina. I cleaned up my room and changed the sheets. Kathy was only there for one night before returning to New York City in the morning.

I returned to my apartment the next night and in the morning woke up with a case of the crabs that Kathy had left for me. I was grossed out. I had heard about crab lice but I had never had this problem before and didn't know what to do. One of my more experienced friends told me to go to the drugstore and get A-200 Pyrinate shampoo to wash my crotch and any other affected areas. It worked like a charm. I tossed my crab-ridden bedding into a dumpster.

When springtime finally arrived, I played drums with the Brotherhood at the RISD spring dance. The band sounded authentically soulful and funky. Everybody in the audience had a case of spring fever and the music we played was just what they needed to get down and dance and celebrate the rites of spring. It felt wonderful to play my drums with those guys. Sadly, this was the one and only show the Brotherhood would ever play, at least with me.

10

THE BEGINNING

I was the one who encouraged Tina Weymouth to join our band. This took some doing; she didn't think it was a good idea. I knew she had a wonderful sense of rhythm from dancing with her. I knew she shared the ideals and esthetics that we needed in our band. But she said no. The first time I asked her was in the spring of '73 at RISD. We had just started dating and one night a friend gave us a line of cocaine, a first time for both of us, and we walked all over town and I told Tina that my dream was to start a new band and that I would like for her to be part of it. She said no, but that she would help me and be supportive in any way she could. I said okay, but I didn't forget this idea.

Tina was living in the carriage house of her parents' house at the corner of Hope and Benevolent Streets, right next to the Brown University tennis courts. Much to her surprise, Tina's parents, Ralph and Laure, bought a house in Providence and moved in during the summer. Her father had chosen early retirement from the Navy in protest against the Nixon administration's war policies. After surviving the Pacific Theater of World War II, the Korean War, and the Vietnam War, he'd had enough. He was turning his nuclear expertise instead to working on environmental protections and the cofounding of Veterans for Peace.

He went to work for a forward-thinking design group in Providence called REDE—an acronym for the Research & Design Institute. I liked him

Tina's carriage house at RISD.

a lot and Tina's mother was especially wonderful. They gave Tina a little old blue Plymouth Valiant with Florida plates to drive. Tina was kind enough to use it to help me move my drums around. Her father had renovated the carriage house and put in a bathroom and shower. She was kind enough to let me set up my drums and practice there. I had been keeping them in a huge loft downtown on Pine Street, but I couldn't really afford the rent anymore. Tina's carriage house was ideal because Tina was there to encourage me and no one ever complained about the noise.

One beautiful September day, my friend Marc Kehoe, who knew I played the drums, asked me if I would help him create some music for a student film he was making about his girlfriend being run over by a car. I told him I would love to and asked him to meet me over at Tina's place. He said he was going to bring another friend, a guy who played guitar.

When Marc arrived with a tape recorder he had borrowed from the RISD Film Department, he introduced me to the guitar player, his friend David Byrne. Marc's directions to us were simple: Make a cacophonous

racket that fades up, builds to a frenzy, and then fades out. I said that I could do that. David plugged in his Fender Musicmaster, which he had covered with leopard-skin contact paper, and we cut loose with the rising and fading cacophony. I think we got what Marc was looking for in the first take. When we were finished, David said that he could play "other stuff," too. I said great, I had been thinking of starting a new band to play for our RISD friends. Would he be interested? Yes, he said he would.

I barely recognized David even though we'd been in the same dormitory during our freshman year. At that time he had a full Rasputin beard, cut his hair very short by himself, wore secondhand clothes, and rarely spoke to anyone. My roommate, Huey Roberts, called him Mad Dave. David and I didn't have any classes together so I didn't really know him. I remember him playing a violin (not very well) with Marc, who went by the stage name Walter Kapusta and played the accordion in front of the RISD Refectory at dinnertime. One of the songs they played was "Pennies from Heaven." He had dropped out of RISD after freshman year to transfer to the Maryland College of Art and hitchhike across the USA with Marc, but now, a year or so later, he was back. RISD refused to readmit him as a student, but that was okay with David. He thought art school was a scam. He moved in with Marc and Huey and their girlfriends, Naomi and Elisca, in a house on Brown Street. David no longer wore a beard but still had a serious five o'clock shadow, and his hair was bleached blond, almost white, which contrasted with his black eyebrows and the profuse black hair on his arms. He wore black leather trousers that he said he had made himself. It was a wild look, very proto-punk.

David Anderson, a young friend of my family's from Kentucky, had recently come to RISD. I knew he was a good guitarist, so I asked him if he would be interested in joining our band. He agreed to do so. Then I asked another friend, Hank Stahler, who played bass, to join us. Hank was up for it, so now we had the possibility of a four-piece rock band. A couple of times a week we would gather at Hank's apartment on Benefit Street to learn and rehearse cover songs. We started with "All Day and All of the Night" by the Kinks and "I Can't Explain" by the Who. These were two songs that I suggested and everyone agreed that they would be cool to play. When we had more or less mastered them, we learned "Liar, Liar" by the Castaways.

Then we decided we needed a song so the audience could slow dance, so
I suggested "Tracks of My Tears" by Smokey Robinson and the Miracles.
Digging into the soul vibe, we also learned the current hit "Love and Hap-
piness" by Al Green.

Rehearsals at Hank's apartment were loads of fun and very relaxed. Even
with all the RISD students in the neighborhood, Benefit Street was quiet
and peaceful but I don't recall anyone ever complaining about the noise we
made. Hank had a pet rabbit that roamed around the apartment occasion-
ally dropping little pellets. It was a very bohemian scene. We would usually
drink a few beers and smoke a few joints to loosen up, except for David
Byrne, who always said that the herb made him feel paranoid. He stuck
with the beer.

One day, David came to the painting studio that Tina and I shared in a
building called Carr House, on the corner of Benefit and Waterman streets.
Tina and I were in our final year at RISD and making paintings for our
senior show exhibition. Tina was doing her rather large abstract *Battleship*

Tina and me during our RISD years.

canvases and I was working on a large abstract painting I called *Gene Krupa*, after the great drummer who had recently given up the ghost. Even though there was much talk that with the advent of conceptual art, painting was dead, Tina and I still believed. We loved the act of painting and believed it would always be a powerful medium. We still do.

When David came to us on that winter afternoon, he said he had been writing a song and he hoped we would help him with it. He said he was writing it in a style somewhat like Alice Cooper, who was hugely popular at the time, but that so far he just had one verse written. He showed us his notebook and read to us the first verse: "I can't seem to face up to the facts / I'm tense and nervous and I can't relax / I can't sleep 'cause my bed's on fire / Don't touch me, I'm a real live wire." I really dug this. It reminded me more of Lou Reed than Alice Cooper. David said he had asked a Japanese girl to help him write a bridge in Japanese to emphasize the psychotic mind of this character, but she had freaked out at the prospect and left him standing there. I suggested that since Tina spoke French why not have her write the bridge in French? Tina put down what she was doing and got straight to work on it. She thought that we should look to Alfred Hitchcock, whose Norman Bates character took offense to women that he saw as being loose. These are the lyrics that she came up with for what we call the middle eight, or the bridge:

Ce que j'ai fais çe soir là
Ce qu'elle a dit çe soir là
Réalisant mon éspoir
Je me lance vers la gloire, OK

What Tina wrote has been described to me as very classical poetic French by several different contemporary French writers. They said that nobody speaks or writes like this anymore. The English translation is this:

What I did that night
What she said that night
Realizing my hopes
I launch myself towards a glorious destiny.

The voice of a true psycho killer speaking.

Meanwhile I got to work on writing some other verses and this is what I came up with:

You start a conversation, you can't even finish it.
You're talking a lot, but you're not saying anything.
When I have nothing to say, my lips are sealed.
Say something once, why say it again?

And:

Listen to me now. I've passed the test,
I think I'm cute. I think I'm the best.
Skirt tight, I don't like that style.
Don't criticize what I know is worthwhile.

And:

I passed out hours ago.
I'm sadder than you'll ever know.
I close my eyes on this sunny day.
Fa fa fa fa, that's what I say.

David had already come up with the chorus:

Psycho Killer, Qu'est-ce que c'est,
Fa fa fa fa fa fa fa fa fa fa, better
Run run run run run run run away.

This sounded very cool, like a mash-up of the Velvet Underground and Otis Redding. Tina showed David how to spell "qu'est-ce que c'est."

Continuing with the psychotic theme as we were brainstorming, I shouted, "We are vain and we are blind! And Tina said, "Yeah, yeah, and I hate people when they're not polite." David wrote it all down in his little spiral notebook.

Yeah yeah yeah yeah yeah yeah yeah yeah yeah yeah
We are vain and we are blind.
I hate people when they're not polite.

It was our first songwriting experience together and it was proof enough to me that we should do more of this in the future. I was determined, one way or another, to make it happen.

The next song written during this early period was called "Warning Sign." The song was built around a drumbeat I was playing in rehearsal one day. In retrospect, I realize the beat owes a lot to the one Ringo Starr created in "Tomorrow Never Knows." I wrote the lyrics, all of them, while lying on my stomach next to the rabbit on the floor of Hank Stahler's apartment. I imagined the song to be somewhat in the style of the Velvet Underground. This is what I came up with:

Warning sign, warning sign,
I see it but I pay it no mind.
Hear my voice, hear my voice,
It's saying something and it's not very nice.
Pay attention, Pay attention.
I'm talking to you and I hope you're concentrating.
I've got money now, I've got money now,
C'mon baby, c'mon baby.
Warning sign of things to come (turn it over, turn it over)
Someone's talking on my telephone (when we're older, when we're older)
Hear my voice, move my hair.
I move it around a lot, but I don't care (what I remember)
Warning sign, warning sign,
Look at my hair, I like the design.
It's the truth, it's the truth.
Your glassy eyes and your open mouth.
Take it easy, take it easy,
It's a natural thing and you have to relax,
I've got money now, I've got money now.
C'mon baby, c'mon baby.
Warning sign of things to come (turn me over, turn me over)

Love is here but I guess it's gone now (hurry up babe, hurry up babe),
Hear my voice, move my hair.
I move it around a lot, but I don't care.
Do you remember
What it is that you remember
Baby remember
Baby remember.

Much later, when we recorded this song for Talking Heads' second album, *More Songs About Buildings and Food*, David added the words in parentheses and took credit for writing the entire song. It appears that he had forgotten that I wrote these words and when I confronted him, he said he would correct the credits on future pressings.

Anyway, in early 1974, we had enough of a repertoire consisting of cover songs and two original songs to play some kind of show. Since we were all art students and making art was our thing, we decided to call ourselves the Artistics.

11

FREE COCKTAILS!

In our senior year at RISD, we were encouraged to plan a show of our best work at the Woods-Gerry Gallery, an old brick mansion at which student and faculty work were shown. Tina and I had a show planned for the spring, but our friends, Jeff Turtletaub, Marc Kehoe, Naomi Reichbart, and David Byrne, had a group show planned for February 6, 1970. They printed flyers announcing "MOVIES TALENT SHOW COCKTAILS T.V. LIVE BANDS GUEST SPEAKERS" and put them up around Providence's College Hill. Our band, the Artistics, was supposed to perform and back Marc and Naomi, who would be dressed in gorilla suits while they sang the Marvelettes' "My Baby Must Be a Magician." There were three rooms in the gallery, a big room in the front and two smaller rooms, one on the side and one in the back. The show was hung by the four artists themselves so that everyone's work was displayed equally in all three rooms. I was moving my drums into the gallery and setting up when the word came down from the school's security force that the opening had been canceled due to the advertisement of cocktails. They were afraid this event might get out of hand. The drinking age was eighteen then and, since it was on school property, they had to be careful not to attract a bad element.

Hearing this bad news, I started packing up my drums while Marc decided to return the gorilla suits to Boston right away so he wouldn't have to

pay the next day's rental. We left the gallery and Tina helped me to move my drums back to her carriage house in her blue Plymouth Valiant.

I didn't find out about what happened next until just a few years ago. As I have said, the show was hung so that each artist was equally represented. When everyone else had left the building, David returned to the gallery and rehung the show so that only his work was represented in the main front room. Marc's, Jeff's, and Naomi's work was relegated to the side and back rooms. When you walked into the gallery, you would have thought this was David's solo show.

As if this behavior was not bad enough, David had not been an actual student at RISD for three years. He had been invited to show his work as a guest by Jeff and Naomi, who were, in fact, students. This incident set an early precedent for David's seemingly continual need to aggrandize himself at the expense of his collaborators, as if their contributions were not as important as his. Had I known about this at the time, I would have called him out on it, but I didn't. For some reason, nobody told me. Years later, he treated the rest of us in Talking Heads with similar disrespect, and continues to do so. I have to wonder how his new collaborators will feel. Tina has said that he seems incapable of returning friendship. We learned this from experience.

12

SUMMER AGAIN

Our final year at RISD was almost too good to be true. I moved to a new studio apartment down at the far end of Benefit Street so that I could be alone with Tina. It was a real artist's garret. Tina helped me build a bed frame of two-by-twelve pine boards with woven rope to support the mattress. Every week or so I had to tighten those ropes because the mattress would begin to sag from all the bouncing we did there.

One day while lying in bed Tina asked me if I would cut her hair. She got up and sat at my little table. Al Green was playing on the stereo. The windows were open, the breeze was warm, and we were nude. Tina said, "Just give me a blunt cut straight across the back." She passed me a pair of scissors. As I began to make the first cut, I stopped because my hands were trembling. I was panicking, afraid that I would ruin Tina's beautiful hair. She said, "Don't worry. I trust you." Her words and the delicate tone of her voice filled me with love and happiness. As I carefully trimmed her hair, I said to her, "You know, Tina, I feel like we could be married." She understood what I meant and she replied with one word: "Yes."

Walking down Benefit Street one Saturday morning, I decided to stop for a cup of coffee at Joe's. Sitting outside, I was sipping my coffee when Char-

Tina in our painting studio.

Me in our painting studio.

lie Rocket from the Fabulous Motels pulled up to the curb and jumped out of his car. Charlie had seen the Ziggy Stardust and the Spiders from Mars show the night before at the Orpheum in Boston. He was absolutely thrilled by the show and was raving about it. Charlie said, "Rock and roll is changed forever!" He wanted to be a part of the new scene in music and, naturally, so did I. We were in complete agreement about the power of David Bowie, Lou Reed, T. Rex, and Mott the Hoople. It was a good time for music.

While operating a video camera for Alan Sondheim for a project of his, we traveled to Cambridge, Massachusetts, to interview Henry Kloss of KLH audio speakers for a series of videos Alan was making of brilliant people. Around the corner from Henry's studio was a little store selling all types of African products. They sold dashikis, spices, African drums, books, and records. The music playing over the sound system was mindblowing. I asked the shopkeeper whose music it was and she showed me the album: *Shakara*, by Fela Kuti and the Afrika 70. Pictured on the cover were a multitude of topless African beauties kneeling in a 7-0 formation with Fela in the middle. Fela, to be fair, was also topless. I didn't have much money but I bought that record and also one by Chief Commander Ebenezer Obey.

The African music became a turntable favorite at parties. Fela really got the dance floors grooving and "Soul Makossa" by Manu Dibango was even on the jukebox at the RISD Tap Room, where we all danced at night.

Tina and I worked well in the studio together. We were both preparing a series of paintings for our senior show at the Woods-Gerry Gallery. While we worked we listened to WBRU, the Brown University FM station. WBRU was a formidable station and always played the latest stuff. Tina and I discovered a lot of new music together. We loved this new thing called Reggae, and twice we took the Valiant up to Boston to see a sensational new movie called *The Harder They Come*, starring Jimmy Cliff, and featuring a soundtrack that included many of the best reggae acts. There was also a great new band from Jamaica called the Wailers and we dug them, too.

Around this time, Tina and I had the idea to form the Painting Club. We found out that the school would give each student club a budget according to how many members the club had. Everyone we knew wanted to be in the Painting Club and we signed them up. We recruited over two hundred members. We had two club activities in mind. The first was a field trip to New York City to see the Andy Warhol show at the Whitney and John Cage at the Kitchen in SoHo.

The second was a Valentine's Day Ball with live music by the Artistics. Both ideas were approved by Gordy Allen, who was in charge of student activities, and a modest budget was granted.

We left very early one Saturday morning to drive caravan-style to New York. Tina was behind the wheel of her parents' extra-long Dodge van. Amazingly, we arrived in New York by 10 A.M.

The Warhol show was pretty fabulous. This was his Cow Wallpaper period. Not everyone in our group was crazy about the idea of wallpaper art, but we all dug the floating, silver Mylar "Pillows." After a minimal lunch we made our way downtown to the Kitchen, a vast performing arts space in SoHo that featured performances of modern music, dance, and theater. We were about to see and hopefully hear the father of contemporary art music, John Cage. We all sat cross-legged on the floor and enjoyed an intimate performance of his piece "Music of Changes" on piano followed by a lovely chat where he offered each of us a freshly picked wild mushroom and a tiny, thimble-sized glass of his favorite wine. Cage assured us that he had been collecting wild mushrooms for years and these were particularly delicious.

We thanked him and walked over to a place we had heard about called the Spring Street Bar. In those days, SoHo was still full of many light manufacturing shops and the streets were crammed with trucks of all sizes picking things up or dropping things off. There were no chic boutiques or bistros. After dark it was a lonely place, except for the artists who came out of their studio lofts to hang out at Fanelli's Cafe, its walls covered with framed photos of boxers, or the more artistically hip Spring Street Bar. It was cold on the street, but the Spring Street Bar was warm and convivial. As Tina and I stood at the bar, each of us sipping a bottle of beer, I spied the famous gallerist Leo Castelli at the other end of the bar speaking with Jasper Johns. I realized right then that for an artist, New York was the place to be. The art world may be international, but in New York it was a small world where you could meet great artists in the local bar. There was a jukebox playing music but it wasn't playing anything I'd heard before. Someone had put a handful of quarters in to play the same song over and over again. It was a long, pulsing, electronic song called "Autobahn" by the German electronic band Kraftwerk. Hearing their music for the first time was a mindblower. I made a mental note to buy the album. We got back in the van and Tina drove us all the way back to Providence. On the ride home we started imagining our move to New York City.

The Valentine's Day Ball was a total bacchanal. It was held in the Bank Building, which was an old Greco-Roman-style bank with marble floors and a ceiling that was fifty feet high. It made a perfect ballroom and was decorated to the hilt with hearts and Cupids by members of the Painting Club. A bar with beer and wine was set up in one corner. The Artistics set up in the other corner. We didn't have much of a PA system but we were happy with what we had. The acoustics were terrible but we didn't care. This was our big gig! David Byrne was wearing his leather pants and a shiny black shirt. He looked cool. I was wearing a workingman's jumpsuit I bought at Sears and dyed black. I took off my black leather motorcycle jacket, also purchased at Sears, and put it behind my drum set. I loved that jacket and I felt cool wearing it, but it was too hot to play drums in. Did I forget to say I was also spinning records at this party? I created a soulful mix with James Brown, Marvin Gaye, Barry White, the Ohio Players, Kool & the Gang, Manu Dibango, Eddie Kendricks, and Otis Redding.

The place was packed with revelers. This being RISD, many of the kids

were in costume or their most gorgeous party clothes. Art students in full effect. We sent out for more beer and wine when the supply started getting low.

The room was full of gorgeous girls and boys, as duly noted by André Leon Talley in his RISD News column called "RISD After Dark." André studied at Brown, but he liked to hang with the more stylish kids at RISD and take his meals at the RISD Refectory. He was a very interesting, flamboyant guy who was whip smart, tall, and skinny as a beanpole. He adored Andi and Tina and featured them in his column. He knew what he was doing, too. He became an editor at *Vogue* magazine when he moved to New York.

When the Artistics began to play, the party became even wilder. We ran through our repertoire with gusto. We'd been rehearsing for some time and we thought we sounded good. When anyone asks me what the Artistics sounded like, I say prototypical punk. Our setlist consisted mostly of covers with the addition of our originals "Psycho Killer" and "Warning Sign." We also had a song called "Sick Boy" that David and I had written and another one called "Spin, Spin." We also played:

"96 Tears" by ? and the Mysterians
"Psycho" by the Sonics
"You Really Got Me" by the Kinks
"I Can't Control Myself" by the Troggs
"Love and Happiness" by Al Green
"Tracks of My Tears" by the Miracles
"I Can't Explain" by the Who
"Kicks" by Paul Revere & the Raiders
"Psychotic Reaction" by the Count Five

Our friends Naomi and Marc sang their duet version of "My Baby Must Be a Magician," by the Marvelettes, in a guest appearance that everyone loved.

It must have been a wild night because hardly anyone can even remember it. I remember it as not only a real cool time, but as a night that David and I really clicked onstage—I think we both got a taste of the exhilaration you experience from giving a passionate performance. David was still very,

very raw and awkwardly stiff onstage, but when he got into the song and lost himself in it, you couldn't take your eyes off him. Some people, particularly early on when we were completely unknown, felt that David's unusual performance made them feel uncomfortable. I thought that was a good thing.

Tina and I traveled to New York City again to visit Donald Munroe and Joan Schwartz at their loft in what is now called Tribeca and was very similar to SoHo. Donald and Joan were working on a performance art soap opera they called *Each Day*. After a disco nap, Don took us to a wild new club called Le Jardin up on West Forty-third Street. It was very gay and fantastic for dancing. The music was loud and sensuous, the way a disco should be, with plenty of bottom end. Tina and I always appreciated a great dance track and the DJ played every dance hit we knew and many new underground favorites we'd never heard before. Everybody seemed super happy and high. Don told me that the last time he'd been to Le Jardin someone had stabbed him in the ass on the dance floor and he was so loaded he didn't even notice until someone else pointed out that he was bleeding. There was a lot of Lurex clothing. Remember Lurex, that stretchy, sparkly fabric? Even I had a Lurex T-shirt but it shrank in the dryer, so I gave it to Tina, who looked fabulous in it.

My grandfather in Kentucky, the one we called Pappy, shot himself that spring. He had lived with bipolar disorder his entire adult life and they didn't have the medications for it then that we have now. As a younger man, he had received electroshock therapy, which sounds terrible but actually worked—if only temporarily. He had recently had a diagnosis of cancer, which he regarded as a death sentence, and he must have felt emotionally overwhelmed. He was the sweetest grandfather and always a gentleman. He bought a gun, drove to the Maysville train station, and parked on Rosemary Clooney Street, where someone would be sure to find him. Then he shot himself. My father was the one who called me with the news and he made a reservation for me to fly home to Pittsburgh, then we would drive to Kentucky. My family held up very well on the outside, but on the inside we were never the same. When a person close to you, particularly a family member, kills himself besides the grieving there can be terrible feelings of guilt in the survivors: "Why didn't I see this coming? What could I have

done to prevent this? Why wasn't I there to stop him?" Pappy had been so loved by his friends and community and they rallied around Mammy, who was gracious and grateful. This was a very difficult time. Some time later when I was sick with the flu, I had a vision that Pappy came to me and told me he was feeling well and doing fine. I called Mammy to tell her and we both had a good cry. I miss him to this day.

Tina and I had our painting show at the Woods-Gerry Gallery. Tina exhibited her minimalist Battleship paintings and I showed a bold, colorful abstract series I had been working on all year. I was particularly pleased with my *Gene Krupa* painting, which I'd begun on the day the great drummer died. We had a good turnout for the opening. One of Tina's paintings was purchased by a local architect. A case of white wine was consumed. We were feeling good.

The Artistics only played four shows: the Valentine's Day Ball, the RISD Tap Room, a private party in a concrete bunker, and an outdoor concert in the park on Benefit Street across from the RISD Museum. The last show was so much fun. It took place on a warm afternoon in May when everyone had spring fever bad. The Artistics all wore black and wraparound shades à la the Velvet Underground, a band that we revered. We even had an opening act, a band called Providence led by our friend Wayne Zieve. They did a great cover of "We're an American Band" by Grand Funk Railroad called "We're a Providence Band." They were loads of fun and Wayne had a lot of soul.

When the Artistics began to play, people came running. The smell of marijuana was in the air and the mood was colorful, festive, and celebratory. All around us people were dancing and getting down. Marc and Naomi came up and sang their duet of "My Baby Must Be a Magician." It seemed like all was right with the world. I looked out at all the kids who were gathered around and saw Tina, Andi, Huey, and all my RISD friends. The vibes were so good. My time at RISD was almost up. I had explored Benefit Street from one end to the other and I was ready for a new adventure. I will always be grateful to RISD, not only for a great arts education, but for the many wonderful people I met there who are still an important part of my life.

Due to thunderstorms, graduation was moved indoors to the Christopher Wren–designed First Baptist Church. My parents had arrived the night before. After the ceremony we were invited up to Tina's parents' home. My

parents were already very fond of Tina. I felt certain our parents would get along well and they did. It was like we were from the same tribe.

Tina and I said our sad goodbyes. We planned to move to New York in the fall. We would meet David and many of our other friends there. It seemed like everyone was moving to New York. David and I would form a band. The sense of anticipation was killing me, but first I needed to make some money to get started in New York. To do that I had to return to Pittsburgh, where I had been commissioned by a friend of my father's to paint a mural in the stairway of Eye and Ear Hospital. It took me a couple of months up on a scaffolding, but in the end I had the nest egg I needed to make the move to New York.

13

LIFE ON THE BOWERY

As a kid growing up, I liked to watch the Bowery Boys on TV. It featured a gang of nutty juvenile delinquents in funny situations getting into all kinds of trouble. Before I moved to New York, this was how I pictured the Bowery, as a kind of playful skid-row hangout for ne'er-do-wells and drunkards.

When I first saw the Bowery with my own eyes in September of 1974, it was not the least bit playful or funny. At the corner of Bowery and Houston you were likely to see a bunch of guys drinking cheap wine like Thunderbird or Night Train and hanging on for dear life to the chain-link fence that surrounded the parking lot there. One or two would be vomiting and another would have his pants down around his ankles as he relieved himself and then wiped his ass with his bare hands in broad daylight as the traffic whizzed by. Some of the crazier guys would venture out into the intersection to direct traffic. Others would ask for a handout while "cleaning" the windshields of cars stopped at the light with an oily rag or a piece of dirty newspaper. In those days, these poor drunks were known as bums.

There were also many dreadful flophouses where you would never want to end up. The great American composer Stephen Foster, who composed "My Old Kentucky Home," nearly died in one at age thirty, but was carried over to Bellevue Hospital, where he later perished of an infection at age

thirty-seven. He had thirty-eight cents in his wallet along with a note that read simply, "Dear Friends and Gentle Hearts."

Did I forget to mention the dead bodies? It was not unusual to have to step over or around a body that was no longer breathing as you walked down the street. Most of these corpses were men who drank themselves to death or toppled out of a flophouse window. The long history of the Bowery is one of crime, misadventure, debauchery, desperation, and death. Pickpockets and thieves hung out in every bar. People were drugged, robbed, and kidnapped. Muggers lurked in the shadows. It was a challenging scene for some nice kids from the suburbs like us. I had to keep telling myself that I would never end up a bum and, if things got bad, my family would surely look after me.

Jamie Dalglish, a good friend from RISD and a great painter, had a loft at 52 Bond Street with his wife, Susan. David had been camping out at their place, sleeping on the couch and helping them fix it up. I was happy to find David in good spirits. It was a surprise to find that David was now in a relationship with Andrea Kovacs, another friend from RISD. Jamie and Susan told me that David and Andrea had been doing some crazy stuff together. I'm not sure what that was about, but we loved Andrea. She was getting a master's degree in photography at Yale and was doing very interesting work. Jamie and Susan were very warm and generous people, and a pleasure to be with. Susan was very boisterous and hilarious. She teased us a great deal. Jamie knew that I was planning to start a new band in New York and he told me there was something going on across the Bowery at a place called CBGB, which stood for Country Bluegrass and Blues, the sort of music preferred by its owner, Hilly Kristal. I went over to see what was happening that very night.

I had been dreaming of a place where my as-yet-unformed band could play. I imagined that there could be a place as important to our band as the Cavern Club and the Star Club had been to the Beatles in their early days, a welcoming place for people who craved interesting new music. That night when I walked into CBGB, it seemed lonely and sad, a real Bowery dive. No one was there. No music played, not even on the jukebox. The place smelled of beer, dog shit, and roach spray. I asked the bartender for a bottle of Rolling Rock. Then I heard the sound of a pool game in the back of the

club. I followed the sound, tripping over the uneven floor. There were four guys shooting pool. One of them was dressed in a silver, iridescent sharkskin suit, black shirt, and purple tie with big silver Elvis Presley shades. His hair was about an eighth of an inch long all over. It was a wild look. I watched them play for a few minutes and then I asked them if there was going to be any music that night. The guy in the sharkskin suit said in a heavy Mexican accent, "No, man. Not tonight, but come back on Friday and the Ramones will be here." Hmmm, I thought. Mexican music? I told him, "Okay, I'll be back."

I took the subway back to Long Island City, where Tina and I were enjoying the hospitality of her brother, Yann, and his adorable girlfriend, Julia MacFarlane. Yann was well over six feet tall and super bright, fit, and handsome. Recently divorced from his wife, Lally, the daughter of *Washington Post* publisher Katherine Graham, Yann was now living a more "downtown artist" lifestyle. He was happy that Tina had returned to New York and gave us no end of encouragement. I joined Tina, Yann, and Julia for a glass of wine at the great dining table Yann had designed. It was oval shaped, had leaves so that it could easily seat up to twelve people and was painted bright green. I told them about CBGB and said that in the morning I would get *The Village Voice* and start looking for a loft. Yann, who was a loft-living pioneer, told me to forget *The Village Voice*. "Look in the *New York Times* industrial real estate section. Look for a raw space." That's how he had found his loft. He did all the design and construction work himself and it was really beautiful. He had been I. M. Pei's chief designer for the East Wing of the National Gallery and, later, the Grand Louvre in Paris, but now he was branching out on his own. Yann and Julia were kind and generous to us, but we didn't want to impose on them for too long and wear out our welcome.

I had the first bout of insomnia in my life that night. I felt anxious about finding a place to live, getting a day job, starting a band, and succeeding as an artist. In the daylight hours, I had great confidence and never doubted myself, but at night, when I lay down to sleep, the wheels would not stop turning and I imagined the worst, which to me was failure. I had chosen the life of an artist and the real meaning of that was beginning to sink in. There were no guarantees of anything. We were on our own and we had to be brave.

The next morning, I started the search for a loft. I needed a place where a band could rehearse and Tina could paint, since she had not yet agreed

to join the band. Of course, we would also need to live there. Most of the places I found were either dungeons or run-down factories. One place we went to look at in Alphabet City was on fire; smoke was billowing out the windows and no one was coming to put the fire out. I found this incredible, but it was the reality of the Lower East Side in 1974.

The Ramones were not a Mexican band after all. They were four guys about my age. The guitarist and bass player had stylish shag haircuts like the Bay City Rollers. The drummer was tiny and had a cool, minimalist playing style. The singer was tall, shockingly skinny, and sang with a faux British accent. Their songs were hard, loud, and very fast. "Blitzkreig Bop" is 176 beats per minute and only about a minute and a half long. Sometimes they would stop in the middle of a song and yell at each other about mistakes they'd made or just to say that they didn't feel like playing that song tonight. I had never seen anything like it. With song titles like "I Don't Care," "Beat on the Brat," and "I Don't Wanna Walk Around with You," the Ramones seemed like a conceptual art piece to me and, even though they had a lot of polishing up to do, they were wholly original and I loved them. As I left CBGB that weekend, the pretty girl at the door told me that next week a cool band called Television was playing. I told her I'd be there.

After a couple of weeks of loft hunting, I went to see a place at 195 Chrystie Street between Stanton and Rivington. It was 1,200 square feet on the ninth floor, with a big freight elevator and a clear view of uptown and the Empire State Building. A couple of sinks were the only fixtures it had. It was definitely raw. The toilets were in the hall. The rent was $289 per month. There was no key money because no one had lived there before. As far as I could tell, no one else was living in the building to complain about band rehearsals. It was three blocks from CBGB. I told the agent I would take it. When I signed the lease that afternoon, the owner of the building looked at me with obvious skepticism. He asked me what I was going to be doing there. I told him it would be my painting studio and he just smiled, shook his head, and accepted my check for $578: one month's rent and another month's rent for the security deposit.

I told David that I was starting a band and I really hoped he would join me. I'd heard that over the summer he had auditioned for Charlie Rocket's

new band, a spinoff of the Fabulous Motels, but they said no. He had faced a lot of rejection in his life but he had a strong presence and individuality. His point of view was different from most people's and we shared a real love of art rock. I felt in my heart that it was an artistically sound idea to take a chance on partnering with him. Tina and I may have been the only people in the world who believed in David as a musician and bandmate. David had trouble looking me in the eye when I asked him to start a new band with me, but I heard him say, "I guess so." It was not exactly the reaction I had hoped for, but it was a start.

Tina and David agreed to be my roommates and split the rent. A hundred dollars a month per person plus electricity seemed doable. I went out to buy paint to freshen up the place, white for the walls and two different grays for the concrete floor with which we created a checkerboard effect. Tina drove me in her old Plymouth Valiant. It was the first time I had been to Chrystie Street after dark. The street was lined with female prostitutes of all shapes and sizes. When Tina was with me they said nothing, they respected her. But when I was on my own, they'd ask, "Wanna go out?" or "You need a date?" There were so many ladies to choose from, if that was your pleasure. These were the cheap $5.00 hookers who serviced off-duty cabdrivers and other lustful guys who would pull up in their cars. Their pimp was a fiercely handsome long-haired Latino dude who never said a word to us. He wore the same outfit every day, a funky knee-length brown fur coat with a baseball bat concealed under it. I never saw him use it, but I have no doubt he would have if he'd ever felt the need.

Tina and I had to steel ourselves to live in this nightmare of a neighborhood. So did David. The three of us had grown up in charming suburban parts of the country. Our parents had given us every advantage they possibly could and had been supportive in every way, but we were determined to live an artistic life and to us that meant living in New York City, the cultural center of the universe. If our parents had any doubts about us moving to the Lower East Side, they never said so, although the first time my father visited us on Chrystie Street, he said, "You know, I could never bring your mother here. She would never stop worrying about you." Ralph and Laure Weymouth were more philosophical about it. I think they thought Tina's brother, Yann, would look out for us, and he did, as much as he could. David's parents, Thomas and Emma, came to visit one time and acted

like this hellhole was completely normal. They were Scots and his mother plopped down in a chair and said, "Oooh! Put the kettle on!"

But there was another side of the Bowery. I could walk down the street and bump into Debbie Harry in one of her kooky thrift shop outfits. Debbie and Tina were like roses in a rattlesnake nest. Our friend from RISD, the designer Stephen Sprouse, lived just a block away in the same building as Debbie and her boyfriend, Chris Stein. I could cross paths with Johnny Thunders and his girlfriends of the moment, wondering why he looked like such a mess and yet his girlfriends looked so fine. Robert Rauschenberg lived and worked one block over on Lafayette Street in an old orphanage he had bought and restored. It still had the painted mural of young orphans on the side of the building. Ornette Coleman had a loft and rehearsal space on Bowery. The gorgeous gap-toothed model Lauren Hutton had a place near the corner of Bowery and Bond. Willem Dafoe was living there, too, as did Robert Mapplethorpe, the conceptual artist Vito Acconci, the pianist Charlemagne Palestine, and the feminist writer Kate Millet. The poet John Giorno, who we met at RISD when he did a reading from his book of poems *Cancer in My Left Ball*, had lived on Bowery for years. In 1966, William S. Burroughs moved into his "Bunker" in the same building and Mark Rothko painted his Seagram murals there. There was a huge artistic community, not that it was ever visible from the outside.

Out on the street you would beeline to the place you were going as quickly as possible. There was no promenading. You looked straight ahead and avoided eye contact with anyone you didn't know, and even some you did know. There were a few places to hang out and have a drink. There was Phebe's, which back then was a hangout for the Off-Broadway crowd from the La MaMa Theatre nearby. Some nights you could find Divine holding court at the bar and she was always a hoot.

Farther down the street was the Tin Palace, a jazz club that served decent wine and food; the new tenor sax star David Murray, even younger than we were, was a frequently featured artist. Sometimes he would chat with Tina and me before his set. He was curious about what was happening in the downtown art and music scenes beyond the world of jazz.

One time I walked into the Tin Palace for a drink and saw Mick Jagger sitting alone at the bar, wearing a huge, quilted pimp-style newsboy cap. I did admire the Stones. He was high as a kite. The jukebox was playing

Roberta Flack's "Killing Me Softly" and Mick was singing along at full volume but changing the lyrics to, "Blowing me softly with his lips. Blowing me softly . . . with his lips." I decided I would wait until another time to introduce myself.

As we painted the loft on Chrystie Street and tried to make it nice, I had no doubt that one day we would live in a more desirable area, but for now we needed to concentrate on writing music and work hard on it. We felt like we had something new to offer to the world and we set about to do just that.

14

EARLY DAYS IN NEW YORK

Second Avenue becomes Chrystie Street below Houston Street, which for some reason in New York is pronounced "Howstun." Light manufacturing and clothing sweatshops lined the western side of the street and the long, narrow Sarah Roosevelt Park makes up the eastern side. I will try to give you an accurate impression of Chrystie Street when we moved to the Lower East Side in the late fall of 1974. It was not the East Village and it was not SoHo (South of Houston). Our neighbors were mainly poor Dominicans and Puerto Ricans who had no great love for one another. Shootings and stabbings among the rival gangs were very common.

On the ninth floor, with windows all along the long, northern side of the loft, we had an unobscured view of the city and the Empire State Building, and along the western end of the loft, a view of the park, with its many junkies and conga players. Young conga drummers with wildly varying degrees of skill would practice for hours until they got tired or the coke ran out. Salsa music blasted from every passing car. Garbage was all around. That first summer, there was a famously long heat wave and a sanitation workers' strike. The neighborhood kids opened the fire hydrants to cool off. I saw flaming piles of garbage float down Chrystie Street. I thought I was losing my mind.

The battery from Tina's old Plymouth Valiant was stolen too many times

to count. After we chained the hood of the car shut, the thieves would crawl under the car to steal it from underneath.

Our building superintendent was a pockmarked, paunchy, inhospitable Puerto Rican named Jimmy, and he couldn't believe we were moving into the building to live. He never did anything except call the elevator company a few times a week when it broke down. He kept a pack of dogs on the roof. The building was strictly industrial and the loft was all concrete with none of the charming wooden beams and tin ceilings you might see in other lofts. There was no heat in winter after 5:00 P.M. We shared the toilet in the hall with a shop full of seamstresses and the furniture maker next door. It was so unbearably filthy that cleaning it was out of the question. I boldly spray-painted the entire thing silver—toilet seat, walls, and all—à la Andy Warhol's Factory. There was no shower or bath.

The ceiling was twelve feet high and when we first tried to roll any paint on it, it began to crumble and fall in our faces. Not a good sign. I decided to use loads of paint on it in hopes that it would somehow act like glue and hold the crumbling concrete in place. That sort of worked, but later on when we were rehearsing, the sound vibrations caused bits of the ceiling to crumble and fall around us.

I never saw any rats in our loft, but there were plenty of roaches and mice. The roaches loved to hide in the cracks of our little kitchen table. Sometimes while I slept, one would scurry across my face. In the morning, if I found a mouse feasting inside a box of Raisin Bran, I would simply hold the box top shut and open the ninth-floor window. Then I would hold the box at arm's length out the window and watch the little mouse, or some-times a pair of little mice, launch themselves out into space. I had the feeling that they usually survived the fall only to scamper right back up the stairs to our place.

I bought a water heater to install a shower for the loft, but soon realized I had no idea how to even begin such a job and had no money for a plumber, so for the duration of our stay on Chrystie Street, we took showers at Jamie and Susan Dalglish's apartment at 52 Bond Street, or at Yann's place in Long Island City. We would show up with our own towels and after some polite conversation ask our hosts, "Do you mind if I take a shower?" No one ever said no.

We wrote most of the songs from our first album, the ones that had not already been written in Providence, and many from the second album there, too. These were written during nightly rehearsal sessions. Songs and arrangements would evolve slowly over a period of time through repeated playing. The story that there was one songwriter in Talking Heads is a myth. The great majority of our songs, particularly the early ones, were always a collaborative effort. We did not record them. We didn't even own a tape recorder. We had to remember the parts in our heads. Tina knew a little about reading and writing musical notation, but David and I did not, so with songs like "Tentative Decisions" and "I'm Not in Love," we had to play them over and over until they were ingrained in our memory.

When you walked in the front door, first you had to unlock a large padlock from the huge, twenty-five-pound iron bar that, like some medieval invention, slid across the door. Once inside, you would immediately lock the door from the inside. On the left in our kitchen area was the table, where the roaches would hide between the cracks and where we had a single hot plate and Tina's toaster oven. There was a sink for washing dishes but no hot water. If you wanted hot water, you had to heat it up on the hot plate, and that could take a while.

The loft was one big room. There were no partitions. As you walked past the kitchen area, there was a tiny red-plastic child's table and chair where we kept our telephone; we wrote frequently called numbers on the wall, but there was a small notebook for all the other phone numbers we needed to remember.

Just beyond the phone area was where David slept and kept his things in a small dresser. He had a double-bed mattress on the floor. Across the floor from David's area was where we kept our band equipment, which at the time consisted of my black-and-gold sparkle Slingerland drum kit and David's two guitars, one electric Fender Musicmaster covered with leopard-skin contact paper and one beat-up acoustic guitar that someone had dripped paint on, and his Vox AC30 amplifier. Just beyond the band area was a little sink where we would brush our teeth, wash our hair, and take sponge baths before going off to our day jobs in the morning, and just beyond the sink was the "living room." The living room consisted of my parents' rattan porch furniture from when my father was stationed in Puerto Rico when they

were just married. There were two armchairs, a couch, a coffee table, and a couple of end tables. On one of the end tables was a tiny black-and-white TV that my parents had given me one Christmas.

Tina and I slept in a double bed at the far end of the loft. We hung a bar from the ceiling to put our clothes on and it served as a sort of privacy screen, not that any of us had much privacy.

One night the three of us were watching TV when a startling blast of powdered glass sprayed all over us. We didn't know what was happening, but when I walked over to the windows I found a bullet hole. We all got down on the floor. I turned out the lights and when it appeared that no other shots were coming, we went back to watching TV, feeling weird and scared.

We lived there for a couple of years. It was both heaven and hell. I'll never forget how brave Tina was. You know, what was such a nice girl like her doing in a place like this? I know now that she did it for me, and if things had been different I would have done the same for her. Tina was smart, sexy, and cool and my love for her was immense. She was an artist with fine principles and I had no doubt that we would accomplish wonderful things together.

There were some big differences between uptown and downtown New York City back in those days. They were two completely different worlds, yet Tina, David, and I inhabited both. As much as we would have loved to just live the life of the artist, we had to support ourselves somehow and that meant day jobs if we wanted to have our evenings free. Our friends were a big help to us in finding work. Tina got a job as a salesgirl at the very chic ladies store Henri Bendel, thanks to Susan Dalglish, who was working there and had put in a good word for her. Jeff Turtletaub, our friend from RISD, was starting a new job at the Museum of Modern Art and gave his old job as a photostat man at an uptown ad agency to David. This meant David could quit his job as an usher at the Murray Hill Theatre; it was driving him crazy to watch the same movie over and over. Tina's brother's wonderful girlfriend, Julia MacFarlane, recommended me for a stock boy/shipping job at Design Research, which sold European-designed furniture, housewares, and fabrics. I called the manager, set up a meeting, told her Julia had sent me, and was hired on the spot. None of us were paid very much, but we made enough to pay our rent and buy some groceries and that's all we

needed. Interestingly, all three of our jobs were on Fifty-Seventh Street, the fanciest shopping street in the whole country.

Many of the best uptown art galleries were located on Fifty-Seventh, so during my lunch hour I could meet Tina at a gallery or we could walk over to Central Park and have a sandwich. It was not bad at all, at least for me. The stress of working at Bendel's was a bit much, though, not just for Tina, but for all the girls who worked there. The pressure was on them to look great and to sell, sell, sell. When she graduated to selling shoes, Tina said the customers could be downright crazy, like insisting that their feet were smaller than they actually were, but she had some nice customers, too, like Cher, Bette Midler, and the young Tatum O'Neal.

I was happy with my day job at Design Research. I worked with a couple of poets and a couple of cool black guys and a whole store full of sophisticated, beautiful young women. The salesgirls were always completely sweet to the poets and me. Brian and Chuck and I would unload a big truck once a week and put the stuff in the stockroom or on the sales floor until it sold, and then we would wrap it up and ship it off to the customer or load it back onto a truck for delivery. We stocked designs by Marcel Breuer, Hans Wegner, Alvar Aalto, and Joe Colombo, among others. We also carried Marimekko apparel and fabrics. We had loads of famous customers, too. Jackie O would come in to shop with her sister, Lee Radziwill, and Truman Capote. Kurt Vonnegut, who always wore a trench coat with coffee stains on it, was a regular customer. John and Yoko came in once and bought an all-white leather sofa. Outside on the street, we spotted celebrities galore. Paul Newman and Robert Redford passed by the store chatting with each other on a fall afternoon. Peter Boyle would walk by chatting to himself. Liz Taylor, Diana Ross, Farah Fawcett, and, best of all, Catherine Deneuve were all frequent passersby. There was no threat of paparazzi then, except for Ron Galella, who mainly targeted Jackie O. I got a kick out of seeing these famous people. Some of them were guarded, but others would give you a smile and a wordless wink of recognition. We used to joke around about how we would be and what we would do if we were rich and famous.

After work I would usually take the F train from Fifty-third Street, near the Museum of Modern Art, down to the West Fourth Street Station. Then I would saunter east on Bleecker Street toward Bowery. If it was my turn to buy groceries, I would stop at the Grand Union at the corner of University

Place, where I would usually pick up some pasta, red sauce, and salad to carry home and cook on our little hot plate. If I was feeling rich, I would buy a bottle of decent red wine at the liquor store at the corner of Bleecker, and Lafayette. It was the closest liquor store to us that didn't just cater to winos. Then I would continue down Bleecker schlepping my shopping bags to the Bowery with CBGB straight ahead. I'd walk down to Houston, speeding up so the bums wouldn't bother me or ask me for money, and head east to Chrystie. It's funny, but in a couple of years almost every lawyer or accountant we met would say, "Chrystie Street? I love Sammy's! Have you ever been to Sammy's?" Sammy's Roumanian Steakhouse was a little oasis of kosher cuisine on the Lower East Side. It was old school and you would see limos parked outside during dinner hours. Music business execs loved that place. It's still in business today, and I've still never been there.

We took turns cooking at the loft. David liked to cook and he was pretty good at it, but really, he would eat anything. One time he came home with some fish that he bought from a guy selling from the back of a truck that stunk to high heaven. I asked if we were really going to eat that and David said, "Well, I am!" as he fried it up on Tina's little hot plate with fish grease splattering all over everything. He served nothing else with it, just a big plate of stinky fish. I had worked in a restaurant and tended to make things like chicken and pasta and omelettes. We substituted cottage cheese for ground beef in our spaghetti sauce to save money. We may have been poor, but we were not starving.

Almost every night after dinner, David and I would sit down at our instruments and fool around. You could call it jamming, but really it was the beginning of a musical search for a sound of our own. It was important to us that, while rocking, we did not have a predictable rock and roll sound. It had to be a sound that was all ours. I had no doubt that we could find it. I didn't yet know about the "Law of Attraction," but I was visualizing success every day and every night. I did have some doubts about finding other players who would share our aesthetic to join the band. Most of the bands we were seeing that had a unique thing going on were not about to quit their band to join ours, but that was okay with us. We were just getting started. We were finding our way.

Tina had faith in us and encouraged us every day, but not everyone understood why I was forming a band with David. He was awkward and, with

what we know now, on the high functioning end of the spectrum. At the first meeting, he did not inspire one's confidence. When my father, rest his soul, came to visit us in New York, David was unable to look him in the eye and barely spoke. While we were all having a beer, David turned and left without even saying goodbye. My father thought David was "a very thin reed to lean on." I said that I could see why he felt that way. I told him that one time Tina's parents had invited David and me to dinner at their home. David was painfully gauche that night. While sitting at the dinner table, he seemed to not really understand table manners. At one point, he lined up a row of peas on his knife and let them roll into his mouth. Then he did it again. I know—I said David was different. But when I played music with him, I liked what was happening. His style meshed well with my own ideas of being different and less predictable. He was a superb rhythm guitarist. He was also very willing to make an unexpected move, both musically and physically. He got into music to get out of himself. When you played music with David you came to realize that his eccentricities were not an act. There was something deeply moving about his determination and heartfelt efforts to perform a song, even in the early days. In spite of his shyness, he craved being the center of attention. He was always doing some weird thing like not joining in on a conversation, but then quoting that conversation in one of his song lyrics. At a party he would sometimes stand alone and not speak to anyone while looking very uncomfortable. People would watch him like they might watch a train wreck. Some people felt uncomfortable being near David; others were strangely attracted to him. I knew he wanted to be a star but we still had no idea who would be the front person in our band. David was a very unlikely front person so everything was up in the air.

We went to CBGB on the weekends. Nothing happened there during the week, but weekends slowly began to pick up. One Friday night in late 1974, David and I heard a band called Angel and the Snake at CBGB. There were maybe twenty or thirty people in the place, if that. The lead singer was heartbreakingly beautiful and her voice was clear, sweet, and unaffected. She captivated me. It was impossible not to be smitten. After their set she was standing by the bar. With David standing uncomfortably behind me, I offered to buy her a drink and told her David and I were starting a new band and that we were wondering if she might be interested in singing with us. I said, "My name is Chris Frantz and this is David Byrne." She looked at

At the bar at CBGB.

us, smiling, and said, "My name is Debbie Harry. I already have a band, but you can buy me a drink." Imagine what might have been if she had said yes?

Television were the big men on campus at CBGB. They had been among the first bands to play there and their music was seriously compelling. They built the first stage at CBGB. They only played original songs. At the time, they had dueling front men in Tom Verlaine and Richard Hell, who had been friends in the Sanford School, a private boarding school in Delaware, before they ran off to join the circus in New York. Tom played guitar and Richard played bass. I heard that Richard was from Kentucky like me, so I liked him more already. The drummer, Billy Ficca, hit hard but had a jazzy style of playing that sounded different from any other rock drummer I had heard. The real musical star of the band, to me, was guitarist Richard Lloyd. He was a fiery player who alternated rhythm and lead parts that were both supercool and smoking hot. According to Tina, he was also the cutest member of the band. Television had a kind of messianic, beat-poet sensibility.

I heard shades of the Stones, the Byrds, Neil Young, and Jimi Hendrix in their performances. They were very impressive and highly original.

The first time I saw Patti Smith play at CBGB, I had no idea who she was. I soon found out. She was a downtown poet who read at St. Mark's Church in the East Village. Her work was in the tradition of the Beats like Allen Ginsburg, Jack Kerouac, and William Burroughs. She was accompanied only by Lenny Kaye on electric guitar, and she performed many of the songs that were later recorded for her first album, *Horses*. She chewed gum a mile a minute like a schoolyard speed freak. Lenny wore a brilliantly colored tie-dyed T-shirt and his long hair was down to his waist. I thought, *Where am I, Woodstock?* But then they started to play, beginning with "Real Good Time Together" by the Velvet Underground into "Hunter Gets Captured by the Game" by the Marvelettes. I thought, *How thrilling is this?* Then they dropped the bomb on us with her unique cover version of Them's "Gloria" that began with Patti's now-famous line, "Jesus died for somebody's sins but not mine." By the end of the song, hairs were standing up on the back of my neck and the smallish crowd of fifty or so people applauded with tremendous approval. By the end of the set, I was a fan. Patti said that we could buy her 45 single at Bleecker Bob's Records. The next day I headed over to Bleecker Bob's and who was behind the counter but Lenny Kaye himself! Lenny was friendly and warm. I congratulated him on last night's show and laid down my money for Patti Smith's "Piss Factory" and also Television's "Little Johnny Jewel." I was really excited by all of these new underground bands at CBGB. They were clearly going places. I wanted to go, too.

By mid-November of '74 Tina, David, and I were getting into the swing of New York City life. In those days you could have a lot of fun with no money. Occasionally we would go out dancing at various loft parties and private underground discos where you had to be careful with the punch. If someone passed you a joint, watch out, it might be laced with angel dust.

Once in a while we would splurge on something big like a dinner at Puglia's in Little Italy or a Roxy Music Show at the Academy of Music, but mostly we enjoyed the hospitality of our friends. We did some entertaining in our loft as well. Artists really relied on other artists and our friends were always good to us. Like any other community, artists influence each other and collaborations can lead to marvelous surprises. Looking back at all the excitement of being a young artist in New York at that time, the

most momentous day by far for me and for our band was the day that Tina walked into our loft carrying a 1963 Fender Precision Bass Guitar she had purchased at We Buy Guitars up on Forty-Eighth Street. She had been saving money from work and, when her parents sent her a check for $100 for her twenty-fourth birthday, she was able to buy it. She had done her research; this was a great bass guitar. It was almost as big as she was. I had been trying to convince Tina to join the band for a long time, but she had always declined for very understandable reasons. She thought rock and roll was a boys' club and, at the time, she was right. Rock and roll had mostly been a guy thing unless you were a singer, and there was the whole overtly sexist thing that so many bands displayed. She was also concerned about neglecting her painting. She had played acoustic guitar in a folksy style and she had played the flute and she could read music a bit, but she had never rocked a Fender Bass. In spite of it all, she decided to make the leap, and I can't tell you how happy and thrilled this made me. She still needed an amplifier, and she was saving for one, but now we were a trio.

Tina jumped right in on bass. She may have been a beginner, but she was serious. She was ready to play bass at any time and we rehearsed and wrote songs together almost every night after work. Most of our songs grew out of extended improvisations. One thing RISD had instilled in us was that it was okay to be influenced by those who have gone before you, but you must always add something that is unique unto yourself to the work. Otherwise, it's imitation. So, that was our musical philosophy. You can say what you will about our technique, but from our very first show we sounded like nobody else.

Despite our bad neighborhood and raw surroundings, we had plenty of visitors. One fellow in particular, Michael "Wayne" Zieve, came to visit us and did two very important things. First, he wrote some lyrics for a song titled "Artists Only" and gave them to us to use. Second, he saw that we were searching for a band name. We had been experimenting with names and we would even put them on my bass drum head with stick-on letters to see how we liked them. We tried the Vogue Dots, the Billionaires, the Tunnel Tones, the Videos, but none of them stuck. Wayne said, "I was reading *TV Guide* and they had a glossary of television cameraman terms. When you have a shot of just the announcer's head and shoulders it's called a Talking Head. It's the most boring but also the most informative format in TV. I think you

should call your band Talking Heads." We all agreed that it was a brilliant name that did not connote any particular style of music. Tina and I each had T-shirts made up that said TALKING HEADS on the front in big silver letters and put them on and took a walk to Washington Square Park. My shirt was red and Tina's was black. People would look at us and smile. One guy asked, "Are you guys in a band?" Another said, "Oh man, that's a terrible name!" We were getting more positive reactions than negative, though, and the name stuck. We became Talking Heads, and today that T-shirt of Tina's is on display in the Rock and Roll Hall of Fame.

15

TALKING HEADS' FIRST SHOW

Now that we had a name and enough songs written to play a short set, we decided to go for it. Yes, we were still very raw and jittery and we did have apprehensions, but we felt that the time was right. We could see that there really was something happening with the new bands playing at CBGB. It was not really big enough to be called a movement. It was a small scene with mostly just a few friends in attendance. It was good that the audience was small because if you screwed up not very many people would know. Artistically speaking, the bands playing CBGB were very strong. They were also diverse. Imagine a place where you could see the Patti Smith Group, Television, the Ramones, and Blondie on any given weekend. We wanted in. I went to speak to the owner, Hilly Kristal.

I walked over to CBGB one spring afternoon in May 1975. The Bowery was sunny and bright but you could smell piss and other nasty things wafting in the breeze. As I opened the door to CBGB, the smells did not go away but came in layers to include beer, roach spray, dog doo, and Chanel No. 5.

Hilly was sitting at the bar with his Saluki dog, Jonathan, who was allowed to poop wherever he wanted. Nobody cleaned it up. There were no other customers so I asked Hilly if I could talk to him about something. He nodded yes. I said, "My friends and I have a band and we'd like to audition to play here."

Hilly chuckled and asked, "What kind of music do you play?" I said, "We play in a style of our own." He chuckled even harder and said in his very deep and resonant voice, "Well, I could put you on before the Ramones on Thursday. If I like your live show, you can play before them this weekend. There is no money for the audition and you'll have to work out something with the Ramones on the weekend." I thanked Hilly, shook his hand, and hurried back to the loft to tell David and Tina.

With this good news we started making a set list and running sets of all the songs we'd learned as professionally as possible:

"The Girls Want to Be with the Girls"
"Psycho Killer"
"With Our Love"
"Artists Only"
"I Want to Live"
"Warning Sign"
"Tentative Decisions"
"Love → Building on Fire"
"I Wish You Wouldn't Say That"
"96 Tears"
"No Compassion"

We didn't tell very many people about our audition. We only mentioned it to a few close friends. The Ramones did not attract very many people, either. They said no one wanted to come to this dump on the Bowery. They were from Forest Hills, Queens, and that was a long subway ride for their friends.

The original stage at CBGB was not big but we were only a trio so space was not a problem. As we set up our gear, we realized there were no monitors, which meant we would not really be able to hear ourselves. But of course we didn't have any monitors in our rehearsals, either, where David sang through a little guitar amp. It would be fine.

We decided to wear black and white. I wore black Levi's with a white oxford cloth Brooks Brothers shirt and black wraparound shades. I felt clean cut, but hip. David was dressed all in black with gray suede Hush Puppy loafers. Tina looked chic, as usual, in a white shirt, black trousers, and red sneakers.

We played our set as best we knew how and we made a few mistakes, but nobody seemed to notice. The audience of about twenty people clapped dutifully after the first couple of songs, but as we warmed up, so did they. It was wild to play for real people in a real underground rock club, and we loved it. Finally we had arrived in New York. To me, it felt like my dream band had finally materialized. I was in love with our new band and this was the life for me. There was no doubt in my mind that we would succeed.

As we cleared the stage to make way for the Ramones, Hilly said we had passed the audition.

I heard Johnny Ramone, the guitarist, say to him, "Yeah, they suck, so they can open for us. They'll make us look good."

Our first show at CBGB.

On the weekend there were more people in the audience, but attendance was still pretty sparse. Maybe we had fifty people in the house, but that was fifty more than would have been there before Hilly started booking bands. We were all hoping this show would lead to many more. Yann Weymouth and Julia McFarlane brought the famous rock writer from *Life* magazine, Albert Goldman. Albert laughed and said we reminded him of an episode of *The Twilight Zone*. My favorite coworkers from Design Research came. A group of our RISD friends were there and between sets we all ran across the street to Jamie and Susan Dalglish's loft at 52 Bond Street and partied.

Tina, David, and I were elated. With the exception of Johnny Ramone, nobody told us we sucked. Quite the opposite: People were intrigued by our quirky little band.

Guys were entranced by Tina, such a pretty thing with so much power. This didn't bother me a bit. I was confident that Tina and I already had a very strong bond. David made a big impression, too. Even in these earliest shows he delivered the songs in a little high-pitched voice and an uneasy earnestness that was very uncommon in rock and roll. After the weekend, Hilly wondered how soon we could come back. We said, "As soon as you like."

16

THE RECORD COMPANIES

There were a few daring record company guys who started showing up at our gigs. Most of the record company people did not want to come down to the Bowery to see a new band. It was way out of their comfort zone. They found new bands from their manager friends. Mark Spector, from Columbia Records, was one of the few who did come to CBGB. After seeing us play several shows, he took us into the famous Columbia Studios to record a live demo. The room was cavernous and could accommodate a full symphony orchestra. It was considered to be the best sounding studio in New York. Frank Sinatra, Barbra Streisand, Leonard Cohen, Laura Nyro, Bob Dylan, Paul Simon, and Paul McCartney had all made records there. The music for *West Side Story* was recorded there. We drove uptown in Tina's little car with our gear and carried it up to the studio. As we were setting up and the engineer was getting his sounds, Mark explained that he wanted us to run through all the original songs we knew as if it were a live show. We were recording live to two-track tape so there would be no fixing or overdubs. We ran through the set in less than an hour and then listened to the playback.

In some ways we sounded like a little toy band, but at the same time had an undeniably downtown edge. There was nothing smooth or easily digestible about our sound. Still, Mark was pleased with the result and, as

an A&R—Artists and Repertoire—man, would play it for his bosses, letting them know that it was our first time ever in a recording studio.

Matthew King Kaufman, prowling downtown New York looking for talent, was another guy who expressed an early interest in Talking Heads. He had a small independent company called Berserkley Records in Berkeley, California. He had recently released the self-titled *The Modern Lovers* album, which we loved and played a lot in our loft. He offered to record a demo for us, too, and booked us into K&K Studio City in Great Neck, Long Island. K&K stood for Jerry Kasenetz and Jeff Katz, who wrote, produced, and performed the 1910 Fruitgum Company, Ohio Express, The Music Explosion, and Crazy Elephant. They were the undisputed kings of bubblegum music. We had added one of their big hits, "1-2-3 Red Light," to our live shows just for fun, so the irony of working in their studio was not lost on us. Matthew and his engineer, Glen Kolotkin, had us record just three songs: "Artists Only," "Psycho Killer," and "First Week, Last Week." This time we were recording to sixteen-track tape and we spent more time getting the drum sounds right. Matthew seemed very pleased with the results and offered us a record deal. We told him we'd have to think about it and he said, "No problem, man, and you can play this demo for any record company you want." We didn't do that because, on close listening, it was clear to us that we needed more time to develop our skills. Live we were already very strong, but making a great recording was another skill set altogether. In a live setting, you are going for a compelling performance even if the playing is not always perfect. On a recording you are going for something that sounds good, hopefully even exciting after repeated listenings. We were learning how to do this as we moved forward.

We sent the Columbia demo to Bob Feiden, one of Clive Davis's Arista Records guys who had signed Patti Smith and Lou Reed, but when I called him about it after a few weeks, he said he'd lost it.

Then one night in November 1975, when we were opening for the Ramones, Seymour Stein heard us play quite by accident. He had come to hear the Ramones and was standing outside CBGB talking to Lenny Kaye when we opened our set with "Love → Building on Fire." To hear Seymour tell it, he was mesmerized by the song and the sound of our little trio and was drawn to the front of the stage as if by some mysterious force "like a snake charmer." I remember seeing him standing there as if he were a statue, eyes

popping out. After the show, he asked Tina if he could help her take her equipment off the stage. He said, "I'm Seymour Stein of Sire Records. Can we talk?" Seymour always says it was David he was speaking to, but really it was me. I said, "We know who you are, Seymour, but now is not a good time. Could you call us tomorrow?" I gave him the number at our loft.

The next day Seymour called, excited. He wanted us to make a record for Sire. We invited him over to talk. We liked him and we appreciated his enthusiasm but we told him he would have to wait. We weren't ready to make a record yet. We were certain of that. We realized that if we made a mediocre-sounding record the first time out, we might never get a second chance. Seymour was truly surprised that we said no, not yet. He was, in fact, shocked! So, he waited—not patiently—but he waited.

Meanwhile, we started talking to each other about adding a fourth member, ideally someone who could play keyboards and guitar. But who?

17

THE STARS OF CBGB

On some nights, CBGB on the Bowery was like a beacon. I felt it was a sign of great things to come. On other nights, it was an oasis. It was a place where I could be refreshed, and gaze upon all the new rock stars. Other nights, it was a shelter, a refuge from the harsh reality that was life in New York City.

One winter night during a freezing cold blizzard when the snow was up to my kneecaps and still coming down and blowing sideways across Chrystie Street, I decided to make the three-and-a-half-block trek to CBGB. I was wearing a knit ski cap, a wool tartan scarf from Brooks Brothers, and a white Swiss Army sheepskin overcoat with black engineer boots. It was bitterly cold and I trudged as fast as I could to the welcoming interior lights of CBGB. I pulled open the door. The place was nearly empty, but standing in front me by the bar was David Johansen of the New York Dolls. I knew David a little bit from hanging out at CBGB. He was wearing a light blue satin suit, almost a tuxedo, with no shirt underneath. I said, "Hi, David." He took one look at me, had another sip of his cocktail, and said, "You know, Chris, rock stahs, we don't dress fuh the weathuh." Another thing he told me was, "Chris, you're never going to make it in this business. You're too nice!"

* * *

One night in late fall of 1975, Tina, David, and I arrived home after work at our building on Chrystie Street to find the street blocked off. Several fire engines and emergency vehicles were just arriving on the scene. Our building was on fire. You could see the flames and smoke billowing out the windows on the fifth floor. Our loft was on the ninth. It was a dreadful feeling to think that we could lose everything we had. And it was cold outside. The fire chief said there was nothing we could do, let his men do their job and come back in a couple of hours. We decided to go to CBGB. It was 7:00 P.M. and Hilly Kristal was the only person there. We told him what had happened. He expressed his concern and told us to come on in and have a seat at the bar. He served each of us a pint of draught beer and a big bowl of his homemade chili. Over the years there have been many jokes and stories told about the chili served at CBGB. People say that they wouldn't dare eat it—imagine what was in it! Well, I can tell you that we three Talking Heads ate the chili that night with great gusto and appreciation. I'll tell you something else, too: It was really delicious. After a while, we steeled ourselves and walked back to our building. We were in luck. The firemen had put out the fire, which had been in a sweatshop that made polyester clothing. Polyester burns really hot and the fumes were toxic. Our loft was unharmed, but because of the strong fumes of burning plastic, we would have to sleep elsewhere that night. David went to stay with Andrea. Thankfully, Yann and Julia welcomed us to their loft, a half hour away by the F train in Long Island City.

From my first visit, CBGB held a position of great importance in my life. First, it was our ambition to play there. Then, when we were performing there, it was both an incubator for our baby band and our launching pad out into the world. Finally, when we were "too big" to play there anymore, it became a place that we would return to see old friends and check out the latest new talent.

An early CBGB friend and fan was Lenny Kaye. He was full of encouragement and warmth. As guitarist in the Patti Smith Group, in my mind he was at the pinnacle of the CBGB hierarchy. When I was still at RISD, I had bought the great album he curated and compiled called *Nuggets: Original Artyfacts from the First Psychedelic Era 1965–1968*, and we played several

tracks from that album with our band, the Artistics. Lenny always came to our early shows when sometimes there were only ten or twenty people there, and we could hear him cheering at the end of each song. On one hot summer night in 1975, he introduced us to the great Patti Smith herself. She looked us over while snapping her chewing gum and said, "Oh, yeah. You're that art school band. I wish my parents were rich enough to send me to art school." She turned and started taking to someone else. That was it, end of conversation. It was not the conversation we had been hoping for. Lenny had also started seeing Tina's sister, Laura, and I think Patti put an end to that. When I run into Lenny now, he never fails to mention that he still has a soft spot in his heart for the Weymouth girls. As a musician, author, and producer, Lenny is in a class by himself.

Richard Hell was the bass player for Television, and also a poet and the author of the song "Blank Generation." Richard was definitely a kingpin at CBGB. With his choppy hair and torn clothing, he pretty much created the punk look, which was copied, stylized, and sold in the UK, and later in Los Angeles, by Malcolm McClaren. Richard was from Kentucky like me but when I first mentioned the connection to him, he pretended he didn't hear me. Later, we talked a little bit about Lexington, Kentucky, but it was clear that he had no great love for bluegrass. Richard quit Television and formed the Heartbreakers with Johnny Thunders. From what I heard, in 1976 Johnny was in Florida on the ill-fated final tour of the New York Dolls

when he saw posters for a band from Gainesville, Florida, called Tom Petty and the Heartbreakers. He liked the name "the Heartbreakers" and thought these guys will never go anywhere and decided to use the name for his new band. So, Richard was a Heartbreaker for a while but soon formed Richard Hell & the Voidoids and signed a recording contract with Sire about the same time Talking Heads did.

Richard Lloyd of Television was one of the best guitarists at CBGB, maybe the very best. We heard stories that he had been taught to play guitar by Jimi Hendrix, which, while only partially true, explained how Richard's guitar work combined rhythm and melody to great effect and drove Television's sound to a higher level. While Richard was not exactly chatty back then, we had a good rapport. He has written that he did have a big crush on Tina. He was not alone. Richard Hell and Dee Dee Ramone also had a thing for Tina. I was not surprised or jealous that these guys admired Tina. It merely showed they had good taste in women as well as in music. Television had founded the music scene at CBGB. While some say that other artists such as Wayne County had played there first, it was Television who first approached Hilly about doing a residency there. When Hilly said that he preferred country and bluegrass music, Television said, "Oh, we can play that!" Of course they never did, but that's how they got their feet in the door. They even built the first stage, which was barely big enough for the four of them. After we had more or less established ourselves at CBGB, we approached Television about doing double bills together—with them getting top billing, of course. After thinking it over, Tom Verlaine, who saw himself as the leader of the band, agreed. Television and Talking Heads was a bill that not only packed the place but also attracted a diverse crowd of people, including music lovers from as far away as the UK, France, the Netherlands, Italy, and Japan.

Roberta Bayley was the very smart and pretty, no-nonsense young woman who took the money at the door. She was originally chosen to do this by Television, but I guess Hilly never saw any need to hire anyone else. Roberta was also a very edgy photographer who shot the Ramones' first album cover and many of the great early band photos at CBGB. Later, when things got kind of crazy, the very wonderful Deerfrance also helped out at the door before she went off on tour singing with John Cale and relocated to Paris. Between Hilly and the people working the door there was a policy to

not charge band members for admission, even when they weren't performing, so CBGB became a real gathering place for downtown musicians. If the bartenders, Richard and Merv, liked you and your band, beer was on the house, but they did have a full bar if you wanted something harder. Hilly's drink of choice was brandy and Fresca. I never tried that combination, but I did have a few Stoli and grapefruit juice.

After one of our first sets at CBGB, Johnny Thunders came up to me and asked if we were a feminist band. One-third of the band was female and playing bass, which was highly unusual. Also, he had just heard us play a song called "The Girls Want to Be with the Girls" so it was a fair question. I told him, "Yes, we are." And why not? We knew from the start that we could never beat the Rolling Stones or the Who at their own game, so we would have to take a different tack.

Dee Dee Ramone was one of my first friends at CBGB. Joey was friendly, too, but Dee Dee had a lot more to say. I remember once he was trying to quit drugs and he said to me, "When you're not getting high, the days are so long! It's a real shocker."

The guys in the Patti Smith Group were all cool. Besides Lenny, Ivan Kral was the most friendly to me. Ivan was Czech and very handsome. He played the bass and the guitar. Early on at CBGB he shot a black-and-white film, now an underground classic, called *Blank Generation*. Talking Heads was lucky to be part of that documentary. He had the most adorable girlfriend named Lynette. Both of them were bright, beautiful, and as sweet as could be.

Patti's keyboard player was Richard "DNV" Sohl. When he became a member of the band the sound took a quantum leap. He never overplayed but always added lovely textures and colors to the overall sound. He was beautiful, too, in a *Death in Venice* way.

For a long time Patti Smith had no drummer, but when she added Jay Dee Daugherty, that's when the band really started to rock. Jay Dee had come to New York from Southern California as the drummer for the Mumps, but it was with Patti that he found fame and maybe a little fortune.

The Mumps were Lance Loud's band. Lance was a very wild guy who had experienced fame young when his family starred in the early documentary series *An American Family*. We got along well together. Lance's musical partner was Kristian Hoffman, who moved to New York with Lance from

Southern California. The Mumps were a tight little band with Rob Duprey on guitar and Jay Dee Daugherty on drums, until Jay Dee joined the Patti Smith Group. Kristian later worked with Lydia Lunch, James White and the Blacks, Klaus Nomi, and the fabulous Ann Magnuson. Rob Duprey went on to work with Iggy Pop.

The Shirts were all from Brooklyn, which in those days seemed a million miles from Manhattan. They all lived together in a brownstone and kindly invited us to make some demos in their basement studio that their good friend J. R. Rost was putting together. The Shirts signed to Capitol Records, but lead singer Annie Golden left the band to be in Milos Forman's movie version of *Hair*. Then she went on to Broadway and eventually to HBO's *Orange Is the New Black*. Despite many highs and lows, including the untimely death of guitarist Ronnie Ardito, the band has persevered and continues to record. I particularly love one song they wrote called "Tina of the Talking Heads." You can imagine why. The "While David Byrne was squawking / Tina was pure white chocolate" kills me every time I hear it.

Mink DeVille was Willy DeVille's band. He was one of the most colorful denizens of CBGB. Rumor had it he was a Latino from San Francisco when in fact he was a suburban guy from Stamford, Connecticut. He sure did have some soul, though. His vocals were terrific and his band was cool. He had a great drummer named Manfred. Manfred—whose real name was Thomas Robert Allen Jr.—and I used to chat, but conversations at CBGB were often very fragmented because of the volume of the music. You had to shout to be heard and that soon became tiresome.

Robert Gordon fronted a hard-rock band called Tuff Darts. Those guys were super tight and had real tough musical chops, but Robert departed after a few years to pursue his true love, rockabilly music. He worked with Link Wray, Chris Spedding, and Danny Gatton while Tuff Darts recorded an album for Sire with another singer, Tommy Frenzy.

They say Wayne County—later Jayne County, after she transitioned—played CBGB first and that may be. Wayne grew up in Georgia and still had a strong Southern accent. Her band was first called Wayne County & the Backstreet Boys and later changed to Wayne County & the Electric Chairs. She had a wild sense of humor and had been part of the downtown underground scene for years. She wrote songs that were almost parodies of rock songs and were vulgar in the extreme. My favorite was "(If You Don't Want

to Fuck Me, Baby) Fuck Off." She taunted the homophobes and everyone else at CBGB. One famous night when Tina and I were watching, Handsome Dick Manitoba of the Dictators was heckling her and she said that if Handsome Dick didn't stop he would be sorry. Handsome Dick continued to yell obscenities at the stage and Wayne stepped forward and swung her microphone stand like a battle-ax onto Handsome Dick's neck. That was the end of the heckling. An ambulance was called and Dick was carried off to the hospital. Dick survived and later, in CGBG style, a benefit concert was staged to help with Handsome Dick Manitoba's medical bills. I'm pretty sure Wayne County was one of the performers.

John Cale was a frequent performer at CBGB. After his ups and downs with the Velvet Underground, he produced some classic records for Nico, like *The Marble Index*, *Desertshore*, and *The End*; for the Stooges' self-titled debut album; and even the demos for the original Modern Lovers that were later released as their first album on the Berserkley label. He also recorded a number of great solo records that we loved. Recently he had returned to New York to produce *Horses* for the Patti Smith Group and he was performing again. He put together a great band and everybody at CBGB loved his version of the Modern Lovers' "Pablo Picasso." John was a Welshman with an appetite for booze, drugs, and music, like almost everyone else at CBGB. He had already taken a few laps around the track, but he was still going strong.

The Marbles were also early on the scene, an example of how diversified the musical styles were at CBGB. With Fab Four haircuts and a very clean, buttoned-down appearance, they were pure power pop before power pop was a thing.

The Dead Boys came to CBGB from Cleveland, Ohio. We had heard that Cleveland was one of America's great rock and roll towns and the Dead Boys were as hard rocking as they come. Singer Stiv Bators claimed to have been the fan that gave Iggy Pop the jar of peanut butter that he famously smeared all over his shirtless torso. Guitarist Cheetah Chrome was a powerful player in the tradition—if you could call it that—of the Stooges and the MC5. Stiv, Cheetah, and Johnny Blitz had all been in one formation of the legendary Cleveland band Rocket from the Tombs, so they had something of a pedigree already.

Can you imagine walking into a dive bar on the Bowery, making your

way to the stage, and seeing one of history's great beauties for the first time? Imagine then that this woman can sing in a voice that speaks sweetly and directly to you as if there was no one else in the room. This was my experience with Debbie Harry. Her band—originally called Angel and the Snake, but now Blondie—was still finding their way and other bands kept poaching her players. Ivan Kral left to join the Patti Smith Group. Fred Smith left to join Television. When I first met guitarist Chris Stein—who was Debbie's boyfriend and songwriting partner—he looked a bit like a better-looking Alice Cooper. Drummer Clem Burke was a friendly guy who, while standing at the bar, asked me if I thought he resembled anyone. I was stumped. Then Clem said, "Some people tell me I look like Paul McCartney." Keyboard player Jimmy Destri insisted on auditioning for Talking Heads when he heard we were considering adding a fourth member. Understandably, Debbie was annoyed at this. Musicians jumped ship from Blondie in the early days because they thought they could do better with a band that was getting more accolades in the music press like Patti Smith, or Television, or even Talking Heads. Bass player Gary Valentine even went solo after the first album didn't do so well. Some people can recognize a diamond in the rough, and some people can't.

There were some serious journalists down at CBGB, too. Our favorite, a nightly regular, was James Wolcott. Jim was writing for *The Village Voice* and wrote a great piece called "Tired of Glitter?: The Conservative Impulse of the New Rock Underground." Of all the bands to choose from, the *Voice* put Talking Heads' picture on the cover, probably because we had the shortest hair. Jim Wolcott seemed to get our music immediately, even in this early raw stage. He was both friend and fan. We liked him and his friend Trixie A. Balm, who was also writing for the *Voice*. They were smart and sympathetic to where we were coming from. John Rockwell from *The New York Times* was also very early in writing about CBGB and the bands that played there. He was more formal than Jim Wolcott but also very astute. Robert Christgau and Richard Goldstein were prowling around the scene, too. The great Lester Bangs arrived from out of nowhere one day and was hooked on the Ramones. He didn't get Talking Heads and didn't like us at first, but one day he told me he'd had an epiphany. He said, "Now I get it. You guys are so uncool, you're cool." That was one way to look at it.

Terry Ork was Television's manager and ran a little label called Ork

Records. Television's first 45, "Little Johnny Jewel," was on Ork. He also released singles and EPs by Richard Hell, the Marbles, Alex Chilton, Chris Stamey, Mick Farren, Cheetah Chrome, and the Student Teachers. Terry was a sweet guy and he helped and guided Hilly with bookings. Seymour Stein once said to me, "I'd like to do business with Terry, but he's always laughing. I can't take the guy seriously if he's always laughing." His day job was running Cinemabilia, a West Village shop for film fans with books, magazines, and film memorabilia for sale. Richard Hell had worked there and I think maybe Tom Verlaine, too.

Danny Fields was a great character on the scene. Danny seemed to know everybody who was anybody. He had attended Harvard. While working at Elektra records, he signed the Stooges and the MC5. He hung with the Warhol crowd and was buddies with Lou Reed and Nico. His day job was managing editor of 16 magazine and he was one of the first people to write about Talking Heads in his talent-spotting column in the *SoHo News*.

LOU REED

In the early days of CBGB, Lou Reed was practically a regular. I had seen him at a couple of Patti Smith shows and a couple of Television shows. It was a thrill to see him there. He later told us, "I still notice things," and he did. To his credit, he was one of the first and few stars to come to CBGB to check out the new bands. The first time I saw him there I jumped over a few tables and chairs to ask him for his autograph. The last time I'd asked somebody for an autograph was President Eisenhower when I was just a kid and my father took me to the dedication of Eisenhower Hall at Valley Forge Military Academy. Lou, who was wearing aviator shades in the darkened club at 2:00 A.M., signed the piece of paper and then turned on his heels and left.

So we were practically in awe when he appeared backstage at CBGB after one of our early shows. This was right after his *Coney Island Baby* album had been released in December 1975 and I was playing that record a lot in our loft on Chrystie Street. Lou invited us back to his place and gave us the address. We were amused that his apartment was located on the Upper East Side near Bloomingdale's. We had not expected that. So we quickly packed up our gear, took it back to our loft, and then headed uptown. I think this was one of the few times we splurged on a taxi to get to his place as soon as possible.

His building had a doorman and potted plants in the lobby. The door-

man told us that Lou was expecting us, so up in the elevator we went. We knocked on his door and were met for the first time by Rachel Humphreys, who was Lou's transgender girlfriend. Rachel said nothing but waved us in. Except for a couch there was no furniture. Lou said, "This is Rachel. Have a seat." Rachel looked like kind of a badass and was the first transgender person I knew. You could see that she was very protective of Lou, but I guess she decided that we were okay because she went into the bedroom and closed the door.

Tina, David, and I sat on Lou's very ordinary 1960s modern couch and he sat on the floor. He was alternately sweet and acerbic. The first thing he said to us was, "It's, like, cool you have a chick in the band. Wonder where you got that idea?" He then proceeded to critique our set that night and also those of other bands he'd seen recently, namely the Patti Smith Group and Television. He liked what we were doing, but fixated on a song called "Tentative Decisions" over all the others. He loved the words but felt the tempo was much too fast and that if it were played more slowly it would convey a deeper feeling. I'm sure he was right about that, and in future performances and recordings we did slow it down a little, although probably not as much

Lou Reed.

as he would have liked, because at this point our audiences responded best to up-tempo numbers, not slow ones.

Lou got up and walked to the kitchen and fetched a quart of Häagen-Dazs ice cream from the refrigerator. He brought it back and sat down again, cross-legged on the bare hardwood floor, when he said out loud to himself, "I'm gonna need a spoon for this." Tina volunteered to get him one, and when she opened the kitchen drawer realized that there was only one bent and blackened spoon in the place. With a slight grimace, she

brought it over to Lou, who proceeded to eat the entire quart of ice cream right in front of us with that funky spoon. He didn't offer us any ice cream or anything else. It must have been four o'clock in the morning. Lou seemed like he was just waking up.

In between bites, he told David that he should never go onstage in a short-sleeved shirt because his arms were too hairy. He should always wear long-sleeved shirts.

Lou Reed then told us that a band was like a fist. It could be very powerful, but that the record companies would always try to manipulate and massage one finger away from the others and break it off so that they would only have to deal with one individual and not the whole band. I thought it was interesting that he would be telling us this in light of his own history with the Velvet Underground, but we didn't really know the whole story, so we kept quiet about it.

Lou talked and talked and we listened, sometimes in awe and sometimes in disbelief. At some point Lou got up and went to his bookcase, which had only one book in it, *The Physicians' Desk Reference*. He began to tell us what his favorite drugs had been and which ones he was enjoying lately, kind of like when you look through the L.L. Bean catalog except with pills, pills, pills. He showed us the photos of his various favorites, the uppers and the downers, and warned us about the hazards of each one.

Then, after teaching us a thing or two about Dilaudid, Lou suggested we all get something to eat. We took the elevator downstairs and, as the sun was rising, walked across the street to the diner now called Eat Here Now on Lexington Avenue. Tina and David and I had the early riser's special of bacon and eggs and hash browns, while Lou, our hero, ordered a huge stack of pancakes with maple syrup. Lou was a skinny guy, but what a sweet tooth he had!

After breakfast, we had to get some sleep. As we said our goodbyes, Lou insisted that we meet again. He wanted to discuss producing our first album and he wanted to introduce us to his manager. This was heady stuff for a band that had only played a few shows and were new to New York City. Of course, we told him yes, we'd be happy to see him again.

Lou's manager, Jonny Podell, called us to come see him at his BMF Talent Agency office. Tina and David and I trekked up to Jonny's office in midtown near where we had our day jobs. He was a renowned agent for Crosby,

Stills and Nash and Alice Cooper. His cute-looking secretary told us to go right in. Jonny was on the phone talking a mile a minute and motioned for us to sit. We sat across the desk from him. The room was very dark. When the call was finished he took a little vial of cocaine out of his shirt pocket and snorted two hits up each nostril and then, as an afterthought, offered us a toot. We politely declined. Jonny went on and on about how great his client Lou Reed was and how much Lou loved Talking Heads and they wanted to make a deal. He presented us with a contract and told us to look it over. We said that we would.

At first we thought, *Wow, Lou Reed is offering to work with us. Fantastic!* Then we realized we needed a lawyer to look over the contract. There was one lawyer named Peter Parcher who had been in the news a lot lately. Peter had represented Keith Richards when Keith was busted with a quantity of heroin in Canada. Peter managed to get Keith off without jail time so he sounded good to us. I checked with my father, who said Parcher was well respected, so I gave him a call. The next day Tina, David, and I were up-town sitting in Peter Parcher's office. He introduced his partner, Alan Shulman, and said that Alan would be the right guy to look over the proposed deal for us. I passed the contract to Alan, who recognized a big problem immediately. He said, "This is a standard production deal. I would never allow one of my clients to sign this. Lou Reed and Jonny Podell would pay for the making of the record, but then they would own it. They could then sell the record to the highest bidder, no matter what you want. If you had a hit, they would profit and you would get zilch." I asked if there was any way to negotiate the offer and he said, "Look, Lou Reed's reputation now is when he gets up in the morning, he doesn't know whether to take the bus or the plane. If his heart was in the right place, he never would have offered you this shitty deal in the first place. This kind of deal is the reason that so many R&B artists may have had hit records but still don't have a pot to piss in. I would walk away and wait for a real record deal with a real record company." So we did walk away, feeling a little sad but relieved we hadn't made a big mistake. We continued to visit Lou and still respected him and his work, but we would never again think of doing business with him.

19

THE ARTIST'S LUNCH
WITH ANDY WARHOL

In May 1976, Lance Loud and painter Duncan Hannah brought Andy War-
hol down to CBGB to see us perform. We *loved* Andy's work. When Lance
and the Mumps weren't performing at CBGB, he was doing some writing
for Andy Warhol's *Interview* magazine. Lance pitched the idea for an inter-
view with us to Andy and suggested he come to see us play. Andy agreed
and as Lance had hoped, he liked us. Duncan says that Andy's reaction was,
"Oh, they're so cute. Do you think they'd like to have lunch at the Factory
tomorrow and do an interview?" Of course, we agreed. Andy Warhol was
the most famous artist living or dead. At RISD we regarded him as a hero
and we still did. It was determined that Lance would do the interview and
Duncan, who was a painter but happened to own a camera, would take the
photos.

We arrived at the Factory at lunchtime the following day. I guess I must
have called in sick to my day job. We were greeted by the lovely and cheer-
ful Catherine Guinness, who was acting as the receptionist. She buzzed us
in. We knew that the wild old Silver Factory days were over since the ter-
rible day in June 1968 when Andy had been shot by Valerie Solanas. Every-
thing was different now. The new Factory resembled a real office complex
with a view overlooking Union Square. There was a moose head on the

wall and a huge stuffed black-and-white Great Dane called Cecil standing in the middle of the room. Lance and Duncan were already there and we mingled somewhat nervously until Andy emerged from his painting studio in the back, where he had been working on a series of pet portraits with his assistant, Ronnie Cutrone. Andy led us into the dining room, which was more like a boardroom with a large antique table and sideboard, from which we could serve ourselves from an endless supply of Absolut Vodka. Andy didn't have any vodka but the rest of us did. At some point we were joined by the photographer Christopher Makos, who funnily enough was dressed in the same French striped sailor shirt and blazer as Tina. Andy liked that.

We sat down to have lunch. Andy served two types of lunches: the Artist's lunch and the Patron's lunch. We got the Artist's lunch, which consisted of a very nice chicken salad sandwich and some potato chips in a little box. Most of the conversation around the table came from Lance, who had the gift of gab. It's hard to remember what we talked about exactly but I remember that we did mention RISD and how everyone was hoping that Andy would visit there again like he had in the late sixties. Andy was very affable but quiet. We, like Duncan, were only just out of art school and here we were having lunch at the Factory with Andy Warhol! After everyone had finished their sandwiches, Andy piped up, "Don't we have any cookies?" Christopher Makos got up and went to a back room and returned with a tray of assorted cookies, but in his haste one of his cowboy boots scooted out from under him and as he slipped and hit the floor, all the cookies went flying. Andy thought this was really funny.

After a few cookies it was time for Andy to get back to work, but before he did, he took me aside and said, "You should go easy on the vodka or you're going to lose your figure." Boy, was he right about that! Lance suggested we all take a photo with Andy and, using Duncan's camera, shot a photo of us with Duncan and Andy.

Our interview started while Duncan took some great photos of us with a couple of Andy's Chairman Mao paintings. Later, the art director of *Interview*, another RISD grad named Mark Balet, said to Duncan, "We can't use these! They have to look like the Andrews Sisters shot by George Hurrell!" So we dutifully returned to the Factory for another photo shoot by Duncan even though we were much happier with his original shots, which captured our own esthetic much better.

Talking Heads with Andy Warhol and Duncan Hannah.

Later, Andy would even do a radio commercial for us, saying "Buy the new Talking Heads Record and tell them Warhol sent you," and he continued to be a fan of our band, although he sometimes mistakenly referred to us as the Talking Horses. He was the most famous and quite possibly the greatest artist of our time, yet he always treated us like we were way more important than he was. He was there for many of our shows in New York, too, and I felt very fortunate to have spent some time in his Factory.

20

THE TALKING HEADS LOOK

One good thing about the Punk/New Wave/Post-Punk music scenes was you didn't have to look like a rock star to be one. If I may say so, Talking Heads were pioneers in this arena. We didn't try to look like the Beatles or the Stones or the Who. Come to think of it, we didn't try to sound like them, either. We did try to look nice, though. I mean, we didn't want to look like slobs the way some bands did, and we certainly didn't have a uniform the way the Ramones and the Clash did. We could wear whatever we wanted to, like street clothes onstage and stage clothes on the street. For the longest time people called us preppy because I would often wear the clothes my mom had given me for Christmas, and she did like to buy at Brooks Brothers. Many times I would loan my shirts to David to wear onstage when he had a shortage of clean clothes. Those Lacoste polo shirts you used to see him in? Those were mine. Tina always had a great sense of style and she never failed to add some extra beauty to our group. Still, the idea behind the way we presented ourselves was really that anyone could do this if they put their mind to it. To a certain extent, we were trying to look like everymen. On the rare occasions when we had any extra money we were not about to go out and buy high-heeled platform boots and satin trousers. No, the image we wanted to convey was that of seriously thoughtful people. We were not afraid to appear straight.

Some of the first professional photos of us were taken by Jimmy DeSana. Tina and I both remember that he approached David at CBGB about taking some photos of us and we went up to his tiny theater-district apartment to take the shots for the picture sleeve of our first single, "Love → Building on Fire." Jimmy was a sweet guy, very clean cut and physically fit. We had heard he was into S&M but saw no evidence of that in his studio apartment. He got that we did not want a rock star image. We were looking for *no* image, something less predictable, and Jimmy captured that for us. We are almost smiling in the early photos; even David, with a ballpoint pen in his shirt pocket, looks happy. Later on, we stopped smiling, but these were more innocent times. Jimmy took a lot more publicity photos of us after Jerry Harrison joined the band; they were unlike any other band's photos at the time. To me they really capture the time, 1975, the chemistry, and the soul of Talking Heads. They gave our image a new feeling.

At the Factory.

21

FINDING JERRY

We were all very fond of the Modern Lovers album that had finally been released by Berserkely Records in August 1976. It was actually a demo produced out in Los Angeles by John Cale during his stint at A&R for Warner Brothers. It sounded great to our ears, but during the recording session, lead singer Jonathan Richman began to have second thoughts about the loud, raw Velvet Underground sound he had aspired to. He decided he wanted to write sweet, quiet songs, and he left the band, John Cale and Warner Brothers in the lurch. Still, that Modern Lovers album became an art rock classic and we felt a musical and conceptual kinship with the band.

During a visit to Pittsburgh, one of my mother's friends, Liz Shoyer, took me aside to tell me about her nephew, Ernie Brooks, who had attended Harvard and had a band in Boston. Liz's husband, Ed, was a law partner of my father's. She said I should get in touch with Ernie. I said that I would and what was the name of his band? Liz said, "They're called the Modern Lovers." I knew that the band had broken up some time ago, but I didn't mention it.

Back in New York, one evening Tina and I stopped into a cool downtown café called The Local. It was owned by Mickey Ruskin, who had owned Max's Kansas City during its heyday. It was a small basement place and the burgers were great. The painter Julian Schnabel was manning the grill. We

each ordered one with a glass of red wine and, as I gazed around the room, I recognized Ernie Brooks, bass player with the Modern Lovers and Liz Shoyer's nephew. I recognized him by his big head of curly hair, as pictured on the back of the album cover. I walked across the room to introduce myself and Ernie was friendly and cool. After making a little Pittsburgh small talk, I asked Ernie what Jerry Harrison, the Modern Lovers keyboard player, was up to. Ernie said that Jerry had enrolled in graduate school at Harvard to get a degree in architecture. I told Ernie we were looking for a keyboard player to fill out our sound, and he gave me Jerry's number and said I should give him a call. He told me that Jerry was also a good guitarist. This was good news.

When I called Jerry, he was very pleasant on the phone. I told him about our band Talking Heads, that we were a trio living in New York, had gone to RISD, loved the Modern Lovers, and were looking for a fourth member. I explained that we were very particular and he was the first person we had asked. He said he had only just enrolled in graduate school and that he'd had a really bad experience with the demise of the Modern Lovers. It had broken his heart. I said, "We do have a couple of offers from record companies on the table." That got his attention. Jerry said, "I'd like to hear you play before

Dinner at The Local.

this conversation goes any further." I told him, okay, I would book a gig in Boston. I called up the Rathskeller, better known as "The Rat," which was the CBGB of Boston, but they were all booked up for the month. Then Hilly gave me the name of a guy he knew in Cambridge who had a place called the Club. I called the guy and we got a gig for the coming weekend. Then I called Jerry and told him to save the date. I told him we were really doing this showcase just for him. It would be our first show in Boston, which was an important market to break into.

On the way up to Cambridge in Tina's car, we got a flat tire on the overpass on I-95 in New Haven. I pulled over to the breakdown lane. It was April and it was cold and raining. We had to take all the gear out of the trunk in order to reach the spare tire and jack. Cars and trucks were whizzing by at high speed and spraying us with rainwater. As I jacked the car up and changed the tire, David, who had been in a cranky mood, started howling with laughter. Tina and I had to laugh then, too. It occurred to us that David was happiest when things were not comfortable. When things were going well, he would become dissatisfied, the opposite of the way most people feel.

We finally found the Club with Tina navigating by map. As we set up to do the show, we realized the people at The Club had no idea who we were. A couple of members of Aerosmith had been drinking there the night before and that was all they could talk about. Also, compared to CBGB, the Club was pretty generic and had a mediocre ambience. Still, we were here to convince Jerry that we were a band worth joining. We put his name on our guest list.

When it was time for us to play, Jerry had still not arrived. We went onstage anyway to a small handful of people. We could tell that most of the audience was not really feeling us. The vibe was less than cool. It was then that I recognized Jerry, standing in the back watching us with great seriousness. He did not look like he was having fun. We played our set and received a small smattering of applause. I went out into the club and brought Jerry back to the dressing room where we all introduced ourselves. Jerry was easygoing, friendly, a good-looking guy. He was circumspect when I asked him what he thought of the band, but said, "Why don't you come by my apartment tomorrow evening and we'll go out to dinner? Better yet, come by the architecture building at Harvard first and I'll show you around."

That sounded promising, so we packed up our gear and drove to a little motel out on Route 128 by the power lines.

After a good night's sleep we drove over to Harvard Square and had lunch at the Wurst Haus. My father always joked, "When you're in Harvard Square, don't go to the best house. Go to the Wurst Haus. German food! Bavarian beer!" David loved a good sausage, so we lingered there until it was time to visit Jerry at Gund Hall, the impressively contemporary Architecture School building. The interior consisted of several open tiers of studios designed in the hopes that if the students could see and hear one another, collaborations would occur. After searching all around we eventually found Jerry, who was working on one of his assignments. We talked about our show the night before and, although we hadn't completely blown his mind, he was intrigued. He could hear that we were at least as eccentric and artistic as the Modern Lovers. Without making any promises, he said that he would come down to New York and jam with us. Great, I thought. Mission accomplished. Jerry said, "There's just one thing: I'm not going to join the band officially until you have a recording contract." That was fine with us.

22

THE SPIRIT OF '76!

We played sixty-five gigs in 1976, mostly at CBGB, but also at My Father's Place out in Roslyn, Long Island; the Ocean Club; Max's Kansas City; the Showplace in Dover, New Jersey; RISD; the Rat in Boston; and Clark University.

Hilly had arranged for several nights of recording for a *Live at CBGB's* album. We cautiously agreed to be recorded while not agreeing to be on the album. We still had strong reservations about having our songs released on a record at this early stage in our development, but I made the mistake late one night of signing a letter with Hilly that I thought was a release form, but was actually a deal memo. So, there was a moment when Hilly could have forced us to be on the album, but to his credit never did. He did ask if he could still use our picture on the album cover and we agreed to that. That's why our picture is on the cover, playing live at CBGB, but we are not on the record.

We first made the trek out to My Father's Place for the first "CBGB" night on June 26. The bill that night was the Patti Smith Group, Television, the Ramones, and Talking Heads. Can you imagine? For some reason, Tom Verlaine hitched a ride with us in Tina's Valiant and for most of the drive obsessed on the weather. Thunderstorms had been predicted. Tom kept saying, "If there is lightning, I'm not playing." I said, "But Tom, it's an indoor gig." Tom replied, "Yeah, but what if lightning strikes the building

while I'm singing into the mic?" I didn't want to argue with Tom so, I just said, "Yeah, that would be a drag."

We arrived at My Father's Place and parked under a railway bridge beside the club. The owner, a character named Michael "Eppy" Epstein, greeted us with a mixture of sweetness and sarcasm. In fact, most of the kids on Long Island at the time were still into the Allman Brothers and the Charlie Daniels Band. The new wave had not reached Long Island yet, so Eppy was on the vanguard. He was also booking many great reggae bands that called his club "I Father's Place."

We had been working on some demo records with a guy called J. R. Rost, who was a close friend of the Shirts, so Tina had the idea to ask J. R., who we liked very much, to come out and mix our live sound for us. He agreed and became our first soundman. Many years later, J. R. told me that this was the time David had said to him, "So, I'm thinking of kicking Tina out of the band. What do you think?" J. R. says when he heard this, "My brain froze." When J. R. asked why, David said, "She's holding me up and not progressing fast enough." Tina had been playing bass for just over one year. J. R. recalled how one day when we were recording at the Shirts' studio and before I got there, David said to Tina for no apparent reason, "I'm gonna play some stuff and I want you to come up with some bass parts." Tina, realizing that this was some kind of audition, declined. They were exchanging words about this when I walked into the room and David immediately dropped the subject. In fact, all three of us were still learning to play our instruments well. It is true that Tina had not played rock and roll before Talking Heads and did not have a repertoire of standard blues and rock bass licks in her musical vocabulary. Her approach was more classical. To this day, Tina never ever plays the predictable thing. She invents every part anew—this was one reason Talking Heads sounded so unique.

It was a great night at My Father's Place. We went on first, followed by the Ramones, who were followed by Television. When the Patti Smith Group hit the stage, they were greeted with a roar of crazy enthusiasm from the not-quite-sold-out crowd. They had toured constantly behind the release of their debut album, *Horses*, and never sounded better. Tina and I had a great time hanging out backstage with Lenny and Jay Dee before the show and it was a great pleasure to see how hard they rocked.

Outside in the parking lot after the show, Tina told Dee Dee Ramone's

Tina with her Fender Precision.

girlfriend, Connie Ramone—really Connie Gripp, but Dee Dee christened her with the family name Ramone—who was more dressed up than usual, how pretty she looked and asked her, "What is that lovely ornament in your hair on top of your head?" To me it looked like a lovely golden coil glistening in the moonlight. Connie shot us a puzzled look and put her hand on top of her head to feel what it was. It seems that there were pigeons roosting under the railway bridge, and one of them had released a big surprise right on top of Connie Ramone's pretty blonde head! We tried our best not to laugh while Tina helped Connie clean it up.

On June 30, we played a five-night run at CBGB culminating on July 4, 1976. The American Bicentennial was a major party all over New York City. Tourists poured into the city and all sorts of parades and special events were planned. I don't know how many of those tourists ended up at CBGB,

but definitely more than usual. The place was packed with lines down the block. It was steaming hot on the Bowery and even hotter inside CBGB. Everyone was sweating and guzzling cold beer.

In between sets the crowd moved out onto the sidewalk under the flophouse to cool off and mingle.

For those five nights we shared the stage with an interesting band from Boston called Orchestra Luna, led by Rick Berlin. They were signed to Epic Records. They were very musical, had an Off-Broadway sensibility and they could rock. One of their singers, Karla DeVito, later sang with Meatloaf and Jim Steinman. They were good and different from what we'd come to expect to hear at CBGB.

At the end of our final set of the week, Tina's brother, Yann, told us some good news: The loft adjoining his in Long Island City was becoming available. The fellow who lived in the loft, an artist named Bill Barrell, who was a protégé of Red Grooms's, had decided to move back to his native Australia. Bill was a lovely guy. To make ends meet, he boarded cats in his loft. His favorite client was Diana Ross. Miss Ross would summon Bill to come pick up her cats any time she went out of town, which was often. Tina and I called Bill early the next morning and, for a small fixture fee, he agreed to turn the lease over to us.

The loft was located at 9-01 44th Drive at the corner of Vernon Boulevard. It was one subway stop from Manhattan and one block from the East River near the big Pepsi Cola sign. We had a view of the United Nations Building and the 59th Street Bridge, but best of all we had our own private bathroom with a shower plus a bathtub in the kitchen! The loft was 2,700 square feet with brick walls and wooden floors, columns, and beams. The ceilings were high and made of white painted tin. The loft had plenty of windows and good natural light. There was a giant freight elevator that opened in our loft, descended to the ground level and then opened right onto the street. This was fantastic for loading our gear in and out. The rent was $300 per month.

None of us were sorry to leave the loft on Chrystie Street, and I didn't even mind losing my two months' deposit. David got a nice little studio apartment in the East Village close to CBGB. He was happy to have his own apartment. Tina and I were, too. As I helped him move in, I was strangely

touched to see that he had bought matching bath mats and toilet seat covers to make the bathroom nice.

The word was out at CBGB: "Did you hear what happened to Chris and Tina? David moved out."

Hilly had a moving business on the side and kindly let Tina and me use his moving truck. Some people might imagine that Hilly was rolling in dough now, but the fact is he needed extra income to keep CBGB in business. A couple of the guys from The Shirts pitched in to help us and drove the truck across the Williamsburg Bridge and across McGuinness Boulevard through Greenpoint to Long Island City. We didn't have a whole lot of stuff to move, but as we opened the door to the freight elevator right on the street, there was much oohing and ahhing at how cool a space it was for working musicians.

Laura, Lani, and Tina Weymouth at CBGB.

Well, our new loft was a very good thing for Talking Heads. It had great ambience for creativity. Yann Weymouth was just starting his own architectural firm called Red Roof Design in his loft next door. Fortunately, Yann loved music because he was going to be hearing a lot of it. We established a rule of no loud music before noon or after midnight.

Long Island City was bustling with manufacturing shops, body shops, taxicab garages, and warehouses. Steinway pianos were made there. It was a busy, thriving place with little pockets of residential areas.

If you arrived by the E or the F train, you would walk through a small Latino area with a small supermarket where we bought our essential things

on the way home to our place. If you took the Number 7 train, one stop from Grand Central, you would walk down Vernon Boulevard through an old-fashioned Italian neighborhood with a Catholic Church, and a few restaurants and bars and a pharmacy. Every store was mom-and-pop style. I particularly liked John's Market, where you could buy big crusty loaves of Italian bread and sausages and great cheeses and fresh produce. John was always very nice to me but became absolutely courtly if Tina was with me. They had a sign by the cash register saying, IT'S NICE TO BE IMPORTANT, BUT IT'S MORE IMPORTANT TO BE NICE.

It was a workingman's neighborhood and after work everything shut down. It could be a long, spooky walk from the subway station to our place at night. It was like the set of a horror movie.

For Tina and me, 9-01 44th Drive became our new home and it was such a vast improvement. I felt like we would be together forever both as romantic partners and as bandmates. For Talking Heads, 9-01 became a composing room, rehearsal hall, and business office. All of our business was done on a single telephone landline, or by talking to a person face-to-face.

We had a really strong work ethic. If we weren't doing live shows, we were working on new songs. David came to me not long after our first meeting with our lawyer. Alan Shulman had explained to us how music publishing works and how songwriting is legally defined as words, if there are any, and melody. Up to this point, I had written or cowritten words to some of our songs. As a kid I loved to write. I'd written poetry that had been published in the school literary magazines. I wrote a record review column in my school newspaper that I called "The Listening Eye." To me, writing went hand in hand with music and art. It was something I loved. So, David came to me and said, "I can't sing songs with conviction unless I write the words. I want to be the one who writes the words." When I look back, I believe that I should have stood my ground, that David was simply demanding a bigger piece of the pie. At the time, though, I thought about how off the wall some of his lyrical ideas were and how surprising his word choices were. I also thought about how different his thought process was from my own. He was not able to look me in the eye for more than a very quick glance, but I told him to keep those lyrics coming. I told him that I really liked the words he had written so far, and that I was with him no matter who wrote the lyrics. I was for Talking Heads and whatever was good for Talking Heads. It was as simple as that.

23

WORDS OF FAITH AND TELL ME STRAIGHT

By the autumn of '76, David and Tina and I felt the time had come to make a record deal. We had a good momentum and we wanted to keep it going.

Standing on the sidewalk outside of CBGB one night I asked the Ramones' manager, Danny Fields, what he thought about Sire Records and Seymour Stein. The Ramones had signed a multi-album deal with Sire. Danny was very forthcoming. He said, "Well, you know, with any record company there will be problems. None of them are perfect, but I can tell you that Seymour has always done right by us."

This is what I'd been hoping to hear. We felt that Sire—being a small independent company, but with major distribution and with offices in an old brownstone on West Seventy-fourth Street in New York—would be ideal for us. Seymour was as keen as ever and he assured us that he would always be available to talk and would try to help us solve any problems we had.

My feeling was that our biggest problem was we didn't yet have a manager. There were a few people lurking around CBGB who were managing bands, but they didn't seem right for us. I felt that no manager was better than a bad manager and we had a good legal team in place to negotiate on our behalf. We decided to tell Seymour we were ready to make a deal. Seymour has said that this was one of the happiest days of his life.

On November 1, 1976, we met with Seymour at Alan Shulman's offices in a skyscraper on the Avenue of the Americas. Seymour arrived right on time, beaming with pride. David and Tina and I signed the agreement and passed it across the table to Seymour, who was quivering with anticipation. He signed, too. Finally! He'd been waiting a year and a half for this, worrying that we would be snatched up by some other company. It wasn't the world's greatest record deal for us, but the advance was good enough that we could quit our day jobs and not worry about paying the rent. Alan Shulman assured us that if our first record did well, the deal could be renegotiated. Talking Heads were now Sire recording artists.

Did I say this was a really big day? Well, yes, we signed a recording contract, but on a more romantic note, Tina and I also decided to become engaged to be married. Ever since that day in Providence when Tina asked me to cut her hair, it had been our plan, but this was the day we made our decision to make it real. We kept it a secret until we could tell our parents on Thanksgiving. I was deeply in love with Tina and had no doubt that our marriage would be a great one. She was the perfect young bride for me—physically, intellectually, and emotionally. I adored her. We talked mostly about art and music. I enjoyed talking about celebrity gossip, but Tina was not keen on that. When I went lowbrow, she went highbrow. Nothing has changed since then except we discuss politics and the climate crisis even more today.

24

SUNDRAGON STUDIO

Sundragon Sound on West Twentieth Street had the slowest elevator in the city. It took what seemed forever to get up to the eighth floor. When you finally got there and the doors opened, you were blasted with the aroma of really good weed. There were two residences in the front of the building that you had to walk by and one of them belonged to a super-cheerful guy who sold weed. How convenient! As you walked past his place and through another door, you arrived in a tiny recording room. This is where we would set up our gear to play. The Ramones had just recorded their second album here. It was called *Leave Home*. Seymour had some kind of deal with the producer Tony Bongiovi—either he owed Seymour a favor or Seymour owed him one. Tony was a skillful engineer who at a young age had discovered how to reproduce the Motown Sound in his parents' garage in New Jersey. After hearing what he had done, Berry Gordy gave him a job. The year before we worked with him, Tony had produced "Never Can Say Goodbye" by Gloria Gaynor. That record was huge in every discotheque on the planet. I was most impressed that he had engineered *Good Times* by Kool & the Gang. I loved Kool & the Gang and, of course, we loved Tony's latest production for the Ramones. All of us in the band had eclectic tastes, but at that time I believe my record collection was the biggest and broadest.

The engineer was excellent and a very sensitive and intelligent guy

Working on our first album.

named Ed Stasium. Ed had recorded and mixed the new Ramones album and knew a little bit about our short history. He had been an art student, too, studying at New York's School of Visual Arts. We were new at recording and Ed did his best to put us at ease. For this single we were about to record, we had asked Tommy Erdelyi—aka Tommy Ramone—to coproduce. He offered to help and we were pleased to accept his offer.

Ed showed us around the tiny studio. The control room was so small we couldn't all be in there at once. The tape recorder was a Studer 16 Track and there was a Roger Mayer Console. There was a little kitchen behind the control room that doubled as a lounge. It was cozy.

Ed set to work close micing the drums. After much tweaking and tuning, we'd gotten a pretty good drum sound. Then Ed miced up Tina and David's amps and surrounded them with blocks of foam. Working quickly now, we donned our headphones and got the mix we wanted to hear as we ran through "Love → Building on Fire" for Ed to get his sounds. Within an hour or so we had a couple of good takes with guide vocals to listen back to. Then we recorded the B side. The song was called "New Feeling." After listening back carefully, everyone agreed on which two basic tracks to use.

David overdubbed some nice big guitar chords and funky, choppy rhythm parts. Tina's playing was melodic, minimalist, bottom-end perfection. As I listened back to my own playing, I felt really good. I actually sounded better than I thought I would. Whew! We added some handclaps to the choruses and Ed flew in some little bird tweets to the introduction.

David went back out into the studio to record his vocals. David was not anybody's idea of a good singer, but he was our idea of a great vocalist. He sang with real feeling and in his weird vocal style you could hear the pain of creation. His style was personal and was not riding on the coattails of any other singer. He sounded heartfelt and could also be very amusing. Tony was a little concerned about the vocal style because he was used to working with very professional R&B singers, but Tommy and Ed told him to relax. We were a brand-new thing.

David had the idea to overdub a horn section. We laughed because we knew horns would really surprise the kids at CBGB. So we said yes to horns. Overnight, a cat named Brad Baker wrote a horn arrangement that was performed by saxophonists Lew Del Gatto and "Blue Lou" Marini. Lou Marini also played trumpet. I was hoping this would make us sound more like a Stax band, but no. We still sounded like Talking Heads.

25

THE BLIZZARD OF '77

After we made a record deal with Sire, Jerry Harrison was eager to come on board. We went up to his rented gray cedar shake summer cottage he shared with Ernie Brooks in Ipswich, Massachusetts, to teach him our songs. Little did we know the heating system would not be working. It was January and there was a foot of snow on the ground. Somehow, after loading our gear in, we managed to rehearse for two days with no heat. Thankfully, Jerry was a fast learner. On some songs he played guitar and on others he played keyboards. He seemed to understand our musical eccentricities very well and we got along well, too. Tina and I slept in the same sleeping bag on a mattress on the floor to keep warm that night. We were used to cold nights from loft living with no heat at night. We bundled up with watchcaps on our heads. The next morning we had fried clams for breakfast.

Soon after, we played our first gigs with Jerry sitting in at the Rat in Boston. We were booked for two nights. There was a great reaction of approval from the fans, some of whom knew Jerry from the Modern Lovers. This was also the first time we met Ken Kushnick, who came up from New York. Ken had been hired to run Sire while Seymour was off traveling around the world signing new bands. He had been hired the same day we signed with Sire. Coincidence? I think not. Ken was a cool head and enjoyed being involved with the new bands at Sire. He was well-informed

about the music business and he also had a wickedly good sense of humor. We liked that.

After the Rat, we played the student union at Clark University, and the RISD Tap Room, our old stomping ground, where we had played with the Artistics. It was a good feeling to be back there. The Jabberwocky at Syracuse University was next. There is a bootleg recording of this floating around.

Next stop was A Space Gallery in Toronto, where we had been booked by A. A. Bronson, who published a great art magazine called *File* with his friend Jorge Zontal. A Space was a tiny gallery but we attracted the wild intelligentsia of Toronto and enjoyed a warm Canadian welcome. We managed to book a second night in Toronto at the Ontario College of Art, which was also legendary and loads of fun. The support band was The Diodes, who were lovely guys and already Toronto's preeminent New Wave band. Both gigs were cool and we loved Toronto. It's interesting to note that we were invited to play in Canada before we could get a gig in most of America.

While we slept, there was a blizzard with over three feet of snow and high winds, so the next day all the entrances to the USA from Toronto were closed to automobiles. We would have to wait. Tina and I hung out at the *File* magazine/General Idea offices with A. A. and Jorge. Somewhere I copped a big chunk of red Lebanese hash the size of a walnut, which I smoked to my

Closing time at CBGB.

heart's content, sharing with anyone who wanted. It was a very stoned snow day and all good fun until we began to wonder where David was. We walked back to our little hotel and called his room. No answer. I went to knock on his door but still no response. I went down to the front desk to see if he had changed rooms and the lady said, "Oh, Mr. Byrne checked out this afternoon." Had he left a message? "No, he did not." I wondered where he had gone. All the bridges to the USA were closed. After making a few calls, I found out that David had taken a flight back to New York without even telling the rest of us. Where had he gotten the money for an airplane ticket? When I told Jerry he said, "Oh, well in that case, I'm taking a plane home, too." This left Tina and me alone to drive the band's gear 350 miles home from Toronto following the biggest snowstorm of the decade.

It was another three days before the Peace Bridge to Buffalo opened, by which time several more feet of snow had fallen. At this point we were driving my parents' hand-me-down silver Ford Country Squire station wagon with the faux-wood paneling on the sides. It was roomy enough for the band and all of our gear. It was a smooth ride, like a boat. Before we arrived at the Peace Bridge, I had a premonition that our car would be searched, so I decided to eat what was left of my hash. Sure enough, the U.S. Customs officers made us pull over to the side and unload the car so that they could inspect the contents. We got out of the car and stood there. Tina was freezing in her little jacket. They were not sympathetic to traveling musicians. They opened every case and even removed the hubcaps from the wheels. Finding nothing illegal, they told us to pack everything up. We were free to go.

It was sunny now, and after putting everything back in the cases and reloading the car, we split. There was no one else on the road until we caught up with the snowplows that were running two abreast down Interstate 90. I swear the banks of snow on either side of the road were over twenty feet high. The wind was still howling and the snow was still drifting, but Tina and I followed the snowplows cautiously all the way to Syracuse. Meanwhile, the hash I had eaten was coming on very strong. I was tripping, but not so badly that I couldn't drive. We traveled on intrepidly. On the radio they were still advising people not to drive unless it was an emergency, which was not comforting. We stopped in the Village of Horseheads to fill up the tank and buy a sandwich. It was like the set of *The Shining*, and we hopped back into the car and drove like hell back to New York City.

26

TALKING HEADS '77

In early April we returned to Sundragon Studio in New York City to record our first album. We set up in the little recording room, this time with Jerry on keyboards and guitar. Tony Bongiovi was our coproducer with Lance Quinn. Lance was a great guitarist and a sweet, self-effacing guy. Tony brought him along, I think, to soften Tony's own strictly business style and personality. Also, Tony was not a musician and needed Lance to figure out any musical issues for him. There was not much of the artist in Tony and I really don't think he understood where we were coming from. We were happy that Lance was there. He was from Maryland and he and David could joke around in Baltimore accents. It was our really good fortune to have Ed Stasium behind the console as engineer. Ed did most of the work while Tony sat there on the phone or read *Pilot* magazine and talked about his new airplane to anyone who would listen. Tony had produced the current number-one record in the country with Meco's disco cover of the *Star Wars* theme. The irony of working with him was not lost on us who were determined to create a record that was both artful and unexpected. In this quest, Ed was our secret weapon.

I felt that we were in good shape playing-wise from all the live shows we'd been doing. David was a bit nervous. He was awkward when meeting new people. Tina was calm, cheerful, and on point. The addition of Jerry

was a great step forward for our overall sound and for the beauty of the songs. Making this first album was something I had been dreaming about since I first heard the Beatles. I knew how important it was to all of us that it be really good. I don't mean just sounding good; of course, it must sound good. We felt the music must convey a modern message about the importance of taking charge of your own life and to hell with the idea that rock stars are somehow more important than everyone else. We were celebrating our own everyday lives and philosophically reaching for a higher level of expression, something that was far greater than the sum of its parts. We also wanted our records to be fun to listen to. We were never about showing off. We were about playing from our hearts.

Tony asked us to do six or eight takes of each song, far beyond the point when a great take had already been recorded. That's when we realized he was listening for something other than Talking Heads music. We felt Tony was condescending to the band, reading magazines about airplanes while we worked. He was repeatedly rude to Tina. Let's just say he appeared clueless and was not a gentleman.

On the other hand, Ed and Lance were full of encouragement and positive reinforcement, which is what a young band needs when recording their first album. We were just learning the difference between a good live performance and a good studio performance. In a live performance, little

inconsistencies and wild moments go by quickly and are soon forgotten. On a record, you hear them over and over, which can be so annoying you never want to hear the record again. When I had any questions about my timing, Lance reassured me that it was good. Under the microscope of the studio and headphones, you can sometimes get overly picky. There was a stopwatch mounted on the console, and he could check the time of each bar. He was impressed that my timing was completely consistent and that was a big relief to me.

As we played and recorded the basic tracks, David sang what are called guide vocals, which would later be resung by him. After we were all satisfied with the basic tracks, it was time to do the vocals for real.

The first song David sang was "Psycho Killer." Again, Tony was bugged by David's singing style. I don't know what he was thinking, but he went into the little kitchen behind the control room and returned with a carving knife. With great seriousness, he told David to get into character and to hold the knife in his hand while singing the words. In the control room, jaws were dropping. David said, "No, that's not going to work." We decided to take a break. David told us he could not sing with Tony in the room and wanted Ed to kick him out of the studio. Ed had another idea. He said, "Why don't we try moonlighting when Tony isn't around? You know, before he gets here or after he leaves." That was agreeable to all and Tony never even knew the difference. He was busy anyway, building a new studio uptown that would be called the Power Station. That was his main concern, not this little band called Talking Heads.

Toward the end of the recording sessions we invited the downtown modern musician and cellist Arthur Russell to come play his cello on "Psycho Killer." We had considered adding an entire string section, but then thought better of it. Cello was all that the song called for. In the end, we made a separate "acoustic" mix of the song with Arthur's cello that can be found on some of our boxed sets.

We finished the basic tracks, guide vocals, and a few guitar and keyboard overdubs in less than two weeks. Back at our loft, we got a phone call from Ken Kushnick, who asked, "How would you like to tour Europe and the UK with the Ramones?" I smiled, sat down, and let that sink in.

27

ON TOUR WITH THE RAMONES

It would be difficult to overstate how excited we were to be invited to join the Ramones on a tour of Europe in the spring of 1977. Our first album had not come out yet, but we had released a single called "Love → Building on Fire," so we got the gig on the strength of that single and our reputation as a good live band from the CBGB scene in New York City. Plus, we had successfully opened for the Ramones before. Seymour Stein and Ken Kushnick at Sire Records proposed the idea to us. Seymour knew that the young European audience would be crazy about this double bill and we only needed about two seconds before we said yes. I had never been to Europe and neither had Jerry. David was born in Scotland and so had a UK passport, but I don't think he had actually been there since he was two years old. Tina had been to Europe many times with her family, but this would obviously be a completely different kind of trip.

Ed Bicknell, an agent at NEMS in London, booked the tour. NEMS Agency (North End Music Stores) was founded by Brian Epstein to book the Beatles, so that sure sounded good to us. The tour would be something like thirty-four shows in thirty-eight days.

We gathered at the Swissair check-in desk at JFK airport on the afternoon of April 23. We brought our own guitars, but we would hire the rest of our equipment, including my drums, in Europe. As we arrived at the airport, I

saw Dee Dee Ramone very carefully getting out of a cab and then walking painfully, with the help of a cane, to the terminal. I asked him what had happened and Dee Dee said, "Oh, Connie Ramone stabbed me! She stabbed me in the ass!" Connie, as mentioned earlier, was Dee Dee's girlfriend at the time and evidently they'd had a fight. Some say Connie was a junkie and a prostitute. I don't know. She was always nice to me. Dee Dee was trying to make the best of it, knowing that sitting down on a plane for the next nine hours would be torture for him.

We all got checked in. The touring party at that point consisted of the four Ramones, their tour manager and soundman Monte Melnick, lighting designer and T-shirt man Arturo Vega, and the four Talking Heads.

While I was making a stop in the men's room, Dee Dee came in, followed by Monte. They were having a bit of an argument. Monte said, "Give me that cane, Dee Dee!" and Dee Dee said, "No, Monte! No! Leave me alone!" As I washed my hands, they had a scuffle, and Monte eventually prevailed, grabbing the cane away from Dee Dee. He unscrewed the handle and proceeded to pour all kinds of painkiller pills and downers into the toilet, while Dee Dee looked on in horror. To be fair, he did let Dee Dee keep enough painkillers to last through the flight, and by throwing the rest away he probably saved Dee Dee from being arrested at customs in Switzerland, where they were no doubt wise to hollow canes. Swiss customs were notoriously vigilant and hard on rock stars.

The flight was delayed for a few hours, which meant that when we arrived in Zurich we had to go straight to the sound check for the first show at a place called the Volkshaus, a lovely old concert hall in the center of town. We were met there by a veteran British tour manager, Mike "Mickey" Stewart, soundman Frank Gallagher, and stagehand Ian Ward. Mickey was a real pro—I never saw him lose his cool. He was considerate and a real gentleman. Ian Ward had an angel's head of curly blond hair, a sweet disposition, and the body of Tarzan. Frank Gallagher—a bawdy Scotsman with the wildest eyebrows in the business and a former cook at the famous Hope & Anchor pub in London—was to become our soundman and close friend for many years.

While the Ramones did their sound check, we got to work setting up our gear, showing Frank and Ian how we liked our various settings. The Volkshaus was the biggest theater we had ever played, and certainly the

oldest and most beautiful. The real proscenium stage itself was the largest we had ever played on. It was about ten times the size of the stage at CBGB. The sound system was from an outfit in London called Concert Sound and it was big and powerful. Frank and Ian carried it in the truck along with all of our gear from gig to gig. I had a very good feeling despite not sleeping all night. I felt like we had arrived at a new level of success even though we had yet to play the show.

When the Ramones finished their sound check, it was our turn. "Drummer!" I got up onto the riser and followed Frank's instructions to hit each drum as he called out their names: "Kick! Snare! Rack Toms! Floor Toms! Hi-Hat! Crash Cymbals!" I had never had what they call full concert micing before, and the level of volume was awesome in the empty, cavernous Volkshaus. Then it was Tina's turn. She played the intro to "Psycho Killer" for Frank. Then he called out "Bass and drums together, please!" and so on, adding David's Fender Music Master and Jerry's Telecaster and then Jerry's keyboards into the mix. Then Frank said, "Singer! Sing into the mic!" David stepped up and sang something like, "Whoa, whoa, ummmmmm, sumaha-sumaha, whoa, grrriiip, ayyyyyyyy, yayyyyy, sumaaaaah!" Our crew had a good chuckle at that. Then Frank said, "Okay, we're pressed for time, but play one song all together." As the opening act, if you're lucky enough to

get a sound check, you are always pressed for time. We ran through "Psycho Killer" one time and then it was time to eat. We were all extremely excited, but we were hungry and not too excited to eat our dinner. Inside the Volkshaus was a very fine bistro, and the promoter provided dinner for us, so we sat down at a long table with the Ramones and the rest of our touring party. We in the Talking Heads—that's right, I just said *the* Talking Heads—were a bit jet-lagged, but full of excitement and anticipation for the tour ahead. The Ramones were not so happy. Johnny's mantra was, "This is grim. This is really gonna be grim." Dee Dee was in agony from his recent stab wound in the ass, but trying not to show it. Joey said nothing and stared at the floor. Tommy was more with it than Joey, but not really conversant, either. Arturo and Monte were much happier and way more fun. We were offered a choice of steak frites or chicken with ratatouille. To drink, we could have whatever we wanted—wine or beer or something softer. It was a civilized meal until our very sweet waitress brought out green salads for everyone. Johnny Ramone stood up and shouted, "What the fuck is this?" I said, "Johnny, that's a salad. It's lettuce and tomato." Johnny, getting pretty upset, screwed up his face and said, "This is not fucking lettuce! Oh, this is grim. This is so fucking grim." We just looked at him like he had lost his mind. The other Ramones said nothing. I guess they knew better than to try and reason with Johnny, who had apparently never seen any green salad other than iceberg lettuce before. Johnny got up, stormed out of the restaurant, and went back to the dressing room. It's probably just as well because the Sacher Torte for dessert and espresso in demitasse cups would have really freaked him out.

When the time came for Talking Heads to go onstage, David, Jerry, and Tina needed to tune their guitars. There was only one strobe tuner for both bands to share and Tina went to look for it. Johnny Ramone was sitting at a table with the tuner in front of him and when Tina asked for it, instead of giving it to her, he said in a loud whine, "Somebody bring me my guitar!" There was no response and the dressing rooms were not very large so Tina, who was not afraid of Johnny, suggested, "Why don't you go get it yourself?" Tommy Ramone came over to Tina and whispered, "It's dangerous to talk to him. I fear for your safety." One of the crew must have had a talk with Johnny after that because we got the tuner moments before we went onstage and everybody was able to tune up. Neither Tina nor I were afraid

of Johnny. The other Ramones were cool, but he was not. He was a classic bully.

When we hit the stage there was a lukewarm welcome for us. We were somewhat known, but only by reputation—no one had actually heard our music before. The place was packed. We kicked off our set with "Love → Building on Fire," which really got the kids going. Many in the audience were younger than us, and they were there to party and have a good time. A few of them were doing this new thing called the pogo, which consisted of hopping up and down as high as possible in time to the music. We had never seen anyone pogo before. Certainly no one had done it at CBGB. One young kid, standing right in front of the stage with his back to the band, was wearing a raincoat with a very prominent Nazi swastika armband. He was blatantly disrespecting us and the people around him. We just ignored him, which is usually the best way to treat somebody like that, but about halfway through our set I lost my cool. In between songs I got down from the drum riser—something I had never done before and haven't done since—walked over to the kid who still had his back to us, slapped him on the head, and pointed to the exit. The kid was taken aback and looked scared. Tina and the rest of the band looked at me, like, *whoa*. I went back to the drums and we continued with the show. By the end of our rather short set we really had the crowd going. We got our first encore of the tour. This was a very good sign for us because, more often than not, support bands are not shown much love by the audience. But when the Ramones came on, there was punk pandemonium. The Swiss are known for their reserve, but the Ramones brought out the wildness in them. With a full house and a full PA system, the Ramones were an unstoppable blitzkrieg of sound. In their Perfecto leather jackets, with their passion and their sheer volume, they really were magnificent.

That night after our show, Frank Gallagher invited Tina and me up to his room for some strawberries and cream. Really, that's what we had; Frank had ordered from room service. We had only met each other that afternoon but Frank said, "I want to join the family." Being a Scot, he loved that David had been born in Dumbarton, not far from where Frank grew up. But, even more than that, he loved our music and our demeanor, which was very different from the many other bands he had worked with. I think

he immediately recognized that we represented something new and un-usual, and he wanted to be part of it.

Early the next morning we boarded the bus that would carry us from show to show. This was not a tour bus with bunks and bars and stereos and TV sets. It was a tourist bus from England with thirty seats and an aisle down the middle, the type that carried tourist groups around the continent. The driver was a young man named Paul and it was his first time out of the UK, but that was cool. For most of us it was our first trip to Europe, too. Paul was actually a mechanic and he had stored an entire spare motor in one of the baggage bays under the bus in case of emergency.

We were on our way to Marseilles in the south of France, a distance of about five hundred miles. Johnny Ramone claimed the front seat next to the driver. Tommy sat in the seat behind him. Joey sat behind Tommy and Dee Dee sat behind him. This was the Ramones' seating arrangement for the rest of the tour, and Johnny was not pleased if anyone decided to move for any reason, such as to see a castle or quaint village as we passed by. The rest of us sat wherever we pleased and evidently drove Johnny crazy with our conversation about art and historical events. The first day on the bus, Tommy privately asked us to please not upset Johnny with our conversa-tions. It seemed Johnny did not have much tolerance for other people's in-terests, particularly Tina's and Jerry's. Even as the rest of us were amazed by the vistas from the winding road through the Alps that day, he maintained that this trip was grim.

No matter. Everyone else was having a good time and shared a great sense of anticipation for the upcoming gigs. Because of the strict rules about how long a bus driver can stay behind the wheel without sleeping, we stopped to spend the night in Grenoble. Tina realized that we were not too far from where her Aunt Mayette lived, and she called her from our hotel. She wanted to let her cousin Yves, a marine biologist who lived near Marseilles, know that we would be playing there the following night. Jet lag was hitting us pretty hard at that point, so we went to bed earlier than usual that night. Tina and I slept well despite the lumpy and sagging mattress we shared. Even a cheap French hotel seemed very romantic to us.

Waking for an early departure the next morning, I crossed the street from the hotel to buy cigarettes at a Bar Tabac. I was surprised to find businessmen

in coats and ties smoking and enjoying a glass or two of wine before work at 8:30 A.M, but I remember that they all looked healthy and slender enough.

Back on board the bus that morning, even Johnny was in a good mood and looking forward to the show that night. As we drove south to Marseilles, the landscape changed to more of a desert scene with sandy ground and rocky cliffs. Arturo Vega, who'd been the "Mexican" in the sharkskin suit I'd met my first time at CBGB in 1974, turned to me and said, "You know Chris, this reminds me of my home in Chihuahua. I feel like I'm at home."

In Marseilles, Tina and I were thrilled that our hotel was right on the Old Port, with fishing boats tied up directly in front. It was like a Brigitte Bardot movie. The skies were sunny and it was very warm; we were relaxed. As we checked into the hotel, the lady at the front desk was clearly skeptical of the Ramones and expressed this to Mickey Stewart, who easily managed to sweet-talk her, persuading her that they were really very nice boys from New York City.

Tina and I went up to our room to freshen up. Not long after that there was a knock on our door. It was Dee Dee. We invited him in and he started talking about how he would like to get a tattoo in the shape of the old-fashioned hotel room key. I don't think he had any tattoos yet; those would come later. Then he cut to the chase: "Are you going to be using your Carbona?" Phonogram, the company that distributed Sire records in Europe at that time, had provided each band member with a little travel kit of things we might need on the road. There was a sewing kit, a toothbrush, aspirin, Fernet-Branca herbal liqueur, maps, and, among other things, a small bottle of the spot remover known as Carbona. Tina and I were not even sure what Carbona was so we said, "Sure, Dee Dee. You can have it." Later on, when the Ramones recorded a song called "Carbona, Not Glue," we realized what was up. If you inhaled Carbona fumes, you would get a brain-damaging high.

Before sound check, we were treated to an excellent afternoon dinner of bouillabaisse, the spicy fish stew of Provence, by our promoters, Jenny Bier and Hervé Mueller. Both of them looked impossibly thin and chic in skin-tight jeans, tailored western shirts, and cowboy boots. Jenny was a young British woman, supercool and living in Paris, and Hervé was a leading rock writer and critic for *Rock & Folk* magazine. He was friends with Jim Morrison and was one of the last people to see Jim alive. We liked them

immediately. They had been contacted about promoting our concerts, first by Phonogram, and then by Ed Bicknell from NEMS, because the usual promoters in France had passed on anything punk. In our early days, this was usually the case. Jenny and Hervé were real go-getters and managed to get decent-sized crowds at our shows by saying we were denizens of CBGB and New York. We may not have been popular yet, but to those in the know, we were a very chic new band.

After lunch we walked over to the club where we would perform that night. It was close to our hotel and located in the oldest part of Marseilles. As we entered the club, I remember thinking that the ceilings were very low and it would be difficult to even see the band. Lots of music clubs had the same problem. The Ramones crew was setting up for their sound check. These were always fun to watch because their sound check was almost as great as their live show, plus the band would stop and argue with one another about things. I don't know if they realized how hilarious this could be to onlookers. This time, after playing one song and launching into the second number, everything went quiet. The power had gone out. Monte threw his hands in the air while Frank and Ian scrambled to find out what the problem was. Somehow they got the power back on and the band resumed playing, but after a few more chords, silence. This happened several more times until, finally, Mickey Stewart told us that not only had the power failed in the club, but in that whole quarter of Marseilles. It was clear that this show was not going to go on. He advised us to get the hell out of there before things got ugly. It was a weird feeling to come all the way to Marseilles from New York by way of Zurich and not be able to play the show due to circumstances beyond our control, but so be it. As we left through the front door, we could see that the line went around the block. At the front of the line was Tina's cousin, Yves, and his wife. Tina expressed our regrets and off we slunk, back to the comfort of our hotel, just in time to watch the sunset over the Vieux Port.

Danny Fields arrived from New York to see that the show had been canceled, so Tina and I decided to join him and Dee Dee for a walk around Marseilles after dark. To us this was the land of *The French Connection*, the movie about the French heroin trade starring Gene Hackman, and we were on guard, but there was really no need for it. Hardly a soul was walking the streets, and the area around our hotel had a few bars where workingmen

were drinking, but it wasn't really a nightlife scene. We wandered around, window shopping and looking for some type of action, but it seemed like Marseilles was dead that night. We all went back to the hotel, had a glass or two of rosé, and called it a night.

The following morning we were on the bus early for the long ride back to Geneva. If the routing on this tour seemed a little crazy, it was. This is often the case with rock and roll tours. This time we did not take the scenic route, but instead hauled ass up the super highways. When we arrived in Geneva, Mickey Stewart said that since we would be sleeping in a men's hostel, Tina should cover up and pretend to be a boy. The guy who checked us in was none the wiser and it was actually a very nice hotel. Joey Ramone's brother Mitch, now known as Mickey Leigh, had arrived from New York. He was a very sweet guy who had the thankless task of being Johnny Ramone's guitar tech. The show was held in an elegant old venue called the Salle du Faubourg. The walls and ceiling were made of beautifully carved wood paneling and the acoustics were marvelous. There was even a small balcony. We rocked the joint. Talking Heads was the perfect opening act for the Ramones. If there had been any doubt, this performance sealed it. Musically we were tight, snappy, just off-kilter and unusual enough that the audience was pleasantly challenged to figure us out. Not everyone in the Ramones audience loved us, but enough of them did to make this an exciting combination. We got the crowd grooving and then the Ramones came out and completely slayed them. There was true pandemonium in the house. Really, it was amazing, a quantum leap from our nights on the Bowery.

That night, Tina's uncle Luco came up on the train from Paris to see our show. Anyone who knew Luco considered him one of most cultured men alive; he moved in high social circles. He absolutely loved both bands and was visibly proud of Tina. He gave her a box of Swiss chocolates, saying, with a wink, it was the only thing the Swiss were really good at, before sharing a bottle of wine with us in the dressing room. He apologized that he would be out of town when we played Paris. Then Luco had a conversation with Dee Dee about how he shaved his head along with his face every morning. Dee Dee said that maybe he should try that.

Our next show was at La Cigale in Lyon, so it wasn't too arduous a journey, and the views from the bus were gorgeous. When the distances were not too great, Mickey Stewart, unbeknownst to Johnny Ramone, directed

the driver to take the scenic route and the winding back roads. The mountains from Geneva to Lyon were a real trip. I spent most of the time just staring out the window while others napped or read books and magazines as Johnny grumbled audibly from the front of the bus.

Arriving at La Cigale in Lyon, we were pleasantly surprised to be greeted by a gang of young fans. It turned out that most of them were in bands themselves, with names like Marie et Les Garcons, Starshooter, and Essence. Our reputation preceded us. They were already fans of the Ramones *and* Talking Heads. The gig was great. Most of the audience loved us and we got an encore. We played "Thank You for Sending Me an Angel." Then the Ramones came on and the whole room blasted off. No one there had ever seen anything like the Ramones or Talking Heads, and the entire room was infected with a contagious musical fever.

After the show, the members of Marie et Les Garcons invited us back to their apartment for a party. We made friends with them easily even though Tina was the only one in our band who spoke French. There was a good feeling of camaraderie and much beer and wine was consumed. It was a wonderful party but we decided to call it a night because the next morning we were driving to Paris. Marie et Les Garcons promised they would be coming to Paris to see us play there.

The next day we rolled into Paris in the afternoon. As we drove through town, we were all mesmerized by the sheer beauty and opulence of the city. The architecture, the monuments and bridges across the Seine, the smoky cafés—all were even better in real life than they were in the movies. We were all happy except for Johnny Ramone, who was mad that everybody spoke French and, yes, the place was so grim. As we drove down the Boulevard Saint Germain past Café de Flore and Les Deux Magots and turned right onto Boulevard Saint Michel, Johnny spied a McDonald's and let out a whoop. Finally, a restaurant that appealed to him! He wanted to stop the bus right then, but Mickey Stewart explained that we were only a few blocks from our hotel and he could walk back there after we got checked in. Turning onto the very narrow Rue Racine, we came to Hotel Racine, where we would be spending the night. The hotel was on the corner of Place de l'Odeon across from the Odéon-Théâtre de l'Europe and one short block from the fabulous Jardin du Luxembourg. It was a relic from another era, and perfect for our first night in Paris. Tina loved it, too,

with its narrow staircases, ancient plumbing and fixtures, and squeaky beds and floors. The little lady who checked us in asked if we would like to have breakfast in our room the next morning. We said yes, we would have café au lait and croissants.

It was April in Paris and we had the day off, so Tina, David, Jerry, and I decided we would explore while the Ramones went to McDonald's. Tina and I enjoyed Jerry and David's company. St. Germain was a bustling area filled with students, bookstores, record shops, boutiques, and cafés. The weather was chilly and damp as it usually is in late April, but we didn't mind. This was the *life* for us, and to think the music we made had brought us here was fantastic. Now we were walking the same streets and alleyways as the beat poets, the great jazz cats, the Existentialists, the Surrealists, and Ernest Hemingway. With Tina by my side walking the streets of Paris, I knew I was leading a charmed life. We stopped at a Tabac to buy some Gauloises and Gitanes cigarettes. Except for Jerry, we were all smokers and the French cigarettes had a really strong kick to them. They smelled like cigars and they made me feel dizzy.

We didn't have much money to spend. Seymour Stein had given each of us a per diem of five US dollars and admonished us to "please don't tell the Ramones." You can imagine that five bucks didn't go far. I had some savings, but not much. None of us had credit cards yet. We had to be very frugal.

At some point we left David and Jerry to browse in Shakespeare and Company. We all had books to read; Jerry was reading a series of spy novels called *The Destroyer* and David was still reading about cybernetics. Tina was reading about the Arthurian legend and I was reading mostly rock magazines and *Lui*, a French men's magazine. I didn't read much French but I loved the photos of Maria Schneider, Isabelle Adjani, Uschi, and Jane Birkin. Tina and I made our way across the Seine and took a short tour of Notre Dame. After that, we headed to the newly opened Musée National d'Art Moderne, also known as the Centre Pompidou. Outside the museum was a large public square filled with street performers and musicians. One fellow was stripped to the waist and breathing fire. Another guy juggled knives and swallowed swords. Musicians of every style wailed away and their sounds all bled together to create a truly psychedelic soundscape. Tina and I wandered among them, smiling and laughing. Look out for the mimes!

Whatever art we saw that day was overshadowed by the museum's wild

new style of architecture designed by Renzo Piano and Richard Rogers. All the air ducts and electrical pipes were on the outside of the building, which resembled some kind of crazy factory. It was a very daring and controversial design for its time. It was New with a capital N and we could dig that.

Feeling hungry, we walked around looking for a cheap café to have a sandwich and found ourselves on the Rue St. Denis. This was like walking through a funky French movie set with street-walking prostitutes leaning in doorways, yelling at one another and teasing passersby. Some of them were actually wearing striped sailor's shirts, berets, and high stiletto heels, like a *New Yorker* cartoon version of a Parisienne prostitute. Some of them were just plain scary. We kept walking.

Tina and I finally found a café that we could afford and shared a ham and cheese sandwich on a baguette and a couple of beers. It was luxurious and romantic. We lingered over this little lunch and allowed the colorful ambience to sink in before we walked back to our hotel for a *cinq á sept*. We were awakened from our dreams by a rowdy Frank Gallagher, who had picked out a nearby restaurant for dinner. Frank had been touring for years and he was an avid foodie who was particularly fond of French food. Tina and I got dressed and we strolled down the street to Le Procope, the oldest restaurant in Paris. Thomas Jefferson and Benjamin Franklin had dined there regularly during their times in Paris. It's been renovated now, but in 1977 it was really down at the heels. A sweet older lady brought us our coq au vin and a carafe of Bordeaux and complimented Tina on her command of the French language. Tina told her that her mother was Bretonne and the lady smiled with approval.

After dinner, as we strolled back to our hotel, we heard some cool-sounding jazz wafting up from a little cellar bar. Tina and I decided to check it out. It was a hip, candlelit nightclub with red tablecloths and a beatnik vibe and who should we find sitting there but Danny Fields? He invited us to join him and we ordered a couple of cognacs. I asked Danny where the Ramones were and he said, "They're back at the hotel. They never go anywhere." I wondered out loud what they might be doing in their hotel rooms with no TV or radio and Danny said, "Well, they're not reading the Bible!" Our budget did not permit us any more drinks that night, so we said good night to Danny and headed back to Hotel Racine. The night porter let us in and smiled as we tiptoed up the stairs to our squeaky, sagging bed.

We were up early the next morning when our cafés and croissants were delivered to our room. Tina was reminded of how much she loved good French bread and butter and coffee in the morning. Taking a shower with a handheld nozzle and minuscule shower curtain was a bit of a challenge, but we managed and felt greatly refreshed. We were traveling to Normandy and the port city of Le Havre for another show. Le Havre is a pretty rough industrial city and was somewhat of a letdown after Paris. As if on cue, Johnny said it was grim and this time he was right. We played the Salle des Fêtes and during the sound check and during the show we were kept company by a small army of police and firemen, who had no doubt been warned about us dangerous punk New Yorkers. The Salle des Fêtes was a grand old ballroom with polished granite floors and very high ceilings with a proscenium stage probably built around the time of Napoleon. The kids in Le Havre were rougher and tougher than our usual audiences and some of them did not really get where Talking Heads was coming from. For the first time in a long while, we did not get an encore. When the Ramones hit the stage, however, they went nuts and we realized that maybe the presence of the police was not such a bad idea. The Ramones rocked the crowd so hard that the kids didn't want their show to end. When it did, we heard cries of "*Revenez sur la putain de scène!* (Get back on the fucking stage!)"

After the show, the promoter, who seemed like he may have had ties to organized crime, took us to a restaurant he owned and gave us a fine sampling of Normand cuisine. He told us not to worry. "One day you will be popular even in Le Havre."

After another night in a lumpy and squeaky bed, we boarded the bus to head back to Paris. I'm not sure how they found us, but the kids from Marie et Les Garcons and their girlfriends appeared at our hotel and we all went to eat dinner at Le Procope. We had the night off before our biggest show yet at Le Bataclan and we were all relieved to be back in Paris after the gritty, industrial vibes in Le Havre.

In the morning, we moved to a hotel near the Place de la République, which was closer to Le Bataclan. Le Bataclan is famous now for the terrible terrorist attack there in 2015, but in early May of 1977 it was one of the most beloved theaters in Paris. Opened in 1865, the Chinese-style theater had seen the likes of performers such as Buffalo Bill Cody, Colette, Edith Piaf, Maurice Chevalier, and Lou Reed, John Cale and Nico, billed as the

Velvet Underground in 1972. This was a prestigious gig for Talking Heads and we were delighted to be there. As we waited in the adjoining café to do our sound check, Tina was surrounded by cute French boys who asked her lots of questions in French like, "Is it true that you know Richard Hell?" This really pissed off Johnny Ramone and David Byrne, who preferred to be the center of attention at all times. I think they both felt jealous that our fans were naturally drawn to Tina and it annoyed them that she was fluent in French. If some young fan asked Johnny a question he would just say, "Speak English!" David simply scowled into his beer and refused to speak to anyone.

We went backstage to do an interview with France Radio 1. Most of the questions were addressed to Tina for the obvious reason that she was the only one among us who spoke French. Not only that, but the interviewer told us that Tina spoke in a very classic and proper French that hardly anyone of our generation does anymore.

We were amazed at the backstage hospitality. There was a tower of fruits de mer, ham and cheese on baguettes, very good wines, beer, and espresso, as well as an enormous bouquet of fresh flowers.

During our sound check, Jerry was badly shocked when he touched his lips to the microphone. He stumbled back and fell to the ground. These kind of shocks were not always fatal but they could be. The crew and everyone else who saw this rushed to see if Jerry was injured. Thankfully, he was just seriously stunned. We took a few minutes to let him recover. It was a grounding issue. You had to be extra careful in these old theaters and probably in the new ones, too, if you were playing an electric guitar. The electric current in France was 220–240 volts, twice as powerful as the current in the USA. When we knew for sure that Jerry was going to be okay, we hurried through our sound check before they opened the doors and let the young punks rush in. Some of them had been waiting all afternoon.

Frank Gallagher had gotten his hands on some great Lebanese hashish and invited me for some "hash under glass" in the crew room. To avoid carrying a pipe or any other paraphernalia, you would take a band badge or a safety pin with the sharp end pointed up, set it on a table, stick a piece of hash on it, and light it on fire. Then you would blow it out and quickly cover it with a glass. When the glass filled with smoke, you would tilt the glass just a little bit and inhale the smoke through your mouth and into

your lungs. The hashish in Paris was the best. A few puffs and a couple of Alsatian beers felt just right. A very fine buzz, indeed, and I was ready for showtime. I had come to believe that I played better if I was feeling loose—not too drunk or stoned, mind you—but loosened up.

We had a feeling this would be a great show. When the people come in and start to dance and jump around, the sound always gets better. The warm bodies soak up the sound and reverberations. A sold-out show always sounds better than a less-than-sold-out show and a hot room always sounds better than a cold one. The audience was stomping and chanting before we even walked onstage, and when we made our entrance, we were greeted with pure adulation. Paris was hungry for punk. Not that we were the least bit punk. We were post-punk before there even was punk, but we came from New York and CBGB and that was all this crowd needed to know. From the opening bars of "Love → Building on Fire," they soaked the music up with powerful thirst and enthusiasm. Tina rocked her bass with perfect determination even while frozen in one spot. Jerry was a little bit reticent to get too close to his mic, but dug in like a Trojan warrior in tight pants. From my position on drums, I could only see David from the rear, but he was wiggling and wailing with that strange high-pitched voice of his and acting as if every nerve in his body was on fire. As for me, I was transported to a place where everything was clear, passionate, and beautiful. Even though my fingers were blistered and bandaged from playing so hard every night, I felt nothing could go wrong. The sound mix was as good as it gets and the entire sold-out crowd of 1,500 people rocked in unison. We got not one but two encores—and could have had a third, but it was the Ramones' time.

If Talking Heads stimulated the left brain of these cool Parisians, the Ramones show clobbered their right brain. From Dee Dee's first "One, Two, Three, Four!" the standing-room-only crowd surged forward and back, from left to right. No one was in danger of getting hurt, but they were definitely "pulsatin' to the backbeat" of drummer Tommy Ramone. By the end of their set, two wild transvestites had climbed onto each end of the stage to shimmy and boogaloo in miniskirts and high heels. Oh, it was so great. It was paradise.

After the show, Mickey Stewart told us that both bands and crew had been invited out to dinner by Jackie, our Phonogram label representative. We accepted with pleasure and even Johnny was happy to go, knowing he

could get a steak and French fries. After drying off while the crew packed up, we took one more look around the historic theater, soaking up the good vibes. Within a year we'd be back to headline our own show at Le Bataclan.

We all climbed on the bus after saying goodbye to a gathering of adoring fans, including the kids from Marie et les Garçons. All of us were in high spirits. We drove across the Seine and up Boulevard Raspail; at the Rodin statue of Balzac we went around the block and turned onto Boulevard du Montparnasse, parking in front of La Coupole. It was late but not too late for dinner at this amazing restaurant. La Coupole had been well known as a meeting place for artists ever since it opened in 1927. Big-time artists like Jean Cocteau, Giacometti, Josephine Baker, Man Ray, Georges Braque, Brassai, Picasso, Simone de Beauvoir and Jean-Paul Sartre, André Malraux, Jacques Prévert, Marc Chagall, Edith Piaf, Ernest Hemingway, Marlene Dietrich, and Ava Gardner. Now they could add the Ramones and Talking Heads to that fabulous list.

There were sixteen of us, so we sat at a long table in a quiet corner where we could see the fantastic giant floral arrangement under the dome in the center of the restaurant. The Ramones all sat at one end and we sat at the other. David always enjoyed eating things that he considered unusual, so he, Jerry, Tina, and I ordered escargots to start. Jackie from Phonogram called for champagne. The British crew was in heaven. They were bon vivants, too, and not all bands treated them this well. Most of us had steak frites and much champagne was consumed although the Ramones stuck with beer. When the main course was finished, Jackie called for strawberries and whipped cream. While we were waiting for our dessert, suddenly the two transgender groupies who had danced onstage with the Ramones appeared. One of them zeroed in on our bus driver, Paul, who was only nineteen and newly married. Paul, who was stocky with a sweet face and rosy cheeks, was very naïve and innocent to the ways of the world. He had just told Tina that he wanted to come to Paris to see if it would be a nice place to bring his new bride on a holiday. When this transvestite sat down on his lap, he blushed brightly and squirmed to get away, but she wasn't going anywhere and she wasn't letting Paul go anywhere, either. When the strawberries and whipped cream were placed in front of Paul she asked him, "Paul, do you like fraises? *Moi, j'adore les fraises!*" Then she pulled up her blouse to reveal a tiny hormone-induced breast. She stuck her finger in the whipped cream,

circled her nipple with it, and asked Paul again, "Paul, do you like fraises?" He was frozen with embarrassment and said nothing as she pressed her Chantilly covered nipple to his lips. At this point Mickey Stewart, sensing Paul's humiliation, stood up and said it was time for us to go—and off we went. Paul was visibly relieved to get back behind the wheel. Because he was so innocent, he never knew that the naughty girl on his lap was really a man, and we certainly didn't tell him.

The next day, Joey and I were the first ones down to the lobby. We chatted about the Bataclan gig and how wild it was. Joey said someone had set off some smoke bombs in the lobby of the theater while we were onstage. He and I stepped outside and took a few photos with some fans and our new friends from Marie et les Garçons. When Tina arrived we got on the bus. That night's show was in Orleans and a group from England called Eddie and the Hot Rods had been added to the bill. The venue was the Palais des Sports, which was like a big gym for a crowd of a thousand people. Eddy and the Hot Rods were cool guys and great showmen from the UK Pub Rock scene.

One of many great things about touring Europe is that the distance between shows is usually not too great. We arrived in Brussels by lunchtime. The only problem was that we found a single cup of coffee cost us our entire per diem. So we savored that coffee and waited until sound check when the promoter would provide us with some sandwiches and good Belgian beers. Before the show we did interviews with a fanzine called *Mor Mag* and Belgian Radio. Again, most of the questions were directed to Tina. Funny how people like to speak and write in their own language. The gig was at the university in a lecture hall that resembled a small amphitheater and it was clean as a whistle.

When showtime came around, we were thrilled by the reaction we got from the mostly male audience. The students went nuts and, for some reason, threw some potatoes and stuffed animals at us. Evidently, that meant they liked us. We got two encores and signed many autographs after the show. As usual, the Ramones killed. This young audience would loyally follow both bands from that day forward.

The following day, May 6, we rolled into Amsterdam, probably the hippest and most progessive city on earth. It still is. We would be staying at the Hotel Wiechmann, on the canal just off the Leidseplein. As the

bus turned onto Prinsengracht, the very narrow street where the hotel was, we were blocked by a poorly parked European car. Mickey Stewart asked us all to follow him off the bus. He told each of us to hold onto the bumpers and underbody of the car and lift it out of the way! So the members of the Ramones and Talking Heads, to our own amazement, picked the car up and carried it out of the way and onto the sidewalk. Mickey said we were lucky it wasn't a Cadillac.

The Hotel Wiechmann was where all the bands stayed. It was one of those tall but narrow historic townhouses that line the canals of Amsterdam, and the bands loved it because you could walk almost anywhere you wanted to go from it. As we checked in, we learned that Dr. Feelgood was also staying there. Tina and I climbed the very steep and narrow stairs right behind Joey Ramone. We had tiny rooms on the fourth floor and with our duffel bags it was a real hike. I remember collapsing onto the bed with Tina to take a short nap when there was a knock on the door. Getting into the tiny room was no problem, but there was no room to open the door from the inside without standing on the bed. It was Joey, who wanted to make sure that we didn't forget him when we left for the show. I assured him that we would never leave him behind.

The show that night was at the Paradiso, famously one of the best music venues in Europe. Hippies squatted in this big nineteenth-century church in 1967 and tried to turn it into a music and performance place. That same year the police kicked them out, but then the city took over and turned it into a subsidized youth center.

There were still a lot of hippies in Amsterdam, to be sure, but there were also many people who loved the concept of punk even if they didn't fully embrace the lifestyle themselves. They spoke English very well and were well informed about music and art. They made our bands feel welcome. Dutch Radio played our first single, "Love → Building on Fire," before any other station in the world. The Dutch people that we met and came to love completely embraced the new.

When we arrived at the Paradiso we were impressed that the venue was still very much a church. In fact, services were still held there a couple of times a week. The main floor was all standing room with a large stage where the altar would be. The stained-glass windows remained. There were two balconies. It was very dark inside. The dressing rooms were downstairs

under the stage, rustic but clean and bigger than most. As we walked in, Frank Gallagher grinned and said I should check out the choir loft. I walked up the stairs to find what looked like a little café where the guy behind the counter asked if I would like to see the menu. When I read it, I realized this was a hashish bar. They had a full range of varieties and prices for sale. Back home you would go straight to jail for this, but here in Amsterdam people were skinning up hash and tobacco spliffs in public. I bought a little piece of the black to save for later.

The Ramones were doing their sound check and, with the booming acoustics of the Paradiso, they sounded like a horde of bikers on choppers at full throttle, but with melodies. Somehow over all the crazy commotion, Joey always hit the notes and it was almost always a happy sound. You wanted to punch the air with your fist at every chord change. At least I did.

The Paradiso was definitely hot by the time we hit the stage and our band was in terrific form. We were surprised to see that many people down in the front knew the words to our songs and were singing along, particularly on "Psycho Killer." They chanted along as if we were at a soccer match. From behind the drums I could see the balconies were heaving in time to the music. The excitement level was energizing to the point that we played harder and harder. David and Jerry and Tina all broke strings on their guitars. It's not easy to break a string on a bass guitar, but Tina did it. We were learning what it took to put on an exciting show and the Dutch reciprocated with keen appreciation. We only had time for one encore and then the Ramones came on to take everything up to an even crazier level. They were not just loud, they were *sublime*. Downstairs in the dressing room we could see the floorboards above our heads throbbing in an unsettling way, but all was cool. The Blitzkreig Bop was in full effect. After the show, when we were all still soaked with sweat, Dee Dee motioned me over to the dressing room toilet and closed the door behind us. Someone had given him a little cocaine and he offered to share it with me. He put his index finger to his lips to say not to tell anyone. It was only a tiny amount but it was really good. Then Dee Dee said that one day we'd get together and do a whole gram. We laughed and joined the party in the dressing room where the Heineken was flowing and some very tall and gorgeous Dutch girls were all over the Ramones. We were introduced for the first time to Hans DeVente, a giant of a man who called himself our biggest fan. He was with Fer Abrahams,

who had been playing our single on Dutch radio. Both of these guys became lifelong friends, but particularly Hans, who worked for Sony product development and would show up at our gigs around the world. He had access to the very best in portable recording devices and has a huge archive of our live performances that he recorded with our permission.

After the show we went back to Hotel Wiechmann to change before going to a club the girls in the dressing room had invited us to. In the lobby, Tina and I met up with Dee Dee and Willy DeVille and his girlfriend, Toots. Willy was on tour with his band Mink DeVille and it was good to see him, although I don't think he ever understood or cared for Talking Heads. Toots was a real tough cookie and super jealous of any girl who even looked at Willy. In her black bouffant hairdo, black mascara, pencil-thin black leather skirt, and black stiletto heels, she resembled one of the Ronettes or maybe one of the Shangri-Las. She had been known to use a knife and some people were afraid of her, but she seemed to like Tina and me and we were cool with her.

As we walked to the club, it became clear that Willy and Toots were very loaded, but it was a beautiful Friday night in May and Amsterdam was heavenly. We laughed together while exchanging touring stories with Willy. Then Toots tripped on the cobblestones and pitched forward, poking her chest on an iron bollard used to keep cars from driving up on the sidewalks. She rolled off the bollard and landed hard on her side. It was a terrible fall and we feared the worst, but as Willy helped her up she just brushed herself off and said not to worry, she was fine. Toots felt no pain. Not yet, anyway, but the next day we heard she had several broken ribs and some internal injuries, too.

The club was cool. David and Jerry were already there. Jerry was hitting it off with the ladies and David was dancing by himself. The DJ was spinning punk and reggae and Tina and I had fun dancing on the tiny, packed dance floor until some very tall Dutch girl accidentally stomped on Tina's foot. At five feet four inches tall, Tina said she felt like a dwarf in Holland. There was no sign of Dee Dee, Willy, or Toots. At the time I wondered where they had gone, but now I know they had probably copped something they liked and gone to get high.

The next day, the hotel provided a fine Dutch breakfast of ham and eggs, cheese and yogurt with fresh fruit and pancakes. It was fun to have breakfast with Dr. Feelgood, who were cheerful and had enormous appetites. I

sat across the table from the singer Lee Brilleaux, a fine lad, and the drummer, who was known as The Big Figure. They were pub rockers reacting against much of the seventies music the way we and the Ramones were, but they had been doing it longer. We had seen them perform at the Bottom Line in New York City when the great guitarist Wilko Johnson was in the band and the Ramones had been their support act. They were influential to the British punks and they never failed to rock the house.

Now we were on the bus to Eindhoven to play a club called Effenaar. Johnny Ramone was in a bad mood again. Who knows why? Danny Fields turned to us and said, "The Princess and the Pea," which put everything Johnny ever said into perspective. Hans and Fer were at the sound check and interviewed Talking Heads for a radio show called *Supporting Act*, which is what we were. It was a great show and not too much of an anticlimax after the Paradiso. We got a hard-earned encore.

The following morning, May 8, was my twenty-sixth birthday and the bus took us to northern Holland to the town of Groningen. In 1977, there was not much happening in Groningen. Our hotel was a Dutch Seaman's Hostel for men only so we had to sneak Tina in as a boy again. She did make a very cute boy. The hotel was completely Spartan with bathrooms and showers in the hall. The color scheme was ship's gray on gray. After a little nap we headed over to the Huize Maas club to play the gig. The club was not very interesting; it seemed like the music was secondary to the drinking. The people running the place were not interested in us at all and the dressing room for both bands was the size of a broom closet. Then something wonderful happened. Just before Talking Heads was about to play, a huge gang of Dutch Hell's Angels roared up to the front of the club. They were out for a Sunday ride and thought they would check out these New York bands that were playing. They completely outnumbered the other customers and the thing is, they were really nice people. They were wearing the Angels' colors but they seemed like well-mannered, educated guys and not a thing like their American brothers. As we climbed onstage to play, they came to the front of the tiny stage and actually paid attention. They were fascinated by our weirdness and cheered us on after every song.

Of course, the Angels loved the Ramones, too. Maybe even more. And after the show, they invited us to join them at another bar nearby. Since it was my birthday and there was nothing else going on, Tina and I said yes

and Dee Dee came along, too. One Angel in particular took us under his wing and rolled a big hash-and-tobacco spliff for me. We shared it with pleasure, had a couple of Grolsch beers, and were in the middle of a political discussion when, suddenly, the police walked in. They ignored Tina and Dee Dee and me but very calmly asked all the Angels to go outside. Our Angel friend said that we should get out of there right away and we did. Looking back as we quickly walked away, we saw the cops lining the Angels up against the outside wall of the bar and frisking them. That was the end of my birthday party.

The bus rolled back to Amsterdam the next morning to the Hotel Wiechmann for a much-needed night off after playing seven in a row. We walked over to the Leidesplein with David and Jerry where we met our biggest fan Hans (who was wearing a badge that said I MAY BE FAT BUT I'M NOT STUPID) for a dinner of spaghetti bolognese. Then we walked around the corner to the famous Melkweg, which was second only to the Paradiso in terms of music and partying. It was a Monday night, so there was no live music, but people were stoned on all kinds of things, primarily acid. The air was thick with hash and tobacco smoke and the DJ was banging. He had no idea we were there but played our single "Love → Building on Fire." People danced. How sweet it felt.

After more great shows in Rotterdam and Utrecht, we turned our sights to the UK. As the bus rolled onto the ferry from the Hook of Holland to Harwich, I felt like our tour of the capitals of Europe had been a complete success and I was sorry to leave. Now we were heading to London, which was going to be really wild. We would be playing the Roundhouse on the Queen's Jubilee Weekend and every punk musician in London would be there. We had a particularly rough crossing of the North Sea, with many seasick passengers vomiting overboard and all around us. We finally arrived in the port of Harwich and as the bus rolled off the ferry onto UK soil, Mickey Stewart turned on the bus radio to play some music and what we heard the announcer say was, "This is the BBC. Now, from the city of New York in the United States of America, these are the Ramones with their latest single, 'Sheena Is a Punk Rocker'!" The feeling on the bus was euphoric. We were part of a new vanguard arriving in England right on time and ready to take it to the stage and make history.

TALKING HEADS IN LONDON

From the ferry landing we reached London in high spirits, if still a bit queasy from crossing in a Force 8 gale. The Ramones had flown up to do a few dates in Scandinavia without us so we were on our own for a few days. We stayed in a no-name hotel in an unmemorable part of town. When I stood up from a brief lie-down on the bed, Tina burst out laughing. The back side of my black jeans was completely covered with bright orange lint from our cheap, bright orange bedspread. With some difficulty I managed to get it all off with a piece of gaffer's tape before we went out on the town. Mickey Stewart took us to a well-known music club called Dingwalls to see Johnny Kidd and the Pirates. They were old school, wore pirate suits and eyepatches and were not really our cup of tea, but they'd had a number one single in the UK in 1960 with "Shakin' All Over," and it was fun to hear some pre-Beatles British rock and roll.

The next day, Friday the 13th of May, we played a Talking Heads showcase, the first of two nights, at a club called the Rock Garden in Covent Garden. This was the first sunny day we'd had since Marseilles and Tina and I enjoyed walking around. The club was a tiny honeycomb of dark rooms and the show was sold out. It's always a good idea to play a smaller place that you know will sell out, rather than a larger room that may not, especially for your debut in a cultural capital like London.

We rocked the joint and played two encores. London's music press was out in force and the reviews that followed were glowing. In those days the UK had three main weekly music papers: *Melody Maker*, *New Musical Express*, and *Sounds*. There were also some cool punk 'zines like *Sniffin' Glue*. The weekly papers had to come up with news scoops to sell magazines every week and Talking Heads was right up their alley. So were the Ramones. Together on tour we were big news.

The next day Tina and I decided to visit Malcolm McLaren and Vivienne Westwood's shop on King's Road. SEX was a tiny boutique selling crazy tartan and leopard-skin bondage trousers and uber-gay Tom of Finland T-shirts. There was no way we were going to wear any of it, but two doors down, Tina, who felt the cold, bought a black jacket made of quilted paper.

As we strolled down King's Road we expected to see some punks and, sure enough, a small group of punk kids passed by with their Doc Martens, spiky hair, and drunken stagger. If you read the papers, you would think the punks were everywhere in England causing madness and mayhem, but we figured that it was actually the same small group of kids that showed up at all punk events over and over again. The media loved them and they loved the media. It was fun for these kids to horrify their stodgy British parents and scandalize the government, and it was a hoot for us to observe.

Linda Stein, who co-managed the Ramones with Danny Fields, had just flown in from New York and took us out to dinner that night before the show. She loved our band and was excited to show us off while the Ramones were away and Johnny wasn't looking. When we got to the Rock Garden it was completely sold out again. We slowly made our way through the packed house to the cramped backstage area and began to get tuned up to play, when Linda came rushing in to tell us ecstatically that John Cale and Brian Eno were in the audience. She said she would bring them back to meet us after the show. We already knew John, famous for his work with the Velvet Underground, pretty well because he'd been living in New York and hanging out at CBGB while producing the Patti Smith Group's debut album, *Horses*. David had been invited to sit in with him as a guitarist along with Lou Reed and Patti at one of John's shows at the Lower Manhattan Ocean Club. John was a pretty wild guy in a Welsh poet sort of way and we liked him a lot. His productions of the Stooges, Nico, and his own solo work were impeccable. Of course, he had also produced the Modern Lovers

demos that were later released on Berserkley Records after Jonathan left the band, so Jerry was particularly well acquainted with John. It would be good to see him after the show. As for Brian Eno, I had all of his albums and we were big fans. We felt a kinship to what he was doing in his early solo work with songs like "Baby's on Fire" and "I'll Come Running (To Tie Your Shoe)." He had also released a live album with Cale, Nico, and Kevin Ayers titled *June 1, 1974*. John and Brian were considered to be leaders of the rock avant-garde, a position that we respected and aspired to. But now it was time for us to rock.

The show was wonderful despite the cramped little stage and the sweaty, smoky, dripping-hot atmosphere. We were used to these conditions from our shows at CBGB.

This was our set list:

"Love → Building on Fire"
"Uh-oh, Love Comes to Town"
"Don't Worry About the Government"
"Who Is It?"
"Take Me to the River"
"Tentative Decisions"
"The Book I Read"
"New Feeling"
"A Clean Break (Let's Work)"
"I'm Not in Love"
"Psycho Killer"

ENCORE
"No Compassion"
"Thank You for Sending Me an Angel"

In keeping with the old showbiz rule, "Always leave them wanting more," we did just that and left the stage. I knew we had made a strong, mostly good impression on all who were there and, most importantly, on Cale and Eno.

Linda quickly brought them backstage along with producer Chris Thomas, who had just produced the Sex Pistols' album after working with

the Beatles and Roxy Music, among many others. We shook hands all around and I heard John tell Brian, "They're mine, you bugger!" I asked Linda to get Brian's phone number. I should have known that she already had.

After the show we were taken to the Speakeasy Club. "The Speak" had been an important musician and record business hangout, but we had the feeling it was well past its prime. John Cale was there with his manager, Jane Friedman, who was also Patti Smith's. John was a hard drinker back then and was feeling no pain. Jane was dispensing drink money to him, but not wholeheartedly. Chris Thomas was still with them and had a quiet chat with David. Who knows what they talked about? Thomas had passed on producing Talking Heads' first album, which we had yet to finish recording. He had been our first choice mostly due to his work with Roxy Music, but it wasn't to be. Tina found the ambience at the Speakeasy depressingly awful so we said good night and we split back to our no-name hotel.

The next day was a Sunday and Tina and I went to the Victoria and Albert Museum. It had been several years since either of us had made a painting but we still thought like painters. We spent hours taking in as much of the collection spanning five thousand years of art and design as we could. The Japanese collection was particularly gorgeous. A kindly security guard, a grandfatherly man, asked us if we were enjoying London. "Oh, yes," we said. He asked us if we would be sticking around for the Queen's Jubilee weekend and we told him yes, we would be playing two concerts at the Roundhouse that weekend. "What type of music do you play?" he asked. I told him we played dance music and he said, "Oh, I love to dance!" and winked at Tina.

Even though many restaurants in London were closed on Mondays, Linda was able to set up a lunch with Talking Heads and Brian Eno at my request. I thought it was a good idea to meet with him while the Rock Garden show was still fresh in his mind. The four Talking Heads, Brian, and Linda Stein met at a pub called the Hungry Horse. I would say that the lunch couldn't have gone any better. We didn't talk business but we did find Brian to be very likable and interesting. He had the bearing of a Jesuit priest, but I had heard of his reputation with the ladies so I knew he was far from one. He was soft spoken and courtly, and it was clear to me that he was also keen to make a good impression. We all had a good laugh, especially

Tina and Linda, when he explained to us what an item on the menu called Spotted Dick was. Brian was very complimentary of our sound, which he later described as "The rhythm section is like a ship or a train—very forceful and certain of where it's going. On top of that you have this hesitant, doubting quality that dizzily asks, 'Where are we going?' That makes for a sense of genuine disorientation, unlike the surface insanity of the more commonplace, expressionist punk bands." Brian invited to us his flat for tea the following day and of course we accepted with pleasure.

That night we went with John Cale and Jane Friedman to see Kevin Ayers perform at The Rainbow. It was a very old-fashioned, laid-back, and romantic show with a tropical island stage set in keeping with the theme of his latest album, *Yes, We Have No Mañanas*. At the party afterward, John introduced us to Kevin, who was totally charming and puffing on a big Cuban cigar. Years later, Kevin would be our houseguest in Connecticut for a couple of days and cooked us the most delicious fish dinner. Tina and I had produced some demos for his daughter Galen that he liked and we talked about the possibility of doing some work together, but sadly, he passed away at his home in the south of France before we ever got together again.

When we woke up on Tuesday, Tina felt she was coming down with a cold and needed to rest, so David, Jerry, and I took a cab over to Eno's flat in Maida Vale not far from the historic Abbey Road Studios. It was a quiet, rainy day. Brian was welcoming and I was impressed by how unpretentious and anti–rock star his surroundings were. He was wearing an Adidas tracksuit. Gone were the feather boas and makeup of his stage persona. Over cups of tea we talked about many things including how, as a recording artist, you don't have to have hit records to stay in business as long as you keep your expenses down. We also talked about using the tape recorder as simply another musical instrument and how not bothering to read equipment manuals could allow interesting, unexpected musical events to happen. That was fine with me. I've never read a manual in my life.

Brian was excited by Jamaican dub mixes and showed us his copy of Dr. Alimantado's *Best Dressed Chicken in Town*, which I also had in my record collection. We both loved Lee Perry. He also had high praise for Fela Kuti's work and I explained that we loved him, too, and that I had bought his and other African records at a multicultural store in Cambridge, Massachusetts, during our RISD days.

It was a very calm and happy afternoon with great mutual admiration all around. I was pleased to see David feeling about as comfortable as David could be in Brian's presence. It was also good to see that Jerry, who had not really been a fan of Eno's music, was beginning to appreciate Brian's point of view.

After a few very fine cups of tea and a couple of hours of great conversation, I excused myself to go check on Tina back at the hotel. David and Jerry stayed at Eno's place, where evidently the discussion turned to one of David's favorite topics, cybernetics. Jerry thinks David never really understood it, but it made him feel smart to talk about it. In 1948, Norbert Wiener defined cybernetics as "the scientific study of control and communication in the animal and the machine." Whatever happened, there is no doubt that our meeting that day with Brian set the stage for some great, groundbreaking work together in the future.

Just before we had left New York City to go on the tour, I'd been walking across Fifty-seventh Street when I saw my friend and painting teacher Richard Merkin. He had heard about Talking Heads and asked me how it was going. I told him we were about to go play in Europe and the UK. He said that he would write a letter of introduction to his good friend, the great British Pop artist Peter Blake. Peter was well-known for designing and creating the cover of the Beatles' *Sgt. Pepper's* album. In fact, he'd been well-known and highly respected before that—it was why the Beatles chose him. One of the many feathers in Merkin's cap was that he is one of the characters on that album cover. He gave me Blake's number in England and told me to call him, so when we got to London I did.

Peter Blake answered and asked, "Can you meet me for lunch today at Mr. Chow's, and do you mind if I bring a friend?" We had the day off so I said we would love to and, of course, do bring a friend.

I gathered everyone together and we took a cab over to Mr. Chow. I do love those London cabs where the whole band could sit in the back. Peter Blake was waiting patiently, dressed like a country gentleman in a three-piece tweed suit and sporting a neatly groomed Van Dyke goatee. He smiled broadly, invited us to sit down, and said how pleased he had been to hear about us from Richard Merkin. After ordering for the whole table he talked a little about art, but then quickly turned the conversation to the London music scene. He asked us if we had heard of Kilburn and the High Roads. I

replied that I had heard a little about them from a sweet guy I'd met at CBGB called Humphrey Ocean. Peter smiled and said, "Here he comes now!" Sure enough, Humphrey Ocean, tall and lanky, came striding over to our table with a tiny guy who walked with a cane and a pronounced limp. They both sat down with us and Peter said, "You already know Humphrey and this is our friend Ian Dury." Ian was dressed like a gypsy or a tinker, a real ragamuffin. He had pierced ears with dangling cross earrings and an oily, curly Gene Vincent–style hairdo. He said, "'Allo Tawlkin 'Eds." I later learned that his Cockney accent was a complete put-on, but he certainly fooled us. Ian was not the only British musician to adopt a working-class accent to disguise a more posh background. Joe Strummer, amusing us with Cockney rhyming slang, springs to mind. Both Ian and Humphrey had been in Kilburn and the High Roads, a group of pub rockers who were now considered to be important predecessors of British punk. Ian had been an art student taught by Peter. Humphrey had been an art student taught by Ian. All were painters and music lovers, our kind of people. As the meal wound down, I invited them all to our upcoming show at the Roundhouse. Peter said that he was living in Bristol and rarely came to London anymore. But it just so happened we'd be playing in Bristol so I said I'd put him on the guest list. Peter picked up the tab for all of us. What a kind and generous man.

DEEPER INTO THE UK

The Ramones landed in the UK from their Scandanavian gigs. Dee Dee especially loved the show in Finland. When I asked him why that show in particular, he said, "Because it's right next to Russia!"

Frank Gallagher went out to Heathrow Airport with Tommy and Johnny Ramone to pick up their girlfriends, Claudia, Robin, and Roxy, who were arriving from New York. Roxy had brought Johnny a new black leather Perfecto jacket because his had been stolen from the stage while the Ramones were performing at the Effenaar Club in Eindhoven, Holland. The Perfecto jacket was a very important part of the Ramones' look, so you would think that Johnny would be grateful, but no. To Frank's horror, while still inside Heathrow, Johnny began slapping Roxy, yelling and hitting her around the head. This would explain why Tommy's girlfriend, Claudia, looked shell-shocked when she arrived at our hotel and Tina said, "Hi! Welcome to London!" Roxy never said a word to anyone about this or anything else. I suppose she was forbidden to speak to anyone. Dee Dee told me she came from a wealthy family and her last name was Whitney, but we never found out if she was one of *the* Whitneys. Somehow, I think not.

Our first show of this leg was in Liverpool at a basement club called Eric's. It was in the alley next door to the historic Cavern Club, where the Beatles had rocked and rolled. In their wisdom, the city fathers had allowed

the Cavern Club to be destroyed and replaced with a parking garage. Eric's had exactly the same floor plan and architecture as the original Cavern Club: a long, narrow staircase leading down to a cellar with vaulted ceilings of brick and stone, a tiny stage, and no windows or ventilation. If it hadn't had the Beatles myth attached to it, it would have been a pure hellhole, but like CBGB, the kids loved it. By the time we climbed onstage the air was smoky and thick and the stone walls were dripping with condensation. Our crew had set up a fan to cool us down but it was just blowing hot air across the stage. Tina, who had a bad cold and fever, felt alternately like she was tripping or dying. My hands were so slippery and wet I was having trouble hanging onto my drumsticks after playing the first song. David was fucking up his parts, forgetting his words and skipping entire verses, but no one in the audience seemed to notice or care. To my right, Jerry, who was normally cool and calm, was streaming sweat and turning bright pink. We were all gasping for air. The kids in the audience were going nuts from the first song—I mean, they were really going wild and not just a little bit. There was no barrier between the kids and the tiny, low stage; they were right in our faces. I can't remember a single girl in the crowd of young men, although evidently the NME sent enfant terrible Julie Burchill to review the show. She adored the Ramones in every way but dismissed Talking Heads as sounding like we'd been locked up in a closet with our Sam & Dave records for too long. Ha! That's still one of my favorite descriptions of our band and not too far from the truth, despite Julie's mean-spirited intentions.

We got two encores and ran upstairs and outside for some fresh air. Our soaking-wet hot bodies emanated clouds of steam. The good news was Tina's fever had broken. She was feeling good again!

We could have slept late the next morning, but the maids in our Liverpool hotel ignored our DO NOT DISTURB sign and knocked loudly on the door until we got up. Tina and I decided not to fight it and went downstairs for breakfast. The dining room, with lace curtains and white tablecloths, was really like a scene from *A Hard Day's Night* with proper British businessmen in suits drinking tea and looking askance at us. No matter, the full English breakfast with eggs and bacon and fried tomato with toast, jam, and coffee was just what we needed. We felt good and ready for more action.

We would get plenty of more action. It was a lovely day and Tina and I had a serious case of spring fever. The next stop on the tour was Leeds Poly-

technic University, where we would play in the same refectory where the Who had recorded their classic album *Live at Leeds*. The room was packed with punk students wearing shades, ripped T-shirts, and badges while guzzling pints of lager in, thank God, plastic cups. It was a large room, and there was plenty of space to pose and pogo. The crew set our gear up on ten large modular wooden boxes that formed the stage. By just walking onto the stage, we got a huge reaction. I wouldn't really call it an ovation. It was more like an eruption. This audience was primed! As always, we played our show with all the passion and humor we could muster. David was really milking his nutty onstage idiosyncrasies, playing off the audience's reactions, and the kids loved it. How could such a nerd be so much fun? It was great to see more young women in the audience, too, and Tina's presence on bass guitar was not lost on them. This audience was so enthusiastic we got three encores! If I repeat myself with the encore thing, this is because the number of encores you get is real evidence of how you're doing and evidently we were doing something right.

The wild welcome that we received from this crowd, however, paled next to the reaction the Ramones received. When they hit the stage to the strains of Ennio Morricone's theme for *The Good, the Bad and the Ugly*, plugged into their Marshall amplifier stacks with a scream of feedback, planted their feet wide apart and Joey intoned, "You're a loudmouth, baby! You better shut it up!" the entire audience surged forward with such force that the modular stage was pushed back twelve feet or so until it hit the back wall! The Ramones wobbled a bit, but Tommy didn't miss a beat as their famous backdrop waved back and forth. Lesser bands may have been freaked out by this, but not our Ramones. Dee Dee looked so defiant that Jerry dubbed him "The Noble Savage" and I had to agree, although I'm pretty sure Dee Dee was not without sin.

Following the show, as Tina was boarding the bus, Johnny Ramone grabbed her by the collar of her jacket and dragged her back down the steps. She turned around and he said, "Oh, I thought you were Roxy!" No apology. He was angry because he thought Roxy was getting on the bus before him. Everyone around the bus, including many fans, were witnesses but Tina just said, "Watch where you're going, man!" He didn't bother Tina after that but wherever we went we'd hear Johnny shouting, "Roxy! Roxy!" at his girlfriend. Finally, Linda Stein told him to quit hitting and yelling at

his girlfriend in public or he was going to wind up in jail. Linda, a former elementary school teacher, knew exactly how to talk to a disobedient child and Johnny got the message, at least for the time being. Johnny's abusive behavior was something we and Linda did our best put an end to, but this was a very deep-seated problem. Tina and I spoke to the band, but the other Ramones seemed unable to do or say anything about it. They looked the other way and Tommy in particular asked us to please not confront him about it. It seems that the entire band was bullied by Johnny. They were unwilling to speak out about it.

The next day, Saturday, May 21, we arrived in Glasgow, Scotland. It was a bright sunny day, a rare occurrence in Scotland, according to Frank Gallagher, one of our resident Scots. David and Frank had both been born not far from Glasgow and our collective mood was very high. After checking into the Ivanhoe Hotel, we took a long walk around the city where many young people who looked a lot like David were out promenading and window shopping while eating from brown paper bags of fish and chips. Tina observed that the boys were cuter than the girls. Glasgow was a tough town, but on this day, with the fair weather, people were happy to be alive.

Incredible as it seemed to us, the Ramones and Talking Heads were performing at the University of Strathclyde on the same night Television and Blondie were playing at the Glasgow Apollo. This felt like a bad booking practice, but so hungry were the Scots for the music of these new American bands that both shows were completely sold out. If we thought the crowd reaction in Liverpool and Leeds was something wild, nothing had prepared us for the sheer, savage ferocity of the Scots. The Celts really know how to give it up and turn it loose, and boy did they ever. Thank goodness they loved us or I probably wouldn't be here to tell this tale. Clem Burke from Blondie and Fred Smith from Television came by to check out our set and were impressed with the addition of Jerry to our band. They, too, were in awe of the crowd reaction, especially when the Ramones made their entrance.

After our shows, a group of us New Yorkers hit the pubs. The beer was good and so was the Scotch. It seemed like a dream for all of us to be transported from the Bowery to the city of Glasgow on the same night. Frank Gallagher asked me if I knew the difference between summer and winter in Scotland. He said, "In summer the rain is warmer." This was a good thing

because it had started to rain, and when we got back to our hotel we were locked out. After much ringing of the bell and pounding on the door, the night man eventually arrived to let us in. He scolded us for staying out too late, but then he smiled and said, "Look. I've saved you some sandwiches." I loved his little egg salad sandwiches cut into triangles with the crust trimmed off. They were a sign of civilization.

In Manchester at the Electric Circus, the kids wore black plastic "bin bags"—what we in the USA call garbage bags—over their clothing like ponchos, and we wondered if this was a new punk fashion statement. We found out soon enough that the bin bags were protection from a disturbing new trend in the UK known as "gobbing." Gobbing was the act of spitting high into the air with the goal of landing the gob somewhere on the band onstage. In the bizarro world of punk rock, gobbing was considered a sign of approval. It was something new and ultra punk. The more a band was loved, the more they were gobbed upon. We got our fair share of gob, but when the Ramones hit the stage there was a veritable blizzard of gob. I felt badly for the band, but even more so for the crew who had to wipe the drums, guitars, and other gear down after the show. Besides being just plain gross, the gobbing was a real health hazard. Joe Strummer from the Clash got hepatitis from being gobbed. After the show we talked about how punk had become a kind of ugly club and wondered how much uglier things could possibly become. The Punk movement was really picking up steam.

At the Outlook Club in Doncaster, all we got was polite applause, and Tina noted even more misogyny than usual directed at her from the mostly young male audience. After the show one young fan told me about a new band he liked called XTC. I said I'd keep an eye out for them.

En route to Birmingham for the twentieth show of the tour, Mickey Stewart suggested we stop in the countryside near Nottingham for lunch at the oldest inn in England, Ye Olde Trip to Jerusalem, established in 1189. They served great steaks and all sorts of ales. We spent all of our combined per diems and then some. Afterward, at Tina's request, we did a quick tour of Nottingham Castle. Dee Dee loved castles, and who doesn't? It was fun for everyone, even Johnny, to get off the bus and soak up the historical vibes and get a little fresh air.

After another crazy, wild show at Barbarella's in Birmingham, where we

had to climb a high metal ladder to get to and from our dressing room, we all got on the bus again and drove straight to London. We had a better hotel this time, the Kingsley on Bloomsbury Way. I remember taking a long hot bath with Tina, and then doing our laundry in the same bathwater. As I was shaving, I looked in the mirror and for some reason had a vision of how I would look forty years down the road. A little jowly perhaps, but not too scary, thank goodness. It could have been worse.

We had the next day off and we decided to take a bit of a busman's holiday and ride down to Sussex University in Brighton to catch the Clash's White Riot Tour. The support acts were the Jam and the Slits. We just managed to catch the tail end of the Slits' set. They were wildness personified onstage. From where I stood at the back of the hall, I couldn't understand a word they were singing but I'm pretty sure I was receiving their message. Tina and I really enjoyed their defiance and playfulness.

The Jam was up next. They were the most technically proficient band of the night by far and they looked sharp, too. Everything about them screamed Mod. They wore sharkskin suits with white shirts, skinny ties, and two-tone dress shoes. At this point, I was still wearing Levi's and Lacoste. Though they were only a trio, they had a big sound very reminiscent of the Who or the Small Faces in their early days. They had been playing together for about five years but their first album, *In the City*, had just been released three days before. They were already getting solid radio airplay and were clearly a big draw on this tour. Evidently, they were kicked off the tour later when Paul Weller's manager dad asked for more money.

After a short break, the Clash hit the stage with a huge, high-contrast banner of an image from the 1976 Notting Hill riots flying behind them. Their first album, *The Clash*, was only a month old and so extremely raw and politically charged that their US label, Columbia, refused to even release it. Gnarly as it was, I dug their fiery sound. The songs "White Riot" and "I'm So Bored with the USA" were both invigorating and hilarious to me. "Police and Thieves" was one of my favorite reggae tunes and the Clash rocked it really well. The university audience in Brighton was well charged and completely receptive to the type of rebellion the Clash instigated. Also, I couldn't help but notice they had a great drummer in Topper Headon. He was the one who was driving this train with no frills, just some good hard rocking.

Just before the Clash finished their set, Mickey Stewart took us back to the dressing room so that we, but especially the Ramones, wouldn't get mobbed by fans.

The Slits were there partying with a few friends and offered us some warm beers and passed their spliffs. They were really friendly and welcoming, especially the singer Ari Up and her mom, Nora Foster, who later married Johnny Rotten. Viv Albertine was interested to meet Tina, too, and years later asked her to play bass on one of her solo albums. I might add that Viv turned out to be a very good writer with two excellent books to date. We were all relaxing and having a lovely time when the Clash burst in. An extremely agitated Joe Strummer glared at us as if to say, "Who the fuck are you?" It was his dressing room, after all. Then he spotted Joey Ramone sipping a beer in the corner and his expression relaxed and widened into a huge grin. Suddenly, we all were welcome.

We played a place called the Friars Club Aylesbury on the following night. This was a magical gig. We didn't know what to expect but a name like the Friars Club conjured up the image of a funky pub owned by Rodney Dangerfield. In fact, it was a new entertainment hall that held 1,250 people and it was really well run by friendly staff. Musicians loved this gig and many of our favorites had played there. David Bowie, Mott the Hoople, The Pretty Things, and Free had all played there, as well as prog rockers like King Crimson and Genesis. Iggy Pop had recently kicked off his Idiot Tour there with David Bowie on keyboards. This was the big time, but it felt very relaxed and comfortable, no pressure at all.

The audience in Aylesbury was somehow wild yet genteel at the same time. You had the feeling that these were people who not only loved music, but also knew a thing or two about the history of music, as if they all had taken a course in music appreciation. While we represented something new to them, they recognized our musical roots and art school background and they signaled their approval with tremendous enthusiasm. The guys from our distributor, Phonogram, who were supporting the tour, came backstage to pat us on the back after our third encore of the evening. They could see clearly that their investment was not in vain.

The next day's gig at the Civic Hall in Guilford was canceled because punk music concerts had been banned by the town government. Punk was in the news all the time in England and this day turned out to be a real punk

milestone. The Sex Pistols released "God Save the Queen" in May 1977. The song was promptly banned by the BBC and the Independent Broadcasting Authority. It rocketed to the number one spot on the NME chart and to number two on the official UK Singles Chart. Rod Stewart's "I Don't Want to Talk About It/The First Cut Is the Deepest" held onto the number one spot, although from what we could see there was no way that Rod was selling more singles than the Pistols at that moment in time.

We played a last-minute show at the college in Slough because our scheduled show in Hastings had also been canceled due to fear of punk. There was not much of a crowd, even though a lively band from Ireland called The Boomtown Rats had been added to the bill. Still, we played a fine show and the kids who were there were extremely happy we had actually come all the way from New York City to play their little college.

The Greyhound in Croydon was a crazy gig. Located just across the Thames from London, this hotel ballroom got all shook up by the Ramones and Talking Heads. The capacity crowd was completely charged up and ready to go when we hit the stage. Our band was so tight and on point by this time that I felt like we had no worries at all until I looked over at Tina. There was blood running down the front of her bass guitar and she was in a world of pain. When playing the type of music we played onstage, you had to play hard and fast. The audience wanted to see passion and potency. You had to show dominance in your performance. As a result of pushing herself night after night for over a month, the calluses on Tina's right hand had blistered underneath to the point that they had split open and were bleeding. The punks loved seeing blood so she made it through the night, but that show was really not fun for her. To make matters worse, the scene in the dressing room seemed as if every asshole, poseur, and punk in London had been let in to hang out with the bands from New York. The Damned were there and they were cool except for their drummer, Rat Scabies, who actually tried to pick a fight with me. I still don't know why. I just told him to calm down or get out of our dressing room and he cooled down. There was a thing called amphetamine sulfate that the punk bands were snorting and after a while it made them very cranky. In fact, they even called it Crank. I suspect that Rat Scabies was riding that train,

but who knows? The Damned's bass player, Captain Sensible, was as sweet as could be, especially to Tina. There was one girl backstage whose early Goth hairdo and makeup made her look remarkably like Siouxsie Sioux of Siouxsie and the Banshees. I mean, exactly. So, I tried to introduce myself. I told her my name and asked her if she was Siouxsie. She looked at me as if I had lost my mind, like how could I possibly mistake her for someone whose look she had totally copied? That was it for me. Time to go back to the hotel bar!

The most memorable things about the Colston Hall gig in Bristol were that the hall was very large compared to the clubs we'd been playing, and that Peter Blake, the great British pop artist who had designed the cover of *Sgt. Pepper's Lonely Hearts Club Band*, had come to see our show. He seemed to like our performance. After the show we talked about art. He spoke of how his early influences were Robert Rauschenberg and Jasper Johns. I told him that we also held them in very high esteem and that we had lived in the same neighborhood on the Bowery. Peter said that he knew about the Bowery and SoHo in New York and how hip it was, but he had grown to love the country life. Maybe one day we would be able to say that, too. We thanked him again for that wonderful lunch at Mr. Chow's and bid him good night. Then we did an interview with Nick Kent from the NME. We hadn't really done very many interviews up to that point but it was clear to us that Nick was more interested in talking to David than the rest of us. Nick was all dressed up in the classic rock drag of Keith Richards back then. I wonder who he's dressing up like now?

After playing a relaxed show in Swindon in a little shopping mall club that had a very fancy rotating bar, we had a much-needed good night's sleep. At breakfast the following morning, Tina asked Mickey Stewart if we could possibly visit Stonehenge. He said we'd be driving right by it on our way to Plymouth, so why not? When everyone was on the bus we set off. As we approached the ancient megaliths, Mickey asked Paul the driver to follow the signs to the monument and park. Hearing this, Johnny Ramone went apoplectic. "What? *What?* We're not fucking stopping at Stonehenge! It's just a bunch of fucking old rocks!" Dee Dee stood up and said, "C'mon, Johnny! I want to see Stonehenge. *Everybody* wants to see Stonehenge. C'mon!" Johnny was not pleased, and sat in his seat fuming while everyone else got off the bus. It was a beautiful morning, very quiet and still, with no tourists

or anyone else around. On this day, June 1, 1977, there was no protective fencing around Stonehenge. You could walk through and around the gigantic stones and touch them to your heart's content. Dee Dee exclaimed that he would like to carve his initials into one of the stones, but quickly smiled and said he was just kidding. We didn't stay long, but we did feel those Druidic vibes rising up from the site. We felt them loud and clear.

As we checked into a very fine country hotel in Devon, Mickey made sure that Tina and I got Tamar the honeymoon suite. In just over two weeks, Tina and I would be married and he was kind to give us this special treatment. The room was very luxe and romantic and Tina and I made the most of it. Because of the jealous way David reacted, we kept public displays of affection to a minimum, but behind closed doors, we really got it on. This was a heavenly moment.

The hotel was located way out in the country in the moors of Devonshire. Tina and I took a little hike in the fields and spotted a few of the famous wild horses that lived there, followed by a wonderful bath in the huge honeymoon suite tub. Then we went downstairs for tea and a sampling of strawberries with Devon's famous clotted cream, which was simply divine.

The gig at Plymouth's Top Rank club was a good one. Johnny was still angry at us about our love of art, history, and culture. He said so as if this was ruining his life. I just looked at him and said, "Johnny, this tour will be over soon. Let me just say, in spite of all your bad moods, we are very happy to be here with you guys and one day you will realize that we are the best opening act you have ever had or ever will have." Johnny would never be what you would call a nice guy, but years later, after some punk kicked him in the head, fractured his skull, and put him in the hospital, his attitude improved and we actually became friends.

The bus rolled south to the charming town of Penzance, where Tina, Joey Ramone, Joey's girlfriend Robin, Joey's brother Mitch, and I took a cab to visit Land's End, the westernmost point of mainland England. The craggy cliffs overlooking the sea were absolutely breathtaking. Tina posed me by the edge of the cliffs and took my picture. I did the same for her. One hundred and fifty miles across the water in Brittany is where Tina's mother had been born and where Tina's great-grandfather, the poet Anatole Le Braz, had collected folklore and legends and written some unforgettable stories.

Tina was feeling the pull of her roots and remembering sailing with her sisters over there. Like music, the sea can be very seductive and the memories it creates stay with you forever.

We went to the sound check at the Winter Garden in Penzance and, as the bartender was setting up for the night, I asked him for a drink of sparkling water. It was the first warm afternoon we'd had in England. He gave it to me and I asked if I might have some ice in it. He looked at me with a smile and said, "I'd love to but we lost the recipe."

The gig in Penzance was good. Very relaxed. No stress. There were a lot of surfers in the audience, a first for us.

After the show, back at the hotel we were interviewed by a stylish young woman named Leigh Blake for *Ritz* magazine. Leigh was crazy about Talking Heads. She was an interesting person, kind of wild, who regaled us with tales of London in the sixties. She actually knew the Beatles, the Who, and Jimi Hendrix. Little did we know she would be following us back to New York and move right in.

For the big Queen's Jubilee weekend we had a day off to travel back to London, where Mickey Stewart had booked us into the fabulous Portobello Hotel in Ladbroke Grove, near the Portobello Road. The hotel was one of the early boutique hotels, filled with antiques and charming ambience. It was popular with artists and eccentrics of all types. To this day, it's my favorite hotel in London. True to form, Mickey had reserved the "Four-Poster Room" for Tina and me. The big four-poster bed with canopy was super romantic. One of the great things about the hotel was the restaurant and bar in the basement that was open twenty-four hours a day. This was unique in London at the time. The bar and kitchen were manned mostly by cool young people. In fact, one of the night bar men was Damon Albarn, who told us, "I've got a band." The young women who cooked our full English breakfasts, particularly Nicola McQuaid, were fabulous and just flirtatious enough, but not too much.

The area around the hotel, Notting Hill, was hip and shabbily chic. There were loads of cool bistros, wine bars, and pubs. Down at the Portobello Road there was a huge flea market and all kinds of punk and reggae delights to be had, not the least of which was tiny little Rough Trade Records. They were selling a lot of punk records out of there and our seven-inch single, "Love → Building on Fire" was in the front window.

The nation was celebrating Queen Elizabeth's twenty-five years on the throne. Millions of people came to London to celebrate and try to catch a glimpse of her as she paraded through London in her golden carriage. There were some very fancy parties around town. Most of the people we were coming in contact with were not crazy about the monarchy, or this royal family. In fact some, like Frank Gallagher, vehemently despised "the Royals." The Sex Pistols couldn't have timed the release of their single, "God Save the Queen," any better. Even though the record had been banned by the BBC, you could still hear it on offshore Radio Caroline and other pirate radio stations. It could also be heard blasting out of pubs where the Queen's tipsy subjects sang along with Johnny Rotten.

I'm still not sure if the Sex Pistols' song was a real revolutionary, antimonarchical song, or just really good marketing. Whatever the case, it really pissed off the squares. The Pistols were banned from performing anywhere in the UK by this point, so in another brilliant marketing move, Richard Branson of Virgin Records paid for a party-boat record release party on the River Thames.

The music press was all invited. The band snorted a lot of speed and then performed a few songs, including "God Save the Queen," before police boats pulled alongside and killed the party. When the boat returned to its dock, the cops arrested manager Malcolm McLaren, fashion designer Vivienne Westwood, artist Jamie Reid, and some others while the band sneaked

away. This event made all the news outlets in London very happy. It was front-page news all over England.

We played a show at the Odeon Theatre in Canterbury with the Ramones and The Boomtown Rats. Tina thought the Rats were so civilized after being on the road with the Ramones, especially their manager, Fachtna O Ceallaigh, who went on to manage Bananarama and Sinead O'Connor. Irishmen can be tough, but this crew was charming. Singer Bob Geldof would become super famous when he dreamed up *Live Aid*, but for some reason we were not invited to play that gig. Oh, that's right. By 1984, David had decided that Talking Heads, one of the world's great touring bands, should stop performing live.

The next day was the big gig we had all been waiting for. The Roundhouse in Chalk Farm was built in 1847 as a railway turntable, but had for decades been a performing arts center. So many fantastic shows had taken place there. The Rolling Stones, Jeff Beck, the Yardbirds, David Bowie, Jimi Hendrix, Pink Floyd, Led Zeppelin, the Incredible String Band, the Doors with Jefferson Airplane, and Otis Redding had all rocked this joint. We were sold out for two nights at 3,300 people per night. This was the biggest crowd we had ever performed to and we were amazed at the number of fans in the UK. The Ramones had played here the previous summer as a support band to the Flamin' Groovies and set off the UK punk explosion when the young guys in the Sex Pistols, the Clash, and the Damned had been inspired by them to form bands of their own.

Over at the Portobello Hotel we were getting ready for the show. Mick Jones from the Clash was doing an interview with a journalist on the front steps. Mick was wearing a bright blue soccer uniform and holding a ball in his lap. I was wearing a rumpled white oxford cloth Brooks Brothers shirt that I had washed in the bathtub, but didn't iron, and black Levi's. For good luck, Tina was wearing a black linen shirt with blue stripes and a blue silk collar made for her by our friend Moki Cherry, our upstairs neighbor who was married to jazz trumpeter legend Don Cherry. Jerry was in a black T-shirt, black jeans, and Capezio Jazz Oxfords that he had painted yellow. David was wearing a light yellow button-down collared shirt and wheat-colored Levi's with no belt, and gray Hush Puppy loafers. We felt cool.

The Phonogram people came to pick us up and take us to the show. They would be riding in a van and had provided a beautiful, blue Bentley

limo with a fur carpet for Talking Heads. Thinking of our reputation in this world of punk, we declined the limo and told them to ride in it with their wives. We would take the van. When we got to the Roundhouse, I asked our driver to take us to the backstage entrance. I banged on it and banged on it, but no answer. The Ramones were already inside and the door had been locked. So, I went around to the front entrance, and cut to the head of the long line of rockers saying, "Excuse me, excuse me!"

When I got to the front I told the guy that Talking Heads were at the stage door and locked out. He told me to wait a minute while he got his boss. He came back with a tough-looking geezer who looked like he hadn't slept or shaved in a week. I explained the situation to him and he said, "Only a Yank would be so polite about this. Follow me." He led me through the theater to the stage door and we motioned the band to come in with their guitars.

It so happened that this guy was our promoter, John Curd, and would continue to be our promoter in London for years. He was rough around the edges but did a great job for us, and vice versa.

There was a third band on the bill called the Saints, from Australia; they were also signed to Sire Records. They had a cool single and album called *Stranded*, which, like most punk rock, owed a debt of gratitude to the Stooges. They kicked off the show at around 5:30 in the evening with a fast and hard-rocking set. Evidently, they are still performing, which would make them the only band that played the Roundhouse that night that is still together.

Seymour and Linda Stein came backstage to wish us all well. Linda was co-managing the Ramones with Danny Fields, but she was also rooting for Talking Heads. Her husband, Seymour, had signed both bands, after all. This was a very big night for Sire Records in London and Seymour's reputation as an A&R genius was sealed.

After this night, he would discover and sign loads of new British bands that no one in the States had even heard of and they would have many hits, but on this night I think Seymour was even more nervous than we were.

We did our best shows when we were nervous. In fact, if we weren't feeling nervous we psyched ourselves up by jumping up and down, hyperventilating, and imagining everything that could go wrong. This was one way we kept our edge, by stimulating our adrenal glands.

As important as every show is—and we played each night as if it were

our last—this show at the Roundhouse was particularly crucial. The number of journalists, photographers, radio people, and cultural tastemakers in the audience was staggering. Johnny Rotten poked his head into our dressing room and said, "Sorry, I was looking for the Ramones." Frank Gallagher, who was giving us our preshow pep talk, said to him, "Well, then FUCK OFF!" Then he turned to us smiling and said, "It's just another gig. Heads down, turn it up, and see you at the end."

We walked out to the stage as the DJ, Andy Dunkley—"The Livin' Jukebox"—was finishing up his set. The crowd was a teeming mass of punks, music lovers, and out-of-town Jubilee celebrants. It was our biggest crowd yet. Tina, looking cool, strapped on her Fender Mustang bass and plugged in. Jerry, very much in the moment, put on his Fender Telecaster. David, already wearing his Gibson hollow-body 12-string guitar, stepped up to the mic and said, "The name of this band is Talking Heads." The words to our first song started out like this:

When my love
Stands next to your love
I can't compare love
When it's not love
It's not love
It's not love
Which is my face
Which is a building
Which is on fire
On fire

When the band kicked in full force on the word "fire," the crowd surged forward with a gigantic wiggle and shimmy and I knew then that everything was going to be all right. We got 'em going on the first number. The sound was fantastic and huge and the band was playing with a new power that we had developed over the past six weeks of nightly shows with the Ramones. There is no better way to improve your performance than by playing repeated shows in front of a live audience. At the end of our set, we received two very solid encores. We had made our mark and we turned the stage over to the Ramones.

The gobbing had not been too bad for our set, but when the Ramones came on and Dee Dee shouted "One, two, three, four!" the gobbing was relentless. In the bright lights it appeared to be a monsoon, but the Ramones soldiered on regardless. The audience adored them and couldn't get enough. They went from song to song without a word or a pause, until about half-way through the set when Joey said, "We've got a new single out. It's called 'Sheena Is a Punk Rocker'!" Everyone in the Roundhouse, myself included, thrilled to the undeniable supremacy of the Ramones. Damn, they were good!

The second night at the Roundhouse was every bit as great as the first. The Ramones were the stars, but we were the artistic upstarts who nearly stole the show, not that any band could really steal the show from the Ramones. Linda Stein had arranged an after-party at a restaurant called Country Cousins with hot dogs and drinks. I still have the image burned in my memory of Tina surrounded by the bass players Dee Dee Ramone, Captain Sensible, and Sid Vicious. Tina is showing them her bloody fingers and they are all grimacing and Sid says, "But, Tina, have you ever tried using a plectrum?"

The next morning we were off to Heathrow Airport and then back to New York City. We said goodbye to all of our wonderful crew. They had been such troupers and really a great help to all of us. Tina and I gave each of them a Swiss Army knife with TALKING HEADS engraved on it. There were bear hugs all around and, for Tina, kisses. We knew we would be back as soon as we could and that these guys would be there for us. But first, Tina and I had a wedding to attend in Kentucky.

OUR WEDDING IN WASHINGTON, KENTUCKY

When we returned to New York from London, we had a lot of things to do. We had booked four days at the ODO recording studio located under the newly opened Studio 54 with our engineer, Ed Stasium, to finish recording David's vocals and make a few fixes and final overdubs on our new album. Tina carried her bass on a very hot day in its extremely heavy case on the subway from our loft in Long Island City. When she paused to rest for a moment on the steps of the CBS "Black Rock" building on the corner of Fifty-second Street and the Avenue of the Americas, a car full of kids hung out the window and screamed, "Tina! You rock!" This made her feel good despite the heat and the jet lag. She felt even better when Ed told her that her parts had been played perfectly with no fixes required. If only she had known before schlepping her bass all the way across town! Bobby Grossman, one of our RISD friends, took a studio shot of the band by the recording console and also a photo of Jerry's torso to be used for the single sleeve of "Psycho Killer."

There were ten days until we would be married in Washington, Kentucky, a village of five hundred people where my grandfather was born. My grand-mother still lived there in the stately Georgian-style home my grandfather

had grown up in. My grandparents bought it and carefully restored it after they retired. Tina had visited Washington with me a few years before to meet my grandmother, who we called Mammy, and they hit it off very well. When it came time to decide where our wedding would be, Washington seemed like a winning choice. We wanted a smallish, low-key wedding to be attended by family and a few good friends.

We were fortunate that my mother, Suzanne, and Tina's sister, Nanu, took care of all the arrangements while we were off on tour. Together they handled everything perfectly. When we arrived in Kentucky, there were three days of parties for us and our guests that were hosted by my grandmother's very generous friends in their beautiful homes. Our friends from New York City were charmed to find out that Southern hospitality was a real thing and the Kentuckians were thrilled to meet all the stylish, young New Yorkers. To be welcomed with such great warmth made Tina and me feel very happy and relaxed, indeed.

Tina and I had to get our marriage license at the courthouse five miles down the road in Maysville, Kentucky. Before we could do that we had to be examined by my mother's cousin, Dr. William Cartmell, who had been practicing medicine in Maysville for fifty years. He looked at Tina and said she was going to make a very pretty bride. Saying it was a formality, he asked us if we were any kin to each other. We said no. He looked us up and down and said, "Well, you look okay to me. You all have a happy marriage and take good care of each other."

The rehearsal dinner that night was held across the river in Ohio at a charming new place called The Winery, where they made their own wine. The guests sat outside at tables on the deck overlooking the great Ohio River. It was a gorgeous, sunny evening and not too hot. All of a sudden we were serenaded by a brass band that had appeared out of nowhere, led by my mother's good friend Harriet Cartmell, Dr. Cartmell's wife, who happened to be the mayor of Maysville. The band played "Strangers in Paradise" and "My Old Kentucky Home." Then, as mayor, Harriet presented Tina and me with the keys to the city.

After a lovely dinner and many happy toasts, my brother, Roddy, drove me back to my motel in a Lincoln Continental Mark IV that our father's friend loaned Tina and me. Quel luxe! Tina was sleeping with her family at the farm of my grandmother's friends, Andy and Mary Louise "Hula"

Duke. I was told she got the nickname Hula because once, as a student at the University of Kentucky, she was observed by some boys through her dormitory window dancing the Hula in the nude in front of a mirror. The nickname stuck. She was a grand dame now and a pillar of the community, but still loads of fun.

The next morning was our wedding day. Tina's sister Nanu and her husband, Fred, hosted a fine, big breakfast for everyone at Caproni's Restaurant by the river. My grandmother, Mammy, gave a beautiful toast about how a marriage can have many challenges, ups and downs and twists and turns. Then she showed Tina and me a big knotted white cord, asked us each to hold to one end, and said, "When things get really bumpy, and they will, Chris and Tina, you all just hang onto this!"

Tina's ivory silk gown consisted of a long-sleeved blouse tucked into a long straight sheath, over which were buttoned two panels of tiny pleats. It was designed and sewn by Virginia Hatley, Tina's dear friend who had worked with her at Henri Bendel. Virginia had recently married Tina's

June 18, 1977.

former boyfriend from RISD, Peter Coan, who now practiced architecture with Tina's brother, Yann, at their new company Red Roof Design. The gown would have a second life thirty-seven years later when our son, Egan, married the exquisite artist Elizabeth Wendelbo, of the Xeno & Oaklander electronic duo.

Tina's sister Danielle was the matron of honor. The bridesmaids were Tina's sisters, Lani, Letitia, and Laura, and my little sister, Ruthie. They were the prettiest bridesmaids I have ever seen before or since, dressed in white gowns, sewn by Tina's sister Nanu, with crowns of silk wildflowers in their hair. Tina's nieces, Laura and Erica Dorwart, were the flower girls and their little

brother, Marc, was the ring bearer. The ushers were my brother and best man, Roddy; Tina's brother, Yann, and my cousins Tommy Fryman, Holton Cartmell, and Jeff Allen. Like me, the men were dressed in khaki summer suits and identical striped blue, silver, and red rep ties from Brooks Brothers.

My mother's roommate from college and close family friend, Jean Marie Edwards, arranged the flowers with the utmost simplicity and elegance.

We were to be married in the little white clapboard Washington Presbyterian Church next door to my grandparents' home. Because Tina's parents were Catholic and mine were Episcopalian, the service was performed ecumenically by Catholic and Episcopal priests as well as the presiding Presbyterian minister. The service was brief but very traditional. Tina and I were fine with tried and true wedding traditions. Our lives were creative enough as it was, and we didn't want an alternative wedding. For the moment, we chose to be relaxed and informal, but, at the same time, completely committed. We wanted people to know that we were serious about our union.

Tina's father walked her proudly down the aisle as I waited at the altar in the hot little church. Tina arrived at the altar looking absolutely adorable. No veil. She really was a vision of loveliness with a crown of silk wildflowers and a bouquet of Lily of the Valley. I was a very happy young man. We exchanged our vows with confidence, but when Tina got to "lawfully wedded hu-hu-husband," she dissolved into a laughing fit! I could feel a large drop of sweat fall from my forehead and land with a splash on my lapel in exaggerated slow motion. Evidently, the word "husband" was just too much to take seriously, and who could blame her? I laughed heartily, too. But then I said, "Tina," and she kissed me on the mouth.

Everything else went according to plan and, after we were pronounced man and wife, we walked back down the aisle to the lawn outside the church. It was cooler outside and Tina and I were in a state of bliss as we kissed and held hands and mingled with all the guests. Seymour and Linda Stein were both dressed in white and clearly enjoying themselves, along with Ken Kushnick, who was our main man at Sire Records. My high school friend Pat Hannah took a beautiful photo of this gathering on the lawn, a moment I often recall with a feeling of great tenderness.

Everyone was relieved to get outside into the cooler air. We walked a short distance down the road to the Broderick Tavern, where we celebrated with champagne and a classic white wedding cake. I cut the cake with Tina's

father's dress sword from the Naval Academy—the same one, I'd been told, he had threatened to run through some of his daughters' boyfriends (but fortunately not me). Music was provided by a portable record player playing the new *Rumors* album by Fleetwood Mac, chosen because it was popular and inoffensive. We didn't have an official wedding photographer, but Tina's mother, Laure, took some great photos of the wedding party—except for my grandmother, Mammy, who was off flirting and showing the sights to an old college beau, James Cogar, who shared her interest in historic preservation. James had been the president and curator of the restoration of Colonial Williamsburg in Virginia and was currently planning the restoration of Shakertown in Kentucky.

After a little while, the party moved over to Maysville to Harriet Cartmell's mother's place. Her name was Rebecca "Beck" Hord and she, too, had been the mayor for many years. She and Harriet hosted a buffet supper for all of us in the wedding party and our guests in her stately home filled with art and antiques. Seymour Stein, an avid collector himself, just stared with his eyes bugging out and said, "Look at *this!*" As we dined on country ham, corn pudding, tomato aspic, transparent puddings, and other Kentucky fare, everybody loosened up and got to know one another. My parents and Tina's parents were clearly happy and relieved. They really liked each other. My parents were crazy about Tina and I think Tina's parents were fond of me, too, although Tina said on the drive to the wedding they had told her, "You know, you don't have to go through with this. We always say this before a wedding." It seems they weren't sure that I would be emotionally strong enough for Tina. Fortunately, forty-two years later, I'm still strong and so is she, in fact, now more than ever.

Not wanting the party to end, we Talking Heads and some of our friends changed our clothes and drove a few miles down the river to a roadhouse where the Boxtops were playing. The band sounded great from outside, but the place was packed to bursting and this was not the type of joint to give us VIP treatment. We were pretty tired and tipsy by this point anyway, so Tina and I went back to the Dukes' farm. They had given us their luxurious master bedroom for our wedding night, and we slept together for the first time as hu-hu-husband and wife in a big brass bed. Our mothers were greatly pleased that we were no longer "living in sin."

31

HONEYMOON INTERRUPTED

On June 19, I awoke beside a sweet and sexy, sleeping Tina Weymouth Frantz. I won't lie, the hangover I had was a dreadful one and I was parched with thirst, but to see Tina sleeping so peacefully in her supercute wedding trousseau nightie did wonders to ameliorate the pain in my head. In fact, in spite of being hungover, jet-lagged, and generally exhausted, I felt really good.

Downstairs, our parents and the Dukes were already enjoying a fine country breakfast of bacon and eggs with grits and fresh fruit. After brushing my teeth and drinking a few big glasses of cold water, I woke Tina as gently as possible with a long, sweet kiss. In spite of not really being a morning person, she was beaming. We took a shower together and, feeling greatly refreshed, joined our family for breakfast. We were offered Mimosas to drink and, boy, they tasted divine. We lingered over breakfast, basking in the love and affection our parents were giving us. All was right with the world.

As a wedding present, my parents had given us a weeklong honeymoon at the Cloister at Sea Island, Georgia. Tina and I would be driving those 750 miles in the Country Squire and it was time to go.

Both of us were wistful to leave little Washington, Kentucky, and our

Newlyweds at Hurrah.

parents. Tina was especially wistful, but Sea Island was paid for and waiting! So we had a look at the map and off we went, like the bride's nightie.

It was hot—unreasonably hot and humid—and the Country Squire had a slow oil leak, so I had to stop every fifty miles or so to open the hood and add a quart of oil. It was a beautiful drive south through the Appalachian Mountains and then over to the coast. After about twelve hours or so we arrived at the Cloister. It was 2:00 in the morning. I had warned them we'd

be running late and the night man took us to our beachside bungalow. We were really excited and feeling frisky until we got inside and Tina cried, "Oh, no! Twin beds!" Sure enough, there were neatly made up twin beds with a table and lamp between them. I tried to calm her down, but she was so disappointed and tired that I promised her we would take care of it in the morning. We both crawled into one bed and went straight to sleep.

Early the next morning, I found our housekeeper, a charming, plump Sea Island lady by the name of Sassy. I told her about our problem and took her into our bungalow and she said, "Oh! What you all want is the Honeybed!" She simply removed the table between the two beds and pushed them together. She pulled off the twin white sheets on each bed and replaced them with pink pillowcases and king-sized pink sheets over both beds and—voila! The Honeybed! Why hadn't I thought of that? Tina was very happy now and when Tina is happy, I am happy. When Sassy left, we thanked her and christened the Honeybed with newlywed passion.

Tina and I enjoyed the food and the beach at The Cloister. The atmosphere was that sort of Deep South luxe that is undeniably wonderful. Every detail was perfect in traditional southern, colonial style. There were many other newlywed couples there and you had to dress for dinner, meaning a jacket and tie for men, summer dresses for the ladies. We came prepared, as we always do. It was a far cry from the Bowery. The other guests seemed kind of square to us, but they were nice and friendly. There was a big buzz that President Jimmy Carter was arriving soon, which we thought was a hoot. We were fans.

After two more days of sun and swimming in the sea and much Honeybedding, Tina and I had to interrupt our honeymoon to fly up to New York to be the opening act for Roxy Music's Bryan Ferry's solo show at the Bottom Line. We did not know Bryan personally and we wouldn't have agreed to this for just any band, but we were big fans of Bryan and Roxy Music. We knew that his audience would be very receptive to Talking Heads. Also, to play at the Bottom Line put us in a bigger league with Lou Reed, Patti Smith, and Bruce Springsteen. It was still a nightclub, but it was the big time. To play there meant that we had truly arrived in New York City. The band was only offered $200, but knowing a good opportunity when he saw one, Seymour offered to pay for our round-trip airfare. We agreed.

Tina and I drove to the Brunswick, Georgia, airport and caught a flight

to LaGuardia Airport the day before the show. We met David and Jerry at our loft for a rehearsal in order to sound our best. Our last show had been two weeks before at the Roundhouse in London. We got our thing together, the band sounded good, and we stuck to the same set list we had played on the Ramones tour. We knew it was a crowd-pleaser.

They say that New Yorkers are a tough crowd, but they never intimidated us more than fans in any other city. New Yorkers were among our best and most responsive audiences. So, Tina and I met David and Jerry at the Bottom Line on Mercer Street at the appointed hour for sound check with all of our gear. As often happens when you're in the supporting slot, the headliner was running overtime and there was nothing we could do about it. It was their show, but this time was worse than usual. Bryan Ferry had apparently told his road manager to make us wait outside. No explanation, just: "You'll have to wait outside until we're finished." So we went outside on the sidewalk on Mercer Street to wait. People were in line for the show already, some of them fans of ours who said, "Hey, Chris and Tina! What are you doing out here? You're supposed to be inside!" Sounds funny now, but at the time it felt ludicrously disrespectful and inconsiderate of Bryan Ferry. We thought, *No wonder Eno quit working with him.*

After well over an hour of sweating in the heat outside we were allowed to come in with barely enough time to set up our equipment before the show started. When we got to our tiny dressing room we were greeted by none other than supermodel Jerry Hall, Bryan's girlfriend, who said, "Hi! How are youuuuuu?" in her Texas drawl. She was so beautiful and refined. Her skin, her long wavy hair, her almond-shaped eyes, and her figure: Everything about her was perfect. We recognized her from the cover of Roxy Music's *Siren* album. Tina told her that Bryan must be a little insecure to make us wait outside on the street. Jerry Hall said, "Oh, I don't know about that. I think he's just plain ruuuuude!" Not long after that she was dating Mick Jagger.

We hurried up and got ready for the show. Let's just say that that night at the Bottom Line was like a homecoming for Talking Heads: We stepped onstage to a loud, long, and rousing ovation. We played our opening set with everything we had in us and then some. It was hot and we were sweating until we were drenched, but our playing was flawlessly funky. I was having an out-of-body experience behind the drums. On my drum riser, I

felt like I was floating above the audience and they were all smiling back at me. The whole band was great. We stole the show from Bryan Ferry. He was good, maybe even great, but *we* were the ones who rocked the party that night. In his review of the night, John Rockwell from *The New York Times* wrote, "The show opened with Talking Heads, who were even better than Mr. Ferry. This was the lower Manhattan group's 'big-time' New York debut, after a hugely successful tour of Europe. It was also the first time that this observer, long an enthusiast of the original trio, had heard them fully rehearsed in their new quartet configuration. Jerry Harrison, the new guitarist and keyboard player, is now fully integrated into the band's idio-syncratically abrupt, exactly colored sound. Talking Heads played mostly new material on Thursday, and much of it had an almost disco feeling. This is interesting because it offers one possible avenue to commercial success, and because it formalizes a similarity between minimalist disco (K.C. and the Sunshine Band) and minimalist underground rockers that had never previously been made overt."

Mission accomplished, Tina and I flew back to Sea Island the next morning for Honeymoon Part 2. We really relaxed into a couple of more days of sea, sex, and sun.

It seemed so short, though. On Sunday, we started the drive home to New York, going up the Georgia coast through wonderful Charleston, South Carolina. We spent the night in a very cheap motel (Free TV!) on Emerald Isle, North Carolina, a place that I knew from my youth, and frolicked in the big waves of the Atlantic Ocean. We ate fried fish and shrimp and hushpuppies and washed it all down with icy bottles of beer. We went to a disco and danced to "Rock Steady" and "I Feel Love." We slept like babies. The next morning we took a wake-up swim in the sea before driving all the way back to New York and the real nitty-gritty, but I wasn't worried and neither was Tina. We were good together.

32

THE SUMMER OF SAM

Tina and I returned to our loft in Long Island City to find that David, who was not exactly a people person, had moved his houseguest from London into our place without even asking. Leigh Blake was a journalist and fashion person who had interviewed us over in the UK. We liked Leigh. She was smart and fun, but we had just been married and had not been expecting to have a new roommate. She had managed to get herself to New York but now she was broke and had nowhere to live, so we took her in. In appreciation, she gave Tina a beautiful Kenzo dress and a set of British National Health hospital pajamas. Tina looked smashing in both. Because she was good with the press, we asked Leigh to be our unofficial publicist. We already had a publicist, but Leigh could help, and she was happy to do so. We had a lot of fun together.

We had four nights, July 5–8, booked at a famous nightclub called the Village Gate on the corner of Thompson and Bleecker Streets. The Village Gate was a basement jazz club that had featured Duke Ellington, Miles Davis, Tito Puente, Nina Simone, and Aretha Franklin, among many other big names. Jimi Hendrix and the Velvet Underground had played there, too. Now the Village Gate was booking Talking Heads, Blondie, and the Patti Smith Group during the month of July. We had a different support band

each night. We especially liked the Erasers, who were an all-girl outfit and friends of ours.

This is the set list from our first night:

"Love → Building on Fire"
"Uh-oh, Love Comes to Town"
"Don't Worry About the Government"
"Take Me to the River" (Al Green)
"Happy Day"
"The Book I Read"
"New Feeling"
"Pulled Up"
"I'm Not in Love"
"Psycho Killer"
"No Compassion"
"Warning Sign"
"Love Is All Around" (The Troggs)

This was the time when the .44 Caliber Killer, later known as Son of Sam, was stalking the city, shooting young women and their lovers. As if New York did not feel dangerous enough already, now there was a killer on the loose. People were uneasy and wondering where he would kill next. There was also an interminable heat wave going on. Even the toughest New Yorkers were teetering on the edge of sanity.

On July 13, Tina and I decided to have a little barbeque on the roof of our loft. Thanks to a slight breeze coming from the East River, it was cooler up there than it was inside. We were going to start mixing our album the next day and everyone was in the mood for a celebration. We were drinking wine and beer and grilling hamburgers and chicken as we gazed at the sunset over Manhattan. From our rooftop you could see most of downtown, midtown, the Upper East Side, Harlem, and the Bronx. As the sky became darker and darker, the lights of the city came on. I was watching the cars zooming across the 59th Street Bridge when I noticed something strange. All the lights in the Bronx had gone off. There was only darkness. As I was pointing this out to Tina and our friends, the lights of Harlem went off. One by one, the Upper East Side, then midtown and, finally, downtown

went dark. We all just watched in amazement at the abruptly dark outline of the New York City skyline. Thankfully, the lights were on in Long Island City and would remain on. We went downstairs to turn on the TV. The news was not good. In some parts of town looting was going on. In other parts of town fires were raging out of control. I've heard some people say that hip-hop was born that night when future DJs and rappers could find turntables, mixers, microphones, and PA systems by smashing the windows of their favorite electronics store and walking right in. Any way you look at it, New York was madness that night.

The next day was not any better. Even in daylight, there was still burning and looting in some areas. No one could get to work and the news was telling everyone to stay home. It was still hot as hell and, of course, there was no air-conditioning. Eventually we got a call from Ed Stasium that the mixing would begin at Media Sound on Fifty-seventh Street later in the week if possible. The power came back on in most areas after twenty-five hours, but there was widespread arson and looting. More than a thousand fires had been set and something like 1,600 stores were broken into.

When things settled down, we entered Media Sound on Fifty-Seventh Street, which had once been a church, with an air of confidence. We felt as if we had great tracks and we believed that Ed would take them to an even higher level in the mix. Mixing is when you take your master tape with sixteen or twenty-four or more tracks recorded on it and "mix" it down to two stereo tracks, left and right. You can add equalization and effects and delays as you do the mix to make the record sound as sonically exciting and interesting as possible.

We had booked the studio at Media Sound during the day. Aerosmith was working on *Draw the Line* in the same room at night. Tina and I were the first in our group to arrive and, when we walked into the control room, the first thing we saw was that the huge plate glass window looking out into the studio had been completely wallpapered with pages from sleazy, hard-core porno mags. It was a really bad vibe for Tina, and I was not very happy about it, either. I pulled them all down and put them in a paper bag for Aerosmith to enjoy someplace else. I'm not one to act holier than thou, but ugh! I teased Jerry about it because he was always saying what a great band Aerosmith was.

Ed got to work. Tony came and went, talking about bullets, as in "My

latest record is number 10 with a bullet in *Billboard* but it's only number 19 with no bullet in *Cashbox*!" Having a bullet meant the record was expected to rise up the chart. This was all new to us, but we didn't care about bullets. We were happy to have any record at all. Mixing is a very detailed process and not for the uneducated ear. You have to be able to listen attentively to the same song and various elements of the song coming in and out all day long without losing focus. Some of us are better at this than others. Ed was really good. He was using noise gates on every track to lower the noise floor, but otherwise not a lot of studio trickery. One day, while mixing the song "No Compassion," we noticed that the snare drum sound was not as powerful as we felt it should be. I'm not sure how I thought of this, because I'd never mixed a record before, but I asked Ed if we could send the snare drum signal out through a speaker in the studio and re-mic it, using the studio as a large chamber. Ed looked at me and said, "Aha!" He tried it and it worked really well in an early gated-reverb style.

On July 27, Ed mixed "Psycho Killer" parts one and two. I think it was clear to everyone who heard it that "Psycho Killer" should be the first single from our album. Even though it was the first song we had ever written together, there was something undeniably urgent and compelling about "Psycho Killer" and we hoped it would cross over beyond the CBGB crowd to listeners around the world.

Waiting for the subway back to our loft, Tina and I admired the new "Radiant Baby" drawings in the Fifty-third Street station across from the Museum of Modern Art. These white chalk line drawings on empty black advertising panels had everyone wondering who had made them. They were popping up in subway stations all over town. Eventually, we found out they were made by a young guy from Kutztown, Pennsylvania, named Keith Haring. As drawings, they were unforgettable.

The police finally caught Son of Sam on August 10. The twenty-four-year-old mail carrier David Berkowitz told investigators that he had been getting directions to kill from his neighbor's dog. He had killed six people and wounded seven others with his .44 caliber pistol. People started asking us if "Psycho Killer" was written about him. We said, "No, the song had been written years ago when we were art students."

33

GARY

Gary Kurfirst came to see us on August 25, 1977, when we were beginning a four-night run at CBGB. We had asked Ken Kushnick to be our manager and he wanted to do it, but he also very logically said, "If I were your manager, there wouldn't be anybody at Sire Records to fight for you." So, knowing that we had a new album coming out in the fall, Ken brought Gary down to find out if he had any interest. Ken had known Gary since 1971, when they co-managed a band called Stepson. Gary had street smarts and vast old-school music business experience combined with forward thinking. He was the one person Ken believed should manage Talking Heads. We had gotten this far on our own, but record companies don't really like to talk business with an artist. They prefer to talk to a manager and to think of the bands as stars. Record companies, more than anyone else, want you to be a star.

We had seen and heard enough about bad managers that we were circumspect when we met Gary. After our second set of the night, we were introduced by Ken. Gary was wearing one of those silver Porsche racing jackets. He had long hair and a scruffy beard. Gary was only four years older than me but he seemed much older and wiser. He loved our show and invited us to meet him for dinner at a Japanese restaurant next to Carnegie Hall, where his office was. We all agreed.

None of us had ever eaten sushi before. Raw fish? What a wild idea. Gary

ordered for us while we tried out the hot sake. David mostly kept quiet, as usual, but, boy, he loved the Japanese food. He had always had an adventurous appetite and this new style of cuisine was heavenly to him.

He ate everything that was put in front of him. Tina and Jerry and I loved the food, but we were more interested in conversation with Gary. We were feeling him out.

What we found out was that, like the Ramones, Gary had grown up in Forest Hills, Queens. While still in high school, he began promoting concerts. The first concert he promoted was the Ronettes at the El Patio Country Club in 1966. Next came the Shangri-Las. In '67, he put on shows by the Young Rascals, Donovan, and Janis Ian.

In the summer of '67, Gary made a bold move. He leased the Village Theater in Manhattan's East Village, where he promoted shows with Cream, Vanilla Fudge, Moby Grape, Canned Heat, the Yardbirds with Jimmy Page, the Jeff Beck Group, Otis Redding and Carla Thomas, Wilson Pickett, the Doors, and the Who.

Then one day when Gary wasn't looking, San Francisco promoter Bill Graham bought the lease for the Village Theater out from under him and renamed it the Fillmore East. Gary was not happy about that but he had an idea. In the summer of '68, at the Singer Bowl in Flushing Meadow Park, he staged the New York Rock Festival. The bands he booked were Jimi Hendrix, Big Brother and the Holding Company, the Doors, the Who, and Janis Ian. Eighteen thousand people showed up. The enormous success of this festival, both culturally and financially, inspired the 1969 Woodstock Festival of Art and Music in which he also had a hand the following summer.

All the while, Gary had been managing a popular Long Island Band called the Vagrants with Leslie West on guitar. They acted as support band at many of the shows Gary promoted until one day Leslie quit the band to form Mountain with Cream producer Felix Pappalardi on bass and vocals. Gary managed Mountain, who had an enormous hit with "Mississippi Queen." He told us that one of his greatest regrets as a manager was refusing to allow Mountain's performance at Woodstock to be used in the subsequent Warner Brothers film because they were not offering the band any money. He thought that was a rip-off. He did not foresee how much free publicity the band would gather and, as a result of his refusal, no one even knows about Mountain's triumphal performance at Woodstock.

After negotiating a Mountain contract, Gary became close friends with Chris Blackwell of Island Records. Chris suggested that Gary should manage some of his Island artists. Gary agreed and became the manager for Toots & the Maytals, the Mighty Diamonds, and Peter Tosh. Gary loved Toots and had traveled all over the USA with him. He told us about how he had negotiated a huge advance when he signed Peter Tosh to Columbia Records for *Legalize It*. Peter demanded to be paid in cash and that Gary deliver it to him in Jamaica. When Gary arrived in Kingston, he checked into his hotel and waited nervously for Peter to arrive. It was not wise to have that much cash on you in Kingston in 1975. Each day Peter sent a Rasta messenger to tell Gary that Peter would come the next day. This went on for days. Finally, Peter did arrive and Gary handed over the $250,000 in cash in a duffel bag. Peter was pleased and Gary was possibly even more pleased to no longer be responsible for all that cash.

At some point along the way, after not knowing why he felt so tired and bad, Gary was diagnosed with a thyroid problem and had to take a long rest. Now, with the help of modern medicine, he was coming back. He had no other clients at that time. We made a verbal agreement for Gary to manage us on a trial basis for one year. If either party wasn't satisfied at the end of one year, they were free to go. We never felt the need for another manager. Gary was the best.

34

MINI TOURS

Gary didn't waste any time. He set us up with an agent at William Morris named Stu Weintraub. Our first album, *Talking Heads: 77*, was released on September 16, 1977. Because we now had a manager, an agent, and a record to promote, more doors were open for us. But we were still unknown to most of the world, so our work was cut out for us, too. One of the first gigs under our new management was a Beefsteak Charlie's in Scarsdale. I know it sounds like a lousy gig, but in fact it was fun and the pay was good. While the last customers were finishing their steak dinners, the waiters began pushing all the tables and chairs out of the way. There was no real stage, but there was a little elevated area where we set up our gear. We had help this time from a very tall, young, sophisticated black man named Jeff Jones. Jeff's mother was an opera singer named Betty Jones, who had regularly graced the stage at the Metropolitan Opera House. His dad was a civil engineer. Jeff was a graduate of Sarah Lawrence College and we all liked him right away. What he lacked in experience he made up for with his pure enthusiasm. Why he wanted the gig as our roadie, I don't know, but he did. We agreed to pay Jeff twenty-five dollars a day.

We also needed a soundman with a van for our gear and Gary found us just the guy, from Wilton, Connecticut. His name was Gary Scovil. He told us he had just bought his cargo van really cheap because someone had

committed suicide in it. It was like new. Gary had some experience mixing sound, too. We agreed to pay him fifty dollars a day, but only on the days we had shows. He was a curmudgeon sometimes, but he did a good job and never let us down. He and Jeff were about to put a lot of miles on that van.

Beefsteak Charlie's turned out to be a lot of fun. The suburban kids were so excited to get a taste of downtown New York City underground rock. When we finished our set, they hollered for more.

The next show was at a club in Woodstock, New York, called Joyous Lake. We would be opening for Charlie Mingus's Big Band. Some friends who were very hot interior designers, Ronnie and Victoria Borus, said we could stay at their country house just outside of Woodstock. We did our sound check and went to a nearby Middle Eastern restaurant for dinner and to pass some time. Tina's sister Laura and Leigh Blake had come up from New York with us. At the end of dinner, Leigh had the idea to play the game "Killer," where you draw lots to select a "killer." The rules are that none of the other players knows who the killer is. He kills by making eye contact and winking when no one else is looking. If he winks at you, you wait a little while and then say, "I'm dead!" The first person to identify the killer wins. So, we enjoyed a few rounds until a last round went on for too long and someone said, "Hey, nobody's died!" That's when half of us guessed simultaneously that David must be the killer! He had been unable to make eye contact with any of us long enough to wink, which explained why he had never been killed either. We all laughed explosively, especially David, who suddenly began to choke and change color. It was scary. At Jerry's urging, Laura, who was closest to him, managed to help him to his feet and very effectively administer the Heimlich Maneuver. She was so effective that not only did she unblock David's windpipe, but she caused him to projectile-vomit his baba ghanoush like a firehose right across the room. The other diners in the room were paying attention now, but trying not to look. A very flustered waiter asked our table to please leave. I said, "But we haven't paid." He said, "That's okay, just please go!"

I don't know who gave David the car keys, but he backed Tina's Valiant right into a three-hundred-year-old stone wall.

Traveling a short distance to Joyous Lake, we took a few deep breaths, pogoed a few times, and walked out onto the stage. To our surprise, at the

table right in front of the stage was the wizard of all rock stars, Todd Rundgren, with a very tall, statuesque, super-sexy redhead. The Joyous Lake was not a big place and it was nowhere near full for us, but there was Todd and his girlfriend, Karen Darvin, who began making out and feeling each other up during our first song and continued to do so for the entire show. I don't know if they were listening or not, but they were having a really good time. After the show, Todd said he would like to see us again and next time he would bring us something. He did. At UC Berkeley Todd and Karen came backstage with a big pot of delicious homemade organic chicken soup. I believe Todd would have liked to produce our next record, but we had our hearts set on Brian Eno.

Back in the dressing room, the great Charlie Mingus was getting ready to play. He was getting old and not feeling very well. I introduced myself and reminded him of a gig of his five or six years earlier at the Encore Club on Walnut Street in Pittsburgh, where I was working a summer job as bartender. It was a jazz brunch and my job was to keep the Bloody Marys flowing. Charlie and his band were playing and some ladies in the back were talking very loudly. Charlie cut the band and asked, "Will you all please keep it down over there? We would appreciate that." The ladies quieted down and the band started playing again. This was some serious jazz, you know, not background music. Then the ladies started talking over the music again. It sounded like a hen house. In between songs, Charlie looked over at me and said, "Pass me one of those Bloody Marys." Charlie took one sip, leaned back, and threw it across the room, where it landed with a big red splash right in the middle of the noisy ladies' table. The room went very silent then, and the band resumed its set.

Charlie looked up at me with a smile, slowly shook his tired head, and drawled, "Oh, yeah."

It's dark on those Woodstock country roads at night and not easy to navigate but, after a few wrong turns, we finally found our friend's farmhouse where we were going to spend the night. We smoked a joint out on the porch, took a deep breath of mountain air, and went to bed. Tina closed the door to the bedroom where we were sleeping. As she was climbing into bed with me, the door slowly opened again but no one was there. I got up and shut the door, but before I could get back in bed, it swung open again. We thought, "That's weird." We weren't scared, though. We decided to leave

the door open, but guess what? It suddenly closed by itself. I tried not to think about it and went to sleep. No sooner had I nodded off than I began to hear unintelligible whispering in my ear. If I sat up it would stop, but if I lay down it would begin again.

We didn't get much sleep that night but no harm came to any of us, and we all had strange stories to tell in the morning. When I called our hosts to describe our experience, they said, "Yes, we think the house is haunted. What do you think?"

35

LET'S WORK!

Talking Heads: 77 was released to good, and even great, reviews in *The New York Times, The Village Voice, Rolling Stone,* and every UK music paper. We in the band were ready to work. Nineteen seventy-seven was a great time to be in a touring band, but Gary, at the same time, realized that there really wasn't a touring circuit for new bands with our style of music. The big promoters weren't interested. So by talking to college student promoters, club owners, and local independent promoters, Gary managed to put together a really great little tour for us. We played college campuses, like Oberlin, U.C. Berkeley, Penn State, Rutgers, and UCLA, across the country, usually in the student union or gym. We played the clubs, we played abandoned supermarkets, and we played small theaters where the vibes were great.

The day our album was released, September 16, 1977, we started the tour at the New Yorker Theater on Yonge Street in Toronto. There was a giant figure of King Kong climbing the Empire State Building on the marquee. We did two shows. The first one began at midnight! Our Toronto audience turned out for both shows and I think every new wave kid in the entire Province of Ontario was in the house. I have no doubt that a certain degree of rapture was achieved by everyone in attendance.

We drove over to Boston and played two nights at The Rat, where Jerry introduced us to David Robinson, the drummer from the Modern

Headlining at the Bottom Line, NYC.

Lovers. He was starting a band with his friend Ric. They were going to call it the Cars. Like us, they had some big plans. Good times at the Rat on those nights. The place was packed and sweaty, and they were selling plenty of beer. The Rat truly was the CBGB of Boston. Before the second show we taped a radio interview over in Cambridge with a guy who called himself Oedipus. He broadcast from the basement of a building at MIT on the student radio station. He called his late-night show *Nocturnal Emissions*. Oedipus got Talking Heads right from the start. Eventually, he became the top cat in Boston radio at WBCN and kept Talking Heads in heavy rotation.

We made the short drive down to Providence to play a new joint called Lupo's Heartbreak Hotel. Some of our good friends, Dan Gosch, Rudy Cheeks of the Young Adults, and Josh Miller came out to see us. At the original Lupo's, the drummer, me, sat in the storefront window and the band played to two rooms divided by a plaster wall that ran from the middle of the stage to the back of the club.

It was a weird setup. Everyone was seriously checking us out because we were already legendary in Providence thanks to our RISD/Artistics history. Add to that the fact that we had actually made a real record deal and released a real record. Another RISD grad, a bit older than we were, named Martin

Mull had released a record or two, like *Martin Mull and His Fabulous Furniture,* but he created more impact on the TV show *Mary Hartman, Mary Hartman.* Some of the Lupo's crowd were skeptical at first, but after a couple of drinks and a great effort on our part to really deliver the goods, we won the whole room over. We were not rock and roll poseurs. When we rocked, our performance came from the heart.

We returned to New York for an invitation-only live recording session at CBGB. Ed Stasium engineered the recording. It was a beautiful October night in New York. We invited all of our friends and radio people and the music press. This recording would be used for radio promotion and to promote our tour on the *King Biscuit Flower Hour,* a nationally syndicated radio show. The audience, knowing we were being recorded, were even more intense than usual, which was great. We didn't know it at the time, but this was the last time Talking Heads would play CBGB. After the show, Ed took us uptown to the Power Station to mix the concert. There were still table saws and carpentry tools all around, but in one control room the electronics were finished enough to mix. The sound and quality of the performance on this live recording got us a lot of gigs.

A couple of days later we were booked in the Student Union Social Hall at Buffalo State College, where we performed following a lecture by Clive Davis for a rock and roll writers' conference. Clive talked about "a Janis Joplin" and "a Barry Manilow" and "a Patti Smith," as if they were manufactured products. At first I thought this was a bad thing but then I remembered Lou Reed saying, "I wish RCA would treat me like a product and sell as many copies of my record as they did their televisions and refrigerators." A group from *Creem* magazine, including Billy Altman and Lester Bangs, were there and we hung out with them after the show. They were fun guys. We drank a few beers and smoked pot with them, except for David, who still said pot made him paranoid. Lester was pontificating about the importance of remaining uncool in the face of coolness. He was referring to us. Ha!

We played a couple of really wild shows at the Jabberwocky at Syracuse U. and a place called Nite Court in Ithaca, New York, with an opening act called the Sweaty Tools.

We made our Chicago debut at a folk club called the Quiet Knight. The weather was cold and wet but the room was respectably full. People in

Chicago were not sure what to make of us, but we won them over with our energy and attitude. The word got out and our second night was sold out.

Then we traveled to Milwaukee, home of Jerry Harrison, and played the Electric Ballroom. We met Jerry's parents, who were lovely people. You could see Jerry in both of them. Jerry's mother was a painter and a good one. Jerry's father was in advertising. We visited their house, where Jerry had grown up playing in bands and sailing on Lake Michigan. It was good to see where our newest Talking Head came from.

The next show, in Schaumburg, Illinois, was at a club called B'Ginnings. It was owned by Danny Seraphine, the drummer from the band Chicago. We noted that clubs owned by real working musicians always had the most comfortable dressing rooms. This one had several overstuffed leather couches and we all took a much-needed siesta before the show. The food was good, too!

We weren't just playing shows in the towns we visited. We also did interviews with the local papers and visited FM radio stations that might or might not be promoting our shows or playing our record. We learned that if you visited a station with a Warner/Sire promotion man, that might be the only time that particular station played your record, but at least they played it once. After we left, the format returned to Elton John, Foreigner, Debby Boone, and the Eagles.

We also made appearances at record stores. When we rolled into Minneapolis we visited the legendary Oar Folkjokeopus record shop. Even though the clerks could be condescending, it was the hippest record store for miles around and the only shop carrying Punk and New Wave in Minneapolis. Let's just say the clerks did not condescend to us. We met Andy Schwartz, who would soon be running *New York Rocker* magazine. We performed at Jay's Longhorn, *another* steakhouse that pushed back the tables after dinner for the bands to play. They had a scene germinating with bands like Suicide Commandos, the Replacements, and the Suburbs. The Longhorn was the CBGB of Minneapolis, and every show we played there was packed.

Returning to New York City to headline the Bottom Line was a trip. All of our friends were there. The opening act was a magician named Jeff Sheridan. They say New Yorkers are a tough crowd, but we never found that to be the case. The audience was lively from the moment we walked out onto

the stage and it was a killer set, if I do say so myself. We played two sets that
night:

"Artists Only"
"Love → Building on Fire"
"Uh-oh, Love Comes to Town"
"Don't Worry About the Government"
"Take Me to the River"
"The Book I Read"
"New Feeling"
"A Clean Break (Let's Work)"
"Stay Hungry"
"Thank You for Sending Me an Angel"
"Who Is It?"
"I'm Not in Love"

ENCORE
"Pulled Up"
"No Compassion"
"1-2-3 Red Light"

There was not much time to rest. The next night we played at Haver-
ford College, and then we traveled on down to Richmond, where we played
a Halloween party at Virginia Commonwealth University in the Franklin
Street Gym. The last band to play there had been Parliament Funkadelic,
and they had set off a pyrotechnic bomb at the end of their set. It was not
their intention to do anything except create a dramatic stage effect, but the
force of the blast knocked down the kids in the front of the audience and
shattered all the big plate-glass windows in the lobby of the building. Natu-
rally, the security people at the school were a little wary of us, a punk band
from New York City.

In fact, it was the *audience* in Richmond that was wild and crazy. We
loved their enthusiasm. Many were in costume and they were mostly
drunk or tripping or both. At the appointed closing time, while we were
still playing the tail end of our show, the armed security men pulled the
plug. The kids were not happy about it. I call them kids but we were not

much older. We just laughed, hollered "Good night!" and got the hell out of there.

The next day we drove up to Pittsburgh, PA. The dominant concert promoters in Pittsburgh were Pat DiCesare and Rich Engler. They never wanted to have anything to do with Talking Heads. Every time we played Pittsburgh we had to promote the shows ourselves with the help of Gary Kurfirst. For our Pittsburgh debut, we played at Antonino's Pizza Parlor on Craig Street right between Carnegie Mellon University and the University of Pittsburgh. It was a tiny place and packed. My mom and dad were there with a couple of their friends, beaming with joy. Our opening act was a fire-eater who had enjoyed a few too many drinks before the show. He told dirty jokes as he put flaming torches down his throat and rolled his tongue around the torches. Everyone in the house was transfixed.

By the time we took the stage for the first of two shows, the audience was full of great pizza and Iron City beer. The Ramones had played this tiny joint the week before us. They must have been really loud, because even we, who always played at a modest volume, sounded super loud in the tiled interior of Antonino's. We made the best of it and turned what could have been a lousy gig into a legendary night in the 'burgh. I had imagined we would play a nightclub or a small theater. While it was not exactly the type of gig I had imagined my triumphant return to Pittsburgh to be, it was the night the new wave arrived in Pittsburgh.

The next day we drove back east to Rutgers U. in New Brunswick, New Jersey. The kids went nuts, hundreds of them. The year before we could barely even get a gig in New Jersey.

All of us in Talking Heads had parents who had worked hard to make a good life for us. None of us were rich growing up, but we were not poor, either. David had always made it clear that he felt that Tina and I had advantages that he did not. So it came as a bit of a surprise to see how nice his family's home was when we visited David's folks outside of Baltimore in Columbia, Maryland. Columbia was a planned community developed by James W. Rouse, who emphasized human values over mere engineering and economics. The town was comprised of ten villages, with footpaths and bike trails connecting them. Every building we saw was built of red brick and neatly landscaped. Since this was his neck of the woods, David was behind the wheel of the Country Squire. When he realized he had just passed by

his family's home, David decided to turn around by driving over a carefully landscaped median strip. I said something like, "Wait a minute, man!" but it was too late. The Country Squire was now teetering on the median strip like a seesaw with neither the front nor the rear wheels touching the ground. David thought this was hilarious—and looking back, it was—but we were stuck. Tina got behind the wheel while Jerry, David, and I somehow managed to push the car over the pretty roses and boxwoods and off the median to the other side of the road, hoping that no one had seen us. At David's childhood home, Tommy and Emma Byrne were waiting to greet us sweetly with cups of hot tea and trays of homemade shortbread. David had been born in Dumbarton, Scotland. After moving first to Ontario, Canada, when David was two, the Byrnes had settled in Maryland and had lived there for over twenty years. Tommy was an electrical engineer at Westinghouse and Emma was a teacher of special needs children. Their home was cheerfully decorated with plenty of color and light. Tina noticed a number of Spin Art paintings on paper plates prominently displayed on the living room walls and asked Emma if these had been made by her special needs kids. "Oh, no!" Emma proudly replied in her Scottish accent. "Our Davy made those!" "When he was a little boy?" Tina asked. "Noooooh! In art school!"

Two days later we had another big New York gig. This time we'd be playing the Eisner and Lubin Auditorium at NYU. Tina's sister Laura and Leigh Blake met us backstage and we caught up on family news and downtown band gossip. We had a couple of days off to rest and do our laundry before we were back out on the road. Tina and I visited CBGB to say hi to Hilly and all of our friends there. I remembered the words of our good friend Lenny Kaye when I asked him what it was like to play all those great gigs in Europe and across the USA. He said, "There are some great venues around the world, and we are happy to be able to play them, but there really isn't any place better than CBGB."

When we played upstate at the student bar at Binghamton University, our opening act was a hip new comedian named Richard Belzer. They called him "The Belz." We thought he would be a good choice because he was funny and smart and a real New Yorker. Our mistake. As funny and hip as Belzer was, the kids just wanted to rock. They pelted him with ice cubes and booed him off the stage. Tina and I saw what was happening and brought him backstage to our dressing room. He was clearly shaken

and very upset. I offered him a chair and a joint, which he accepted and we sat with him while he smoked it and calmed down. I wouldn't blame him if he never opened for another rock band again, and I doubt that he ever did.

We rarely opened for anyone else after the Ramones tour of Europe. We continued playing around the Northeast at the Shaboo Inn, in Willimantic, Connecticut, and the tiny Hot Club in Philadelphia. We traveled back up to Maynard, Massachusetts, outside of Boston, where we met Ed Stasium in the afternoon to record a live set with a live audience at Northern Studios. This recording would then be distributed by Warner/Sire to radio stations across the country. When I heard the playback, I thought to myself that not only did we sound better than before, but that there was no other band that sounded like us anywhere. We were still unique.

Later that night we opened a show for the Ramones at the classic Orpheum Theater in Boston. The Ramones had already done their sound check and we set up for our show in front of all their gear. When we asked who the lighting man was, Arturo Vega said that he was. We told him, as usual, that we just wanted white lights. Arturo apologized and said, "Johnny says you can't use the Ramones' lights." Incredulous, I said, "Arturo, what are you talking about, we can't use the lights? You expect us to play in the dark?" Gary Kurfirst had just arrived from New York and I explained the situation to him. He went over to talk to Johnny. Gary said, "What are you trying to do, give Forest Hills a bad name? You're from Forest Hills. I'm from Forest Hills and I'm ashamed of you right now! You know what, we don't need your fucking stupid lights!" Gary walked back to our dressing room and said Johnny was still not going to let us use the lights. This was so silly. We walked onstage with just the theater's house lights on. The audience couldn't have cared less and we played a killer show. From my seat on the drum riser, I could see the balcony moving up and down as fans pogoed and danced. Gary made a big impression on the Ramones. A few years later, they asked him to be their manager.

We played the Capitol Theater in Passaic, New Jersey, and The Bayou Club in Washington, D.C. (where, from the balcony, the opening band threw balloons filled with milk at us while we were onstage). On Tina's birthday, November 22, we played the very beautiful Finney Chapel at Oberlin College in Ohio. I remember Jerry playing their huge, fantastic organ before our show until someone hooted, "Hands off the organ!" We drove to Detroit

and played a "New Wave Invasion" concert with the Ramones at the Masonic Auditorium. Detroit Rock City. Motown. Home of the Stooges and the MC5. Well, those days were gone. Detroit had fallen on hard times. Downtown was dead, the perfect lesson in what not to do to a city. The kids came in from the suburbs to see us. They just wanted to have something to do, but once they heard us and saw us, they wanted more.

We had three days over Thanksgiving to get down to the Capri Theater in Atlanta. The show had been booked for weeks when one day Gary got a call from Columbia Records. They wanted to know if we would allow Elvis Costello to open for us. They were offering us two thousand dollars to add him to an already sold-out show. We agreed to do so and it was a fabulous show out in the Buckhead part of town. People had come from far and wide for a taste of live, new music. After the show, both bands were invited to a party at the Fans' house. The Fans were a band from Atlanta who had shared the stage with us at CBGB and we liked them. They loved Roxy Music and the Velvet Underground and you could hear it in their music: they were not playing country or blues. They had a big old house that was great for parties. We went and so did some of the guys from Elvis's band. Musical instruments were all around and some people started jamming. I couldn't help but notice a couple of cute chicks doing a Yoko Ono–style vocal. They were dressed in vintage thrift shop clothes. It was a very bohemian scene, but so much more relaxed than in New York City. Also, the sweetness of a deep Southern accent, particularly from the women, was music to my ears. We couldn't stay very long (we had to be in Nashville the next day) but we did talk for a good while to a group of kids who'd come up from Athens, Georgia, to see our show. They said they were starting a band and they wanted to come up to New York and play. I gave them our number and asked, "What's the name of your band?" They replied, in unison: "The B-52s."

The next afternoon I drove to Nashville on the Interstate in the pouring rain. Incredibly, I did not have a hangover from the party the night before but the rain made me really drowsy. I saw a sign that said NASHVILLE 20 MILES and I decided to tune into the radio station that was supposed to be promoting our show at the famous Exit Inn. The rest of the band was dozing. I tuned in to the station and I heard Tina's bass line from "Psycho Killer" and turned it up. "Hey, check it out. We're on the radio!" We were

still taken by surprise and thrilled any time we heard one of our songs on the radio. Everyone perked up their ears. Then the DJ drawled, "Well, that was the Talking Heads, folks. Punk is coming to Nashville for the first time and probably the *LAST* time tonight at the EXIT INN!"

It wasn't the last time. I can remember a Halloween concert we played a few years later at Vanderbilt that was a complete bacchanal among other great shows in Nashville. The Exit Inn was a good time that night. It was mostly an older crowd who worked in the music business and wanted to see what all the New Wave fuss was about.

The women in the audience were very impressed by Tina's fashion sense, which was so different from what they were accustomed to seeing a woman in show business wearing. Tina had developed a style of her own that did not scream *show business* in any way. Usually, her style was as understated as the guys in the band. They also liked the songs and the energy onstage. We found out later that Adrian Belew was in the audience that night.

After the show Tina went into the office, as she always did, to settle up with the promoter. Our accountant had correctly surmised that Tina had the best head for figures and was consistently reliable and organized. It wasn't the first time she'd seen a loaded pistol on a promoter's desk as he counted out the money he owed us. Tina could tell they were surprised that she, so pretty and petite, was also the road manager, but they never tried to shortchange her. They probably figured there would be hell to pay if they did. She counted out the money in front of the promoter exactly as Gary had instructed her but then, to the promoter's astonishment, she returned the extra bills that he had miscounted. Apparently, it was a first for this guy. He would be on the phone about it with Gary the next day to invite the band to return. But by then we would have outgrown the Exit Inn.

Next stop, San Francisco.

36

CALIFORNIA

Tina was born in Coronado, California. David had visited San Francisco in his hitchhiking hippie days. Jerry had lived in LA for a while while making the demos that were eventually released as the first Modern Lovers album. But I had never been out West, and I was really looking forward to being there. In the mid-sixties I became a serious Beach Boys fan and had a poster of a guy surfing a mammoth wave on my dorm room wall. Though I had never surfed, I felt a spiritual connection to those who did. Then there was the psychedelic age in San Francisco that I had read so much about in news magazines. The new radio format called FM in the late sixties played so much psychedelic music that being in Pittsburgh listening to Brother Love on WAMO-FM, I really felt like I was missing out on something. The Jefferson Airplane, the Grateful Dead, the Charlatans, Big Brother and the Holding Company, they all seemed so wild. My time had finally come. We were booked to play two weeks of shows in California.

On December 1, 1977, Gary flew to San Francisco with us and our guitars. The rest of the gear would meet us there with our crew.

I was immediately impressed with the natural golden quality of the afternoon light in San Francisco. We rented cars and drove to the Miyako Hotel on Post Street in Japan Town and checked in. Staying in the Miyako was Gary's idea and a good idea it was. Lots of bands stayed there. You could

get sushi and hot sake from room service. The deep Japanese-style bathtubs were luxurious beyond anything we were accustomed to. We loved the place. We had one night off before our first show. Gary took us to dinner in the Japan Center next door. David, who had brought his girlfriend Mary Clarke with him, was in absentia. We had dinner for the first time at one of those Japanese places with the little boats that float by as you sit at the counter, each one carrying a serving of sushi or sashimi. We devoured the raw fish with gusto and washed it down with hot sake and Japanese beer. At the end of the meal, you would count up your different colored plates and pay accordingly. Tina and I returned to the hotel for a romantic evening, as we sometimes did, and a hot Japanese-style bath while Gary and Jerry explored the chilly San Francisco night.

Bill Graham was the big rock music promoter in the Bay Area, but because of his history with Graham and the Village Theater, Gary thought we shouldn't play for him until he begged us to do so. So we worked with smaller club and college promoters until that day arrived. And it did.

The Old Waldorf was a club on Battery Street in the financial district that every band played at some point in their careers. You either played it on your way up, or you played it on your way down. If you were Jerry Garcia or Jorma Kaukonen and living in San Francisco, you played it for fun whenever you felt like it. It wasn't a place the kids went to hang out like CBGB, but it was a good place to hear original music. The capacity was 650, and the room was filled with long tables set up at ninety

One of life's greatest pleasures is to dance with your little sister.

degrees to the stage. The room was 130 feet long and 50 feet wide. The stage was only twenty inches high. The walls were red brick. I believe they sometimes served food. There was a dance floor off to the side, but you couldn't see the stage from it. The sound was okay as long as the band kept their stage volume down, which we always tried to do. The room was not really conducive to a lively audience get-down, but we did our best. There was a semi-full house that night but we were nowhere near sold out.

We walked out onto the stage to a smattering of applause. The smell of good weed was in the air. David made his usual announcement saying, "The name of this band is Talking Heads," and we were off. I quickly spotted our friend Damita the Punk Lolita in the front row. Damita, who was twenty-one but looked much younger, was a friend from CBGB, the Ocean Club, and the whole downtown scene. She did some exotic dancing and traveled between New York, San Francisco, and West Hollywood. We all adored Damita. If Damita was in the house, you knew you were in the right place.

After the show and three encores, we taped an interview with KFRC-FM in the dressing room, took some photos, and then headed back to the Miyako Hotel bar for a few Mai Tais. A colorful group of fans followed us back to the hotel.

Our second night at the Old Waldorf was recorded for live broadcast by KSAN, aka Jive 95. Tina asked, "Don't they know that being called 'Jive' is not a compliment?" We had visited the station that day and done an interview with Howie Klein. Howie was the resident punk/new wave expert at KSAN and a good guy. Years later he became an executive at Sire Records and Reprise.

It was Saturday night and the word was out that Talking Heads had come to town. Attendance was much better than the night before. Our set built slowly until the crowd was stomping its feet and pounding on the tables with approval. We played three or four encores and after the show we hung out with the fans at the club until we were all feeling no pain.

Sunday, after breakfast, we drove down to U.C. Santa Cruz. We did an on-air interview at KLRB in Carmel. Clint Eastwood was the mayor and I think he also owned the radio station. It was all very upscale. We made an instore

appearance at Cymbaline in Santa Cruz, signing copies of our album before sound check time. The venue was a small theater called the Kresge Town Hall. It was nestled among the beautiful, tall redwood trees and was a very dreamy and laid-back place. The students were high on the best herb. They seemed gentle, sweet, and smart. The only thing missing was flowers in their hair. From the stage I could see guys lying on the floor embracing their girlfriends with great tenderness. Other couples were dancing with no self-consciousness whatsoever. I think most of the kids had no idea who we were. They just wanted to have some fun. It was a seriously mellow Sunday evening among the redwoods.

In San Jose we played a place called Bodega, where Neil Young was known to do surprise sets. I could see why he liked it. The room was all wooden beams and planks with a Wild West flavor. We visited KSJO to promote the show and the record.

The Keystone Berkeley was right on the main drag at 2119 University Avenue. Some say it was a biker bar, but most people knew it as a super-funky, occasionally experimental music club. Jerry Garcia played there all the time with various bands. Herbie Hancock and Ray Charles and B.B. King had graced the stage. Gary knew it was a good place that local people loved to go to hear some good music. We visited KTIM in San Rafael for a lunch hour radio show and then rolled across the Bay Bridge to Berkeley. We stopped in at KALX to schmooze and promote the show. They played "Psycho Killer" and "Uh-oh, Love Comes to Town." The poster someone had made for the Keystone gave the impression that we were a creepy punk group. This would continue to happen for a while. For some it was a surprise to see that we were actually the opposite of punk. We asked Damita to stand at the door with a clicker and take a headcount of how many people came to see us. As usual we were being paid a flat fee against a percentage of the door money. Gary didn't trust the club to give us an accurate count, so Damita's presence at the door ensured fairness.

The opening band was called Leila and the Snakes. "Leila" was actually Jane Dornacker, who had performed with The Tubes. She was pretty wild. So was the other singer, Pearl E. Gates. They wore vintage clothes and were totally camp. Pearl later had her own band, Pearl Harbor and the Explosions, and toured the USA with us before she married Paul Simonon from the Clash.

Jane moved to New York City, where she had great success as a weather and traffic reporter until the day her chopper plunged into the Hudson River and she was tragically killed while broadcasting live on the air.

After three nights at the Keystone Berkeley and one night at the Keystone Palo Alto and much wandering around the streets of San Francisco, we flew to Los Angeles, where we had no idea what to expect. While we were in the air, I glanced over at Tina, who was looking sensational. She had been playing exceptionally well, too. She was everything I'd imagined she would be. We were both ready for an airplane nap, but before we dozed off I gave her a kiss and she said, "Oh, *mon amour.*" I whispered back, *"Oui, ma chérie.* The next thing you know we'll be in LA."

Los Angeles was very bright and sunny, just like it was supposed to be. Tina remembered that she used to drive a carpool van full of kids to school here in Palos Verdes when she was in high school. We picked up our bags, rented a car, and drove to the Sunset Marquis in Hollywood. Most of the CBGB bands stayed at the Tropicana, but Gary wanted us to be at the Sunset Marquis, which was not the fancy boutique hotel it is now. It was a medium-priced rock and roll hotel. It resembled the set of a sixties TV sitcom, but it was more refined than the Tropicana. There was a courtyard with a swimming pool surrounded by tables with umbrellas. You could mingle with other bands and Hollywood schmoozers by the pool and order room service and drinks. It was a friendly scene, as if it were happy hour all day long. I said a brief hello to Christine McVie and Dennis Wilson, who were hanging out looking a little the worse for wear, but smiling.

That night a driver picked us up and drove us to a Datsun dealership over in Pasadena, where KROQ was doing a live broadcast. This was the first and only time we made an appearance at a car dealership, but it was worth it. We were welcomed by Jed the Fish from KROQ. The guy on the air was none other than Rodney Bingenheimer, aka the "Mayor of the Sunset Strip." Rodney was a true tastemaker. If Rodney said you were "great," people would want to check you out. He was a passionate glam rock Anglophile. Rodney's English Disco had been a real scene where underage girls danced to David Bowie, T. Rex, Mott the Hoople, Slade, Suzi Quatro, and the Bay City Rollers. These same rock stars would then hang out at his

club when they were in town, drinking and drugging. As the glam rock days faded away, Rodney discovered Punk and New Wave. He loved the Ramones and Blondie and he said on the air that night that Talking Heads was great. After that, we were added to the KROQ playlist in almost perpetuity.

In the morning, Tina and I woke refreshed and decided to take a walk down Sunset Boulevard. The thing is that nobody walks in LA, so you feel kind of weird as all the cars whiz by. We only walked a few blocks down to the Old World restaurant, where we had Bloody Marys and a nice lunch under a huge billboard of Diana Ross. After lunch we crossed the street to visit the world-famous Tower Records. There was only one Tower Records then and this was it. We had never been to a record store with shopping carts before. According to what we'd heard, Elton John would come in and fill a big shopping cart with records to buy. We didn't have the cash to buy anything, but it was exciting to see our album on display with a poster for our three upcoming nights at the Whisky a Go Go, which was just a few blocks away.

Later that afternoon we had our photo taken on the corner of Sunset and Alta Loma with some huge, brightly-colored plush animals that a vendor there was selling. It's one of my favorite photos from that time. After the photo was taken we all piled into the car and drove down to Huntington Beach, where we had a two-night gig at the Golden Bear. We did our sound check and were hanging out backstage with the Warner's promotion man, munching on tacos and drinking Coronas, when David decided to take a walk with Mary Clarke. I always felt a little wary when David would wander off at the airport or before a show, but so far he had always returned in the nick of time. Tina, Jerry, and I would breathe a sigh of relief. This time David was really late, so late the promoter was worried they would have to cancel the show. There were no cell phones to call him back then. Finally, the club got a call. David and Mary had been arrested for jaywalking! Mary had said to the arresting officer, "You've got to be kidding! We're from New York!" To prove he wasn't, he took them to the police station, where they were detained and, finally, ordered to pay a fine before being released. David, who was strangely elated by the mishap, joined us onstage to start the show over an hour late, and we pulled out all the stops to play an edgy set for the surfers, college kids, and fellow music lovers. I guess we were worth waiting for. We got three encores that night.

We made an instore appearance at Greg Shaw's Bomp! Records store. Greg was a music writer, historian, archivist, and publisher. His fanzine *Who Put the Bomp* was going to do a feature on Talking Heads. He was excited about punk, new wave, and power pop. Greg had a strong connection to Sire Records. He had released early singles by the Modern Lovers, Devo, Iggy Pop, and the Flamin' Groovies, who were another Sire band, and had written for *Rolling Stone, Creem,* and the *Los Angeles Times.* He had come to see us play at CBGB and it was a pleasure to visit his shop in LA.

We were booked for three sold-out nights at the Whisky a Go Go. We had been hearing about the Whisky for years; in fact, it's still going strong. Famous shows by the Doors, Janis Joplin, Buffalo Springfield, and Led Zeppelin had happened there. Now it was our turn.

Gary introduced us to Elmer Valentine, a founding partner of the Whisky, the Roxy, and the Rainbow Bar and Grill. Elmer and Gary were old friends and Gary knew that Elmer could be very helpful to us going forward, and he was. We played the Whisky this time and, if all went well, we would graduate to the Roxy next time.

Happily for Tina and me, two of our closest friends from RISD were at the first show. Andi Shapiro was testing the Hollywood waters in hopes of becoming an actress, and Mary Lambert was becoming a really superb filmmaker. Both of them were pleasantly surprised that we were even in LA, never mind playing the Whisky a Go Go. We invited them backstage to catch up and it was wonderful to see them.

We were going to play two sets that night, so we had to pace ourselves and not party too hard. We were sharing the stage with a band called the Heaters. They were a good band with two very talented young women on vocals—one of whom also played bass—and three guys. They played a more traditional form of rock and roll than we did. In fact, *every* band in LA played a more traditional form of rock and roll than we did. Visiting Los Angeles helped me realize how cutting edge we really were, and it also made me realize that a lot of people in the music business had no interest in cutting edge. After our first night, Robert Hilburn of the *Los Angeles Times* wrote that he preferred the Heaters because they were more listenable. We were simply too weird for him. He didn't get us.

We were not discouraged by one less-than-stellar review. We could see

most of the people at the Whisky had come to hear us and we could tell they were thirsty for the new. Sometimes the new takes a while to sink in.

Warren Beatty was at the Whisky that night. He was always on the prowl for something new, but what was really nutty was when we returned to our room at the Sunset Marquis, the phone rang. It was well after midnight. Thinking that it was David or Jerry, I picked up the phone and said hello. A smooth voice on the other end asked to speak to Tina Weymouth. I asked, "Who's calling, please?" The voice on the other end replied, "Tell her this is Kim Fowley." I told Tina who it was and passed the phone to her. Kim Fowley, who wrote and sang "Alley Oop" in the sixties with the Hollywood Argyles, was the manager and producer of the Runaways and a legendary LA music biz eccentric. He had been at the show and was so impressed by Tina that he told her, in so many words, "You should quit Talking Heads and make your own album. I'll produce it and I'll be your manager." Tina laughed and said, "Thank you, but I love my band and I'm going to stay with my band. Good night." Tina hung up the phone, which then kept ringing and ringing until we called the front desk and asked them to hold our calls until the morning.

We flew home to New York on December 18. Brian Eno was in town and Tina's brother, Yann, and Julia MacFarlane had a dinner party for him at their loft next door to ours. Brian seemed as delighted to be in our company as we were to see him again. In a couple of months' time we would be making our second album with him. I looked around the table at the smiling faces of David, Jerry, Tina, Brian, and the rest of the guests and I thought, *How fortunate am I?* Quite literally, my dreams were coming true.

37

FROM XTC TO DIRE STRAITS

We finished 1977 on New Year's Eve at the Main Point in Haverford, Pennsylvania, not far from Philadelphia. This was a great club where we had received a lot of love on our previous visits, but the killing schedule we had set for ourselves was taking its toll. By the time we hit the stage David had very little voice and by the end was coughing up blood. I called Gary Kurfirst the following morning and told him we would have to cancel the New Year's Day show at My Father's Place on Long Island. There was just no way we could do it.

We drove back to New York City to rest up and run errands for our second tour of Europe and the UK, which was to begin in a week. We needed all the rest we could get. David had a bad throat and Tina had bronchitis. Playing a holiday show at the cold, damp, and dusty CBGB Theater had been a big mistake. We never should have done it, but we felt a strong sense of loyalty to Hilly and our New York City fans, so we did it. It's a good thing we had a week off before departing for Europe on January 9.

When we met at the KLM counter, we were all in high spirits—even Jerry, who was in the habit of complaining about everything: the hotel, the elevator service, the food, and the weather. Hard memories of the Modern Lovers would stir him to say things like, "This is the type of thing that makes bands break up!" Sheesh. Well, on this day even Jerry was happy. We

were flying to Amsterdam and Talking Heads loved Amsterdam. We had chosen an opening act called XTC for the European leg of the tour. They had the reputation for putting on exciting shows and, like us, they were defying a lot of rock and roll clichés. Before even meeting them, we liked their style.

Our tour manager, Mike Stewart, greeted us warmly at the airport, driving the yellow Ford minivan that we would be spending the next month riding around in. It was just big enough for both bands and our personal things. Everything else would ride in the truck with our soundman, Frank Gallagher, and stagehand, Ian Ward.

The Apollo Hotel was clean and Bauhaus modern with a wonderfully bright and airy, glassed-in terraced café overlooking the canal where we could conduct interviews with press and radio, eat broodjes (sandwiches), and drink Heinekens to our hearts' content. There was a lot of press to do, too. The Phonogram people who distributed our record were on the case and doing a good job with publicity, so necessary for any tour to succeed.

The first show of the tour was at the Diogenes Club in Nijmegen. We met the guys in XTC at the sound check. They seemed cool and were very enthusiastic. Andy Partridge had a naughty sense of humor. His wit would keep us in stitches for weeks. Colin Moulding was quiet and thoughtful, in a George Harrison style. Barry Andrews was energetic and ready for any type of rock and roll experience. Terry Chambers was a salt-of-the-earth, good-natured lad who had no patience for nonsense. All of them were great players and, together, they created a unique sound. Their first album, *White Music*, was just about to be released. We had much in common musically and after the first show it was clear to all of us that this was a fantastic double bill. We were sold out in advance and we got three encores.

The following night we had another sold-out show at the Eksit Club in Rotterdam, where, six months earlier, Johnny Ramone had his Perfecto leather jacket stolen. This time we had security watching the stage and it's a good thing, because punks in the audience were looking to make some kind of trouble. We didn't take the bait. Talking Heads simply transcended any type of predictable punk behavior. By the end of our set, I felt both Talking Heads and XTC had exceeded the audience's expectations.

It's lucky that we got along well with XTC because it was a long drive in the van to the next show in Hamburg with the windows all steamed up.

Mickey Stewart and David were roasting in front by the heater, while people in the very back, Tina and me, were freezing. Andy kept us wildly amused with tales of his youth, his pornography collection, and the secret videos he'd seen from the bathrooms in Chuck Berry's restaurant. I'm pretty sure this was XTC's first trip to Europe and it was Talking Heads' first visit to Germany, land of my paternal ancestors. The gig in Hamburg was at a tiny jazz bar called Onkel Po's. Artists who had played there before us were Chet Baker, Don Cherry, Dizzy Gillespie, Carla Bley, and Dexter Gordon, to name a few. It was a real who's who of jazz. The idea was to pack the place for our first show in Germany. We managed to sell out for two nights, no problem. The wine they served on tap there was called Wiessburgunder, a pinot blanc, and we all had plenty of it. It was great with Schnitzel.

In Hamburg, of course, we thought of the Beatles and their early days when they would ferry over from Liverpool to play six or seven hours a night, six nights a week for weeks on end at the Star Club and other dives along the Reeperbahn. Mickey Stewart took us on a little tour of those places, but actually, Onkel Po's was more happening in 1978. Representatives from Phonogram were there at our show and hung out with us in our hotel bar way past everyone's bedtime. They were so happy to know that we were fans of Can and Kraftwerk and Tangerine Dream. They were very proud of their "Kraut Rock" and why not? There was a different mind-set in this part of Europe, for sure, and the music of these bands reflected it. Most bands tended to be more cerebral in northern Europe and more romantic in the south. "Kraut Rock" was art music. It was uncompromising and we could dig that very much.

After the two Hamburg shows, we drove back to Amsterdam to a sold-out show at the Paradiso. I was happy to see that the hash bar in the choir loft was still in operation. XTC kicked the show off really well with their song "Radios in Motion." They were strong and quirky onstage and got the kids in the audience, all fourteen hundred of them, super excited. After a short break, Talking Heads walked out to a roaring ovation. The sound was difficult onstage, but we were pros at this point and didn't let that phase us. It was the sound out front that mattered and, by all reports, it was fabulous. Our biggest fan, Hans DeVente of Sony, recorded the show for bootleg posterity and it did sound wonderful to us. We would

have loved to hang out in Amsterdam, but we had three shows in Belgium to do.

We checked into the delightfully fading but still grand Hotel Metropole in the center of Brussels. Every band from the Everly Brothers to the Beatles and the Stones had slept there. While waiting for our rooms to be ready we decided to have a Belgian beer. The hotel bar was irresistibly inviting in a grand, old-world style with a long curved brass and zinc bar and enormous windows looking out onto the Place de Brouckère. Tina and I each had a croque monsieur and a beer, because that was all we could afford. While we ate we admired a framed photo on the wall of Jack and Jackie Kennedy sitting on the same tufted red leather banquette we were sitting on.

We were amazed to find that, in 1978, the chairs and stools in our very large hotel room were covered in real leopard skin. The bathrooms were also unusually grand with lots of room and a huge cast-iron bathtub that Tina immediately took advantage of. Later, we would wash our clothes in the tub, too. What luxury!

From the Hotel Metropole, we commuted to our shows in Zeldelgem, near Bruges, and also Liege. On the drives we all had a great time joking around with XTC. Andy Partridge was not shy of teasing David about his obvious eccentricities, and David took it very well, considering that Andy's barbs were sharp and frequent. Andy also spoke a good deal about his own not very happy childhood, like the time when, as a young teenager, he was practicing his guitar and his mother hated the sound so much she turned off the electricity to the entire house.

When there was enough daylight in the van, Jerry and David would try to read. Jerry was reading a spy series he loved and David was still trying to read his textbook on systems analysis that I was becoming convinced he just carried around to look smart.

We were squeezed in too tightly for me to read anything but rock magazines or *Lui* with Jane Birkin on the cover, and I was easily distracted by the scenery when the windows were not fogged up, which was almost never. Tina was often laughing out loud or rolling her eyes at Andy's antics.

The wildest gig of the tour happened at the social hall of an old desanctified church called Le Vieux Saint-Jop. Somehow this room had become *the* place for punk and new wave shows. At a capacity of six hundred people,

it was completely sold out. My mother had asked me to call my uncle Jim, who was chief of staff at SHAPE—Supreme Headquarters Allied Powers in Europe—in nearby Mons, Belgium. Uncle Jim was a real music lover. He had played trombone in high school and was very excited to hear our record when it came on the US Armed Forces Network. He came to this crazy old Salle Des Fetes with my aunt Kitty in full military uniform. I think it was obligatory for him to be in uniform at that time. The promoter gave them seats in the tiny balcony next to the lighting man, whose instructions from us were to turn all the lights on full blast at the beginning of the show, leave them exactly like that, and then to turn them off again at the end of the show.

The audience that night was full of young students who were just on the verge of being out of control. They were full of crazy punk nihilism and they loved the XTC show, but when Talking Heads hit the stage the entire building began to pulse and throb. Several songs into the set we could see that there was a sort of dimple in the crowd. Some of them had managed to pogo right through the floor, landing in the basement below. They would then climb back up the stairs and push the crowd so that the kids in front of them dropped through the hole they had created. Nobody seemed to be getting hurt or asking for help so we just kept on rocking, but we could see a big portion of the crowd, mostly boys, creating a sort of sweaty conveyor belt of punks that kept disappearing into the floor. Even though it was mid-January, Le Vieux Saint-Jop was like a steam bath inside. My aunt and uncle were amazed at what they had just seen and so were we. Who knew that Belgian students could be so fearless and so much fun? Now that we knew, we would be back.

Mike Stewart arranged for an Italian restaurant to stay open for us after the show and the pasta was very good. I had fettuccini carbonara for the first time and was enjoying a glass of the house reserve, which is usually half the price and just as good as any other wine on the menu. Suddenly, XTC's drummer, Terry, who was seated across the table from me, started shouting at the top of his lungs, "Where are my chips? I want my *fucking* chips!" Rock and rollers can be such big babies. He appeared to be on the verge of tears. Frank Gallagher told him that, because the place had been held open late especially for us, there was a limited menu and would he please sit down and stop acting like such a provincial twat! Frank had a

good way of diffusing such situations. Terry, still all red in the face, got up and left. Other than that, it was a lovely dinner with XTC.

In the morning we squeezed into the van and drove to Paris. We would only have one night in Paris, which was a shame, but at least we would be playing at the Bataclan. We completely rocked the sold-out joint. Boys were pushing to the front of the stage to stand at Tina's feet. Tina was cool about it. The band was on fire and the audience greeted every song with that flash of joy and recognition that only comes from repeated listening. We had some real fans in Paris and they sang along with almost every song. Because it was the last night with XTC, we invited them onstage to join us for encores of "Take Me to the River" and "Psycho Killer." I wish I had a recording of it. It was really wild and surprisingly good. Later that year, to show our admiration, we invited XTC to support us at our New Year's Eve show at the Beacon Theater in New York.

It wasn't easy to leave Paris and our French fans after only one night, but we had more shows to do. In the morning we took the train to Calais, the ferry to Dover, and another train to London. A UK tour of clubs and universities would begin the next day in Sheffield. Back in New York before we began the tour, Ed Bicknell, our booking agent from NEMS, had sent me a cassette tape of a band he was thinking of managing to see what we thought of them, and if they could open for Talking Heads on this UK tour. On cassette the band sounded a lot like J. J. Cale, with a taste of Bob Dylan and Eric Clapton on top. I told him I didn't know about the UK, but in the States they could be huge on FM radio. I played the tape for Tina, David, and Jerry and they okayed the band to support us on the UK tour. The band was called Dire Straits.

We arrived at Sheffield University and promptly did our sound check. Believing what goes around comes around, Talking Heads were always very conscientious about allowing our opening acts full sound and lights and plenty of time to properly sound check.

Dire Straits were four serious guys who knew how to play. They were not punks. They had chops. They were still honing their stagecraft, but their sound was fully formed right from the beginning. David Knopfler on guitar and John Illsley on bass were the handsome gentlemen of the group and the most sociable. David had founded the band. Pick Withers on drums was an excellent player, but had the bad habit of carrying his sticks around

with him at all times. He was constantly practicing his drum rudiments, even on the back of the headrest of the person sitting in front of him in the van, which was usually me. This drove everyone crazy and when we told him so, he would stop for a while only to begin again. We finally assigned him the seat behind Mickey Stewart, who was driving and made it extremely clear to Pick that he had no patience for paradiddles on his headrest or anywhere else in the van. The quiet one was Mark Knopfler. He was an unlikely front man, but then you could have said that about David Byrne, too. You'd think he would show a little excitement about being on tour for the first time, but no. It was clear that he was not the bubbly type; in fact, he acted like he might be depressed much of the time.

From Sheffield we traveled to Manchester University, which was sold out, and then another crazy gig at Eric's in Liverpool, also sold out. Doncaster's Outlook Club was not full, but we got three encores from the northern kids. Then we headed south to the very groovy Friars Club Aylesbury, which was a favorite venue from our previous tour with the Ramones. Our agent, Ed Bicknell, was there with Dire Straits' producer, Muff Winwood. There was also a supercute young barefoot woman wearing a very pretty white dress who had sneaked her way into our dressing room. Her name was Paula Yates. She engaged Tina in a long conversation, for some reason divulging that her father, a well-known British television presenter, had sometimes kept her locked up in a box when she was a child. It sounded like crazy talk but turned out to be true and years later, when her father died, it was revealed that he wasn't her real father after all. DNA tests proved that her real father was yet another British television producer. Tina turned to tell me to come listen to this amazing creature, but when we turned back around Paula had disappeared and so had Jerry. *Hmmmmmm.*

The Roundhouse show in London was sensational. The bill consisted of Talking Heads, Dire Straits, and Slaughter and the Dogs. The venue was sold out in advance and the vibes were very good all around. Despite having a pretty bad case of bronchitis she had gotten from the combination of nasty weather, overheated hotel rooms, and lack of sleep, Tina looked great and played like the real trouper she was. All of us were getting pretty worn out, but when showtime came, the adrenaline kicked in and we rocked the house. After the Roundhouse set, we were called back for four encores. The press was there in abundance and the reviews in the following days and

weeks were wonderful. Seymour Stein was in heaven and threw a big party organized by Ed Bicknell for us at the Institute of Contemporary Art. Bob Geldof came up to me and said, "You look terrible!" The man has no manners. David Bowie's longtime collaborator Mick Ronson was much cooler and spoke to us about how much he enjoyed the show before Seymour took Mick and us into a back room for some English blow that was always cut with speed. Still, it enabled us to stay awake and enjoy the party, which was a good one. Tina's brother, Yann, was there and so was Leigh Blake. I had a long talk with Mick Jones from the Clash. Ian Dury was there, too, with a few Blockheads.

We played fifteen shows in seventeen days and on the only days off we traveled by train to Manchester to play on *The Old Grey Whistle Test* television show and then back to London again. We were warned that the host, "Whispering Bob" Harris, would ask us one question only and then, rather than lip synching, we would perform two songs completely live. The television studio had a backstage bar for the artists near the green room so we proceeded to get loosened up. When the time came we took our places and "Whispering Bob," who was a charming fellow, asked us "How long did it take to make the album?" Someone said, "Three weeks" and we launched into "Psycho Killer" followed by "Don't Worry About the Government." The sound we heard in the studio was pathetic but the sound of the actual broadcast was much better. Thank God, because every music fan in England was watching. David was wearing a yellow Lacoste polo shirt I had given him because it wasn't my color. I wore a green one. Both shirts had been a gift from my mother. Little did she know she would have a hand in deconstructing the rock and roll wardrobe.

We took the train back to London and drove by van with Dire Straits to the Top Rank in Brighton. We had dinner with Yann and Leigh, which raised Tina's spirits. She was concerned about David's behavior. It seemed like the more successful Talking Heads became, the more cold and dyspeptic David became. He was never a great personal communicator, so if you asked him if everything was okay he would just clam up and pout. In any case, this tour was almost over.

At the City Center in St. Albans the venue was packed with much younger people than we were accustomed to. Thanks to playing live on *The Old Grey Whistle Test* and the power of television, our audience was

expanding. We were met backstage by Tina's sister Danielle and her husband, Mark, who were in the UK with their firstborn baby, Sabrina. Yann Weymouth and Leigh Blake were also there to cheer us on. It was a great show, if I do say so myself. People were starting to sing along with our songs, especially the choruses of "Psycho Killer." The sold-out house demanded three encores and tried for four.

At the Oasis in Swindon, home of XTC, the audience of nine hundred people almost rioted. Some film crew was shooting parts of the show and the kids, I guess playing to the cameras, went absolutely nuts. Swindon was not known for this type of behavior and XTC were out of town; maybe they could explain it to us. The evening was pretty intense.

The final show of the tour was at the Greyhound in Croydon. For our part, end of tour euphoria had set in. We invited Dire Straits to join us onstage for the encore. We played "Psycho Killer" and "Gloria." I don't think we had ever played "Gloria" onstage before—and we haven't played it since—but somehow we pulled it off with great panache.

We then had three days of interviews, parties, and sightseeing around London. We were back at the Portobello Hotel that we loved so much. Mike Stewart had arranged for Tina and me to have the "Four Poster Room," which was heavenly. David and Jerry each had cabin rooms that were small like a ship's cabin, but stylish with comfy antiques and built-in cabinetry.

During these three days, Seymour Stein began calling insistently from New York. He wanted us to open in Seattle, Washington, for Elvis Costello and the Attractions, whose career was blowing up on FM radio in the US. This was to be the launch of their West Coast tour, and Seymour knew all the big Warners honchos would ride up to see what Talking Heads had grown into if we opened the show. While it was a great idea in theory, Seymour was not taking into account that we had just traveled around Europe and the UK to play twenty-one shows in twenty-three days. Now he wanted us to take an overnight economy flight from London to Seattle to open a show straight from the airport without so much as a sound check. With all due respect to Elvis and his great band, in our exhausted state, there was no way we were going to cross an ocean and a continent to be an opening act for them. Seymour kept calling our rooms, one by one, in hopes of a yes. We all asked the hotel operator to hold our calls. We really needed a break.

On the day we were to fly back to NYC, we were met at the front desk by Leigh Blake, who had a troubled look on her face. She said the staff at the hotel was very upset with us. I asked the lady behind the front desk if there was a problem, but she wouldn't even speak to me. This was especially weird, because she had always been so chipper and friendly. Jerry and Tina were standing with me wondering where David was, because the van was waiting to take us to Heathrow. David finally shuffled up the sidewalk outside the Portobello as we were loading our bags into the van. He made some excuses by way of explanation, saying that he had had an "accident" with the telephone and a desk. According to him, while he was trying to get some sleep, the operator had disregarded his Do Not Disturb to repeatedly put Seymour (who claimed it was an "emergency") through to his room. Finally, he had yanked the phone out of the wall and then hit his head on an open cabinet door. In a fit of anger, he had smashed some furniture, too. Well, I thought, how predictably rock and roll. Mike Stewart settled our bill, including the hefty damages. Our agent, Ed Bicknell, would tell us that the hotel was upset, but not nearly as mad as when they called him to take Richard Hell away. There is still a terrible rumor about what David had done before he vacated his room, one that we have been unable to dispel. Hotels draw the line at this type of behavior. I guessed that the next time we came to London, we would have to find another hotel.

38

BUILDINGS AND FOOD

It's quiet here now on West Bay Street in Nassau, the Bahamas, except for the little conch salad stand and bar by the road where local villagers and a few tourists hang out and drink beer and rum, listening to reggae and soca. You can't imagine how important and happening this little spot once was. Music history was made here. No kidding. The building is still here, but it's accounting offices now: the studio is gone. It's a casualty of the digital age. Everybody has home recording gear now and record labels don't have the budget to fly a group down here to record anymore. Forget about it, it's too expensive.

But there was a time. Talking Heads was the first band to record and mix an album at Compass Point Studios. We worked on three Talking Heads albums here: *More Songs About Buildings and Food*, *Remain in Light*, and *Speaking in Tongues*. Tina and I made the first and second Tom Tom Club albums here, too. Later, when Tina and I began producing other bands, we produced records for Ziggy Marley and the Melody Makers and Los Fabulosos Cadillacs here. It was serious business and we had a ball.

When Tina and I arrived at Compass Point on March 15, 1978, directly from my beloved grandmother Mammy's funeral, David and Jerry, along with Brian Eno, engineer Rhett Davies, and Tina's sister Laura, had already been there for a couple of days. Brian was fresh from David Bowie's *Low* sessions in Berlin. Jerry and Laura met us at the Nassau Airport in a little

open-air vehicle with a striped canopy top made by Volkswagen in Brazil. We piled in and headed to the studio only a couple of miles away. When we drove through a huge cut in the limestone and the beautiful blue-and-green sea was revealed, Tina and I felt like we were dreaming. It was heavenly with poinciana, bougainvillea, and jacaranda, all in bloom. I had never been to a real tropical island before, and I was thrilled. I still feel the same way every time I come here even though the studio is long gone and so many good people are no longer here.

At the studio we were warmly welcomed by a staff mostly comprised of women. The studio was created by Chris Blackwell, the founder of Island Records. Compass Point was in tiny Gambier village, one of the oldest settlements in the Bahamas at the opposite end of the island of New Providence from the capital city of Nassau. It had an unhurried out island ambience and was right across the road from the glistening blue-green southern Atlantic Ocean. Blackwell, who was Jamaican, decided to build the studio in the Bahamas after Bob Marley and so many other people had been shot during a period of great political unrest in Jamaica. Nassau, while still a haven for gamblers and pirates of all kinds, was a far more stable tax-free environment in which to work and conduct business.

Chris had been to see us play at CBGB early on and, although he had passed on signing us because he was putting all his energy into breaking Bob Marley at the time, I think he liked our band. The British singer Robert Palmer brought him to see us, and I think Chris may have regretted that he had passed on us, but maybe not. He had a long history of doing business with our manager, Gary Kurfirst, who had managed Toots and the Maytals, Peter Tosh, and the Mighty Diamonds. In fact, when we first met him, Gary's office was within Island Records' offices and his secretary was none other than May Pang, who had been John Lennon's companion during his "lost weekend" away from Yoko Ono. Chris told Gary that he had built a new studio in the Bahamas and that he would give us a really good rate to be the first band to make a record there. Talking Heads had quite a buzz at the time and it would be good publicity for the studio. Also, Brian Eno, our coproducer, was an Island artist and felt comfortable that he was familiar with the console and recording equipment, which was the same gear he had been using at Island's Basing Street Studios in London. It was a win/win situation.

Entermedia Theater, NYC, 1978.

Everything was brand new and the staff was almost as excited as we were to be there. They were mostly Bahamian or Jamaican and we got to know them all by name. It was good to know that Chris Blackwell had doused the perimeter of the studio grounds with the blood of a freshly killed chicken in Voodoo/Obeah tradition: everything within was protected from evil.

After we'd had a look around the studio, we drove back down twisting West Bay Street along the coast to the little bungalow at Cable Beach where Tina, Laura, Jerry, and I were staying. The house was just steps from the beach and was a very welcome change from our industrial loft in Long Island City. Life was good. David stayed at a different ocean-side apartment with Rhett Davies the engineer and I think he was pleased to do so. We would pick him up on our way to the studio in the mornings. We didn't do that thing where we would stay up all night. We worked mostly in the daytime. Brian stayed at the guesthouse of Chris Blackwell's Ocean View home, a little cottage called Sea Pussy, that was easy walking distance to the studio. We didn't bring any crew with us. We each looked after our own instruments and our own money, as was our custom. All of our gear—amps and drums and keyboards—had been shipped down from New York. Today that would be insanely expensive, but in 1978 it was doable.

As I set up my red Rogers drum kit in the studio, I gave myself a little pat on the back for how far we had come as a band. Three years before we had been listening to Eno's *Taking Tiger Mountain By Strategy* album with fascination in our raw concrete loft on New York's Lower East Side. Now we had completed two tours of Europe, the UK, and North America and we were in a beautiful new studio in the Bahamas with Brian Eno himself working alongside the four of us. I felt particularly good for Tina and how she had not only lived up to our expectations, but had far exceeded them. Her bass parts were sublimely funky without any unnecessary frills and they were uniquely unpredictable. She was not a show-off and she knew how to get down.

The songs we were about to record had all been written long before, mostly even before Jerry joined the band. We had been performing them live on tour. Our playing was very tight and well rehearsed. On the first day of recording Brian said he'd like to try out some ambient room microphone techniques to give the recording a different sound than our first album. This involved placing mics in different parts of the room in different configurations to create a more exciting sound recording. He also brought his EMS Synthi A, a small briefcase-style synthesizer that he would use to "treat" our instruments on separate tracks as the recording was going down. Tina took Polaroids of the studio set up with her SX-70.

The assistant engineer was a good-looking young Bahamian guy from Cat Island named Benji Armbrister. Benji told us, "Relax, man. This is the Bahamas. You can't rush life." I don't know how Benji got the job, because Rhett had to show him how to do everything. But he was a great guy and came to be the best tape operator and assistant engineer I have ever known.

The mood was very upbeat throughout the sessions. We were all on cloud nine—including Brian—and the energy level was high. We sailed through the recording of the basic tracks in the first ten days. We did multiple takes, but usually chose the second or third as the final. Brian only requested two changes in our song arrangements. One was to delete what he called "the Woodsman Section" of "Stay Hungry," where he said David sounded like a lumberjack yelling "TIIIIMBER!" in a forest, and he was right about that. It did sound better without that part. The other suggestion was to try playing our cover of Al Green and Teenie Hodges's "Take Me to the River" as slowly as we possibly could without losing the groove. He was

right about that, too. The slowed-down version was far sexier and had an almost underwater quality that we all loved. When I mentioned I would like to record a small percussion overdub, Brian said, of course, but try to limit the part to only one note for every two bars. I hit a wood Gato Box with a mallet very sparingly and with enough reverb it sounded like a sonar bleep. Perfect! It's interesting to note that "Take Me to the River," originally an Al Green B side, was also recorded during the same time period by Bryan Ferry, Levon Helm, and, of all people, Foghat, but it was Talking Heads who made a hit of it. It became our first Top 40 single.

After a day of recording, Rhett would make us a rough mix on a cassette and we would take this back to our bungalow and listen back on our boombox and dance and dance and dance. To a recording artist there is no better feeling than to listen to your day's work and think, *Damn. This is good!* Even though we had played most of these songs hundreds of times, we had never recorded them and heard them like this. David would re-sing the vocals and we would add a few overdubs, but the artistic quality of the basic tracks was undeniably wonderful.

We had a song called "The Good Thing" that Brian, who loved amateur musicianship, suggested we invite the women who worked in the studio offices to sing on the choruses. Tina led them and sang with them. The idea was that they would somehow sound like Chinese youth in the days of Chairman Mao and, amazingly, they did! They were credited on the album as Tina and the Typing Pool.

Brian would be the first to tell you that he was not a real musician. He was an idea man who communicated his thoughts in the most eloquent English we had heard in a long time. On this album, after the recording of the basic tracks, his production style really came to shine during the mixing. We loved the effects that he had created with his treatments of our sounds. They worked really well and gave the songs an added edge. We also loved the mixes that Rhett, his favorite engineer, achieved with only a little direction from Brian. We developed a great rapport with them and I felt that there was genuine mutual respect among us. We laughed a lot together, because we were truly enjoying ourselves.

After a day in the studio, we would usually wander on foot down the road about a quarter of a mile to a truly marvelous spot called Traveller's Rest, A Restaurant Truly Bahamian. Let me describe it to you. It was situated right

across the road from the beach; you walked up a few concrete steps, opened the screen door and were transported into a relaxing Out Island experience. There were heavy wooden picnic tables and tables made of molded concrete, with beach glass mosaics of fish and octopus. The walls were covered with paintings by local artists and there was a painted mural on the wall of a brown-skinned man sitting in a sea-grape tree next to his boat. There was a bar stocked with many varieties of European beers and Caribbean rum. My personal favorites were St. Pauli Girl beer and Myer's Rum. You could get just about any drink you wanted, but the house specialty was the fresh Banana Daiquiri, which we later realized had about as many calories as half of a banana cream pie, but was so delicious. The sound system played a great selection of Bahamian classics, reggae, and American Soul music. You could order conch or grouper or snapper or minced crawfish or ribs or pork chops or curried chicken, all served with coleslaw and peas and rice. With your dinner you got a salad with homemade dressing and most people agreed that the creamy garlic dressing was the best. You could relax here for hours and sometimes had to, because the service could be slow, especially on a busy night. We were on "island time" and that was okay by me. The clientele was a good mix of Bahamians and tourists and on Sunday afternoons there was live music by a band called De Changers, whose repertoire consisted of reggae, soca, and Bahamian Junkanoo. People would come from all parts of the island to hang out, drink, flirt, and dance. I can remember thinking to myself, on one of those hot Sunday afternoons while dancing close with Tina at Traveller's, that life doesn't get any better than this.

Another place we liked to go for dinner was the Pink Pussycat Club in downtown Nassau, where they served grilled steak, baked potatoes, and salad for six dollars until 2:30 in the morning. We were told that Winston Churchill loved the place and you could see why. It was in an old limestone colonial building where cigar smoke was heavy in the air and croupiers from the casinos would gather after work with their girlfriends to drink heavily. The place had the vibe of a pirate den, which I suppose it actually was.

During our days off, we all liked to go to the beach by our little bungalow. It was a popular tourist spot. Of course, nobody recognized us. We were still a relatively unknown band and, even if someone did know about Talking Heads, they wouldn't expect to see us in our bathing suits on a beach in the Bahamas drinking Planter's Punch.

One night after a mixing session, Chris Blackwell had a small party for us under the coconut trees on the patio of his rather modest British colonial style home. The other guests were mostly Bahamian artists and entrepreneurs like the drummer "Peanuts" Taylor, Ray Munnings, who cowrote and sang "Funky Nassau," and Al Collie, a singer and club owner who was Chris's Bahamian partner in the studio business. Tina and I sat for most of the night with Robert Palmer while he held his newborn son, Jim, in his arms. Robert and his darling artist wife, Sue, were living in a town house on the sea right across the road from the studio. They would continue to be real friends who gave Tina and me a good deal of encouragement in our musical work. Like Chris Blackwell, Robert appreciated the value of a good rhythm section.

Easter is a huge holiday in the Bahamas and we took Brian, who had a genuine love of gospel music, on a tour of various church choirs that Sunday. Wouldn't you know that the one we all agreed was the most inspiring was the singing by the choir and congregation at the little Pentecostal Church of God of Prophecy right next to Compass Point Studios. They had an electric guitar player, a Farfisa Organ, drum kit, and a whole lot of tambourines. The roughness of their sound made the music seem all the more divine.

Brian and Rhett finished up the mixing on April 12. One song, "Found a Job," would be remixed by Ed Stasium at Media Sound in New York. We were all very fond of working at Compass Point, especially Tina and me.

Before we packed up to leave, we had a little meeting with Brian in his cottage to discuss possible album titles. We were all sitting around together enjoying the afterglow of a very fine, par excellence recording experience. Tina asked what we should call an album of songs about buildings and food? I piped up that we should call it *More Songs About Buildings and Food*. Everyone, including Brian, thought it was the perfect title for Talking Heads' second album and so it was.

When we returned from the Bahamas, David and Tina took the Polaroid photos that formed the mosaic of the band on the album cover. This was done on the roof of our loft building in Long Island City. Everybody loved the cover, but later I realized it was "heavily influenced" by Andrea Kovac's work. We should have given her credit for that.

PLANET CLAIRE HAS BIG HAIR

In my life, there are two bands that I feel especially close to: the Ramones and the B-52s. We toured extensively with both of them. When we met the B's at the Fans' party after our first show in Atlanta, Tina and I thought there was something very interesting and unique about them. Actually, they reminded me of a bunch of Southern RISD kids. They were not like any of the other bands. I felt that before I'd even heard any of their music; you could just tell. Ricky Wilson, Keith Strickland, Fred Schneider, Kate Pierson, and Cindy Wilson were their names. We exchanged phone numbers and addresses and they said they would send us their independently pressed 45-rpm single as soon as it was made.

They did send the single of "Rock Lobster" with "52 Girls" on the B side. It was the most fun I'd heard on vinyl in a very long time. The sound was kooky, the lyrics were wildly Dada-esque. The singing and playing were something else—like the Ventures meets the Shangri-Las meets Paul Lynde at Yoko Ono's house. They said they were planning a gig in New York and we encouraged them to call CBGB. They did call CBGB and sent a tape and, strangely, they got a negative response. I didn't know this or I would have marched right over there and vouched for them, even though I had yet to see them play. I can't believe Hilly made the decision. More likely it was some new guy. So the B's ended up playing at Max's Kansas City instead.

My brother Roddy and me after his Urban Verbs show at Hurrah.

Gary went with Tina and me to the show and we loved them. They were the most fun of any new band we'd ever seen and the songs were completely original. Even though Max's only allowed them to play a very short set that night, they made a huge impression on everyone there. Tina and I invited them to spend the night in our loft, but they said they had to get back to Athens, Georgia, and left right away. That was a long haul for a very short gig, and knowing Max's, probably not even enough money to pay for gas.

My brother, Roddy, was the vocalist in a great band in Washington, D.C., called the Urban Verbs. They were very artistic, hip, and going places. Roddy's good friend Bill Harvey organized a gig at the Corcoran School of Art with the Urban Verbs and the B-52s. They had played together at CBGB—yes, the B's finally got their gig at CBGB—and it was a winning double bill. Bill made a poster and put it up around D.C. The demand for tickets was so high that Bill added a second show that night. The B-52s drove up from Athens. Tina and I took the train down from New York with Gary Kurfirst, who was very interested in managing both bands. We arrived just in time for the second show. It was completely sold out and a number of A&R people were in the house, including Karen Berg, who had signed Television to Warner Records, and Bob Krasnow, also of Warner.

The energy and enthusiasm for both bands was elevated to the extent that we New Yorkers were very impressed. Both bands were on fire, too.

I introduced Gary to the B-52s and the Urban Verbs after the show. I remember telling them that Gary would be able to represent them and I recommended they each meet with him next time they were in New York.

Not long after that, while standing in front of the Compass Point Studios, Chris Blackwell asked Tina and me if we could sign any new band in the world, which would that be? We told him, "Either the B-52s or the Urban Verbs." The fact that Gary would be managing the B's swung the deal in their direction. Bob Krasnow went on to sign the Urban Verbs to Warners.

Gary and Chris Blackwell truly loved the B's. Their first eponymous album, produced by Chris Blackwell himself at Compass Point, was a wild success and went gold right out of the box. I was happy for them. Talking Heads did not have any gold records yet, but we did have a huge buzz on our live shows, so when we invited the B's to tour the USA with us, it was a magical pairing. They energized us. We ended up taking the B's to Europe with us, too. Every date was sold out. Their second album, *Wild Planet*, was a similarly huge success. They had it made.

One day I was sitting in Gary's office, just hanging out, when he got a call from the B's. I could tell by the look on his face that it was not good news. After he hung up, Gary turned to me and said, "I can't believe it. They want me to fire Chris Blackwell as their producer." This was a crazy move because not only had both the albums Chris produced been commercial and critical successes, but he was also the president of their record company! Gary said, "Guess who they want to produce them now? David Byrne."

I let that sink in. It seemed the B's were no longer satisfied with being a "tacky little dance band from Athens, Georgia," as they had often called themselves. Even though the Island Records bands were taken seriously and Chris was a far more experienced producer, they wanted the artistic caché they assumed David would bring them. David had never professed any love whatsoever for the B's the way Chris Blackwell had, but he took the gig. The album, later reduced to an EP called *Mesopotamia*, was the B's first non-hit album.

Tina and I, along with our son Robin and his nanny, Louise Kelleher, traveled down to Athens, Georgia, for Cindy's wedding to Keith Bennett on April 21, 1985. It was a beautiful, storybook Deep South wedding, really

wonderful. After the wedding I got food poisoning at the B's favorite Mexican restaurant and lost ten pounds overnight. I said to Cindy, "So that's how you keep your figure!"

We remained friends with the B's through thick and thin. Tina and I were delightfully surprised when, one day in late 1984, they asked us to play with them at the first enormous January 1985 "Rock in Rio" festival outside of Rio de Janeiro in Brazil. They had never had a bass guitarist. Kate played keyboard bass. Keith Strickland wanted to play guitar now and he invited me to play drums. We rehearsed at tiny Charles Lane Studio in the West Village. Tina and I had a ball playing with them. We took a little break for the holidays and then played a couple of warm-up shows in Worcester, Massachusetts, and out on Long Island. Then we flew to Rio.

We brought our baby son, Robin, with us to Brazil as well as Tina's sister, Laura, to look after him when we were busy playing music. Ozzy Osbourne was on the same plane with his new wife, Sharon, who was the daughter of the notorious UK music manager—and some say gangster—Don Arden. This was before Sharon had all that cosmetic surgery. She was doing a good job minding Ozzy, who was in a terrible state. It seemed like he was brain dead.

We checked into the five-star Copacabana Palace Hotel. We had a huge, beautiful suite with an ocean view in the front of the hotel. Ozzy had the same suite just one floor above us. On the street below us, a large gathering of fans were chanting at top volume, "Ozzy! Ozzy! Ozzy!" They went on and on until Ozzy made an appearance on his balcony, waved to the crowd, and raised his arms in the air like a heavyweight champion. The kids screamed with delight and then, when Ozzy went back into his room, picked up the chant again. This went on for days. I went down to the elegant bar for a caipirinha and met the guys from the German heavy metal band Scorpions. They were great guys, but all they wanted to know was, "Where's Tina?"

Later, when we were hanging out at the pool, Robin, who was two years old, said to Keith Strickland, "Keith, don't you just love nipples? Everybody has them!" Everyone around the pool cracked up at that one.

We had another rehearsal day at Gilberto Gil's "Studio In the Clouds" high atop one of Rio's mountains. We were joined by the super-groovy saxophonist Ralph Carney and trumpeter Dave Buck. The horns were so much fun and so were the horn players.

We traveled up the coast to a hip little resort town called Buzios, where

Brigitte Bardot had just spent a much-publicized vacation with her playboy boyfriend. It was a quiet little artist and musician's colony. Tina and I stayed in a little hotel and the B's rented a house together. While we were all out to dinner together, the B's belongings were stolen. That was very unsettling, so they headed back to Rio. Tina, Robin, Laura, and I stayed on for another day. We heard various bands of musicians playing samba tunes while marching over cobblestone lanes. We bought a beautiful wood carving of a nativity scene that we keep at our place at Compass Point.

The B's were scheduled to perform twice during the festival. Day one's lineup was:

- Queen
- The Go-Go's
- The B-52s (with Chris Frantz and Tina Weymouth)
- Lulu Santos
- Eduardo Dusek
- Kid Abelha e os Abóboras Selvagens

We arrived at the site via a large helicopter. As we flew over the festival, we saw that the crowd was truly enormous. The attendance was 1.4 million people over the course of the festival. When it was time for us to go on, Kate was late, still working on her hair and makeup. Apparently, she was always late, but this was not the kind of gig where you can be cavalier about your set time. The gigantic stage rotated so that while one band was performing, another could be setting up, and the one that had performed earlier could be tearing down. Finally, Kate was ready and the B's hit the stage. Tour manager Matthew Murphy breathed a huge sigh of relief and stayed with Tina and me until it was time for us to join the band after the third song. Tina was wearing a huge gold Mylar wig on her head and I was wearing a special matching paisley vest and turban I had had designed by a friend of Fred's. I got up on the drum riser and looked out over the 350,000 people in front of us, took a deep breath, and counted off the next song. Everybody in the place went nuts. When you play in front of an audience that huge, you have to operate on automatic pilot. You can't be concerned about any little mistakes or imperfections. You just rock, and rock we did! Ricky on guitar was especially fiery and fabulous.

After the show, Tina and I went over to the Go-Go's dressing room to say hello, but they were all crying! They had just decided to break up after playing the biggest show of their lives. Of course, years later they reunited.

The second night we played the lineup was:

- Yes
- The B-52s (with Chris Frantz and Tina Weymouth)
- Nina Hagen
- Blitz
- Gilberto Gil
- Barão Vermelho
- Erasmo Carlos

Everyone in the band loved Brazil. Brazilians really know how to party. Tina and I hung out with Frederic Serfati, our favorite promoter from Paris who had flown in for the show. One of our local record company people took us on a little walking tour of Rio at night. We came across a public square where James Taylor was performing unannounced with Caetano Veloso. They were singing Brazilian songs that had previously been banned by "the Colonels," the right-wing military government that ran the country until recently. This was the most marvelous experience. Just two guys with acoustic guitars and beautiful voices singing about freedom and love. James Taylor sang in Portuguese and he knew all of the songs by heart. I was told the night he performed at the festival, they had the highest attendance. Hundreds of thousands sang along with JT in English. The crowd loved the gorgeous melodies and they knew every lyric.

When we returned to the States, the B's started working on their next album, called *Bouncing Off the Satellites*. We hadn't seen them for a while so Tina and I invited them up to our new place in Connecticut for a party in early October. Our accountant, Bert Padell, had told us we should buy a house and we had found the perfect place in southern Connecticut, just over an hour's drive from New York City. The house was a barn-like structure with a large music room for rehearsing. It was built next to a large pond with Canada geese, wild ducks, turtles, foxes, and deer abounding. The neighborhood public schools were good and we had many well-known musicians, writers, and actors living nearby.

We were looking forward to seeing the B's again, but the morning of the party, I got a call from Cindy's husband, Keith Bennett, who said, "I'm sorry we won't be able to make it to the party. Ricky has died." It was difficult to process this. Ricky had always seemed so sweet, healthy, and *alive*. The news was shocking to everyone who knew him, because Ricky hadn't wanted anyone to know he was sick. He was only thirty-two years old.

Gary and his right-hand man Ira Lippy organized a memorial service of close friends that was held at the Brooklyn Botanical Garden, where a young tree was planted in Ricky's honor. Kate, Tina, and Laura stood beside the tree and sang a lovely a capella "Under Your Shade" by George Frederick Handel. Then we moved into a small pavilion, where I had been asked to deliver a eulogy. It is one of the great regrets of my life that, standing on a chair, I was unable to say more than two sentences before I broke down and wept and never regained my composure enough to carry on. I hope people understood that all of a sudden, the grief was simply too much to bear. There was so much love for Ricky. It was a terribly saddening time for all of us who knew him. How would the B-52s ever recover from it?

We lost touch with each other. For a long time the B-52s were inactive. They went silent. They did not return phone calls. Gary wanted to meet with them but they wouldn't respond. Then one day Gary found out they had decided to get another manager. This was heartbreaking for Gary, who adored them, though they probably didn't realize that. Gary was from a different culture than the band, and sometimes I think they didn't understand each other. Gary sent Ira to tell them they had been dropped by Warner and Island, but that he would sign them to his new label, Radioactive. There was a court battle and Gary won. Now the B-52s would have to pay two managers.

Still, they pulled themselves together and created their biggest hit ever with the help of producer Don Was. "Love Shack," from their album *Cosmic Thing*, was a great, great song and a huge seller. Also in heavy rotation on MTV were "Roam" and "Deadbeat Club" from the same album. The B-52s were back!

Tom Tom Club, the musical collective Tina and I formed in 1981, played a few shows with them here and there. We were an excellent double bill.

They invited Tina and me to play with them on a couple of songs when they were celebrating their twenty-fifth anniversary at Irving Plaza in New York City in 2001, and that was a great pleasure. Yoko Ono sang with them that night, too. Backstage, she was a real sweetheart.

Keith sent Tina and me a bottle of Cristal champagne in 2002 when Talking Heads was inducted into the Rock and Roll Hall of Fame. When we drank it, we toasted each of them—Keith, Ricky, Cindy, Kate, and Fred—by name. By the way, they are still touring the world.

40

DICK AND PHIL

In early March 1979, we flew to Los Angeles at the invitation of Dick Clark to perform on his classic teen television show *American Bandstand*. As usual, we stayed at the Sunset Marquis. We loved to hang out by the pool there and chat with the movie stars like Sonia Braga and director Hector Babenko, who had a hit with *Kiss of the Spider-Woman*, with music by Wally Badarou; rock stars such as Phil Collins, Bananarama, and Robert Fripp; and other nutty personalities like SCTV's Rick Moranis. The weather was warm and after a brutal winter in New York, living in a loft with no heat after business hours, I could see why so many people had migrated out there. The living was easier, for sure, at least until you tried to navigate the freeways.

We had a rental car and drove ourselves to the ABC Television Studios, where we were delighted to find the parking lot full of kids of all ethnicities practicing their dance moves and making costume changes. None of them had any idea who we were. Dick Clark taped as many as five episodes in a day and we felt amazed and honored to be featured on this program that we had watched every Saturday for years as young music fans.

Before our segment, Dick Clark himself came to our tiny little dressing room to fact-check the information he had been given about us. He was very bright, friendly, and kind and we were impressed that he had actually done his homework.

We had lip-synched on a few European TV shows, but this was the first time we had done it in America. Everyone on *American Bandstand* lip-synched and it felt a little bit weird on the rehearsal run-through, but we got settled into it. The song we performed was "Take Me to the River." Typically, Dick would ask the band a few questions after the performance and he directed the first question to David: "You don't like to categorize your music, do you?" David replied simply, "Not really, no." Then Dick asked him, "Are you a shy person?" To which David replied, "I think so." I couldn't help but notice that David's very curt response took Dick Clark by surprise to the extent that the hand he held his mic in started shaking. David had managed to make even the unflappable Dick Clark feel uncomfortable. He quickly pivoted on his heels and turned to Tina. He asked her what we were hoping to accomplish with our band and Tina said, "Well, it may sound kind of highfalutin, but we want to make our mark in music history."

When you appear on nationally broadcast television, people really notice and show you respect, whether you are worthy of it or not. After appearing on *Saturday Night Live* the month before, in February, when Bill Murray swept Tina off her feet and danced with her during the closing segment, we went to the after-parties, first at an Upper East Side Italian restaurant, where Tina and I sat with Gilda Radner, who was a very sweet and lovely person.

We want to make music history.

Then we went downtown to an unmarked bar called the Black Rhino Club, owned by John Belushi and Dan Aykroyd. Belushi was being guarded by some big guys to make sure he didn't do any cocaine. He just stood by the bar like a statue and spoke to no one. Shortly after that we played *American Bandstand* and Talking Heads became a household name. We had become almost a mainstream band—not quite, but almost.

Seymour Stein thought that our next album should be produced by Phil Spector and since we were in Los Angeles he set up a meeting. We did love his "Wall of Sound." After hearing the well-known stories about Phil and how he treated women, especially Ronnie Spector, Tina had zero interest in meeting him and even less interest in working with him, but she could see that the rest of us were interested, so she went along with us. We arrived on time with Seymour at his favorite upscale Chinese restaurant called the Mandarin and ordered a round of drinks. I asked for a Mai Tai. As we continued to wait, I had another and then another. When Phil Spector finally arrived—over an hour late—we were all pretty tipsy but excited to meet him. Phil Spector is not a tall man, but he had a very tall woman on each arm. He said to Seymour that they were his bodyguards and were trained in karate. He was wearing a gray, double-knit three-piece suit with a purple silk tie and Beatle boots. Was that a wig or a toupée? He made no apology for being late. Tina started to say something and he said dismissively, "Great bass player but you don't talk. Just keep quiet and play the bass." Tina looked at me as if to say, "Now you see why I didn't want to meet this jerk?" After that, if we spoke to him, he whispered into one of his bodyguard's ears and she would then reply to us. Even Seymour, who had idolized Phil for years and still calls him a genius, was getting weirded out. Finally, I asked Phil what it was like working with John Lennon and he gave me the evil eye and clammed up altogether. At that point, we couldn't wait to get out of there. Seymour could see very clearly that this was not the meeting of the minds he had hoped it would be. Later on he had better success with the Ramones, who agreed to be produced by Phil and who then, with the exception of Joey, really regretted it. Even though we immediately realized Tina was right, none of us would have predicted that Phil Spector would one day become a murderer. We left the meeting with Phil Spector the genius with the impression that he was crazy. As a producer he was as completely wrong for us as Brian Eno was completely right.

41

FEAR OF MUSIC

We had the idea to record our next album right in the loft where Tina and I lived. The music for the album had been mostly written, arranged, and rehearsed there and we felt that the acoustics of our rehearsal space would make for an interesting contrast in sound to our previous two albums. Eno was keen on the idea, too. We hired the Record Plant Mobile for the occasion. We would record the basic tracks on two separate Sundays when there was very little traffic noise leaking in from outside. Robert "Kooster" McAllister parked the mobile truck outside of our building and ran the mic cables up the stairs to our loft on the third floor.

After getting a good sound on all the instruments, we played each song as if we were playing a live show. Brian sat in the mini control room in the truck with engineer Rod O'Brian, who recorded everything. We had been working on these songs for weeks, and our playing was really energetic and tight. We had two highly regarded albums under our belts and this new one had to live up to our own standards of excellence, never mind everyone else's.

The songs we recorded most often grew out of extended jam sessions. We developed a process where we would jam until we had a cool groove and tempo happening. Then we would record a snippet of that on our portable cassette tape recorder and call that an A section. We would then return to jamming until we had created a B section, record that, and then

practice transitioning between, say, eight bars of A, and eight of B. When we felt comfortable, we would improvise a C, or bridge, section. Then we would arrange the various parts and play them together and record that. The music was a real collaboration. David would take that cassette home with him to write lyrics. In the case of "Life During Wartime," the song began as a jam between Tina and me. The entire song, including the vocal melody, is based on Tina's part. It's also interesting to note that, though he did come up with fantastic lyrics, David later credited himself as the sole writer of the song. This happened to us all the time with David. He couldn't acknowledge where he stopped and other people began. This song about urban guerillas became the hit of what would become the album *Fear of Music*.

"Heaven" was conceived as a song in the style of Neil Young. We all admired Neil's songwriting skills. I can remember my roommate from RISD, Huey Roberts, commenting, "If Neil Young's voice gets any higher he's going to sound like a newborn kitten." The lyrics are pretty cynical and it's ironic that some people have chosen this tune as their wedding or funeral song. Can it really be anyone's idea of heaven that it is a place where nothing ever happens? Weird.

I can still hear Beatle-esque qualities in the songs "Paper" and "Memories Can't Wait," although at the time we would not have heard that. "Memories Can't Wait" may be the darkest-sounding track on the album and "Paper" may be the brightest, but both of them boasted new sounds for our band. We were reaching a broader scope.

"Animals" and "Electric Guitar" were a return to our nutty, uncompromising art school roots. There was no chance either one would get any radio airplay, but both songs were so out there musically and conceptually that they screamed "Not Selling Out" to our fans.

"Mind" and "Air" were among the most thoughtful and relaxed-sounding songs on the record. The grooves we established in these songs did not have the high-pressured tempos of punk or new wave. They were more laid back while retaining some of that Talking Heads tension. A song about needing something to change someone's mind was not a new idea, but mixing it up with time, religion, money, and drugs gave the lyrics a deeper meaning. A song about the air not being your friend was one of David's interesting lyrical points of view. He took something everyone needs to survive and made it into an enemy. I remember him telling us that his

Scots grandmother once warned him, "Trust no one, Davy. Even your own asshole will let you down." I think that's what this song is about.

After we got the basic track of "Air," we invited Tina's sisters Laura and Lani to join Tina on background vocals. The sweetness of their three voices combined was simply wonderful and not lost on me. Tina and Brian decided to credit their background vocals as the Sweet Breaths.

"Drugs" more or less speaks for itself. We had been performing the song around the world as "Electricity," but I guess David decided to call this song exactly what it is, a song about the influence and effects of mind-altering drugs. The eventual dub-wise mix on the album is really like a drug experience itself.

"Cities" was as close to a touring song as Talking Heads ever did. Beginning with "Think of London, a small city." Take that, London. Birmingham, El Paso, and Memphis are also brought into the mix with weird David Byrne–style observations about each. David's scratchy rhythm guitar is punctuated by Jerry's Yamaha CP-70 electric piano, but Tina's bass again provides the melody for what is essentially a spoken word vocal.

The album begins with a song called "I Zimbra." The basic track was recorded as an instrumental. There were no words yet. This particular track, with its Nigerian High Life influences and the way it came into being though jamming, was the template for composing our next album, *Remain in Light*. When I say the influences were from Africa, that is for sure. But none of us were African. We were rock musicians who were looking for a way out of what had become a very predictable formula for playing and performing rock and roll. The African music we loved had the energy and the passion of rock and roll, but with one big difference. It was not based on Chuck Berry licks. I played my most minimal drum part ever, consisting of only bass drum and high hat playing a funky disco beat. I did this not only because I liked funky disco, but because I was loath to tread on Tina's, Jerry's, and David's beautifully intertwining guitar parts. Dance music, or "Disco," was wildly unpopular with the punk set, but we never shared this feeling. This song was a giant breakthrough for us, and not a style that I think anyone outside the band had anticipated. We just needed some lyrics. Eno also saw this song as an important move forward for us and suggested we use a sound poem by Dada poet Hugo Ball called "Gadji Beri Bimba." Hugo Ball, a German poet who wrote the Dada manifesto and founded the

infamous Cabaret Voltaire in Zurich, had performed this poem there in 1916. We adapted parts of the poem to chant over our recorded track:

> *Gadji beri bimba clandridi*
> *Lauli lonni cadori gadjam*
> *A bim beri glassala glandride*
> *E glassala tuffm I zimbra*
> *Bim blassa galassasa zimbrabim*
> *Blassa glassala grandrid*
> *A bim beri glassala grandrid*
> *E glassala tuffm I zimbra*
> *Gadji beri bimba clandridi*
> *Lauli lonni cadori gadjam*
> *A bim beri glassala glandride*
> *E glassala tuffm I zimbra*

Our loft had different acoustics from those of a proper recording studio, but we liked the sound we got there. It was pretty raw. The project then moved to the Hit Factory for some additional overdubs and vocals.

Two bassists: Tina with Corrine Marienneau of Telephone.

Like Brian, Robert Fripp was now living in New York City. We would see him around town at various clubs and parties. Robert and Brian were good friends. They had made an avant-garde album together called *No Pussy-footing*, where Robert used a system of delays and guitar effects he dubbed "Frippertronics." Eno thought he could come up with something interesting to add to "I Zimbra." We thought this was a great idea and Robert's part worked out really well. David heard a conga player named Gene Wilder—no, not *that* Gene Wilder—while walking through Central Park and hired him to play on "Life During Wartime" and "I Zimbra." That was a nice touch, too.

Talking Heads was on tour all summer. The first stop, after a twenty-hour flight, was New Zealand, where we were awarded a gold album for *More Songs About Buildings and Food*. The record company guy said, "You're bigger than Rod Stewart down here, mate!" I took a minute to let that sink in. We had a ball in New Zealand meeting delightful people and being chauffeured from show to show in his estate wagon by the promoter himself, Stewart MacPherson. As we drove through the scenic, rolling, green hills and valleys, Stewart would say things like, "I hope you like lamb. Our sheep outnumber our people twenty to one."

In Australia, every single show was sold out. In Brisbane, David and Jerry came to our hotel room all excited because they had received cassette copies of the mixes Brian had made for our new album. We played them on an excellent Sony boom box that Tina and I had purchased in Japan Town, San Francisco. We had used the same boom box to record live demos of the album before we recorded the basic tracks with the Record Plant Mobile. When we heard the mixes we were shocked. These mixes were not good, in fact they were terrible. They sounded very dull and unexciting and not at all the way we had performed them. Tina and I looked at each other in disbelief. I reached into my carry-on bag and pulled out the demos we had made and compared Eno's mixes to our portable cassette recorded demos. Guess what? The demos were audibly more exciting and dynamic than the finished mixes. We were a little freaked out. I called our live soundman Frank Gallagher and asked him to come and listen. Frank listened for a while and shook his head. I asked him what he thought. Frank said, "By the sound of it, Eno could nae mix a rice puddin'."

We decided that after the Australian leg David and Jerry would fly back

to New York to watch Rod O'Brian remix the record at the Record Plant. Tina and I proceeded to London, a twenty-four-hour flight with stops for refueling in Singapore and Mumbai. When we arrived in London we freshened up and went to see our friends Dire Straits headline the Hammersmith Odeon. They invited us to join them onstage for an encore of "Gloria." It was really good times and after the show Mark Knopfler gave us a lift back to the Portobello Hotel in his Volkswagen Beetle. The next day the *New Musical Express* said how excited the crowd was that David Byrne sat in with Dire Straits. It seems that the music press around the world was complicit in giving David credit for everything that any of us in the band did, even when we were standing right in front of them doing it. I couldn't hold this against David, but I do remember that I never once heard him speak up and say, "That was Tina's idea." Or, "Jerry gets credit for that." It seems he never learned about the sin of omission, or if he did, he simply didn't care.

42

PARIS TO JAPAN

We finished up a summer tour of festivals and clubs in Europe with a show at Le Palace in Paris. Our opening act was the B-52s, who were very well loved by the Parisian crowd. While waiting backstage to go on, we were visited by some VIPs. The great jazz drummer Tony Williams came by to say hello. Francois DuCray, the writer who had been an early champion of ours, brought us a fine bottle of wine from his hometown of Bourges. And, just before we were about to hit the stage, one of the Rolling Stones popped into the dressing room and said, "Hey, guys! You wanna do a line?" The rest of the band wisely demurred, but not me. I was the big Stones fan in our band and I felt like I could use a little pick-me-up, so I said yes. We went into another room and the Stone laid out a couple of lines that we both hoovered up. Immediately, I realized it was not cocaine but it was too late. On the way to the stage I did not feel good at all. Waves of nausea overcame me and, as I climbed onto the drum riser to play, I thought, *Why the hell did I do that?* I stared out at the audience and counted off the first song. When Tina, David, and Jerry all looked back at me as if something was wrong, I realized I had counted off the song way too slowly. Strangely, this did not worry me. What worried me was that I felt as if I was about to vomit all over my drum kit in front of an audience of thousands. Fortunately, I didn't. We played the entire set in slow motion, at least that was how it felt to me. The audience

didn't seem to notice; in fact, the reviews the following day said it was our greatest show ever in Paris. These kinds of things make you wonder. Let me also add that if you think I'm referring to Keith Richards, I'm not. Keith was not the only member of the Stones to use heroin.

Coming off the stage, Frederic Serfati, our favorite promoter in the world, was waiting. "Great show!" he exclaimed. I told him what had happened with the Rolling Stone and the white powder. Frederic said that as punishment he would not allow that particular rock star into the wonderful party he had planned for after the show.

The party was at Frederic's good friend Bernard Ossude's grandfather's grand Hotel Particulier in the center of Paris. Bernard was a friend and fan of ours, too, as was his beautiful sister, Diane, who we'd met at Compass Point when she was visiting Chris Blackwell and Natalie Delon. Their grandfather was the great art deco painter and sculptor Bernard Boutet de Monvel, and their great-grandfather, Maurice Boutet de Monvel, was renowned for his illustrations, particularly those he made of Joan of Arc. Part of their personal collection recently sold at auction for thirteen million dollars.

The party was fabulous. On this warm July night, in the inner courtyard of their home, surrounded by art and flowers, we partied in grand style with the belle monde of Paris. Tina was the belle of the ball, although Cindy Wilson and Kate Pierson of the B-52s were getting plenty of attention, too. Johnny Pigozzi took our photo for his vast collection of snapshots. What a wild night it was! Max Bell from the UK reported all about it in the *New Musical Express*. The article was called "Americans in Paris," but pictured only David, who still held a Scottish passport, on the cover. We didn't really care. We thought what was good for David was good for Talking Heads. Was that so naïve?

Next stop: Tokyo! We flew to Tokyo on Japan Air with a brief stop in Moscow for refueling. We had to get off the plane and spend an hour in the transit section of Moscow airport where it was mandatory to change at least ten dollars into rubles. If you used the bathrooms, which had no fixtures but only a hole in the floor, that cost you five dollars. Everyone who worked there had warts on their faces. I couldn't wait to get back on the plane to the lovely, sweet Japanese flight attendants and their never-ending supply of sake and sushi.

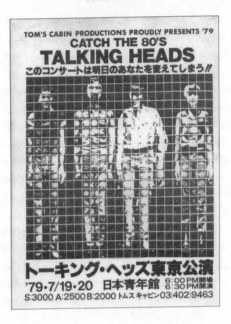

Arriving in Tokyo, we were met by our promoter Hiroshi Asada and his right-hand man, Ken Watanabe, not to be confused with the actor. These guys were young, smart, and hip, just the way we liked our promoters to be. Just one thing went wrong. While the band had all the proper visas and work permits, Gary had forgotten to get a visa so they put him on a plane to Seoul, South Korea, where he had to go to the US Embassy and pay for a rush job of the necessary paperwork and then fly back to Japan. When it comes to immigration, the Japanese do not play. Our crew, Frank Gallagher and Ace Penna, made the arrangements for our gear while we climbed into a very comfortable transit van with Hiroshi and Ken. It was a long ride to the hotel, but when we arrived we were greeted by dozens of cute young Japanese fans. This had never happened to our band before. It was like mini-Beatlemania. We sat in the hotel restaurant and recharged our batteries with more sake and tempura before Tina and I took the elevator upstairs and collapsed exhausted into our very inviting hotel bed.

The next day was a press and photo day. Everything was very well organized by the record company. There was a lot of interest in Talking Heads. We appeared on TV and radio, and when Gary finally arrived from Korea,

we were scheduled for dinner with the record company. These were the top executives at Warner-Pioneer. They took us to a very private restaurant where you roll your own sushi and drink while sitting on tatami mats, surrounded by shoji screens. The men were delighted to see Tina fearlessly swallow a live wriggling shrimp. Tina was becoming a very adventurous eater. After much laughter and toasting, when we stood up to leave, Gary fell over backward through the shoji screen and into the party seated next to us. The Japanese people, including the party Gary landed on, thought this was hilarious. Gary was mortified, but one of our record company guys explained that Japanese people are so regimented and formal that they take great pleasure in seeing other people acting up when they've had too much to drink. Not to worry.

The design crew, who designed the souvenir concert program for the tour, came to our hotel to show it to us. We all liked what they had done. Their names were Toshi Nakanishi, Chica Sato, and Hajime Tachibana. They were super stylish and charming and they were starting a band called Plastics. We were invited to go to their studio to jam. Well, we don't usually go to jam with people we don't know, but this was a hoot. When we got to their studio it was really tiny and full of bright plastic toy instruments. Those were what we jammed on and we really had a good time with them. The sound of the toy instrument jam was cute but mind-boggling, especially with a bad case of jet lag. They have remained our good friends over the years, although sadly, Toshi recently died. When we think of Japan, we think of Plastics.

The shows were great. As is the custom in Japan, we played some matinees as well as nighttime shows in lovely modern theaters, except for in Kyoto, where we played a very funky, deconsecrated temple near the university campus. We spent the night in a very traditional country inn where the men are separated from women. All the men sleep in one room and the women sleep in another. Gary hated that arrangement, not to mention having to sleep on tatami mats with little adzuki bean-filled pillows.

We returned to Tokyo on the high-speed bullet train for some more shows. Ace was overjoyed to find his Haliburton briefcase full of cash, thousands of dollars, exactly where he had left it on the platform of the train station. The cash inside was untouched. Incredible.

After checking into our hotel, I decided to go up to the bar on the top

floor for a drink. It was a very quiet scene in the bar with only one other customer: Iggy Pop. I had seen Iggy around New York, but we had never properly met until now. I introduced myself and he invited me to sit next to him at the bar. He was on a promotional tour and not doing any live shows. We talked a little about David Bowie and Brian Eno, but what Iggy really wanted to talk about was arms dealing, drug dealing, and money laundering. Some of his ideas sounded like nutty conspiracy theories to me, that our government could be involved in such things, but they all turned out to be true. Iggy is no fool and he could really hold his scotch.

We really hated to leave Japan. If you've ever been, you know why. It's the people and their hospitality. For a traveler, this means everything. Also, they have a great appreciation of all the American arts, particularly our music. When Tina and I walked through the park near our hotel on a Saturday afternoon, we were surprised to see all Japanese doo-wop groups, rockabilly bands, soul singers, and jazz cats busking for crowds of people who were dressed in the same style costumes as the bands. They were having a crazy good time and the bands all sounded very true to the originals.

We had a gig booked in Honolulu so that we could spend a couple of days in Hawaii on the way home. Our hotel was right on Waikiki Beach. It was almost sunset when we checked in and, while Tina was freshening up, I decided to take a walk on the beach. The sun was going down and there were plenty of people walking the beach. A young Hawaiian teenager approached me and asked in a friendly way if I was looking for "Da Kine." This was the best strain of Hawaiian marijuana. I had some per diems in my pocket so I said, "Sure, just a little bit." Before I knew it, a big guy was poking a knife in my back and telling me to hand over my cash, my wallet, and the new watch I had just purchased in Tokyo. I said, "You must be joking." He poked me a little harder with the knife and said, "Does it feel like I'm joking?" Feeling like a fool, I gave him what he wanted. A few days later, the Honolulu police called me to let me know they had my wallet. They caught the thief trying to use my credit card. He was going to jail. We definitely weren't in Japan anymore.

43

REMAIN IN LIGHT

Remain in Light, considered by many to be Talking Heads' greatest record, and by some to be one of the greatest recordings of all time, almost didn't happen. After the final show of the Fear of Music tour in Munich on December 19, 1979, we agreed to speak to an independent journalist who had traveled to see us from somewhere behind the Iron Curtain. I remember that his breath was very bad. He opened with the question, "What are you going to do now that David is leaving the band?" David had already spoken to him privately and told him this. Tina and Jerry and I explained to the journalist that we knew nothing about it and left it at that. Everyone was exhausted. We really needed a break and none of us wanted to deal with David's hurtful behavior. It had been a very fruitful and positive year for us. Christmas was coming. It was time for reflection and celebration.

After the holidays, I got a call from David asking if I would play drums on a basic track for a thing he was doing with Brian Eno. Tina thought that, to keep channels of communication open, I should do it. Jerry was nonplussed. So I went downtown to the studio, where I found David, Brian, Robert Fripp, and Busta "Cherry" Jones. We had met Busta before. He was a friend of Gary's who had played bass on some of Eno's records and had a band with Chris Spedding called Sharks. Busta was a very funky cat from Memphis, Tennessee. When I asked him why he called himself Busta *"Cherry"* Jones he

answered with a grin, "Why do you think?" We were asked to lay down a long, funky groove. Busta and I dug in deep and did that very well, I think. Fripp, all the while, was playing his Frippertronics with style, finesse, and with perfect posture while sitting on a high stool. The song would eventually be called "Regiment" on the Byrne/Eno album *My Life in the Bush of Ghosts*. David and Brian then decamped to San Francisco to make the rest of that album and we didn't hear any news from either of them for some months. Tina and I often wondered what they were up to out there.

It was usually up to me to be the person who reminded everyone in the band that it was time to make another record. Tina was ready. Jerry was ready. I was certainly ready. David and Brian, not so much. They were both back in New York, but evidently—and unbeknownst to us—some problem had occurred between them while they were making their album in San Francisco. When I called David, he expressed no interest in making another album with us. I called Brian and he said he wasn't interested in producing another album with us. What to do? Tina, Jerry, and I began improvising in our loft and recording everything on our Sony boom box for reference. After a couple of days, we had a few early scraps of songs that sounded very promising. Then Tina had an idea. She called Brian at his apartment on Eighth Street. She said, "Hi, Brian. I'm having a jam session with Chris and Jerry here in our loft. Why don't you come over and join us?" Brian said, "But Tina, you know I can't play any instruments." Tina told him, "It doesn't matter, Brian. We're just having fun. We're not going to judge your musicianship." Brian thought about it for a moment and said, "I'll be right over."

After jamming a few tunes with Brian, there was a good energy in the room and everyone was having a marvelous time. Then Tina called up David and said, "Hi, David. Brian's over here jamming with us and it's really great. Come on over!" David put down whatever he was doing and came to our place, guitar in hand, within the hour. Psychology is a funny thing, no?

Now things were starting to get interesting. I kept recording these little jams, and by nighttime we took a break to listen back. You could hear all kinds of interesting parts germinating, mutating, and evolving. There was nothing commercial or predictable about these little jams and, as we listened back, you could see smiles of surprise coming over our faces. There was just no denying that Talking Heads still had a great chemistry going on and the beats were good. You could dance to it!

We continued jamming for a week with very inspiring, if unpolished results. The creation of the song "I Zimbra" had pointed us in a new direction. The sound we were creating was a little bit art school, a little bit modern, and had a healthy dose of swinging African and Afro-American polyrhythms.

I suggested we ask Gary to book Compass Point. This time no one disagreed. We were all on board. David talked about how he would like to get away from the idea of the lead singer being in a dominant position. He felt that no one was more important than anyone else and the band should be presented as equals, which was surprising considering the way he usually treated the rest of us. This was music to my ears. Eno chimed in that we should use the recording studio as a tool for writing. He also said he would like to be treated as a fifth member of the band. We welcomed that idea. Since no real songs were written when we arrived at Compass Point to record, this is how we would proceed. The music would be created by the band members out of improvisation. All four members and Brian would be credited as writers. This was our verbal agreement going forward.

It was so sweet to be back at Compass Point. A second studio, Studio B, had been built and that's where we set up. Studio B was brand new and the Jamaican Chinese studio designer Chow, who had designed all of the Island Records studios, was on hand to make sure there were no problems. AC/DC was in Studio A with Mutt Lange recording *Back in Black*. Malcolm, Angus, Cliff, and Phil were lovely guys and this was their first recording with their new lead singer, Brian Johnson, after the death of Bon Scott. Brian had to take a break after screeching each line or he'd develop a migraine. He was under a lot of pressure as the new guy and when he signed on he didn't know he would be expected not only to sing but also to write the lyrics. He did a fantastic job. *Back in Black* became the third-best-selling album of all time.

In Studio B, record sales were the farthest thing from our minds. We began by jamming together in the studio. It felt good to be working with Rhett Davies again. He was the guy who recorded and mixed *More Songs About Buildings and Food*. Weirdly, after only three days of recording, Rhett announced he was leaving. When I asked him why, Rhett said, "Every time you play something that sounds like it could be a hit, Brian says it sounds

too commercial and nixes it. You could be a great pop group, but he won't allow you." Well, we were in accord with Brian. We loved pop music, we really did, but now we were interested in creating sounds that would take us deeper and far beyond what people had come to expect from us.

Brian suggested we call Dave Jerden, who had worked with Brian and David in San Francisco, and we all agreed to that. In the meantime, we would record with a young Jamaican guy named Steven Stanley behind the board. Steven, skinny as a beanpole with a huge puffy Afro hairdo, was only twenty-one years old, but already had a wealth of experience recording reggae music. They called him Youthsound. It was Stevie who recorded the basic track for what would become "Once in a Lifetime." We could have easily continued with Stevie as engineer, but when he would say, "Jerry, play for me," Jerry would just sit there not realizing he was being spoken to. The same thing would happen with David. Stevie's patois was just too difficult for them to understand. I guess they hadn't listened to as many reggae records as Tina and I: We understood him perfectly.

Dave Jerden came quickly to Nassau. He was a fun but no-nonsense guy and a seriously gifted engineer. Tina and Jerry and I took to him right away. Goodbye, Rhett. Hello, Dave.

My personal challenge and Tina's was to conceive and perform rhythm parts that not only grooved like crazy and propelled the song forward, but that also sounded shockingly new. Each song called for a unique part from us that bore no resemblance to any part we'd played before. Because there was no predetermined song structure or lyric, we had no idea where the verses and choruses and instrumental sections might be. So Tina and I created parts that were loops performed live. Then David and Jerry could superimpose their parts over ours. It was a very exciting process that required a lot of forethought. We could not simply revert to the tried-and-true chord progressions and familiar patterns of rock and roll. The fact that Tina and I were married and members of the same band did not mean that we agreed on every single thing, but we always had the band's best interests in mind. In fact, we sometimes made great sacrifices for the better of the band. I believe that Tina did this for me, because she knew how important Talking Heads was to me.

Some journalists have written about interpersonal squabbles during the recording at Compass Point. I don't know where they got that information. While the recording process was very challenging, everyone involved

rose to the occasion. It was important to be supportive of one another. Our friend Robert Palmer and his drummer, Dony Wynn, dropped in from time to time and joined in on some group percussion parts and handclapping, but otherwise all the playing on the basic tracks was by the four core members of the band.

At the end of the Compass Point sessions, David told all of us that he felt he needed more time to work on the lyrics. We were fine with that. We understood and we told him to take his time. Tina and I had a brief moment alone with Brian on the lawn in front of the studio. The sun was shining. The sea breeze was gentle and warm. I told Brian, "I'd like to thank you for being part of this project. We know your involvement made a big difference." I was struck by Brian's tepid response, as if he'd rather not be part of this conversation. This was surprising to me. It was as if he were disconnecting from me.

When Talking Heads made a record, we insisted on paying for the recording costs with our own savings. Ultimately, this could be well over one hundred thousand dollars and that did not include airfare, perdiems, and accomodations. We didn't send Warner or Sire the studio bills. That way, the record company could not bother us by coming around the studio to see what was happening with their money. They couldn't say they didn't hear a hit single. We would deliver to them the finished product. So, for *Remain in Light* and every other Talking Heads record, each band member paid 25 percent of the costs. That meant that "Chris and Tina" combined paid 50 percent of the recording costs. When the *Remain in Light* sessions resumed at Sigma Sound in the old Ed Sullivan Theater building in New York, this fact made David and Brian's attitude toward Tina and me truly appalling. It seemed as if they thought of us as sidemen who were no longer useful to them. At one point Brian actually said to us—in his most bothered tone of voice—"There are too many people in the control room." He was telling us to get out of our own recording session. David was complicit by saying nothing. Now that they had these groundbreaking tracks created by Tina and me together with David and Jerry to work with, they were now pushing us out of the picture. This felt hurtful. Clearly, David had forgotten his earlier statement that no band member was more important than any other. Now it was all about him and Brian, but mostly him. Their treatment of Tina was especially disrespectful: it was breaking her heart and in turn, my own. We turned instead to creating the album sleeve.

Tina's brother, Yann, had told us about the work he had been doing at MIT with an outfit called the Architecture Machine Group. They were inventing software for the US Defense Department and they were creating new graphic images with a humongous mainframe computer. This mainframe computer was as big as a house. Taking a tip from Yann and with his introduction, Tina and I drove up to Boston. We were met by Walter Bender and a charming young guy named Scott Fisher, who showed us around and explained some of what they were doing there. Scott couldn't tell us everything because we didn't have the proper security clearances, but he could show us how to create new digital images. Our intention was to create an arresting image that would somehow take the viewer by surprise. We had brought headshots of each band member, which Scott scanned and digitized. Then he scanned and digitized a photo Tina had brought of four Grumman Avenger airplanes like the ones Tina's father had flown in the Navy. We tried a few ideas but kept coming back to the idea of masks. Scott showed us how we could paint digitally on the headshot of each band member. After several tries with different colors we arrived at an image of the four band members with roughly painted red masks on their faces, and we were excited about that. We decided to keep that one as a possible front cover. Then we took a look at the image of the planes that were originally flying over a gray, flat Pacific ocean. While we worked on painting the masks, another guy from the Architecture Group, working from a different monitor hooked into the mainframe, delighted us by adding a background of the Himalayan Mountains to the photo of the planes. Then he printed the image and brought it to us, very excited to be part of our little collaboration. The working title of the album was *Melody Attack*, so this combination worked perfectly. Digital technology is commonplace now, but in 1980 it was totally cutting edge. Tina and I were very pleased with these images and, thanks to Scott and the other people at the Architecture Machine Group, we felt certain we had the makings of a great cover.

Returning to New York, we arrived at the studio where David was working on the vocal for "Crosseyed and Painless." David had come to an impasse: He didn't know what to do with what would become the "Facts are simple and facts are straight" part of the song. Eno's deck of Oblique Strategy cards, which had served us well up to this point, were no help. David and Brian were both at a loss. This is why it's good to have the band

members present in the studio. I said to David, "You know, there's this new thing called rap. You don't have to sing. You don't need a melody. You just rap the lyrics. Here, just listen to this!" Then I put a brand-new record called *The Breaks* by Kurtis Blow on the turntable. "Why not try that in this section?" David went out to the mic and nailed it on the first take. Bam!

While we were in Boston, Adrian Belew, who was on tour with David Bowie, stopped by the studio and overdubbed radically intense guitar solos on "Crosseyed and Painless" and "The Great Curve." We also added the extraordinary percussionist José Rossy to a number of tracks. Eno's friend Jon Hassel overdubbed a truly freaky and transporting trumpet solo on "Houses in Motion." Finally, the great Nona Hendryx added formidable multilayered background vocals and the recording was done. Oh, wait. I remember Dave Jerden secretly asking Tina to replay some of her bass parts that Brian Eno had erased when he and David thought they had a better idea, but their bass parts killed the groove. Dave was seriously bugged by this: The swing was gone. So Tina replayed her original parts and everything was tight, swinging, and grooving again.

Mixing *Remain in Light* was a daunting task because of the myriad parts that needed to be arranged and edited. It was meticulous work, but Dave Jerden made sure that in the end it sounded new and exciting.

The band and Eno were in agreement that the cover art Tina and I had created enhanced the music and the image of the band. The guys at MIT asked that we not use their full names because they figured that, even though they were big fans of Talking Heads, the US Department of Defense might not like that software designers on their payroll were moonlighting on some rock band's album cover. Therefore we used their computer handles, HCL, JPD, DDD, WALTER GP, PAUL, and added our own, C/T (which stood for Chris and Tina).

We had been approached by an interesting new graphic design firm called M&Co that said they would oversee the entire cover production for us and make sure Warner's quality control did its job. Tibor Kalman designed the lettering for the cover from Tina's instructions and had the clever idea to turn the two As in Talking Heads upside down. We liked that idea. Of course, Tibor, who originally offered to do this job for free, ended up charging us a fortune and taking credit for the whole thing.

Brian had some suggestions for titles; the one we liked the best was

Remain in Light. He said he had gotten the idea from an African poet and author he had been reading who was and remains unknown to us.

Brian called a meeting at his label/management office, EG Records, to determine the songwriting splits. We all arrived chipper and clear-headed. Brian said he had determined that if we each wrote down on a piece of paper what we thought the splits for each song should be, then we could average those out and arrive at a fair conclusion. Before we began recording, knowing that all five of us would be involved in the composition of the music, we agreed that the music writing share would be split evenly among us, but Brian and David reneged on that agreement. When we tallied up the splits and averaged them out, Brian was vexed. He stood up and said, "I have never felt so disrespected in my entire life!" Then he stormed out, leaving the rest of us wondering what had just happened. Brian was lucky we agreed to give him anything. In fact, Brian had wanted the album to be called *Remain in Light by Talking Heads and Brian Eno.* We asked Gary to talk sense to him. Gary said to Brian, "You know there will be a six-month-long promotional tour following the release of the record. Are you ready to commit to that?" Brian replied, "No, I couldn't possibly do that. I don't tour." So Gary said, "Well, we can't say the album is by Talking Heads and Brian Eno because your fans will be so disappointed that you are not on the tour."

We all agreed that writers' credits on the album cover should be "All Songs by David Byrne, Brian Eno, Chris Frantz, Jerry Harrison, and Tina Weymouth." The names were in alphabetical order. When we signed off on the final album cover at M&Co, this is how it was. Well, evidently David couldn't help himself and probably Brian was in on it, but when we received our advance copies of *Remain in Light,* the writing credits on the cover had been changed to "All Songs By David Byrne, Brian Eno, Talking Heads." On the lyric sheet inside the album, the credits had been changed to "All Songs by David Byrne and Brian Eno, except 'The Overload' and 'Houses in Motion' written by David Byrne, Brian Eno, and Jerry Harrison." There was no mention of Tina and me. We had been told another untruth by David Byrne, and so had our listeners. This was especially hurtful because, without our persistence, love, and musicianship, *Remain in Light* would never have been made.

44

THE BIG BAND

Before we released *Remain in Light,* we were invited to play a big festival outside Toronto called Heatwave. They called it the New Wave Woodstock. Other bands that were booked were the Clash—who never turned up— Elvis Costello, the B-52s, the Pretenders, Rockpile, Holly and the Italians, plus Canadian bands Teenage Head and the Kings.

David and Brian had insisted that it would be impossible for the original four members of the band to reproduce *Remain in Light* onstage, therefore there would not be a tour supporting the album. Of course, this was crazy. By working very hard, Talking Heads had established itself as a premier touring band and we had a selection of very exciting new songs to add to our repertoire. There had to be a way.

We decided to try expanding the lineup of the band in order to cover all the parts on the new album. Gary got in touch with bassist Busta "Cherry" Jones, who in turn called up some great players on our behalf.

First he called up Bernie Worrell, the extraordinary keyboard player from Parliament Funkadelic. Bernie had never heard of Talking Heads, but he'd recently parted ways with P-Funk and was game to try something new. Growing up in Plainfield, New Jersey, Bernie used to sit on his mother's lap at the piano and was interpreting Mozart by the age of four. He eventually entered the New England Conservatory of Music. In addition to his love of

classical music, Bernie liked to get down with jazz and funk. He had perfect pitch, too. We all learned a lot from Bernie, who was a wonderful human being.

When Busta called percussionist Steve Scales, he left a message with Steve's mom, who took two weeks to give the message to Steve. She was frightened by the gruff sound of Busta's voice. She thought he might be a gangster and a bad influence on Steve. Steve and his mom lived in Red Hook, Brooklyn, where you couldn't be too careful. Steve was a thrilling percussionist and showman. He had spent several years in Vietnam as a drummer in the US Marine Corps Band. The band would stand on the tarmac in extreme jungle heat in full dress uniform waiting for senators and congressmen to arrive from the USA. Steve said guys would keel over left and right. When we met Steve he had just finished a tour with R&B greats Ashford and Simpson. Steve had never heard of Talking Heads either, but he came to meet me at Sigma Sound one day. I gave him a cassette of some of our set to listen to. When he heard our version of "Take Me to the River" he told me he said to himself, "These white people just want to get down and play some funk." Steve was in.

Dolette McDonald was a tiny thing with a beautifully powerful voice. Stylish and pretty with a charming demeanor, Dolette met Busta working on disco records in New York in the late seventies. Like many soul and R&B vocalists, Dolette was brought up singing in church. Her family lived in northern New Jersey. Her parents were friends with legendary gospel singer Sister Rosetta Tharpe and her husband, the Bishop, who was their pastor. They were not happy at all when Dolette began singing "the devil's music" in New York City. Dolette had that pure gospel gift of being able to sing loud and clear with no showbiz affectations. Dolette had soul in abundance. She, too, had never heard of Talking Heads. After getting the call from Busta, Dolette was scared when she first came to meet us. She needn't have been. She fit right in.

Adrian Belew was a welcome addition on wild-and-crazy guitar. We had invited Adrian to join us onstage at gigs in Carbondale and Champaign-Urbana, Illinois, always great fun. Adrian was living in Springfield, and would travel to our gigs. Like me, Adrian was from Kentucky. He had good Southern manners. He told us that he began his musical adventures as a drummer, but then he got mononucleosis as a teenager and was confined to

bed. He used this time to teach himself to play guitar. Adrian was a fast learner and became highly inventive on guitar. Frank Zappa plucked him from a bar band after seeing him play in Nashville. Then David Bowie hired him on the recommendation of Brian Eno, who had seen him playing with Zappa somewhere in Germany. Now, after playing his ass off on two songs on *Remain in Light,* Adrian would be performing live onstage with Talking Heads.

It was not my idea to invite Busta on the tour as the second bass player. I had a good deal of respect for Busta, but this was clearly an attempt to marginalize Tina. Did we really need two bass players? Busta was playing parts that Tina had already written and recorded, and I felt it was a dumb, unnecessary move to merely duplicate all of her bass parts. Tina held her own, though, and remained exemplary. She opened her heart to Busta as well as the other new players and our stage show became a truly unrivaled performance. Our band was making a transformation. Some people have written that the big band was a way for David to marginalize the original band and to aggrandize himself as the star of the show. I have no doubt that this is what David was thinking but, in spite of any Machiavellian plans on David's part, we were about to take the world to church. In the parlance of P-Funk, we were about to "turn the mutha out!" This felt powerfully good to me.

The idea was to try out the expanded lineup for two shows only: the Heatwave Festival in Canada, and the Wollman Skating Rink in Central Park, New York City. While we had always held rehearsals in our loft, the bigger band would need even more space, so we moved our rehearsals down the street to Pink Floyd's Britannia Row rehearsal space in Long Island City. This building was actually an old movie studio sound stage. Charlie Chaplin had worked there until the movie business moved to Hollywood and better weather. Pink Floyd owned the building and used it to store their mammoth PA system. We had been using part of their sound system for years, so we knew about this place that was right around the corner from the PS1 art museum, also in Long Island City.

Rehearsals were more of a getting-to-know-each-other party with not a lot getting done until I pointed out that we had a big festival gig in five days. This was the first time we had attempted to play the *Remain in Light* songs live so there was a lot of work to be done, but we got it together.

We flew up to Toronto the night before the show. All the bands were staying in the same hotel, so the scene in the hotel bar was nuts, but fun. It

was good to see Pete Farndon and James Honeyman-Scott of the Pretenders, who we'd met one night the year before at Le Sept in Paris. They were sweet guys and formidable musicians, but not much longer of this earth. I wish they had taken better care of themselves.

After a pretty good night's sleep, I woke up nervous, thinking of all the things that could go wrong with our performance later that day. Anxiety is the curse of the performing artist and boredom is the curse of the touring artist. After waiting around the hotel all morning, we were flown by helicopter to the festival. The crowd was enormous. We found out later that upward of 85,000 people were in attendance. Gary had planned it so that Talking Heads would hit the stage right at sunset and then the stage lights would all come on during our show. It was good timing.

To say that we were well charged by the time we hit the stage would not be an exaggeration. The ladies in the band were very circumspect about the rock and roll party favors available backstage. Adrian was, too, but the rest of us guys were partying full on. I remember Adrian was shocked to enter the men's dressing room tent to find us all huddled over the back of someone's beautiful guitar chopping out lines of cocaine. Let's just say that the blow went nicely with the cocktail of champagne, weed,

The big band onstage at Radio City Music Hall.

and Molson Ale. I had given everyone in the band sunglasses as a gift, the great big wraparound kind that you wear after having your pupils dilated at the eye doctor. The whole band, except for David, would be wearing these onstage when we made our entrance.

The B-52s finished a blazing set and it was time for us to do our thing. The crew made the changeover onstage. I'll never forget that Frank Gallagher replaced Tina's broken keyboard stand with an ironing board when no other was to be found. Frank announced, "Boys and girls, it's showtime!" We would begin with the four Talking Heads playing "Psycho Killer," so the audience would get a flash of recognition. All these kids needed was to hear Tina's bass part intro and we had them going. Next we played "Warning Sign" and "Stay Hungry." Then, on "Cities," Adrian, Steve, and Dolette came out onstage to the surprise of some puzzled fans in the front. The crowd was so massive that we could really only make eye contact with the kids down front. After "Cities," Bernie entered the stage wearing cutoff jeans, snakeskin cowboy boots, a fur jacket, and a ten-gallon cowboy hat! We launched into "I Zimbra" and the audience went delirious. The excitement level escalated through the rest of our set, which was crazy because none of these thousands of people had ever heard "Once in a Lifetime," "Houses in Motion," "Born Under Punches," and "Crosseyed and Painless" before. This was the first time we had performed these songs live. *Remain in Light* would not be released for two months, but this crowd was getting the raw uncut version right now and they were pulsating in time to the music. By the time we played the final song of the set, "Life During Wartime," the crowd singing the choruses was drowning out the band. As we left the stage, and heard the overwhelming roar of the crowd, we knew that we were on the right track. We had reached a whole new level. We returned for one encore only, "Take Me to the River." The new players helped to take this song higher and higher to the gospel place it had originally come from. As I played this wonderful song and looked over at Tina, I felt a more powerful love than ever before for her and a touch of the divine in my own heart.

The audience wanted more from Talking Heads but we had no more to give. Those were all the songs we had rehearsed. The kids down front lit a garbage fire under the stage. Poor Elvis Costello would have to wait an hour and a half for things to calm down before following our show, and by the time he did, we were long gone.

The next show was a few days later in Central Park. Our good friends, the band from Tokyo called Plastics, opened the sold-out show at Wollman Skating Rink. We loved the Plastics. It was a hot, sticky afternoon in August. Backstage, Tina and Dolette were making fashion decisions because fashion sends an important message. Tina always felt that she shouldn't wear the same thing that she wore the last time we played a particular town or city, because women in the audience notice these things, so she chose a set of outfits for each different tour. Nona Hendryx joined Dolette on background vocals for this special show. Nona arrived wearing a white Panama fedora and a white unitard that showed off her abundant curves. Seeing that Dolette was upset that she was about to be upstaged by Nona, Tina suggested she wear the fabulous purple Kenzo that Leigh Blake had given her, which was by far the sexier of the two dresses she had brought. Tina would wear the long summer shift my mother had given her to wear to our rehearsal dinner in Kentucky, but she would hike it up to keep cool under the hot stage lights. The two of them looked chic and cool and utterly feminine in flowery summer dresses. It was a girl-power move that made everyone happy. For my part, I wore white jeans and a black T-shirt emblazoned with the words NEW YORK CITY.

The set we played was the same as the one we'd played at Heatwave. The effect on the audience was just as dramatic. Again, we hit the stage just before sunset. The venue was completely packed with even more people outside on the hills looking over the walls. I always have at least a little bit of butterflies before a show, but I think we all had more confidence that night knowing what this band was capable of. We walked onstage to an increasingly loud roar of welcome. Here in New York we were a local band and this was one beautiful homecoming. From my position behind the drums I could see the entire band and their interactions. I could see David instantly sweating up his clothes. I could see Tina smiling, cool as she wanted to be. I could feel the powerful effect this super-funky new music was having on the crowd. They were not expecting the quantum leap our band was making right before their eyes. David said to the crowd, "We're not the same as we used to be."

Some people have called that evening in Central Park our band's most magical moment and maybe up until that point it was, but this band had a magical moment every time we played. With each city we visited, we never failed to bring the party and ultimately, the church.

Tina in Kenzo.

After the show, we all headed down to the Mudd Club to celebrate our wild show in Central Park. Drinks were on the house and the dance floor was packed all night long. The DJ played all of our hits. We danced to our own songs and that felt really natural and good. When Tina and I finally got home, took a shower, and got in bed together, we felt lucky to have each other, but something was missing. I got up to put on some music. I chose Al Green's album *I'm Still in Love with You*, and by the time I got back in bed and took Tina in my arms, nothing was missing at all.

TOM TOM CLUB

After our world tour with the big band and rocking the party in every city we visited, Gary told us that David wanted to make a solo album. I'm glad Gary told us because David gave us no warning that he wanted to do this. When we asked Gary how long this solo album would take he said, "Your guess is as good as mine."

When Jerry heard of David's solo project, his reaction was "Well then, I'm making a solo album, too." Seymour Stein gave both David and Jerry deals to make their solo albums.

Tina and I had no interest in making solo albums. We were very happy with our roles in Talking Heads. Our accountant, Bert Padell—whose clients included Alice Cooper, Blondie, Madonna, Robert De Niro, and Faye Dunaway—advised us, "You gotta do something. You only have two thousand dollars in the bank." The big band, fabulous as it was, had cost a fortune to keep on the road.

Tina and I decided to make a record as a collective with some other people, but first we would need a record company to back us. We felt by definition every band was a collective, including Talking Heads. When Gary went to Seymour about a deal for Tina and me, Seymour flat-out passed. He told Gary he couldn't afford three solo albums from Talking Heads.

Gary prodded him over a period of time and Seymour finally agreed to offer us a fraction of the amount he had offered David. It was not enough money to make a good single, never mind an entire album. It seemed to us that Seymour had not been paying attention to the real chemistry of Talking Heads. He, too, had come to believe David's lies of omission, as if Tina and I had merely been riding David's coattails.

Singer-songwriter Garland Jeffreys, who had a hit with a song called "Wild in the Streets" and was a friend of Lou Reed's, invited Tina and me to be his rhythm section on a new album he was making. We liked Garland and appreciated the offer but we didn't really want to be someone's sidemen. Bert Padell advised us against this idea, too.

Still, we had to make a living. Fortunately for us, Gary knew better than Seymour Stein the extent of our value to Talking Heads. In a moment of great empathy and deal-making, he called his old friend Chris Blackwell of Island Records. Gary knew that Chris liked us and we liked him. Chris had passed on Talking Heads, something that he had come to regret. Also, Tina and I had encouraged Chris to sign the B-52s, which he had, producing their first two albums that went gold right out of the box. Chris told Gary, "I understand the value of a good rhythm section. Have them come down to Compass Point and record a single. If I like it, they can make a whole album."

Tina and I were listening to a lot of dance, early hip-hop, and reggae music. When we would go out at night in New York, this was the kind of music we were grooving to at the Mudd Club. We thought we should make a record that would delight the downtown New York community that we were a part of, something unpretentious and downright funky for our friends to shake their asses to.

Who should we ask to produce this record? We felt there was only one man for the job and he was Lee "Scratch" Perry, the Upsetter, the Jamaican genius producer of the Wailers, Max Romeo, George Faith, and many others. Blackwell set up a meeting with "Scratch," who by good fortune was in New York City staying at the Howard Johnson's on Eighth Avenue where all the Jamaican bands liked to stay. When we arrived at the hotel at the appointed nighttime hour of 11:00 P.M., we phoned upstairs to Scratch's room and a woman's voice said, "Give us ten minutes and then

come on up." We waited in the coffee shop, where I saw Gene Simmons from Kiss, sans makeup, eating a late-night breakfast. It was not a pretty sight.

We knocked on Scratch's hotel door and it was opened by a young, petite, foxy-looking Chinese-Jamaican woman named Valerie, who worked for Island Records in Jamaica. She was assisting Scratch with his business in New York. Scratch had heard about Talking Heads and he was agreeable to meet with Tina and me. We told him what we had in mind to do and he said, "Yeah, man, me can do it. Will be great!" Then the phone rang. Scratch answered it, said a few words, and then passed the phone to me, saying, "You talk to him." Playing along, I took the phone and said, "Hello?" The voice on the other end said, "Hi, this is Steve Winwood." I was an enormous fan of Steve Winwood and had bought all the Spencer Davis Group, Traffic, and Blind Faith records. He said he was calling from England and I told him who I was, that Tina and I were meeting with Scratch about a project and—could he possibly call back later? Steve was completely cool and said, "No problem."

Before we left, we set the date with Scratch to meet at Compass Point. Valerie wrote our contacts down in her book and after smoking some good herb to seal the deal, feeling very excited, we said, "Good night. See you in the Bahamas." Scratch said, "Yes, man. Irie. I will be dere."

In March of 1981, we packed up our gear and flew down to Nassau. We would be moving into a new apartment building behind the studio on a hill overlooking the sea. In the Bahamas, rather than a street number, each building has a name. At Chris Blackwell's request, Tina came up with the name Tip Top and I named our little apartment Tom Tom Club. Tina's brother, Yann, and his partners, our friends from RISD, Peter Coan and Franklin Salasky, designed the interior for us. When it was finished, Chris Blackwell told us it was the most beautiful apartment he had ever seen. It was a large open space, similar to a loft, with gorgeous tile work, cathedral ceilings, and a terrace facing west with an ocean view. We paid for it in exchange for our first Tom Tom Club record. We thought we would be spending a lot of time there and we did. We were the first to move into the building while most of the other apartments were still being finished, and we were very happy to be there. It was a welcome change from living in Long Island City.

On the day we were scheduled to begin recording, Scratch was a

Tina gave me this bike for my thirtieth birthday.

no-show. This was not a huge concern, because the Jamaican producer had been known to run late for his appointments. Still, after waiting for two weeks, Gary finally reached Scratch on the telephone. He told him, "Chris and Tina have been waiting for two weeks. Are you coming or not?" Scratch said, "Yeah man, I'm coming, but I need to be paid a thousand dollars an hour." Gary said, "It sounds like you're trying to price yourself out of this gig, that's way too much money." Scratch replied, "No problem, man. We make the album in eight hours." This was clearly nuts and Gary told him so.

Tina and I decided to ask Chris Blackwell if we could produce the record ourselves with the young Jamaican engineer Steven Stanley, who had worked on *Remain in Light* and was waiting in the wings. Chris said, "Great idea. Go for it."

So Tina and I went into Studio B to cut a single. Grace Jones was in Studio A with Sly and Robbie, Wally Badarou, Barry Reynolds, Mikey Chung, and Sticky Thompson, with Alex Sadkin engineering. They were just beginning the great *Nightclubbing* album. Chris was requesting ideas for songs that Grace could cover and Tina and I suggested "Warm Leatherette" and "Walking in the Rain." Both of these songs were fantastic.

After two weeks of waiting around, I was more than ready to begin, but I was a nervous wreck inside. We didn't have any songs written. We began

Tom Tom Club in Studio B at Compass Point.

by using the same process we had used on *Remain in Light*. I would lay down a foundation of drums first. I programmed a percussion track on a drum machine to play along with so that the tempo would remain consistent for any future editing. After getting a seriously great drum sound on my kit, Stevie said we were ready to roll tape. I had a strong groove in mind to play, but much to my chagrin I soon realized that the Myer's Rum I had been drinking all day to calm my nerves had taken its toll. I had always been a guy who could hold his liquor, but listening to the playback I realized that I was drunk—in fact, too drunk to play. Tina and Stevie and assistant Benji Armbrister told me to go home and go to bed.

Despite my blowout the first day, we quickly made up for lost time to create the basic tracks for three songs over the next couple of days: "Wordy Rappinghood," "Genius of Love," and "Lorelei." For the beats I had in mind, I wanted something very club-wise and easy to dance to. I would lay down drums, Tina would add a bass line, then we'd take turns adding a simple keyboard part. For instance, for "Genius of Love," Tina played the Prophet-5 part, the *dee-deet* of bar one, then the *dee-deet* of bar two, and repeated that two-bar pattern for the whole song. I then added the corresponding syncopated *deet-deet* that lead back to the downbeat of Tina's *dee-deets* of bar two. Simple, but powerful. We made a pretty good team.

These were the days before sampling and sequencing, so if you had a particular sound in mind, you might have to create it yourself. For what would become "Wordy Rappinghood," I had the idea to put the sound of Jah knocking on the one at the top of every measure. None of the drums we had available made that God-like *BOOM*, so I drove downtown to Nassau's only music store. In the window sat a big fat tympani. I asked the clerk if I could try it out, and with one hit of the mallet, I realized this was the sound I had been hearing in my head. Usually tympani come in pairs, so I bargained the price down and said I would buy it if the man could deliver it to the studio right away. He did, and I overdubbed the huge booming sound at the top of every bar. Tina then added a low chunky part on the Prophet-5 synthesizer. Then I added a different sound. We can't even remember which one of us added the little galloping part.

At the end of three days, Chris Blackwell came to listen. He said, "Make an album. But first, make a single."

We agreed that Tina's sisters, Laura and Lani, would be ideal for creating a beautiful vocal blend with Tina the way they had on the Talking Heads song "Air." We flew them down to Nassau to become a part of our collective. Having Laura and Lani singing with her as they had done since they were kids gave Tina the confidence she needed. No lyrics had been written yet and Tina was torn over what direction to take. Then it came to her. She needed words, therefore the song should be *about* words! Assuming an eight-bar verse-and-chorus cycle of the rhythm bed the two of us had laid down, Lani, Tina, and Laura stood together in front of a single mic and sang in unison, *What are words worth? What are words worth? Words!* every eight bars. Then Stevie added two more mics and the ladies stood facing each other in a semi-circle so their voices would bleed into each other's mics as they double- and triple-tracked the same lines for a group effect.

This was a start, but we still needed a verse and a chorus. Stumped, the three went for a walk on the beach to clear their heads. Lani spontaneously began to skip and sing an old schoolyard chant remembered from their childhood. That gave Tina an exciting idea. When they arrived in the control room, she said, "You may laugh, but we would like to try something." They went to their mics in the studio, Stevie rolled the tape, Tina gave the count-in, and this is what they sang: *A ram sam sam! A ram*

Laura, Tina, and Lani sing "Genius of Love."

sam sam! Kuni kuni kuni kuni ram sam sam! A ka yéh yoopi a ka yéh! A roo a roo a ni ki chi!

When I heard this completely surprising vocal part, I thought, *Hallelujah!* Stevie and Benji were now dancing around the control room with pure joy. They couldn't believe how much fun it was, a totally unexpected surprise.

Now that we had a chorus, Tina set to work on verses of rhyming couplets all about words. I suggested that she simply *rap* the words which, without any practice, was actually harder than we thought. Stevie recorded her one line at a time so that she could give each line its own character and sound. To put the icing on the cake, she wrote some couplets in French. This song was destined to be truly international.

Now we needed some funky rhythm guitar and Stevie knew just the guy, a Bahamian cat named Monte Brown from the funk outfit T-Connection. Monte created a fast-driving syncopated rhythm part that inspired the girls to add another singing part at the end of the song: *You don't stop, you don't stop, you don't stop, and you don't stop!*

During the mixing of "Wordy Rappinghood," Stevie added a few effects, including a typewriter sound from a vintage sound effects record. He took his time mixing and, when he was finished, we called Chris Blackwell in to have a listen. I wish you could have seen the look on his face. After listening one time, he asked to hear the song again, beaming with pleasure.

I asked him what he thought, and he replied, "I think you should make a whole album. Meanwhile, we will release this song as a single. What do you call it?" "'Wordy Rappinghood,'" said Tina. Then he asked, "What are you going to call the band?" We already knew. In unison we replied, "Tom Tom Club." We never considered any other name.

46

GENIUS OF LOVE

We still had no record deal for Tom Tom Club in the USA, but Island quickly released the single "Wordy Rappinghood" in Europe and there was nothing but good news. In Belgium the record went to number one in the pop charts. In the Netherlands it went to number two. In Spain it landed at number three. In the UK it charted at number seven, France at number nine, and Ireland at number ten. These chart positions were higher than any of our Talking Heads records had reached, and on import in the USA, "Wordy Rappinghood" hit number one on the Billboard Disco chart.

This felt very good to Tina and me, but now we needed a follow-up single and album. We returned to Studio B at Compass Point.

We were determined to make music that sounded nothing even remotely like Talking Heads. We didn't need to compete with our own band. We were going to do our own thang.

Tina and I had started recording tracks with drums, bass, and keyboards. Back at the apartment, Tina, with Laura, made vocal demos over those recordings on Tina's TASCAM Portastudio. One of these was a super-funky little number that stood out from the rest. The source of inspiration for the groove was a new song by Zapp called "More Bounce to the Ounce." We loved this song in part because it was played at a slower, funkier tempo by far than so many other dance tracks of that period. It was very relaxed

Ready to lay it down.

and sexy while still maintaining a raw, hard edge. Produced by none other than Bootsy Collins of P-Funk and James Brown, and Roger Troutman, this song really turned us on. It was our departure point. Tina wrote some amazing words in tribute to our favorite soul, funk, and reggae artists, but wanted a third verse. I gave her these closing lines: "He's the genius of love. He's got a greater depth of feeling. Well, he's the genius of love. He's so deep!" She loved it and declared me a genius! So "Genius of Love" became the title. It wasn't until we were back in Studio B that she grabbed our attention with a throw away opening line, *Whatcha gonna do when you get outta jail? I'm gonna have some fun!*

After building a number of basic tracks, we invited Adrian Belew down to Compass Point to play some guitar. By this time, he had already performed on David's and Jerry's solo albums. We liked Adrian very much, so we also invited his wife and two young children to join us for two weeks. We paid for their airfare and expenses. They stayed with us in our apartment. His kids were very cute and sweet and we all had a wonderful time together. Adrian overdubbed guitar on six songs and on the seventh, an instrumental called "Tom Tom Theme," he masterfully played the strings of a grand piano with drumsticks. I dug that. With promises to return, Adrian left us in Nassau at the end of April to join and record with King Crimson

in London. We learned in June he used the guitar effect he'd come up with for a song we'd written called "L'Elephant" on a song King Crimson would call "Elephant Talk." Cool.

We had talked to Adrian about becoming a permanent member of Tom Tom Club as a singer and guitarist. Somehow, this was misinterpreted by Adrian. We later found out by reading an interview he did that he thought we were asking him to replace David in Talking Heads, as if we could do that. In addition to sharing credits and writers royalties with Adrian on the seven songs he played on, we showed our appreciation by asking Chris Blackwell—who was somewhat reluctant—to give Adrian an album deal. Adrian didn't share his plans with us, but returned in September to record that album, *Lone Rhino*. By that time, however, we had completed *Tom Tom Club* and departed Nassau. I guess prog rock was where he was really at.

After Adrian left, Laura and Lani returned to record the rest of the album vocals with Tina. I completely adored the vocal blend these sisters got together. Tina likened the sound to "naughty Catholic school girls," and who was I to disagree? Stevie was very particular in recording their vocal blend and the end result was gorgeous and unlike any other vocals I had ever heard.

Tyrone Downie, the young keyboard player for Bob Marley and the Wailers, played grand piano on "L'Eléphant." This was our antiwar song, although you might not realize it since the lyrics are all in French.

Monte Brown came to the studio again to play a lilting Bahamian-style rhythm guitar part on "Genius of Love." This sat well in the groove along with Adrian's snaking, slithery picking part.

We invited the incomparable Uziah "Sticky" Thompson, who was working with Grace Jones in the studio next door, to play his unique style of Jamaican percussion on "Lorelei" and "As Above So Below." He hit it out of the park, adding parts that sounded as organic as the jungle itself.

Finally, before mixing began, we invited Sly and Robbie to join Tina and me in adding handclaps on the backbeats of "Genius of Love." Stevie had the four of us stand in a circle around a Neumann U 87 microphone and clap along for the duration of the eight-minute track. Then he asked us to do it again and again and again until we had four tracks of handclaps, which he then mixed down to one. My hands were sore but what awesome clapping! Sly and especially Robbie were not prone to exaggeration but when they heard the playback with the line "Reggae's expanding with Sly and Robbie"

Robbie said, "Man, bus it straight to Paris! This is a hit!" Tina and I had that feeling, too. So did Chris Blackwell.

We still felt like art students when thinking about album covers and we loved the process, but this time we acted more as art directors. Tina and I decided to invite our friend Jimmy Rizzi to try his hand at it. Jimmy worked in a childlike style that Tina called "urban primitive." He lived and worked in a tiny SoHo storefront on Sullivan Street, where we would sometimes drop by and smoke a joint. He always had a good supply and we enjoyed his company. We called Jimmy up and proposed that he bring his art supplies down to Compass Point and create an album cover for us. We did not have to twist his arm. Jimmy arrived, hung out with us in the studio and by the pool, and within a few days we had a super-wild album cover that featured Jimmy's idea of what everyone who worked on the album looked like. Tina printed the lettering for the song titles and credits in her own hand. Later, Jimmy and Laura flew to London to create an amazing animation video for "Genius of Love" from thousands of Jimmy's drawings with directors Rocky Morton and Anabelle Jankel of Cucumber Studios. Their studio was in the same building David Bowie posed in front of for the cover of *Ziggy Stardust and the Spiders from Mars*. The video was delightful and was featured by comedian Steve Martin in his first TV special. At the moment, it has over 11 million views on YouTube.

We still didn't have a deal for the USA, but by the time Chris Blackwell had sold 150,000 "Genius of Love" twelve-inch singles imported from the UK into the USA, Seymour woke up and saw the light. He asked Gary how much we wanted for the album. Gary said, "I'm sorry, Seymour, but I don't think there's enough money in the world for Chris and Tina to make a deal with you." Seymour said, "Oh Gary, just tell me how much they want." Gary, who knew how much we loved boating, said, "Enough to buy a yacht."

It's such a wonderful feeling to have created a hit record. It was not a feeling I ever expected to have. Back in New York City, I was walking west on Houston Street and as I turned up Sixth Avenue, where a number of basketball courts are located, I stopped in my tracks. Every player had his boom box tuned to WBLS and they were all blasting our "Genius of Love" megamix out into the atmosphere. The feeling I got inside brought tears of joy to my eyes. Then one day Tina and I were riding in a checker cab downtown with Gary and David. Gary said, "Guess what? The *Tom Tom Club*

Tina by the pool at Compass Point.

album went gold today." I wish he had picked another time to tell us this good news, but I guess he had his reasons. It should have been a time for celebration, but David glumly looked out the window and said nothing at all.

Talking Heads had no gold records yet, but frankly, we were never about quantity. We were about quality. So was Tom Tom Club. *People* magazine, of all places, gave us an interesting review: "Tom Tom Club . . . is led by the Heads' husband-and-wife rhythm section of Frantz (drums) and Weymouth (bass). They feature the euphoric, witty side of the Heads most in evidence on the group's first two albums. In the clever, funky Wordy Rappinghood, Tina presents 'a rap race with a fast pace.' As her sisters Lani and Laura chant, 'What are words worth?' Tina intones, 'Eat your words, but don't go hungry / Words have nearly always hung me.' Tina's too modest. Her rhymes put Debbie Harry's 'Man from Mars, eating cars' in the tricycle class. And all eight cuts have irresistible bounce. People tend to think of the Heads as the tool of Byrne's artistry. These discs suggest the talent and inspiration has always been deeper and more shared."

BURNING DOWN THE HOUSE

Tina and I went to the big P-Funk, Bootsy Collins, and Brides of Funkenstein show at Madison Square Garden, and what a wild and mind-bending show it was. Before the band had even taken the stage, the audience was chanting in unison, "Burn down the house! Burn down the house!" There were not a lot of white people in the audience. This crowd was black, or as the record business had taken to calling this segment of the population, "Urban." The chanting created a feeling of somewhat dangerous good times ahead. While Tina and I were not complete strangers to this scene, we were not exactly relaxed or in our own element, either. The show was unbelievably funky and very long. We were invited to the after-party upstairs, where we spoke briefly to a very distracted Bootsy Collins and to Bob Krasnow, who had signed Funkadelic to Warner. "Kraz" had also signed my brother's band, the Urban Verbs, to the label after a Brian Eno–produced demo brought them to his attention.

With the success of the Tom Tom Club album and all the hip-hop versions of "Genius of Love" by Grandmaster Flash and the Furious Five, Jekyll and Hyde, and many others including even the comedian Rich Little, people were asking us what we were going to do next. The Tom Tom Club grooves and vocal style were becoming a huge influence on R&B music. Well, we were going to make a new Talking Heads record. Tina and I saw

Talking Heads as the mothership. We loved our first band like it was our first child and no way would we ever abandon or neglect it. To say that David and Jerry were shocked at the success of our Tom Tom Club record would be a fair assessment, but neither of them talked to us about it. Jerry once said that he wished he had thought of the catchy "dee-deet, deet deet, dee-deet" keyboard part that Tina and I had come up with for "Genius of Love." David never mentioned our record at all until one night, following the Broadway opening of his collaboration with the great Twyla Tharp called *The Catherine Wheel*. We were all standing around at the Studio 54 after party with Twyla and Mikhail Baryshnikov. The DJ spun an extended version of "Genius of Love" and the dance floor went wild. David leaned in to ask, "How did you get that hand clap sound?" That was it. He never mentioned the song again except to say in the press that its success was "merely commercial."

Speaking of Twyla, she and David had a budding romance. Tina and I were very pleased, because Twyla had a good influence on David. He

Tina Weymouth and Grandmaster Flash,
New York City, 1981 © Laura Levine.

seemed more grounded and friendly when he was with her. But then one day after returning from a tour of Japan, we received a phone call from Twyla asking if we knew where David was. We told her that David had decided to stay in Japan for a while. What we didn't say was David had found a new girlfriend in Japan, one that, much later, he would end up marrying.

Whatever David and Jerry thought about Tom Tom Club, by 1981, according to our contract, it was time for a new Talking Heads record. We had bought some time by releasing a really good live

album called *The Name of This Band Is Talking Heads*, but we needed new music. Tina and I asked David and Jerry to join us at our loft in Long Island City to begin songwriting. I recorded everything on our boom box. The first day we began with an up-tempo jam, over which I hollered, "Burn down the house! Burn down the house!" just like I had heard at the P-Funk show. This was how that song began. It evolved to become one of our greatest house rockers and our first and only top-ten hit.

We would sometimes switch instruments during these jam sessions. This is how "Naive Melody (This Must Be the Place)" came about. Tina played rhythm guitar, Jerry played keyboard bass, and David played some freaky little sounds on the Prophet-5 using the modulation wheel. I played the drums because no one else knew how. On "Swamp," I began with a bluesy, rolling keyboard bass part. Tina played the bass foundation on which "Slippery People" was built. David was eager to play, too, but Jerry, not so much.

All in all this should have been a happy time, but Jerry was not himself. He is an only child and his mother had been diagnosed with cancer. Naturally, Jerry was stressed about it. He began showing up to these writing

Don't smile. People will think you're making money.

sessions hopelessly hungover or still drunk from the night before. Some days he didn't show up at all. On those days we got our upstairs neighbor Eagle-Eye Cherry, the fourteen-year-old son of Don and Moki, to sit in on keyboards, which was fun, but Tina and I were worried about Jerry. David, never much of a people person, said, "We should kick him out of the band." I had a better idea. I called up my father and had a heart-to-heart talk about how they would handle a situation like this at his law firm. My father said, "We've had problems like this from time to time. What we do is recommend the person take a leave of absence with pay to get detoxed and straightened out. We don't tell them how they should do it, but we tell them in no uncertain terms that it must be done one way or another if they want to come back to work." I had a talk with Jerry. He acknowledged he had a problem. He said that he would rather not take a leave of absence, but he would get straightened out. He did. He began arriving at rehearsals on time and clearheaded and we all went back to work.

On Valentine's Day of 1982, Tina decided to go off the pill. She had been taking birth control pills since before we met, but now she was thirty-one years old, our financial prospects were better than they had been, and we were considering having a child. I was pleased with her decision and after a night on the town I said to her, "Let's practice!" I didn't know she would get pregnant right away, but that's what happened. This was a very happy turn of events for us, but we didn't tell anybody yet.

We all agreed that, unfortunately, working with Brian Eno was no longer an option. He had simply become too demanding. For example, he would only fly on the Concorde and expected us to pay for it. Brian had done a lot for Talking Heads, but Talking Heads had done even more for Brian Eno and his reputation as a producer. Tina and I visited the great T. Rex and David Bowie producer Tony Visconti in his room at the Hilton Hotel in New York to ask him if he would be interested in working with us. As he packed his bags before flying to London, Tony said, "You don't need a producer. All you need is a great engineer."

When the band had written enough material for an album, we recorded the basic tracks at Blank Tapes in New York with engineer Butch Jones at the controls. Butch had mixed our 1982 double live album, *The Name*

of This Band Is Talking Heads. He was a charming person and an excellent engineer to work with. We decided to produce the album ourselves as a band.

The basic tracks were recorded quickly and almost effortlessly. Since Adrian Belew had run off with Robert Fripp and King Crimson, David thought we should scout out a new guitarist for an upcoming tour of Japan, the US, and Europe. Gary put the word out and right away our splendid Warner's promotion person, Benita Brazier, called us from LA. She recommended we check out Alex Weir, who had worked with his cousins the Brothers Johnson and also with Quincy Jones. Instead of a traditional audition, we asked Alex to come to New York and overdub some guitar parts on the album we were working on. It worked out beautifully. Alex was a magnificent rhythm player with chops for days. His lead parts were not bad, either, as we soon found out when we invited him to tour with us.

The promoter in Japan was the famous Mr. Udo. He was the biggest promoter in Japan. When he met us at the airport—a tiny fellow with

slicked-back hair, huge sunglasses, and a floor-length mink coat—he was very warm and welcoming. Mr. Udo told Gary that Talking Heads were great and everything, but the band that would really sell tickets in Japan was Tom Tom Club. So, we said that Tom Tom Club, who had never toured before, would open for Talking Heads. We would do a mini-set.

We rehearsed both bands and found ourselves working with a new tour manager/soundman, who was the absolute worst. In Tokyo, he repeatedly knocked on Laura and Lani's door in the middle of the night. He slipped mash notes under their door. When they didn't respond to his unwanted advances, he gave Tom Tom Club shorter and shorter sound checks until we had none. Tina asked him why he hadn't been giving us our per diems and he reached into his pocket and threw Yen in her face. A lesson was learned: When a person has a very long résumé, chances are he has been fired a few times. We were stuck with him for the Japanese tour, but as soon as it was over we fired him.

For the upcoming tour of Europe, we asked Jeff Hooper, a veteran of some other Talking Heads tours and a good friend of Frank Gallagher's, to take over the soundboard. We never had any worries with Jeff. He was a lovely Welshman and the favorite soundman of Tom Jones and Shirley Bassey, two of Wales's most enduringly popular artists. For tour manager on the upcoming European tour, we hired Matthew Murphy. Matthew had a warm, kind, easygoing way about him that was greatly appreciated by us and the other members of the band and crew, as well as the promoters.

We didn't know then that this would be Talking Heads' final tour of Europe.

We didn't have Busta on second bass anymore and Bernie had taken a job producing Rita Coolidge's next record, so we recruited Raymond Jones, the keyboard player from Chic. Also, we brought Tyrone Downie from the Wailers to play keyboards with Tom Tom Club. Tyrone and the rest of the Wailers' extended family had been going through a difficult time since the untimely death of Bob Marley the year before.

Here are some highlights of the tour.

At the Montreux Jazz Festival, when we were getting ready to go onstage there was a knock on the dressing room door. I opened the door and

standing before me in a khaki-colored anorak, blue jeans, and sneakers was David Bowie. I had heard from Adrian that he had a home near where we were, next door to Charlie Chaplin's widow, Oona. "May I come in?" he asked. I remembered when we were performing at Radio City Music Hall and I saw him dancing in the wings all by himself. I replied excitedly, "Hell, yes! Of course you can. C'mon in!" He said hello to all the men in the group. The ladies had a separate dressing room. There was a lovely assortment of backstage munchies on the table and Bowie zeroed in on that. He asked politely, "Are you going to be eating those nuts?" I said, "Please, help yourself." He filled up one big pocket of his jacket with nuts. Then he asked, "How about those cheeses? Are you going to be eating those nice cheeses?" Again, I said, "Please, help yourself." Bowie neatly wrapped up most of the cheeses in a napkin and put them in his other pocket. Then he said, "Well, have a great show. Break a leg. Can't wait to hear Tom Tom Club." And with that he was off. Byrne looked burnt.

In London, we played two nights at Wembley Arena. Gary and Chris Blackwell tried to come backstage without the proper passes so the security told them to fuck off. Gary said, "But I'm the band's manager!" Chris said, "I run their record company!" Security said, "Sure you do," and escorted them both outside to the car park.

Backstage at the Rock Werchter festival in Belgium, I was killing time with Jake Riviera, the founder of Stiff Records who also managed Elvis Costello and Nick Lowe. Jake was teasing me that we would never be as big as Elvis Costello when all of a sudden a United Nations motorcade roared up behind us with two motorcycles and a stretch limo with US flags flying from the hood. It was wet so the uniformed driver put boards across the grass so that his passengers would not have to get their shoes muddy. Two very-well-dressed, good-looking ladies got out and waved to us. Jake Riviera exclaimed out loud, "Who's that?" I replied, "Oh, that's my mother and her roommate from college. The guy behind them is my uncle. He's the chief of staff of NATO."

In Italy, it seemed to us that the kids used our shows as an excuse to go wild. In Milano, for example, the promoter Fran Tomasi was working with the Communist party in order to keep the ticket prices low. The ticket price was *twenty-five cents*. It was a huge outdoor show in a beautiful park. When we hit the stage there was pandemonium all around. To my right, in the

distance, I could see exploding Molotov cocktails that the kids were hurling at the police. The police, in return, were firing tear gas grenades into the crowd and the gas was wafting back onto the stage. Our eyes and throats began to sting badly. Steve Scales said to me, "I was in 'Nam, man. This is some motherfuckin' tear gas! I'm getting the hell out of here!" I took Tina, who was pregnant and showing, by the arm and led her back to the dressing room trailer. Fran Tomasi and his crew circled the backstage area to protect us. Fran cut up large sections of grapefruit and told us to rub the juice all over our faces. It worked! Then he pleaded with us to get back on the stage before things got worse. Oh, and why were the kids rioting? Twenty-five cents was too much to pay. They thought the concert should be free. We did get back onstage and "Life During Wartime" never sounded better.

Palermo, Sicily, was too crazy to even talk about except that the stage in the old football stadium was built cockeyed so that the whole thing listed to the left. The generator to power the sound system arrived at the last minute with no fuel in it. No one was allowed on the grass except for local dignitaries, so most of the audience was seated miles away from the stage in the bleachers. The *carabinieri*, who were there to protect us, ate all our food and drank all of our wine and beer while we were onstage.

In Athens, after a visit to the Acropolis, Tom Tom Club was pelted onstage with round, plastic orange juice bottles and cans full of beer. Gary Kurfirst leapt onto the stage to protect Tina from the flying objects. We couldn't take any chances and left the stage after a few songs. Five thousand kids had paid to get in, but 20,000 broke down the fences to fill up the bleachers behind us. They only saw our backs. The promoter said soccer fans throw stuff when they love you. But we could see people were actually aiming for the security police who, although they were there to keep the audience off the playing field grass, chose to take cover behind the band onstage. After the Talking Heads set, we made a fast exit in a large transit van that was surrounded and rocked back and forth by the audience until we could finally pull away. Our promoter, who thought it was a great show, had an after-party on the roof of our hotel with champagne, langoustines, and beautiful vegetables all served from huge ice sculptures of the Greek gods. We tried to have a good time, but we were still in a state of shock. We now knew why most rock and roll bands never toured in Italy and Greece.

Flying into Budapest behind the Iron Curtain was a trip. At immigra-

Baby Robin!

tion, we had to sit at a typewriter and fill out a form that was twenty pages long. All the questions were in Hungarian. Try that with two hours of sleep and a bad hangover. Onstage in Budapest we were surrounded by Soviet soldiers with machine guns and German shepherds. Not a good vibe, but the crowd loved us.

Tyrone had some sort of a breakdown at the airport in Belgrade. He unzipped his pants and waved his cock at the armed security while screaming, "I want to go back to America where black people are black and white people are racist!" The guards backed away, but kept their guns pointed at him. Gary and I took him by the arm and led him to the airline counter and bought him a ticket to Munich, where he said he had some friends who would help him. That was the last we saw of Tyrone, until years later in Paris when I turned on the TV and there was Tyrone on some talk show looking great and speaking perfect French.

One week later, we started a thirty-eight-show US tour at the County Bowl in Santa Barbara, California. Sly and Robbie with Black Uhuru opened the show. At the Sunset Marquis, Michael Rose gave me a pound of fabulous Humboldt County weed. The Black Uhuru fans had showered him with herb and he begged me to take some of it. He couldn't bear to throw it out.

Tina was showing her pregnancy more and more, to the amazement of our fans. She wore fitted clothes so people would know she was pregnant, not fat. She was such a trouper. David and Jerry had another bass player waiting in the wings, but Tina told them in no uncertain terms that she was doing this tour. The other guy could go home. The moment she realized she was pregnant, she quit smoking and drinking. After the show, instead of partying madly with the rest of the band, she would retire to our room and take a long bath, do yoga, and read. She was looking radiant and gorgeous, taking good care of herself and the little baby inside of her. Our relationship grew even stronger—although I didn't manage to give up partying the way she did . . . and I should have. It would have been better for everyone.

When this exhausting tour was finally over Tina, Jerry, David, and I traveled back to Compass Point Studios, where we worked some more on the album that would be called *Speaking in Tongues*. This time we were working with one of the hottest engineers around, Alex Sadkin. Alex was now a fixture at Compass Point, where he worked with Grace Jones, Bob Marley, and Third World. He was our downstairs neighbor at Tip Top and was a wonderful, handsome man. Our other neighbor at Tip Top was "the Prophet" Wally Badarou. Wally overdubbed the genius synthesizer parts and solo on "Burning Down the House."

On November 3, 1982, Tina was playing her last bass part on our last song when who should burst into the studio but P-Funk's Bernie Worrell, who had been playing with Talking Heads for years, and George Clinton. They were in Nassau for the Black Music Convention over on Paradise Island.

After howls of laughter and big hugs all around, George walked over to Tina and said, "Haven't you had that child yet? I'm gonna scare that child out of you!" George put his face next to Tina's swollen belly and made a sound like, "Bwhooooohooohahahahaha!" Our son Robin was born the following morning after Tina's long night of labor at Rassin Hospital in Nassau. As he was being born, a rooster was crowing outside the hospital room window. Baby Robin was healthy, beautiful, and a born music lover.

Tina and I began a new stage of our lives, parenthood and family life. I still wasn't sure I was ready for fatherhood, but I was so in love with Tina and the baby that I felt like everything was going to be fine.

48

LIFE AT COMPASS POINT

After Robin was born in 1982, Tina and I decided to stay at Compass Point as long as possible. David and Jerry flew back to New York, but our manager, Gary, and his wife, Phyllis, were living just down the road at their place with their young son Josh. Our apartment at Tip Top was beautiful, comfortable, and clean with magnificent ocean views. It was a good place for a newborn baby and his parents.

Let me tell you a little bit about our life and our friends at Compass Point. Compass Point is located next to Gambier Village, named after Royal Navy Officer Admiral James Gambier, born October 13, 1756, in New Providence, the Bahamas. After Nassau, it's the second oldest settlement in the Bahamas. Gambier Village is inhabited by many old and mostly very poor black Bahamian families with names like Poitier, cousins of the actor Sidney Poitier, Cartwright, Bethel, and Morris.

Robert Palmer and his adorably sweet wife, Sue, and their two children, Jim and Jane, lived just across the road. They were the best neighbors ever, always welcoming and generous. Tina and I spent many an evening at their place enjoying their hospitality. Their home was a little two-story white-row house with a cedar shake roof on the sea directly opposite the recording studio. We'd talk about music with Robert until all hours. Robert was a true scholar of music history and, like us, he loved James Brown, Marvin Gaye,

Aretha Franklin, and the whole Muscle Shoals crew. He was also very well informed about the latest musical happenings in the UK, Europe, and around the world and introduced us to many artists we did not know about. He had spent a good part of his youth living on the island of Malta, where he listened to North African radio, so he had a strong love of African music, too. Robert was excited by any successes we had with Talking Heads and Tom Tom Club. He would say to us, "You did it. You really did it!" His enthusiasm was a wonderful thing. I remember him saying to us that like a great person, great music must not only have personality, it must also have character.

Wally Badarou was our neighbor across the hall. He was from that part of Nigeria now known as Benin, but he had been raised in Paris. Wally's family were all doctors and lawyers and Wally himself had studied law before becoming one of the world's great composers and studio musicians. He had already played keyboards on many of the dance and disco hits created in Paris when he recorded a session with M on the international hit "Pop Muzic." I think Wally played all the parts of that record except for the drums.

Chris Blackwell heard about Wally and invited him to come to Compass Point to work with a new supergroup he was forming to make a record with Grace Jones. Wally knew nothing about Grace Jones or Chris, but he

Joe Cocker, Robert Palmer, and me at Robert's place.

took a chance and flew to Compass Point. On the plane to Nassau he met guitarist Barry Reynolds, who was also on his way to Compass Point. Barry had recently had a hit with a song he wrote with Marianne Faithfull for her 1979 comeback album, *Broken English*. When they arrived at Compass Point, neither Chris nor Grace was anywhere to be found. Eventually, they met Sly and Robbie, Mikey Chung, and Sticky Thompson and together they became the Compass Point All Stars.

Wally and his bride, Genevieve, became good friends of ours, not only back then at Compass Point but to this day. We always look forward to seeing them when we travel to Paris.

Steven Stanley also lived at Tip Top with his wife, Dawn, and their baby girl, Dawnette. They were so much fun. Stevie bought a fast Japanese Mitsubishi sports car that he kept in immaculate condition, washing it every day to protect it from the salty sea air. With the success of Tom Tom Club, Stevie was getting lots of work recording and mixing the B-52s, Lizzy Mercier Descloux, Ian Dury, and loads of reggae artists. We have worked with many great recording engineers over the years but none as wild and crazy in the control room as Stevie. He called Tina "the Queen" and he called me "the Mastermind." His dub mixes were to die for and his energy was unsurpassed. Did I say *was*? Stevie is alive and well in Kingston, Jamaica, where he has his own studio and is still a force in the reggae world. He recently mixed a reggae version of "Wordy Rappinghood" by our good friend Mystic Bowie. What goes around comes around.

Grace Jones lived just up the road next door to our manager, Gary Kurfirst. Grace was a creature of the night, although sometimes she would venture out in daylight. I remember the time I thought I should start getting more exercise. Grace said she would show me her workout routine. So, for my first time ever working out, my trainer was Grace Jones in a bikini. Can you even imagine? She showed me things I would never have dreamed of doing, like lunges, both forward and reverse. "This is for your glutes, man. This is for your ass. Do it!" Then she showed me squats. "Very important, Chris! Do it!" This continued with different exercises and many repetitions until Grace was glistening with tiny beads of sweat. I was not glistening. I was dripping. One late night after singing in the studio, Grace was hungry so she asked Stevie and Benji to ride with her to town to get "chicken in a bag." There was a little place they knew that was open all night. With

Grace behind the wheel they headed into town. The police stopped Grace for speeding and asked to see her ID. Grace gave the cops her passport and when they opened it up they found a big fat spliff. Grace, Stevie, and Benji were all led off to jail. Stevie and Benji, who never smoked or drank alcohol in their lives, were released, but Grace had to stay and face the judge the next day. Bahamian drug laws were draconian back then, but the judge gave Grace a choice: Face jail time or leave the island. Grace was on the next plane out. Evidently, all is forgiven now. Grace was recently the star of the Bahamas Film Festival with the documentary of her life, *Bloodlight and Bami*. Tina and I never miss one of her shows and we both agree that Grace Jones now is better than ever.

One time when Black Uhuru was recording, I sat by the pool with the founder of the group, Duckie Simpson. We had known each other for a few years since the first time Tina and I visited Jamaica and Chris Blackwell sent Duckie and Michael Rose to meet us at the airport in Kingston. Duckie is one of the most badass-looking Rastas of all time, but he is also a really sweet guy. This particular day Duckie turned to me and said, "Chris, man, you know who my favorite woman in all the world is?" I said, "No, Duckie, who she is?" There was a long pause. Then Duckie said, "Princess Di." I smiled at him and asked, "Really?" Duckie said, "Yes, Chris. One day you will read in the *Daily Mail* this headline: 'Princess Di Runs Off with Ragamuffin Dread.'"

Ian Dury came down to make a new record with his musical partner, Chaz Jankel, and Sly and Robbie. They had a lovely young nurse named Louise with them to deal with Ian's health issues, should any arise. He had suffered from polio as a child and had to take good care of himself. Tina's sister Laura was visiting with us. She had been dating Chaz back in London so this was a happy reunion for them. Tina and I invited them all up for a dinner of barbecued chicken. At the time our drink of choice was Myer's Rum and orange juice, also known as a Yellow Dog. I was taking my time grilling the chicken outside on my little hibachi when I noticed our guests were all just staring at the food with great anticipation. I realized that I should serve dinner as soon as possible. When we sat down to eat, Ian, Chaz, and Louise curled their arms around their plates as if to keep anyone else from taking their food. They wolfed down the barbecued chicken, peas and rice, and salad and asked for more. Tina and I just watched, bemused.

After dinner Ian said, "Oh man, that was good. First real food we've had in days!" It turned out that Quincy Jones had just won a Grammy award for his big hit "Ai No Corrida." When accepting his award, Quincy quite properly said, "I'd like to thank the writer of this song, Chaz Jankel." Who knew that Sly and Robbie watched the Grammy Awards on television? Well, they did and in typical Jamaican fashion used it as a bargaining point to demand more money for their services. Yes, they had already agreed to a fee, but now that there was a Grammy Award, "the fee gone up." That's where Ian and Chaz's food money had gone. By the way, there were no hard feelings. Sly and Robbie performed beautifully. Food money came from England. Tina and Laura added background vocals to "Spasticus Autisticus," which appeared on the 1981 album *Lord Upminster*. We all had a great time together and before they departed Louise gave Tina her phone number, saying, "If you ever need a nanny for baby Robin, I'm your girl."

Our good friend Mick Jones of the Clash brought his new band, Big Audio Dynamite, down to Compass Point for a little rest and relaxation. They stayed across the road from us, next to Robert Palmer's place. Much beer and rum was consumed on their first night at Compass Point and they mistakenly left their cameras and boomboxes overnight by the pool. In the morning everything was gone. The kids from the village took them and that was that. Later that same morning there was a knock on my door. I opened it and standing there in a T-shirt and a wet bathing suit was Joe Strummer. He asked me, "Have you seen Mick? I've followed him down here to try to patch things up, but my luggage got lost."

I pointed him in the right direction and checked on them later. Everyone was getting along fine. Tina and I took them for a ride on our powerboat, *Cool Runnings*, and really enjoyed their company. Years later, Tina and I went to see Joe's last performance with his band the Mescaleros in New York at the Bowery Ballroom. After the show we went backstage to say hello. Joe's dressing room was overflowing with well-wishers. Roberto Benini, Jim Jarmusch, and Cerys Matthews were all squeezed into the tiny dressing room. I said "Hi, Joe!" and Joe came out and brought me a Heineken. Cerys Matthews opened the bottle for me with her teeth. Joe gave us bear hugs and then called his young drummer over to say hello. He

said to him, "You know how I'm always asking you to play more like Chris Frantz? Well, this is Chris Frantz right here. A proper drummer!" While I felt a little embarrassed for the young drummer, I felt damn good that Joe had said this.

Lee Perry came to Compass Point to make an album. It turns out that the real reason Scratch never showed up to produce the first Tom Tom Club was because of some perceived injustice that Chris Blackwell had committed against him. Instead of producing our album, Scratch recorded a song called "Chris Blackwell Is a Vampire" under the pseudonym "Pipecock Jackxon." Apparently, all was now forgiven because Scratch was in the studio making a new record on Blackwell's dime. Scratch was staying at Tip Top and he seemed to be doing well. Everyone said Scratch was crazy, but some people thought it might be an act to keep unwanted people away. The housekeepers at Tip Top were scared to death of him and wouldn't clean up his apartment or go anywhere near him. One day I was walking by his place when I heard howling laughter. His door was open so I looked inside. There was Scratch sitting on a barstool in front of the kitchen stove with a stack of glowing red-hot coins on each of the electric burners. He was tossing paper money onto the burners, too, which burst into flames. To add to the insanity, Scratch had filled the bathtub with sand, water, and a half dozen or so dying conchs that stunk to high heaven. It's no wonder the maids were freaked out and it was clear to me that his madness was not an act.

Another time, Scratch asked me to drive him to the liquor store. He said the Bahamian herb was useless and he wanted some Tia Maria. The liquor store was closed so we went to Traveller's Rest for a drink or two. Scratch was knocking back the sweet Tia Maria when a wave of sadness swept over him. You know the famous scene in *On the Waterfront* where Marlon Brando says, "I coulda been a contender!"? That was how Scratch was feeling. He told me, "Chris, man, I blew it. I could've worked with the Clash or Talking Heads. I could've worked with Paul McCartney or Tom Tom Club, but I blew it." I told him, "But Scratch, you are recognized as the greatest reggae producer of all time. Don't beat yourself up about this." He said, "Yeah, man. But that was yesterday and this is today." This, in a nutshell, is the curse of every great artist: How do you remain relevant in a changing world? I guess the answer is to stay alive and keep working, and this is exactly what Scratch has managed to do.

* * *

Once in a while, there is trouble in paradise. In 1983 at the Compass Point Christmas party, we were introduced to the British folk artist John Martyn. He was honeymooning with his new wife, Annie Furlong, and he was going to be recording *Sapphire*, an album with Barry Reynolds producing. Tina and I did not know much about him, but we understood that he was revered by many in the UK. We offered John and Annie a ride back to Tip Top, where they were staying in the apartment below ours. On the short ride home John started getting belligerent and began insulting Tina and me. Evidently, he imagined we were musical know-nothings and was jealous of our success. I tried to ignore him, but he punched me in the back of my head while I was driving. That was the beginning. Annie managed to calm him down a bit and when we got back to Tip Top we all said good night. Annie seemed all right. She was pretty. She had been the manager at Windmill Lane Studio, where U2 recorded most of their music, but something was not right with Martyn. At night we heard him screaming in tongues. We didn't know what to think. The sound traveled up the stairwell to our place. Was it Gaelic? Was it nonsense? Was he having the DTs? Whatever it was, it was a horrifying sound punctuated by cackles of manic laughter.

On New Year's Day, Lee Perry came upstairs to visit us and see baby Robin, who was just one year old. Scratch sat at my drum set with Robin in his lap and played a one-handed drumbeat while scat-singing some happy-sounding lyrics. It was early in the afternoon when John Martyn burst in, shouting at Scratch that it was time to get going or he would miss his plane. Some fool had put John Martyn, of all people, in charge of getting Scratch to the airport on time. Scratch just ignored him. Then John really got crazy and called Scratch "a good-for-nothing, useless old nigger." I asked John very firmly to leave, but he just continued cursing at Scratch. Finally, Scratch got up, said goodbye, and left with John following him down the stairs berating him. He seemed to realize that John was even more crazy than he was.

A few nights later, very late, we heard him screaming bloody murder and saw through his open window, in full view of anyone who walked by, that he was holding his naked wife's head underwater in the kitchen sink while beating her neck and shoulders with his free hand.

We banged on the door with a fish cudgel and John Martyn opened it. By this time, a crowd had gathered to see Annie lying soaking wet, bruised and naked on the floor tiles. We were all sickened. Louise and Tina covered her nakedness and took her upstairs to the safety of our apartment where they took pictures and she slept for the first time in days. She told us he had wanted her to stay awake to watch him "work" *and* watch him sleep. Rather than calling the Nassau police, who had a brutal reputation, the studio staff took over caring for Martyn. Louise, who was traveling the next day, took Annie back to her family in Ireland at her request. But when Annie's brothers met them at Shannon Airport and Louise tried to explain what had happened, they rudely told her to mind her own business.

Robert Palmer quickly squeezed a few more vocals out of Martyn and he was sent home. Everyone at Compass Point breathed a great sigh of relief. His album was finished without him.

That was a terrible and horrifying time, but it was not at all typical of life at Compass Point. More often life there was relaxed and idyllic. Chris Blackwell did his best to make it that way. He built a gorgeous Spanish-style villa on a cliff overlooking Old Fort Bay called Terra Nova. He lived there with his girlfriend, the French actress Natalie Delon, ex-wife of Alain Delon. They hosted the best parties. One New Year's Eve the guests were Dennis Hopper, Timothy Leary, Elia Kazan and his daughter, Sonia Braga, Robert and Sue Palmer, Wally and Genevieve Badarou, and many other happy revelers. After midnight, I took Sonia Braga and another woman by boat to the Junkanoo parade in downtown Nassau. I knew the waters very well by that time, but it was still a crazy thing to do on a windy, moonless night. I invited Hopper and Leary to join us, but they respectfully declined because they could see how high on rum and cocaine I was. Can you imagine being too high for Timothy Leary? Well, that night I was. We made it back safely, but not until well after noon. Tina, at home with baby Robin, was understandably worried and upset and told me to shape up. She needed me to be a more responsible husband and father.

One day at Robert Palmer's place, I was introduced to a new neighbor who had moved into the home where Grace Jones had been living. His name was Emil Schult. Emil was an artist who had worked closely with Kraftwerk. As a student of Joseph Beuys, he had studied at the Academy of Art in Deusseldorf. Emil created the famous *Autobahn* album cover and

many more for Kraftwerk. He also wrote lyrics for them. When I'd met him in 1982, he already had an idea for a song called "Artificial Intelligence." Always well informed, Emil was full of great ideas. More recently, we visited Emil at his studio in Germany, where he was working on a grand project to be exhibited in China. Tina and I were very happy to join Emil and his family for cakes and coffee on a Sunday afternoon at their home. It's so great to see your old friends thriving.

One terrible night in Nassau, in July 1987, Alex Sadkin was thrown from a Jeep and killed. He hit his head on a rock and never woke up. We were close friends with Alex by this time. Everyone who knew him was shattered.

Alex had been scheduled to produce Bob Marley's kids' debut album for a new record company called Virgin America. They were called Ziggy Marley and the Melody Makers. It so happened that Tina's brother Loric was working at Virgin America at that time and when the search began for someone to produce Ziggy, Stephen, Sharon, and Cedella Marley, he suggested Tina and me. No one could fill Alex Sadkin's shoes, but we would do our best. We listened to the demos and thought the songs were very good; in fact, we wondered if they might have been written by Bob. We had a meeting over dinner in New York with Rita Marley and the A&R exec from Virgin, Nancy Jeffries. It was decided we should fly to Jamaica to meet Ziggy, who would be performing at the Reggae Sun Splash Festival in Montego Bay. We met very briefly with Ziggy, who decided that we were okay. We produced two albums for him.

The first, 1988's *Conscious Party*, was made in New York, where, on the first day of recording, Ziggy asked, "Why Chris Frantz bring his wife to the studio?" I told him she knew more about musical composition than I did and she was my musical partner, as well as my wife. Ziggy was only nineteen years old and had a lot to learn. Still, the songs were great and the band, a group of young Ethiopians called Dallol, was perfect. We had some special guests, too. The great Hugh Masekela came in with the young South African cast of the Broadway show *Serafina* to sing on "Dreams of Home." Keith Richards played lead guitar on "Lee and Molly." Jerry Harrison played Hammond organ on "Tomorrow People." Tina and Laura Weymouth sang on "New Love." The album became a hit, won a Grammy Award for

The Compass Point All Stars with Desmond Dekker, Joe Cocker, and me.

Best Reggae Album and, after their father's *Legend* album, was the second-best-selling reggae album of all time.

The next album, 1989's *One Bright Day*, was recorded at Compass Point after Ziggy and the band had been touring the world for months on end. The songs were written and they were good, but Ziggy's voice was shot. He had torn up his throat with a bad singing habit of producing a sound on the inhale as well as the exhale so his vocal cords, perpetually in tension, were shot. He needed to rest his voice. So we just kept recording basic tracks with the band until we had eighteen basic tracks to work with.

The Marleys were staying in a seaside mansion that Bob had purchased many years before. When Tina and I visited them one evening, the house was lit by candlelight—not because it was romantic, but because Rita refused to pay the electric bill. For some reason she insisted that the studio should pay it. One day we invited Ziggy out for a boat ride on our little motorboat, *Cool Runnings*. We picked him up at the Marley place and went for a spin around the area. It's lovely to see the island from the water and we hoped to connect more closely with Ziggy. He had been treating his band with great disrespect and he was not communicating well with us. We had a good cruise around the neighboring beaches when I pointed out his home to Ziggy. It was over a mile away. Ziggy asked me to stop the boat and said that he wanted to swim home. I said, "You know, it's a lot farther away than it looks. Distances can be deceiving over water. Let me take you closer, then

Tina and I producing Ziggy Marley and the Melody Makers.

you can swim." No, Ziggy insisted. He would swim from here, and with that he jumped into the water and started swimming. Tina and I decided to keep an eye on him because we really were at least a mile from shore. It's a good thing we did, too. Ziggy started waving his arms the way a drowning man would do. When we pulled alongside of him his face was contorted in pain. He had a terrible cramp in his leg. I put out the ladder and leaned over the side of the boat to help him climb in. Ziggy, ever contrary, said, "No, man. I'm not getting in. Throw me a line and tow me ashore." If you've ever been towed in the water by a powerboat, you know that it's no fun. Even at very low speed the water gets up your nose, down your throat, and it's difficult to keep your grip on the line. It's like torture, but Ziggy insisted that this is how he would like to go home. So we towed him in as slowly as possible with frequent stops to let him catch his breath. When we finally arrived at the Marley home, Ziggy marched up the stairs to the house without saying another word or even goodbye.

Eventually, we had to leave the *One Bright Day* sessions—which had run way overtime—because we had a Tom Tom Club tour booked. Gary and Chris Blackwell made sure we were paid. When you're in the music business, people will try to take advantage of you. We were not happy with the

final mixes, but the album still won a Grammy and Tina and I felt honored to have worked with the scion of the Marley family and his brother and sisters—even though they had no idea what we'd brought to the success of their greatest two albums.

The last project Tina and I worked on at Compass Point was in 1994. One day at our home in Connecticut, I got a phone call from a guy in LA named Tomas Cookman. Tomas represented a band from Buenos Aires, Argentina, with the nutty name Los Fabulosos Cadillacs. He wanted to know if Tina and I would produce their next album. I told him that I was sorry but I had never heard of them. Tomas explained that they were huge in Latin America. Their last album had been a big hit and they were longtime fans of Talking Heads and especially Tom Tom Club. He made me an offer I couldn't refuse. He said, "The band has a gig coming up in San Juan, Puerto Rico. We'll fly you down to meet them and see them perform live, and if you're still not convinced, there will be no hard feelings." Tomas met me at the airport in San Juan, and took us to the Hotel El Convento in the old part of San Juan where I got checked in, and then we went straight to the show. The guys in the band were very sweet and friendly. I apologized for my inability to speak Spanish, but they didn't seem to care. Some of the guys spoke some English. The lead singer, Gabriel Capello—who went by the stage name Vicentico—spoke a few words to me, as did the tattooed bass player, Señor Flavio, but mostly I spoke with the sax player, Sergio Rotman, who was fluent in English. I found out that it was his idea to ask us to produce them, and that it was the band's dream to make a record at Compass Point.

The Cadillacs were phenomenal live. It was a big band, nine people onstage, with horns and percussion. In the outdoor amphitheater, the audience went wild and sang along with every song. When the band played their latest hit, "Matador," the whole theater seemed to levitate. It was a consummate performance, but with a delightful taste of punk.

I told Tomas and the band that I was on board, but I needed to double-check with Tina. I called her up, gave her my review of the band's performance and character, and she was on board, too.

We booked Compass Point with the new studio managers, Terry and Sherri Manning. We began recording with our favorite new engineer, Doug McKean, who became forever known as Señor Doug. The band was

completely professional and so well rehearsed that most of the time Tina and I could just sit back, listen, and say, "That was great!" The drummer, Fernando Ricciardi, is one of the greatest drummers I have ever heard. It seemed they could play in any style. Though they began as a ska band, they had expanded their musical horizons to include rock, reggae, salsa, and thrash metal.

One thing we could help the Cadillacs with was arranging some special guests. They wanted to invite Debbie Harry, Mick Jones from the Clash and Big Audio Dynamite, and reggae superstar Big Youth. I made the calls and everyone said yes right away. Mick Jones was on tour, but would over-dub his guitar and vocals on "Mal Bicho" at a studio in Atlanta. Sergio and Tomas flew up there with the tapes and worked with Mick on that. Debbie Harry came to Compass Point and stayed in Wally Badarou's apartment next door to us. She recorded a fabulous vocal duet with Gabby on a lovely ska version of "Strawberry Fields Forever." The guys in the band were gaga for Debbie and she herself was not unfazed being surrounded by Latin men. She wished she could have stayed longer. Finally, Big Youth flew in from Jamaica and wrote a few lines to toast on a song called "Queen from the Ghetto." I remember Gabby marveling at how this particular song had evolved to include lines like "She go along like she fat so / but Jah Jah know she's the Queen of the Ghetto." Big Youth was something else.

After the last day of recording, we had a little party by the pool to celebrate drummer Nando's birthday. The percussionist, Gerardo "Toto" Rotblat, brought some conga drums and shakers and we were having a little impromptu jam session and beach party with beer, rum, and some nice spliffs, when all of a sudden the police arrived. Some silly neighbor had called them to complain. The officer was dressed in his neatly starched, white Bahamian police uniform. His shiny shoes reflected the moonlight. Before he could say a word, Big Youth, who was no stranger to police problems, walked up to him and said very clearly, "Officer, did anyone ever tell you that you bear a strong resemblance to the great Marcus Garvey?" The officer smiled and was completely disarmed. He told us he did not want to ruin the party, but could we try to keep it down so he didn't get any more complaints?

Mixing was done in Miami at Blackwell's new South Beach Studio by Steven Stanley, who blew the Cadillacs' minds. He even did special dub

mixes of every song especially for Sergio. The album, *Rey Azúcar,* was a hit in 1995; I think it sold platinum in Latin America. And the Cadillacs became our lifelong friends.

We'll love Compass Point forever. In fact, I'm writing this chapter from our little apartment at Tip Top on the hill overlooking where the studio used to be. Tina is by my side, working on her book and still looking very beautiful. Some places, like some people, you make a real connection with. For me, Compass Point is one of those places. I'm always happy to be here, and I'm always grateful to be anywhere with Tina. How I adore her!

STOP MAKING SENSE, PLEASE

To backtrack a bit, Talking Heads finished recording and mixing the *Speaking in Tongues* album at Sigma Sound in New York in February 1983, with Alex Sadkin at the controls. David sang his non sequitur–lyric vocals, with Nona Hendryx and Dolette McDonald providing great background vocals to "Slippery People." Dickie Landry from the Philip Glass ensemble added some heavily treated sax to "Slippery People," too. I felt that "Burning Down the House" could use a little something extra and invited Steve Scales to add concert toms to the intro and outro. He did and—*bam!*—we had a hit. The mixes Alex did were perfect.

We were honored to have one of the greatest living American artists, Robert Rauschenberg, create a limited edition cover and package for us. Without telling us, David made a second album cover for the regular release. We had agreed the cover of the regular release should have been a photo of Rauschenberg's design, but David, true to form, went behind our backs and by the time we found out it was already a fait accompli. Rauschenberg told Tina and me that he felt hurt that David had worked around him. Still, Bob's cover was a real thing of beauty and his design ultimately won the Grammy award for best album cover.

We made a video for "Burning Down the House" at the East Village club called the World. This was the first Talking Heads video that the actual

Bernie Worrell, Steve Scales, Tina, me, David, and Jerry at the premiere of Stop Making Sense.

band appeared in. Julia Heyward, who we knew as an important downtown artist, was the ghost director and editor. It's interesting to note that one of the actors in the video, Rockets Redglare, was later found to be one of the last people to visit Sid Vicious and Nancy Spungen at the Chelsea Hotel on the night in 1978 that Nancy was stabbed to death. Julia did a great job for us and the video went immediately into heavy rotation on MTV.

David had big plans for the production of our upcoming tour. We had never had any stage production before so this was a major leap for us. Basically, David raided the ideas from Robert Wilson's stage productions. He even hired Wilson's lighting designer. If you have to raid someone's ideas for staging, Robert Wilson is an excellent source.

We rehearsed for weeks in what is now known as Chelsea Piers on the Hudson River. The piers were mostly abandoned then, but Malcolm Forbes's yacht, *Highlander*, was tied up there and on some mornings the crew would bring us trays of Bloody Marys. They were fans.

We learned to play all the new songs from *Speaking in Tongues* with Bernie Worrell, Steve Scales, Alex Weir, and two new background singers: Lynn Mabry from the Brides of Funkenstein, and Ednah Holt from the Ritchie Family. Dolette had been invited to work with the Police and later

Sting, probably for a lot more money, so off she went and who could blame her. We also learned a couple of tunes from David's solo album, *The Catherine Wheel*, and Tom Tom Club's "Genius of Love."

David was increasingly demanding and imperious. There was a lot of tension. In fact, the first production manager, a very experienced pro, quit after a few weeks of rehearsals, saying the gig was giving him an ulcer.

This tour in 1983 covered the USA. We were playing every outdoor amphitheater and proscenium stage that could accommodate the rolling risers. Tina and I toured by bus with baby Robin and nanny Louise; the rest of the band traveled by plane. One time when they were all sitting at the gate about to fly out of LaGuardia Airport, tour manager Matthew Murphy said, "Where's Bernie? The plane is boarding." Alex Weir said, "I know where he is. He's in the bar." So Alex ran to get Bernie. The lighting in the bar was dark. Alex grabbed him by the arm and said, "C'mon, Bernie! Let's go!" and started to drag him to the departure gate. The guy resisted and said, "Hold up. Whoa! Hold up, baby!" By the time they got to the gate Steve couldn't believe his eyes. He told Alex, "That's not Bernie. Bernie's already on the plane. That's Ray Charles!"

David insisted that we all wear muted colors, especially no white because that would "pop" too much under the lights. All the chrome mic stands and drum hardware were anodized black. Nothing was supposed to reflect light. Then, of course, David came out wearing the biggest white suit anyone had ever seen. If the lighting person missed a cue, David would stop singing and yell at her. If one of the singers was not standing on her mark, there was hell to pay. But this ungentlemanly behavior on David's part was not only directed at women. At Red Rocks Amphitheatre in Colorado, he hurled his microphone at our monitor man, Rick Coberly. After the show, Tina and I had to go to the crew bus to beg Rick not to quit the tour. Rick was nursing a lump the size of an egg on his forehead with an ice pack. Thankfully, Rick decided not to quit, but I never saw David apologize to him. Rick was the finest monitor man in the business. After our tour he went to work with Michael Jackson and his brothers on the Jacksons' *Victory* tour in 1984.

While performing in Eugene, Oregon, at the Hult, venue director David Pelletier introduced us to the great American author and Merry Prankster Ken Kesey. Ken invited us to his farm for dinner. Parked in front of his

home was Further, the Merry Pranksters' bus on which they toured the USA and turned on anyone and everyone who wanted to do LSD in the late sixties. I noticed rusty razor blades on the floor of the bus and Ken said, "Yeah, my kids come out here to snort coke. They think I don't know." After a hearty dinner of spaghetti bolognese prepared by Mountain Girl—whose real name is Carolyn Elizabeth Garcia—Ken said he had a proposition for us. He said he would normally ask his friend Jerry Garcia of the Grateful Dead to work with him on this, but there was a bad heroin problem, so he was asking us. His idea was to stage an opera based on Henry Wadsworth

Longfellow's epic poem "Songs of Hiawatha." Being a fan of Kesey's writing and a person who had repeatedly read "Songs of Hiawatha" as a young kid, I thought this was a splendid idea. Ken said we should think about it and let him know. I said that we would, but in the van on the way back to our hotel David said no, he wasn't interested. I still wish we had said yes to Ken's idea. What a missed opportunity. I guess David had other plans.

It was a no-brainer that the *Speaking in Tongues* tour should be captured on film. As the tour progressed, the band and production got tighter and tighter. *Nobody* had a rock show this hot. One day we were approached by a young filmmaker named Jonathan Demme and his fellow filmmaker girlfriend, Sandy McLeod. They wanted to make a film of the show. David, Tina, and I had seen Jonathan's movie *Melvin and Howard*, about Melvin Dummar, the good Samaritan who rescued billionaire recluse Howard Hughes from a motorcycle accident in the Nevada desert, and we liked it a lot. So, we decided to roll with the idea. Sandy McLeod, who never got enough credit for all she did, followed us on tour, making notes of everyone's onstage moves and how the show progressed from one song to another. The show began with David alone on a barren stage with a boom box and a guitar. With each new song another band member appeared. Risers were rolled out by the crew. Stage monitors and amplifiers were hidden underneath the risers. Halfway through the show the band took a short break, and screens were rolled down with words and images projected on them as the band performed the second half of the show. It was a very cinematic production, even before the movie was shot.

We shot the movie, *Stop Making Sense*, over three nights at the Pantages Theatre in Hollywood; the title is derived from lyrics in the *Speaking in Tongues* track "Girlfriend Is Better": "As we get older and stop making sense / You won't find her waiting long / Stop making sense, stop making sense. . . ." We paid for the movie ourselves—that is, the four core members of Talking Heads. Gary had to go to Warner Bros. for some money when we decided to shoot a third night. We were excited to learn that cinematographer Jordan Cronenweth, who had shot *Blade Runner*, would be our director of photography. The first night was more or less a wash because of missed camera cues and various other problems, like the band rushing the tempos out of nervousness and too much cocaine. (The men in the band, anyway. The ladies—Lynn Mabry, Ednah Holt, and Tina—were not guilty of this.)

The whole Speaking in Tongues *tour posse with Gary Kurfirst.*

After the second night of shooting went very well, Tom Tom Club had to get up early to appear on *Soul Train*. We didn't mind because this was a dream come true for Tina and me. We showed up on time at the TV studio and then had to wait for several hours, as one does, for host Don Cornelius to arrive. In the room where we were asked to wait, there was a big table with one single pink frosted donut on a plate. I didn't touch it and neither did anyone else in the band, but while we were getting made up for TV, our soundman Jeff Hooper decided to eat it. Not long after that we heard a commotion and shouts of "Who ate Don's donut?" from a production assistant. You would have thought someone had been shot. We thought this was hilarious and told them to go buy another donut, for crying out loud. When Don finally arrived we taped our segment, but Don proceeded to introduce me as Chris Paris two times before he finally got it right. This made me really nervous, but Tina, Laura, Lani, Bernie, Steve, and Alex were cool as ice. The taping went fine. From watching *Soul Train* on my little black-and-white TV in Providence to actually performing "Genius of Love" on the show was a leap not lost on Tina and me. After ten years, we had finally made it!

The final night of shooting was really great. The band performed like we had no limits, in no small part due to our spirited audience. David's performance was truly fantastic, but so was everyone else's in the band. From

my seat behind the drums, I felt blessed to work with such mighty players. The film crew was impeccable as well—when you see the movie, you'll know what I'm talking about—especially Jonathan, who was juggling two films at the same time: As he was working on *Stop Making Sense*, he was also involved in reshooting another movie he'd directed starring Goldie Hawn called *Swing Shift*. Goldie had agreed to a gritty warts-and-all style, but when she saw the result she apparently hated it and made Jonathan reshoot all of her scenes. So Jonathan was not always present for our shoot. That's Hollywood! Still, as a director, he understood the kind of movie we wanted and made sure we got that, but his real genius was in selecting the crew with Sandy. Everyone involved in the production of *Stop Making Sense* was at the top of his game.

After the last show we allowed some VIPs to come backstage. A dear friend from RISD, the filmmaker Mary Lambert—who is perhaps best known for the original, 1989 film version of Stephen King's *Pet Sematary* and her nine videos for Madonna—was the first to hug and kiss Tina and me in a night of much hugging and kissing. Robbie Robertson of the Band came backstage with Peter Gabriel, who actually appeared to be taking notes. Many members of the Warner team were present, including its chairman, Mo Ostin. There was a big crowd surrounding and congratulating us. Then the crowd parted to allow one man to pass. Brian Wilson of the Beach Boys walked right past David, Jerry, me, and everyone else to make a beeline to Tina. He told her he loved her long blonde hair. He didn't say much, but he said a lot with his eyes. He was clearly smitten with Tina. And who could blame him?

LITTLE CREATURES
AND TRUE STORIES

This chapter begins down at Compass Point in the Bahamas, not long after the *Speaking in Tongues* tour ended in 1983. One early morning I looked out of my third-floor window at Tip Top to see a man in a bathing suit lying facedown on the grass next to the swimming pool. Every once in a while he would move around a little bit, so I knew he wasn't dead, but I didn't recognize him. After a couple of hours I decided to check on him to make sure he was okay. I didn't want to startle him so I kept my distance and said, "Hey, man! Are you okay? The sun is gonna burn you up!" He twitched a little bit and slowly raised his head. "Yeah, thanks. I better get out of the sun." I said, "My name is Chris, I live upstairs." He replied, "I'm Eric, Eric Thorngren, but people call me ET. I was up all night remixing Bob Marley's 'Buffalo Soldier' for Rita Marley and Chris Blackwell. I'm still working on it, but I took a break and fell asleep right here on the grass." It turned out that Eric had been the house engineer at Sugarhill Records. He'd recorded and mixed "It's Nasty (Genius of Love)," "The Message," and "White Lines," all by Grandmaster Flash and the Furious Five. These were some of my favorite records of the period and still are. They are the real essence of early hip-hop and have stood the test of time. While I wasn't sure about the idea

of remixing a Bob Marley and the Wailers track, I figured that, based on his résumé, if anyone could do it, ET was the guy. He invited me down to the studio to hear what he was doing later that night.

I visited ET with Robert Palmer that night. We found him working away in Studio B all alone on what turned out to be an amazing remix of "Buffalo Soldier." Robert and I were taken aback, in the best possible way, by the audacious sounds ET was getting. As Chris Blackwell gave Eric more and more work, he became a regular at Compass Point. He had a great energy and was funny as hell. Robert and I both thought that we wanted him to work on our next records. We all hung out together and partied 'til the break of dawn.

Back in New York City, it was time to mix the *Stop Making Sense* soundtrack album, which would be a separate project from the actual film mix. We felt we needed some new ears on the project and I proposed that we try ET. David, who was normally very attentive, was strangely hands-off during these mixing sessions, and Tina was visiting her family in France, but Jerry and I went faithfully to Soundworks studio every night. ET was very meticulous and excited by the tracks, which were the first ever to be recorded fully digitally by the Record Plant Mobile. Some of the tracks were treated and edited, and we arrived at a very powerful-sounding album that helped to promote the film and vice versa. After its release in September 1984, in the USA it sold two million copies, while also doing very well in the UK, Europe, and Australia.

Our next album marked another musical departure for us. For the first time, David brought us demos of songs he had written, at least for the most part. These demos, recorded on a cassette, were not the wild and funky polyrhythmic songs of *Remain in Light* or *Speaking in Tongues*. In fact, they were a return to singer-songwriter-type songs with a heavy dose of Americana thrown in. I was pleased to see that David had used some lyrics that I had written years ago for a song called "Perfect World." We decided we would produce the album ourselves and, at my suggestion, we asked Eric Thorngren to record and mix it for us. After learning and rehearsing most of the songs at tiny Charles Lane rehearsal studios in the West Village, we moved into Sigma Sound Studios on West Fifty-third Street at the top of the Ed Sullivan Theater building. We recorded the basic tracks in one of the

smaller rooms. The control room was tiny but the sound was great. For me, these songs felt comfortable and much easier to play than anything we had ever done before. We were all in good shape playing-wise, so the arrangements the band created came naturally. What David's demos hinted at very sparsely, we made fully formed. This record would be known as *Little Creatures*. As usual, the basic tracks were recorded by the four Talking Heads, but we did have a few additional musicians come in and overdub parts.

Steve Scales added his beautifully punctuating percussion to a number of tracks. Steve always brightened our day when he came to the studio. He had lost none of his sense of humor or energy level. Since Talking Heads stopped touring, he had been touring the world with Tina Turner and Bryan Ferry and later he would jump on board with Tom Tom Club.

The great Brazilian jazz percussionist Nana Vasconcelos had been introduced to us by Don Cherry. Nana added an instrument called a water drum to "Perfect World." The water drum was a handmade round ceramic pot with a hole on top that Nana would fill with a certain amount of water to create a uniquely wobbly, resonant sound.

Eric Weissberg, who was famous for his picking on "Dueling Banjos" from the film *Deliverance*, drove down from his home in Woodstock, New York, to add a gorgeous pedal steel guitar to "Creatures of Love" and "Walk It Down." He said that when he got the call from our office, he didn't even know who Talking Heads were, but his daughter was a big fan and told him he absolutely had to work with us.

Lenny Pickett, an original member of Tower of Power and leader of the *Saturday Night Live* band, played impeccable tenor, baritone, and bass saxes for us on four songs, including "Television Man" and "Road to Nowhere."

"Road to Nowhere" was perhaps the only song on the album that took some time to gel. We ended up recording it the way we'd done *Remain in Light*. In this case, I went out into the studio alone and laid down a simple marching cadence. No, I did not use a click track. Then Tina, David, and Jerry added their parts. The song was coming together but needed some extra flavor, so I called up my good friend Jimmy Macdonell, who Tina called "the Clint Eastwood of Accordion Players." Jimmy Mac, originally from Lafayette, Louisiana, had a shockingly good Zydeco band in New York City called Loup Garou that played regularly at Tramps. Sometimes they shared the stage there with Buster Poindexter (David Johansen's alter ego).

Jimmy brought along his washboard player, Andrew "El Pantalones" Cader, who performed wearing a suit and hat made from one-dollar bills. Jimmy and Andrew were fabulous and lent the song a truly Acadian feel.

At ET's suggestion, we brought in the crème de la crème of studio background singers: Lani Groves, Diva Gray, Erin Dickens, Gordon Grody, Kurt Yahijian, and Ellen Bernfeld. Behind David's and Tina's voices, they gave the record a sweet sheen that one wouldn't have expected from Talking Heads. These people could sing their asses off. They also added nuance to the melodies, which was a welcome touch.

As for David, he was singing more comfortably than ever. For once he was writing vocal parts that were within his singing range. He had taken to a crooning style that was very different from the jittery, squawking and yelping sounds he had sung in our earlier days. This new singing style reminded me of many years before, when he took one vocal lesson but quit when the vocal coach required him to sing "Send in the Clowns." Now he was singing every song like that. It's funny to recall, but some people weren't ready for the change. They missed the weirdness, but that was where we were at then. We were in what was for us new territory.

We were beginning to enjoy the fruits of our labors and David moved into a big loft on Greene Street in SoHo. The interior was designed by Tina's brother, Yann, and his team at Red Roof Design and was very stylish in a low-key way. On the ground floor of his building was the Phyllis Kind Gallery. Phyllis Kind specialized in outsider art. She was the first to champion and show this type of work in New York, or maybe anywhere. Her stable of artists included Martin Ramirez, Henry Darger, Joseph Yoakum, and Howard Finster, among others. David really liked Henry Darger's watercolors of what the artist called the "Vivian Girls." He collected them. These were paintings of cute little transgender girls. Sometimes they were clothed in sweet little sundresses and sometimes they were nude. Why do I call them transgender? The little girls have tiny little penises. These would probably not work for a Talking Heads album cover, but Phyllis Kind had another artist who would; in fact, he had already made a cover painting for REM: Reverend Howard Finster.

Reverend Finster lived in his own Paradise Garden down in rural Georgia, not far from the town of Athens. Howard was commissioned and within a few days had made us a magnificently quirky album cover that included the

four members of the band and featured David as Atlas holding the world on his shoulders, dressed only in boots and his tighty whiteys. Next to his portrait of Tina, Finster wrote, "Tina, may your mansions be many." On the back cover was a color photo of the four of us dressed up in luridly colored pink, lavender, and yellow silk and satin outfits from a SoHo boutique called New Republic. These were not rock star outfits. They were from another dimension.

With the success of the film *Stop Making Sense*, David was able to make a film of his own that would be called *True Stories*, about some wacky characters living in a small town in Texas, of all places, and it would include a soundtrack by Talking Heads. Our plan was that, while ET was mixing *Little Creatures* in the control room at Sigma Sound, we would be out in the studio learning and arranging the songs that David had written for *True Stories*. David had written some parts for us in the film but his idea was to cast me as a pimp and Tina as a whore, so we declined to be actors in the project as graciously as possible.

The songs David presented for *True Stories* were a mix of Americana, rock, voodoo, and gospel. We thought, "Okay. It's cool. We can do this." We knew that David really wanted to do this record with the actors in the film, but the record company wanted another record by Talking Heads, so that's where we were at. When ET finished mixing *Little Creatures* we immediately rolled the tape again and recorded *True Stories*. The tracks ended up being damn good, even if it was not what many of our fans had been expecting. What they didn't know is that at this point, Tina and I were doing our best to keep the band together.

During the recording of the basic tracks, David gave me the only compliment he had ever given me since I met him. After he heard the playback of the basic track "Puzzlin' Evidence," he said, to no one in particular, "Nice drums." Actually, they were better than just "nice." But David was not one to go overboard with compliments.

We decided to finish overdubbing and mixing the *True Stories* record in Los Angeles so David could continue working on his film. This sounded as if it would be fun, so off we went. We brought our now three-year-old son Robin along with a new nanny. Tina was expecting our second child, Egan, but wasn't really showing yet. When we arrived, David's production company had booked us into a lousy hotel in Santa Monica. Tina and I were

shocked to find our room had no windows, and when I turned on the light roaches ran for cover. We spent one night there and then moved to our old favorite, the Sunset Marquis. Eventually, the guitarist T Bone Burnett told us about a friend who had a nice apartment in Santa Monica to sublet and since we were going to be in town for a couple of months of mixing and making videos, we took it. It was in one of those old stucco Spanish apartment houses that was very dark and gloomy inside. The apartment itself was nice enough, although we were told not to tell anyone we were staying there because sublets were not allowed.

We started recording overdubs at O'Henry Studio, Leon Russell's studio over in Toluca Lake. Someone told us that Bob Hope lived in the house next door. We hired one of LA's most famous studio cats, the percussionist Paulinho Da Costa, to add some magic to "Papa Legba," "People Like Us," and "Radio Head." That last song title inspired some young guys in England to name their band after it. David and Jerry did a few fixes to their own parts and the recording was done. We never did get to meet Bob Hope.

Now it was mixing time and we moved to the Village Recorder studio in Westwood. They had a brand-new room with a Solid State Logic automated console that was all the rage because when mixing it could remember the engineer's moves. If you created a mix and the next day you wanted to change just a few things, the SSL would remember where you left off, so you didn't have to start all over again from scratch. ET loved this.

The thing was, though, some of the mixes were not playing back to ET's satisfaction, so after working on a mix for a couple of days he would have to begin again. It was maddening. Finally he checked the little compartment where the SSL's brain was located and the circuit cards were covered in a thick layer of sawdust. It turned out the console was installed before the carpenters had finished the extensive woodwork in the room. We had the compartment and the Dolby SR racks—which were also caked with sawdust—carefully vacuumed and after that, everything worked fine.

Village Recorders was a famous studio. Originally built as a Masonic Temple, it was taken over by the Maharishi Mahesh Yogi in the sixties and became his LA meditation center. Yes, the Beatles meditated there. Geordie Hormel, the heir to Hormel Hams, bought the place in 1968 and turned it into a recording studio. Everybody recorded there. Sly Stone had famously

taken over one of the little rooms with an endless supply of cocaine, and would wave a pistol at anyone who disturbed him. Fleetwood Mac recorded their 1979 double album *Tusk* there. While we were there, Jimmy Buffett, who was working on his latest record, *Floridays*, would pull up in his Porsche each day with a different young beauty. The great songwriter and bluesman Willie Dixon, dressed in a seersucker suit and straw boater hat, dropped into our control room to hear what was happening. He really liked the song called "Love for Sale" that we were mixing. He said, "You know, this is not the first song to use that title. Cole Porter had a song called 'Love for Sale' a long time ago." Willie wrote some very big hits: "I Ain't Superstitious" covered by Jeff Beck; Cream covered "Spoonful"; Muddy Waters covered "I Just Want to Make Love to You" and "Hoochie Coochie Man"; the Doors did "Back Door Man"; the Rolling Stones did "Little Red Rooster"; and Led Zeppelin did "I Can't Quit You Baby," and that's just to name a few. Willie was a bighearted guy and a real gentleman. Tina gave him a kiss on the cheek when he left to have dinner with Eric Clapton.

The next person to drop in was the actor Lee Majors, who starred in *The Six Million Dollar Man* and *Big Valley* on television. He had been married to Farah Fawcett Majors, but no longer. He told us he was a big fan. When you achieve a certain level of fame, celebrities come out of the woodwork. This was fine with me. Lee was a sweet guy and very curious about our band. It turns out we both had roots in Kentucky.

David hardly ever came to these mixing sessions, unless we were also having a photo session. One such photo session was with the classic Hollywood photographer George Hurrell. I recalled when the art director at *Interview* magazine told Duncan Hannah back in 1976 that his photographs of us should look like George Hurrell's, which we all thought was crazy at the time. Now, here we were in Los Angeles with the real Hurrell. His photos of Marlene Deitrich, Joan Crawford, Bette Davis, Gary Cooper, and Clark Gable, and virtually every Hollywood movie star you've ever heard of, earned him the nickname "the Rembrandt of Hollywood." He was a charming man who regaled us with stories of Vaudeville days and used expressions like, "We're comin' into Altoona," which meant we were almost finished with the session. He was all about the lighting and when he got that the way he liked it, he only took a few shots with that vintage 8x10 camera of his. His photo of Talking Heads is unlike any other taken of us. We

actually look glamorous and sophisticated. This was the photo used for the *True Stories* inner sleeve.

During our time in LA we didn't see a lot of David. I remember feeling surprised that during two months in Los Angeles he never once invited us to his new home in the Hollywood Hills, not even for a drink. We invited him to join us for some great sushi dinners in Hollywood and Santa Monica, but he failed to show. We never did anything together socially because he was "too busy."

People who were more hospitable to Tina and me were our RISD friend Mary Lambert—who had just bought a home in Los Feliz—Dennis Hopper, and Paul Wexler.

Mary was the hottest video director of the time, having directed all of Madonna's videos. Prior to that, Mary had asked us if she could make a video of Tom Tom Club's "As Above, So Below." We said yes, of course. She submitted it to Warner as a demo and when they showed it to their newest star, Madonna said, "Oh! I want her!" We loved spending time with Mary and we still do. During this trip we visited with her often.

We'd met Dennis Hopper in Nassau and he said to call us next time we were in LA. We did call and he picked us up in his vintage Cadillac and took us to his early Frank Gehry–designed home. It was located in a rough section of Venice with groups of men huddled around fires they'd made in fifty-gallon oil drums. When we pulled up he opened the garage door remotely and drove right in, closing the door behind us. We followed him upstairs and looked around admiringly at his fantastic art collection while he made a few phone calls. Warhol, Lichtenstein, Rauschenberg, and Johns were hanging on the walls. My favorite pieces were his own photographs, especially one of Teri Garr in her bra and panties taken, I think, in the same bathroom in which it was hanging.

After his phone calls we got back in the car and drove to another Venice compound, this one surrounded by a high chain-link fence with security cameras. It belonged to the artist Charles "Chuck" Arnoldi, who buzzed us in. He had an enormous studio where he was working on paintings made on large sheets of plywood glued together in multiple layers that he would then dig into with a chain saw, creating a brutally rough surface to paint on. Chuck's was a very brightly colored palette and his work was loads of fun to see.

Next stop was the home studio of a guy whose work I'd admired since my RISD days, Billy Al Bengston. He was legendary in the Los Angeles art scene. I didn't know it then but he and Dennis both came from Dodge City, Kansas. They had probably been friends since they were kids. Billy was a motorcycle racer and a surfer. The work I had admired when I was in art school was a series called Dentos, in which the artist dented various-sized sheets of aluminum with a ball-peen hammer and then sprayed them with lacquer paint in various designs, sometimes featuring a sargeant's stripe. He also painted a Dracula series, various abstract paintings on canvas that as far as I could see had nothing to do with Dracula.

Bengston made us a delicious light lunch of soup, salad, and tea and showed us his new work, which had an Asian feeling, with pastel branches of palms and flowers. Today, he's still painting at eighty-five, but sadly, Dennis Hopper is no longer among the living, which is a damn shame.

Paul Wexler, who we knew well from Compass Point, kindly invited Tina and me to a dinner party at the house of his father, Jerry Wexler. Somehow I got lost on the freeway system in pouring rain. They say it never rains in Southern California, but that's not true. During our stay it rained a lot. We arrived over an hour late, which is not cool at a dinner party, but Paul and Jerry were very understanding. Herbie Hancock was there and we recalled the time we first met at a little late-night Robata restaurant in Tokyo. Herbie was enjoying a big hit with "Rockit," which was mixed by Dave Jerden, who had worked with us on *Remain in Light*.

In case you didn't know, Jerry Wexler was the record executive and producer at Atlantic records who brought soul music and rhythm and blues to a crossover market by making a deal with Stax Records in Memphis and bringing Aretha Franklin and Wilson Pickett down to Muscle Shoals, Alabama, to work with a mostly white but soulful rhythm section known as the "Swampers." Jerry even coined the term "Rhythm and Blues" as a very young man while working at *Billboard* magazine. He also coined the expression "oversouling," which is when a singer tries too hard to sound soulful by using unnecessary melisma and vibrato. Some of the other musicians he worked with were LaVern Baker, Ray Charles, Ruth Brown, Solomon Burke, the Drifters, Dr. John, Dire Straits, Dusty Springfield, Delaney and Bonnie, and Bob Dylan.

After dinner Jerry told us a story about working with Aretha Franklin. Before she came to Atlantic she had been on Columbia Records, where they never let her play the piano on her records. They always had some session cat play the piano and Aretha was only allowed to sing. She didn't have a single hit on Columbia. When she came to Atlantic and was recording "I Never Loved a Man (The Way That I Love You)" down at Muscle Shoals, the Swampers were struggling a bit to get the feel of the song right. Jerry asked Aretha to sit down at the piano to play and sing the song. When she did, the band suddenly heard where the song should go and the studio pianist, the great Spooner Oldham, moved over to the Wurlitzer electric piano and followed Aretha's lead. From then on Aretha played the piano at all her recording sessions. By the way, "I Never Loved a Man (The Way That I Love You)," Aretha's first single on Atlantic, went to number one on the R&B chart and reached number nine on the Hot 100 chart.

While the mixing of *True Stories* continued, we shot two videos that would be included in the *True Stories* film and also marketed to MTV to promote the film and album. Gary Kurfirst felt that MTV was eventually going to ruin the music business with its preference for pretty boys and girls over real artists. He was not wrong.

The first video to be shot was for "Wild Wild Life." We were to appear in various disguises in a lip-synch contest. We made the most of it and had a fun day doing it. Tina and Jerry and I picked out our own characters and costumes. Hollywood is a great place to find such things. I chose to be a heavy metal singer in the style of Ozzy Osbourne, a Hank Willams–style country-and-western star, and a satin-jacketed sports fan with WILD WILD LIFE emblazoned on my baseball cap. Tina played a society lady, and a crazy person who rips off her wig to reveal a shaved head. She also played a smoking hot Apollonia to Jerry's Prince. Jerry also did great impressions of Billy Idol, a shady Latino in a zoot suit, and Bruce Lee. David dressed up as a smooth Salsa guy with a mustache and various nerds. ET's in it, too, as himself. It was great to be in a video with actor John Goodman.

After we had done our bit, various members of the crew approached Tina and me to thank us for being so much fun and easy on the set. They

said they had been told to watch out, that we would be very difficult to work with, but in fact it was just the opposite. I asked them who had told them that and they just shrugged sheepishly and rolled their eyes.

Several days later we made the video for "Love for Sale." The point of the video was to show how rock and roll bands are treated as products and marketed the same way pancake mix, makeup, and cigarettes are. A well-known television commercial director named Melvin Sokolsky was hired to shoot the band doing various funny things, sometimes with special effects that recalled popular TV commrcials for hairspray, roll-on deodorant, and candy bars. These shots were cut in with actual found TV commercials, and at the end each band member was dipped in chocolate and wrapped in shiny, colored aluminum foil. It wasn't real chocolate, of course. It was a special kind of clay, delivered in a tanker truck, that simulates and photographs like chocolate. It was cold and it tasted like Pepto Bismol. I had it poured on my head in lovely slow motion. Tina had it poured all over her as she lay on a moving conveyor belt. Then the whole band jumped into a vat of the stuff and came out "chocolate" covered. Melvin Sokolsky lost his temper and rightfully so when David yelled "Cut!" in the middle of a shot he was making. Sokolsky said, in no uncertain terms, "No one yells 'cut' on my set except me!" It was a tense moment in Hollywood. In the end, all was well and everyone was happy with the results. The assistant director, a very capable young guy, came up to Tina and me and said, "It was great to work with you guys, a real pleasure. You know, we were told that you were real divas and difficult to deal with, but it was just the opposite." I said, "Thanks. I wonder who told you that?" He replied, "The guy who yelled 'cut.'"

Gary Kurfirst used to say that in the end, all you have is your reputation. I'm pleased that Tina and I still have a good one. If anyone ever tells you we were difficult to work with, ask for the source of that information. Then look up the psychological term "projection." This is one definition, according to the Urban dictionary: "An unconscious self-defense mechanism characterized by a person unconsciously attributing their own issues onto someone or something else as a form of delusion or denial."

Our business in LA was finished, but the fun wasn't: There was a party in our honor at the Pacific Palisades home of Mo Ostin, the chairman of Warner. Everyone was given *True Stories* T-shirts with little stick figures on them that David had designed for his True Stories One Sheet. It was good

to meet Quincy Jones, who was riding extra high from his work with Michael Jackson and "We Are the World." I reminded him of the time we met him and his family at Traveller's Rest in Nassau, and he said, "Oh, man, the smudder grouper and the curry chicken are the best! Let's go right now!" I told him I would be going there soon enough and he was welcome to join us.

JAMES BROWN COMES TO TOWN

In 1982, when the news that James Brown was coming to Compass Point to cut a record with the Compass Point All Stars reached my ears, I almost couldn't believe it. It sounded like something I might have imagined in a dream, but Paul Wexler had put it together and made it real. Paul was working A&R for Island after having huge hits at Warner Bros. with Van Morrison and the Grateful Dead. He had also worked with the Go-Gos and Tin Huey, Mavis Staples, and many other bands. Most recently he had produced a good part of the B-52s' *Party Mix!* with Steven Stanley. Paul was a cool guy with music in his blood and we hung out together a lot down at Compass Point. Paul even invited me to play on a Joe Cocker session with Wally Badarou, Earl "Pops" Popwell, and Cornell Dupree. It was a tremendous thrill for me to be part of it even though those particular tracks were never actually released.

James Brown coming to the Bahamas was front-page news in both of Nassau's newspapers. When the Godfather of Soul arrived, he stayed at a little guest house on the beach called Press On Regardless, where U2 and Molly Hatchet and other members of Tom Tom Club had stayed. It wasn't fancy but it had its own dock and a little beach and was easy walking distance to the studio. Of course James brought an entourage, which

consisted of Bobby Byrd, Fred Wesley, the young Reverend Al Sharpton, plus some foxy women. James arrived wearing a white straw cowboy hat and lizard skin, stacked-heel cowboy boots, with the tightest jeans you've ever seen and a red vest with no shirt underneath. He was adorned in turquoise Native American jewelry, looking like a true badass.

That evening, in honor of Mr. Brown's arrival—everyone had been instructed to call him Mr. Brown—Chris Blackwell had arranged a big party at his home and invited important Ministers of Parliament and other Bahamian dignitaries. I was invited, too, along with the whole studio staff and community. It was a beautiful night and a great party, but James insisted on having his hair conked by his longtime friend and bandmate Bobby Byrd before he could make an appearance. The great photographer Lynn Goldsmith had been sent to take his picture, but James was still in pink hair rollers and Reverend Sharpton insisted she be frisked and her camera cases inspected before she could even speak to James. This took a very long time and when Mr. Brown finally arrived at the party alone and two hours late, all the crème de la crème of Bahamian government and culture had left. Although he was too cool to mention it at the time, this did not sit well with Chris Blackwell, who had to do studio business with the government ministers James Brown had just snubbed.

I was not part of the studio session that followed in any way, but from what I learned from Paul Wexler and Wally Badarou, James had a few tunes written that were not up to his usual standards of excellence. The cats on the session were Sly Dunbar and Robbie Shakespeare, Wally Badarou, Mikey Chung, and Monte Brown; Monte had played rhythm guitar on "Wordy Rappinghood" and "Genius of Love." Sly and Robbie had some great groove ideas and everyone decided to go with those. Sly sang a pilot vocal in his inimitable nursery-rhyme style and everyone was digging that. Then James took the mic and added some more lyrics. It was sounding good and feeling good. Then James sat down by Sly and told him to play it *this* way. Sly, being a sweet, good-natured guy, obliged. When James tried the same thing with Robbie, though, Robbie handed him the bass, said, "You

play that bumbaclaat part," and walked out. This was bad, but the session continued with Wally playing keyboard bass, while James insisted on calling Mikey Chung "Montaygo."

My parents had come down to visit that week, and as my father and I were walking past the studio one afternoon, James Brown was standing outside looking at the sea. I said, "Hi, Mr. Brown. I'd like to introduce you to my father, General Frantz." I normally did not refer to my dad as General Frantz, but I knew that James was keen on formality. They shook hands and James said, "Very good to meet you, General Frantz. You have a fine son." They got to talking and my dad, referring to the "James Brown" part in "Genius of Love," said, "You know, Mr. Brown, my son made you famous." I could have died, but James sensed that he was only being teased. He answered, "Well, you know, General Frantz, your son may be a genius, but I was *already* famous." Then my father said that he'd heard that James was from Augusta, Georgia, and that he had a law school classmate who was a judge down there. James, referring to a recent divorce settlement, said, "General Frantz, that's the judge that took away my car! Yes, sir! Can you talk to him and get it back?" My dad said that he couldn't make any promises but would try.

Reverend Sharpton, who was acting as James's manager, had plopped his big, round, velour tracksuit–covered body down by the studio phone in the reception area. His hair was perfectly processed and permed. He spoke to no one and maintained an angry pouting expression on his face at all times. When I said hello to him, he looked the other way.

In the studio, James had reconciled somewhat with Sly and Robbie, although they had taken to calling Sharpton "the Reverend Sodomite," in light of what they, as Rastas, considered his unmanly hair style. After a few days of recording, Sharpton announced that James would be getting 100 percent of the publishing rights. In earlier times, when he was cranking out the hits, James could get away with this, but these times were different. Sly and Robbie would not agree to the arrangement, and when Chris Blackwell got wind of it he pulled the plug on the session.

We bumped into James Brown a few years later when he was making a record with Full Force at Sigma Sound in New York. He was in good spirits and

when Tina asked him how it was going, he said, "Going great! You know, you are all my children." Then his assistant, thinking she must work for the studio, gave Tina a piece of paper with a phone number on it and told her to call Mr. Brown's limo for him. Tina did so with pleasure. After all, it's not every day you get to do something in return for the Godfather of Soul.

52

NAKED IN PARIS

Our younger son, Marshall Egan, was born on August 25, 1986, in Norwalk, Connecticut. He was healthy and strong and welcomed to this earth by all of us Frantzes and Weymouths. Not long before he was born, he came to Tina in a dream as a young man dressed in a medieval buckskin hunting outfit. He said to her very distinctly, "My name is Egan, but I'd like to be named Marshall to please my father." We had been discussing what we should name the baby and this settled it. Marshall was a family name on my side of the family, and Egan means "fiery-spirited one." That he is.

One month after Egan was born, the *True Stories* album and movie were released. Plainly speaking, neither one did particularly well despite "Wild Wild Life" reaching number 25 on the pop chart and the video winning two MTV video awards. Tina and I saw the film for the first time at our local theater in Connecticut. The room was not very crowded when we sat down, but shortly after the film began people started walking out. By the end of the film Tina and I were alone in the theater.

David was still getting mountains of press. He had hired his own publicist separate from the band, so we would read things on Page Six in the *New York Post* about how David had attended Jerry Hall's baby shower. I thought, *Really? Time* magazine put him on the cover and called him

"Rock's Renaissance Man." There was some truth to it—but you know he did not get to this point alone.

Tina and I found a charming barn-style home in Connecticut on a beautiful pond with geese and ducks and turtles and frogs. Tina, being a big nature lover, adored this. We'd had a few good years and our accountant, Bert Padell, told us we should buy a house. We followed his advice. Finally, we had heat in the winter after business hours! We kept the loft in Long Island City, though. We did not want to put ourselves completely out to pasture yet.

This was a wonderful time for Tina, Robin, Egan, and me. We spent many happy days with our children and our extended family. We had a big room to play music in. The first thing we bought when we moved in— before we even had beds—was a Steinway piano. We really wanted to keep this music thing going.

You can imagine our excitement—yes, we still get excited—when Talking Heads decided to make a new album. The band got together in our loft and talked about how we would do this. David was keen on returning to the *Remain in Light* approach and Tina and Jerry and I were happy to hear it. We would create the songs together by improvised layering in the studio. When the tracks were complete, David would write the words and vocal melodies. All was good. Then David wrote me a letter saying that I should not play drums in a rock and roll style on this record. He did not say what other style he was thinking of, only that it should not be rock. I thought about this for a minute or two and decided, no problem, I would play this album of songs with brushes. I enjoyed the sound of brushes on the drumheads. Lou Reed's "Walk on the Wild Side" or Serge Gainsbourg's "The Ballad of Melody Nelson" came to mind. I had played brushes myself on an early Talking Heads song called "I Wish You Wouldn't Say That." I told David that's what I would do and the problem was solved.

We had the idea to go to Paris to make this album, which would ultimately be titled *Naked*. We all loved Paris and thinking of Paris made me think of the wonderful Wally Badarou. Though we knew him from Compass Point, Wally was Parisian and very knowledgeable about the music scene there. Tina and I were very fond of his solo work and his productions. He had produced Level 42, Marianne Faithfull, Carlinhos Brown, and Wasis Diop among many others. We suggested to David and Jerry that Wally could

coproduce the new album with us. They thought about it but ultimately felt that we should work with a more well-known producer, while still inviting Wally to play on the sessions and assist us in finding the crème de la crème of African musicians, many of whom lived in Paris. Wally also recommended we work at Studio Davout and that's what we did.

I suggested then that we consider the British hit-making producer Steve Lillywhite. He had worked with my brother Roddy's band, Urban Verbs, and they all liked him a lot. Also, Steve had a very upbeat personality and a great sense of humor. This element was something that I felt was very important for the upcoming sessions. Steve's track record was very impressive, too. He'd produced the Members, Johnny Thunders, XTC, Peter Gabriel, Siouxsie and the Banshees, the Rolling Stones, and several records with U2. In fact, that very evening I was speaking to U2's manager, Paul McGuinness, at Tramps about how his band was doing. He complained that "Eno keeps making these demands. He wants more and more, always more. Just today I found out we can't use his mixes. The band is not happy with them." I asked him what they were going to do and Paul said, "We're going to do what we always do: Call Steve Lillywhite."

We all agreed that Steve was our man and he was available and excited to produce us. Wally was on board, too. Studio Davout was booked.

Before we left we gathered at our loft and recorded two dozen or more musical jams on my boom box. These were not really songs but departure points from which we would jump off to create songs. This process was fun to do and we were all getting along great like we used to do.

We flew to Paris in early May of 1987. We would be there for a couple of months. We had our two boys with us and Tina's mother, Laure, who was excited to live out her French-grandmother fantasy in Paris. She would help us with the kids and take Robin by train to visit her friends and relations in Belgium and Provence. Our nanny and great friend, Louise Kelleher, would meet us in Paris to help take care of baby Egan. Jerry and his future wife, Carol, had their baby boy, Griffin, and David was solo until Bonnie arrived.

Tina and I were still very much in love and feeling fortunate to be leading such a romantic life together.

Ira Lippy from Gary Kurfirst's office had arranged apartments for each of us. Tina and I and our family would be staying in the apartment of Jean-Francois Bizot, the founder, editor, and publisher of the daring French mag-

azine *Actuel*. Jean-Francois, a big fan and friend of Talking Heads, was in the middle of a divorce and neither he nor his wife would be living in the apartment until the divorce was settled, so he was pleased to rent it to us.

When we arrived from the airport, a real estate agent let us in and gave us a couple of keys. The apartment was located on Boulevard Raspail just near the corner of Boulevard du Montparnasse, where Rodin's statue of Balzac stands. There was a fine patisserie next door and a candy store on the corner that Robin remembers his grandmother never let him go in, saying, "Oh, no. It's bad for you." The apartment was on the ground floor with a terrace in back overlooking a beautifully lush garden. There were at least three bedrooms and lots of comfy Moroccan pillows to sit on. We were just around the corner from La Coupole and Le Dome and we dined there often.

Recording sessions began at 10:00 every morning. After a few missteps, Tina and I figured out how to get to the Porte de Montreuil by Metro. This was the predominantly African neighborhood where Studio Davout was located. There was a lively street scene with plenty of people dressed in their native clothing. The studio itself had originally been a large movie theater built near the end of World War II, but was made into a recording studio in 1966. One of the first hits recorded there was a song written by Serge Gainsbourg for the teenage singer France Gall called "Les Sucettes." It was considered to be scandalous, because it's a song about a young girl who loves to suck on lollipops. France Gall denied any knowledge of the double entendre at her age, and I believe her. The main room where we worked was massive, big enough for a full orchestra. They'd removed the seats from the theater but the floor still slanted downward. Where the movie screen had been was now the control room. The ceilings were very high and the room was very dark with only a few lights so that we could barely see what we were doing. Michel Legrand had worked in that room, as had Herbie Hancock, Nina Simone, Dexter Gordon, Serge Gainsbourg, and Duran Duran. One great thing was the Café Davout on the corner. The blond waitress dressed in stiletto heels and a maid's outfit would deliver our espressos, café crèmes, and beers on a tray right to us in the studio. There were no paper cups. We got real porcelain cups and saucers and glasses. French luxury!

Steve Lillywhite had brought a well-experienced recording engineer named Richard Manwaring with him. Richard had a long résumé that included Human League, Orchestral Manoeuvres in the Dark, and Fine Young

Cannibals. He was serious about his gig, but also had a playful sense of fun. Assistant engineer Jean-Loup Morette was immensely helpful with setting up the band to record and translating from French to English when necessary. I felt we had an excellent team in the control room.

Out in the studio Wally Badarou was already creating new sounds on his Prophet-5 and Yamaha DX-7. Wally never used the preset sounds on his synthesizers—he created his own unique sounds sometimes resembling organ or clavinet and then tweak them even further as the songs took shape. Wally set up with the band and would play on "Blind" and "The Facts of Life" before he had to leave to work on one of his own projects.

Wally introduced us to Yves N'Djock from Cameroon, a great guitarist who played on a number of our basic tracks. Wally also introduced us to percussionists Abdou M'Boup from Senegal and Brice Wassy, one of the Bamileke People from the grasslands of western Cameroon. These guys were phenomenal percussionists and real sweethearts, too. On one song, Brice put on pants made of rattling bean pods that were played by dancing. Imagine the sound of one hundred maracas shaking at once and that would come close to the sound those bean pod trousers made. Abdou primarily played three tuned Bougarabou that resembled conga drums but had a deeper resonance. Abdou was a true Griot, trained from childhood to tell stories, sing praises, and keep the oral history of his people.

Last, but certainly not least, Wally introduced us to Mory Kanté, a great singer and master of the kora, a twenty-one-string instrument with a long neck and a resonator of goat- or calfskin stretched over a large calabash gourd. The player usually sits with the resonator end in his lap while plucking the strings with his fingers like a harp. Mory Kanté was from Guinea and had a huge hit in Europe that spring and summer called "Ye Ke Ye Ke," which had been remixed again and again for dance clubs so we were hearing his music all over Paris. For Talking Heads, Mory played on "Mr. Jones" and "Facts of Life."

We were all surprised at how smoothly the music came together on these sessions. As planned, we would listen to our demo cassette from Long Island City and depart from there. Tina, Jerry, and David were all playing beautifully and those creative juices were flowing like a fine Bordeaux. I felt that we were not only having a really good time, we were making some very strong music as well.

Funny episodes happened, too. One day when we were waiting for a particular guitarist recommended by Wally to arrive, right on time a tall, thin African man walked into the studio. Steve Lillywhite asked him if he was the guitarist and he answered in French that yes, he played guitar. Then Steve asked where his guitar was and he said he didn't have it with him. Steve said, "No problem, you can use one of ours." We played the track for him while setting him up to record. When he played it was clear that he was not accustomed to recording an overdub. He was missing the chord changes and his playing was all over the place. When Steve questioned him about it, he said in French that it was no problem—and that we should keep his part and the rest of the band should rerecord their parts to fit with his! At that moment another young African guitarist walked in carrying his guitar. This was the guy we had been waiting for. The fellow we had just recorded was a messenger who had come to pick up a package to be delivered to our business office. Then we asked the real guitarist to take over but he politely declined because he didn't want to take another African brother's gig. It was one of those *c'est la vie* moments.

Another day a percussionist arrived to play and insisted that he needed to tune his drums. We said, "Okay, sure. *Bien sûr.*" What we didn't know was that he would start a big fire in a trash can in the bathroom right under the control room to heat up his drum skins until they were at the right pitch. There was so much smoke that it set off the fire alarm and Jean-Loup had to urgently call the *pompiers*—the fire department—to tell them that everything was okay so they wouldn't come and hose down the studio and all of our electronic gear.

We did have one guitarist join us from England. Steve was friends with Johnny Marr of the Smiths and thought he would be a great addition to a couple of our songs. We had not met Johnny before but he immediately fit right in. We in Talking Heads had not brought any technical crew with us. We carried our own gear and set it up. We tuned our instruments ourselves. When Johnny turned up he had the most famous guitar tech in England—or possibly the world—working for him: Alan Rogan, the guitar tech for Pete Townsend. I chatted with Alan while he was setting up Johnny's gear and tuning his twelve-string for an overdub on "(Nothing But) Flowers." When he mentioned Ronnie and Keith, you knew he was referring to the Stones. When he told you about working with Eric, you knew he meant Clapton.

I figured by having Alan in the same room we had finally reached the big time.

Johnny played beautifully and with ease. After he was finished Tina and I shared some herb and drank some wine with Johnny, Steve, and his lovely and feisty redheaded wife, Kirsty MacColl. Then Johnny was off back to Manchester. I've never been very much of a Morrisey fan, he always seemed so twee, but I will always be a fan of Johnny Marr. Great guy.

Kirsty MacColl sang like an angel and she could effortlessly layer harmonies the way the Beach Boys did. Steve recommended that she sing backing vocals on a few of our songs and, when we returned to New York and David recorded his vocals, she sang on "(Nothing But) Flowers" and another song called "Bill." We developed a good friendship with Kirsty and enticed her to sing with Tom Tom Club on our album *Dark Sneak Love Action*. She was strong, determined, and did not suffer foolishness. Sadly, in 2000 we read in *The New York Times* that she had perished when she was hit by a powerboat while snorkeling at a seaside resort in Mexico. We miss her still. Her own albums and her work with the Pogues, particularly "Fairytale of New York," are outstanding.

Around this time David had to go to London for some reason. Steve wondered aloud, "Why is he going to London in the middle of recording this record?" Though David didn't tell us, I knew from Chris Blackwell that he had been asked to compose the theme for Bernardo Bertolucci's new film, *The Last Emperor*. Later, David told Tina and me that his main contribution to the score was to hire an arranger to orchestrate a traditional Chinese song, for which he had selected various instruments he wanted the arranger to use. In any event, he won the 1987 Academy Award for Best Original Score, which he shared with Ryuichi Sakamoto and Cong Su, who composed the main portion of the soundtrack.

While David was in London, Tina and I took our family and Jerry, Carol, and baby Griffin for a little vacation at Tina's family home in Brittany by the seaside. Jerry went windsurfing every day. We promenaded with the children by the sea and generally had a ball enjoying seafood and crepes, cider, and Muscadet.

When we returned to Paris, we learned by a handwritten note from

Bonnie that she and David had been married in London. I guess they didn't want to share that experience with anyone else.

Tina and I had to fly back to the US for my cousin Tommy Fryman's wedding down in Washington, Kentucky. I was one of the ushers. Tommy had been a US attorney in Manhattan and would come to our CBGB shows after work in a suit and tie. I remember when Terry Ork asked him if he was a Fed and Tommy replied, "Yes, as a matter of fact, I am." Tommy was a real music lover, and before we met Gary, was Tina's first choice to be our manager. Robin and Egan came with us. Tommy was Robin's godfather and he was marrying Lisa Fiedler, the daughter of one of my mother's good friends. In fact, my mother, who had introduced Tommy and Lisa, was greatly relieved that Tommy had finally popped the question. In her opinion, he had taken way too long to do so.

The wedding on June 20 was lovely and the reception at Tommy's farm, Federal Hill, was especially fabulous. During the wedding photos Robin crawled under the voluminous skirt of Lisa's wedding gown. She was a really good sport about it. After dinner and much wine, I stepped outside with my old friend Sam Dryden to get a breath of air. It was hot. Sam and I were smoking a joint and reminiscing by the family graveyard out back when we saw the silhouette of a really gorgeous woman off in the distance. Sam and I both wondered who this fine-looking woman was. She was walking in our direction through the bluegrass. As she came closer I looked at Sam and said, "I know who she is! She's my wife!" Of course, she was. It had been ten years since Tina and I were married in this same little village in Kentucky and it felt good to be back.

Back in Paris, Rupert Perry, the president of EMI Records UK, invited the band to dinner at a five-star restaurant called Le Toit De Passy, in the 16th Arrondissement. He wished to celebrate not only our new album but also a new deal on which he had been negotiating with Gary Kurfirst for years. The food was wonderful, with sorbet between courses and champagne to drink. Rupert was charming and everything was copacetic until Gary's name was mentioned. To my horror, David hissed, "Gary Kurfirst is a liar!" Then Bonnie piped up, "It's true! He is." Rupert raised his eyebrows but said nothing. We were all frozen with shock that David would act like this. Tina asked, "What did Gary do that you would say this?" David said, "He told me my soundtrack album would be a hit!" I supposed he meant

the soundtrack to *True Stories*, where the songs were sung not by him but by the actors, which was a separate album from the Talking Heads version. Very few people had bought that album. Anyway, that was an unbelievably awkward moment.

Very early one morning the phone rang in our apartment. Tina's mother answered. It was Gary on the line asking her, "Lo, are you ok?" She said, "Yes, everything is marvelous!"

Then Gary said, "Oh, thank God. May I speak to Chris, please?" I picked up the extension in our bedroom and said sleepily, "Hi, Gary. What's happening?" He replied, "Oh, man! I just got a call from *Rolling Stone* asking me to confirm reports that you had committed suicide in Paris." I let this sink in for a moment and replied, "Wow, Gary. No! I haven't even been depressed." I still have no idea who those reports came from and I have no details about how or why I would want to kill myself, but to quote Mark Twain, "The reports of my death are greatly exaggerated."

One other important reason that we were happy to be in Paris was that Tina's brother, Yann, was working very hard on the renovation of the Grand Louvre. Yann had worked for I. M. Pei on the East Wing of the

Yann Weymouth and Robin on a BMW in Quartier Latin, Paris.

National Gallery in Washington, D.C., and now I. M. had asked him to be his chief designer for the Louvre project. Not only was Yann a great architect and designer, but he had roots in France, was very diplomatic, and spoke French fluently with a proper accent. This was important when dealing with President François Mitterand and the French government. He had a little apartment in the Latin Quarter and roared around Paris on a stylish BMW motorcycle. Yann always had

time for us and visited us in the studio from time to time. He gave the band a personal tour of the excavation taking place underneath the Louvre, where archaeologists were unearthing new surprises every day. It was an enormous task that took eight years to complete. There was much protest and consternation from detractors in France, but in the end the project was a huge success. The Pyramid, controversial as it was, became a monument that is beloved by the French and attracts millions of tourists every year. It was Yann who designed it.

We had so much fun in Paris. One night Tina and I took David to see the great Calypso singer Arrow, who had a big hit with "Hot, Hot, Hot." The club was mostly filled with stylishly dressed, dancing West Indian people, and the band was loud and wild. I'm not sure that David enjoyed it as much as we did, but we were trying to keep our connection to him positive.

Another time we went to see U2 perform at a huge outdoor show. We were not only friends with the band, but also with many of the guys in their crew. It was wonderful to see how popular the band had become. I couldn't help but notice how intense their Irish security team had become. When we toured with them as our support act they'd had no security whatsoever, but now they were seriously guarded. We ran into them again at David Bowie's Glass Spider tour the following night, where they were just hanging out in the VIP area near the side of the stage like we were.

Then, because we had never seen Bruce Springsteen before, Tina and I were pleased to accept our friend Jenny Bier's invitation to his show. Jenny was our first concert promoter in France ten years before, when we we'd opened for the Ramones. Now she was running publicity for CBS France. This was another enormous outdoor show on the outskirts of Paris in a big grassy park. We sat in the VIP section with Terry Gilliam of Monty Python and lots of cool French people. The show, great as it was, was seemingly endless. It went on for hours and hours as we all baked in the sun. Tina and Terry and I decided to walk over to the hospitality tent and boy, were we glad we did. They were serving Veuve Clicquot champagne, fresh fruits, and cheeses and langoustines. The French really do it right. I drank the first glass of champagne way too fast, but it was hot weather and I was really thirsty. I went for my second glass, got another for Tina, too, and when I turned around I was face-to-face with Jane Birkin, the muse and lover of Serge Gainsbourg. I had admired her since the days of the hit song "Je

T'aime" and when Tina introduced me to Gainsbourg's *Histoire de Melody Nelson* album, which had been released in 1971, I was hooked. She was much loved in France and appeared in many films and fashion magazines and on television. She even had a handbag named after her by Hermès, although she preferred a simple straw basket to carry her things. Anyway, I turned around and there she was, looking absolutely her own gorgeous self, and I tried to say hello and introduce myself, but the words wouldn't come. For the first time in my life I was completely starstruck and tongue-tied. I could tell by her smile she was amused. She said, "Oh, hello," got herself a glass of champagne, and walked slowly away. Tina thought this was hilarious, but thankfully didn't tease me about it too much.

Later, after the show we met Patti Scialfa, who was very sweet and lovely, and also had a good long chat with drummer Max Weinberg. I commented on how exhausting these long shows must be. I think the show that day went on for four hours. Max told me his hands had been operated on seven times from damage done by drumming so hard for so long. He showed me the scars. There were little X's of scar tissue on each of his knuckles, but he said the surgeries had helped.

The big Warner executives were in town and they took us to a great little restaurant in St. Germain. Mo Ostin, Lenny Waronker, and Eddie Rosenblatt must have been on the way home from Midem, the big music business convention in Cannes. They were curious about our new album and we told them the recording was going great. In fact, we were finished with the basic tracks. We told them we'd soon be headed back to New York to cut the vocals and add some horns. David was bananas for horns and why argue? New York had plenty of great horn players to choose from.

Tina and I were very sorry to leave Paris. It was a happy, romantic place for us and always has been. I think Jerry and Carol felt the same way. Strangely, though, David told us it had been a terrible experience for him. He hated it. But then, he was a contrarian and always had been.

LOU REED WITH TOM TOM CLUB AT CBGB

By the time we were to record the third Tom Tom Club album, *Boom Boom Chi Boom Boom*, in 1988, Tina and I felt it was time for a change in direction. We were in the mood to rock, and who better to rock with than Lou Reed? We had always loved the Velvet Underground song "Femme Fatale," originally sung by the great Nico. Lou had written this song for her at Andy Warhol's request and it's a beauty as, of course, was Nico. We recorded *Boom Boom Chi Boom Boom* at Sigma Sound in New York City. We had recorded some hard-driving rockers for it but in the interest of dynamics and coolness we decided to do a version of "Femme Fatale." Tina and I recorded the basic track ourselves and Tina sang a guide vocal, which is not a final vocal but acts as, well, a guide for the musicians so they know where the changes are. Then I got on the phone to Lou. I had spoken to him not long before that, when he called me up to ask how we had been treated by Seymour Stein and Sire Records because he was thinking of doing a deal with them. I told him that Seymour had always done right by us and had always been in our corner, and I thought it would be fantastic if he was on Sire. So when I got Lou on the phone I said that we were recording a version of "Femme Fatale" and would he like to come over and play guitar on it? Lou was such

a guitar lover and I knew better than to ask him to sing, because that's what everyone expected of him. He answered very matter-of-factly, "Yeah, sure."

Knowing that this was going to really be something, I called up Jerry and David and told them that Lou was coming over to play guitar—would they like to be a part of it? Not surprisingly, they both said yes.

Lou arrived at the studio on time with his guitar the next day and we played what we'd already done. When he heard Tina's vocal I could see that he was very pleased. We had kept it in the key of A the way Lou sings it rather than Nico, which is not the easiest key for Tina to sing in, but it sounded great. Lou told us that Nico had questioned him about certain parts of the song, especially the "whoa, whoa, whoa's" at the end of the song. "What means this 'whoa, whoa, whoa'? Lou is making fun of Nico!"

Lou went out into the studio and tweaked his guitar sound for a while and was then ready to record. After a few different takes he was finished. There was no mistaking that it was Lou playing. He had a style of his own. Later, we made a composite of his different takes and it was beautiful. Meanwhile, David and Jerry had come up with their parts. David played some subtle seagull-sounding parts and Jerry used a new sampling synthesizer called the Emulator to create some breathy and beautiful keyboard washes. It was sounding really sweet. Then Tina suggested that we men sing the "She's a femme fatale" choruses together and we did, letting Lou stand closer to the mic than the rest of us so that his voice would stand out. It did. Everyone was happy, especially Lou.

We had a visitor in the studio that day, Sam Dryden. Sam was an old friend of mine from Kentucky. We used to hang out and drive around as teenagers when Sam was driving a brand-new Chevy Super Sport. Sam was the kind of guy who can make friends wherever he goes and that day he began what would become a fast friendship with Lou that would last until the day Lou died. They went on vacations together along with Sam's wife, Sandy McCleod—who'd had an important role in the production of *Stop Making Sense*—and Lou's girlfriend, the artist Laurie Anderson. Together they would travel to Mexico, Mustique, and the Turks and Caicos Islands. In fact, when Lou and Laurie decided to get married, their wedding was at Sam and Sandy's home in Boulder, Colorado.

After the release of *Boom Boom Chi Boom Boom* we decided to perform

residencies, or multiple nights, on our tour of America. I went to speak to Hilly at CBGB about it. In 1988, CBGB had lost some of its caché as being the hippest gig in town. Many new clubs had sprung up downtown and all over town. There was some serious competition. Hilly dug the idea immediately and we agreed that we would play five nights a week for three weeks. No one had done this at his club before or since. We had different opening acts each night

The night Lou Reed joined Tom Tom Club onstage at CBGB.

and charged $5.00 to get in. We had a special T-shirt made that said TOM TOM CLUB in a luridly colored monster-movie style font on the front and I LOVE THE UNDERGROUND LIFE on the back, with CBGB in small letters on the sleeve. This was the first Tom Tom Club T-shirt ever produced and it sold like hot cakes at five bucks apiece. We wanted to keep things inexpensive for our fans as the cost of live shows and merchandise kept going up and up. This worked in our favor for a while, but then it seemed that people actually wanted to spend more, and if a ticket was cheap the band must not be any good. Crazy!

Anyway, we called up some friends to be our special surprise guests on the encores. Debbie Harry said yes. Dee Dee Ramone said yes. Then I called Lou Reed, who said he would do it but only if we could provide transportation. So I called a limo company and had them send one of their best cars to pick him up.

We were working with a stripped-down four-piece band, so it was impossible to re-create what most of our studio recordings sounded like, but none of the club kids cared about that. They seemed to dig this punk version

of Tom Tom Club and the shows at CBGB were packed every night with lines down the block. Tina and I had a room at the Gramercy Hotel for the duration of our three-week residency. The first night I had one of the worst cases of stage fright ever. My head was swimming and my stomach was churning until we climbed onto the stage to a wild CBGB welcome. The kids went nuts and I calmed down, knowing that everything would be cool. Debbie sang "Femme Fatale" with us at the end of the first week of shows. Is it possible she was even more gorgeous than Nico that night?

At the end of the second week of shows, Dee Dee Ramone joined us, playing guitar on a super-punk version of "Psycho Killer." During the sound check he thought the song was "really tough" to remember, but on that night he rocked it.

Finally, for the encore on our last night of this CBGB run, we brought on Lou Reed. With Lou in the house we couldn't just do one song with him, we did three: "Sweet Jane," "Rock and Roll," and "Femme Fatale." There is a photo of Lou onstage with us that night looking back at Tina and he is beaming with pleasure and pride. Remembering this, I will never forget what he said to us that night in his apartment in 1976, after we'd met him for the first time backstage: "It's, like, cool you have a chick in the band. Wonder where you got that idea?"

HAPPY MONDAYS

In early 1992, our office received a call from the management of the Happy Mondays. They asked if Tina and I were available to produce their new record. The truth is that all we knew about the Happy Mondays was that they were a band from Manchester, UK, and had a string of hits on Tony Wilson's Factory Records. We had known Tony Wilson a bit and we liked him very much so we agreed to meet with the band's manager, Nathan McGough, and the bass player, Paul Ryder. In fact, they took the train up from New York City to Connecticut to meet with us. Nathan and Paul stressed the fact that the band wanted to actually play the songs on their new record, and of course they got no argument from us about that. It seems their previous couple of albums had been very successfully produced by DJs who took snippets of the band's recordings and then looped them into a dance groove that was programmed. You see, this was the time of Nirvana, the era of grunge, long, stringy hair, and flannel shirts. There was great emphasis put on keeping the music raw and unfiltered, kind of like punk but without the discipline. In fact, grunge was the antithesis of the whole Manchester dance-music thing. So Tina and I said yeah, we can dig that. You want to play on your own records? You want to make the record in Barbados? Let's do it.

No one gave us any idea what we were getting ourselves into.

The studio in Barbados was owned by the artist Eddie Grant of "Electric Avenue" fame and formerly known as a member the Equals. Sting had recorded *The Dream of the Blue Turtles* there in 1984, and Mick Jagger and Keith Richards had recently held a writing session there. It sounded like a great place to get some good work done and soak up some Caribbean sun.

Tina and I flew down to Barbados with Robin and Egan and their nanny Shelly. When we arrived we were taken to the house where we would be staying, a fantastic old sea captain's home made of limestone by Crane's Beach. There were security bars on the windows, but no glass, so birds were constantly flying in and out. It was a great house and we loved it.

Bruce Martin, our percussionist and keyboard player with Tom Tom Club, came, too, along with our engineer, Mark "Suave" Roule. They were part of our team. It took several days of troubleshooting to get the studio up to the necessary standards—power surges and fluctuations were a big problem—but eventually everything was ready for the Happy Mondays to begin.

When the band arrived very late one night, we were in for a bit of a shock. They came straight from the airport and informed us that Paul's brother, front man Shaun Ryder, had dropped and broken his six-week supply of methadone at the Manchester Airport. Nathan McGough described the scene of Sean on his hands and knees licking up as much of the methadone as he could from the floor of the airport. By the time they arrived in Barbados, Shaun was dope sick and the entire band and entourage of wives, girlfriends, and the Ryders' parents were in a state of anxious exhaustion. Nobody had told us about Shaun's bad habits. If Tina and I had been different types of people we would have quit right then and there. Instead, we tried to help everyone get settled in. Some of the band was staying in the studio's residential quarters; the rest were staying in private cottages at Sam Lord's Castle, a luxury resort several miles away. We told everyone to get a good night's sleep and tomorrow we would begin setting up to record.

The following day, we waited for the band's gear to be delivered from the airport. While we were hanging out, trying to get to know each other and understand the band's Mancunian accents, we heard screaming from outside the studio. The studio was very private, surrounded by sugar cane fields and located way back from the main road. What the ruckus was about was that Mark "Bez" Berry, the band's dancer and maraca shaker, had been

doing donuts with his newly rented open-air Jeep in the sugar cane field and flipped the car, which landed right on his upper arm, shattering it and nearly cutting it off completely. Somebody brought Bez into the studio lounge while we tried to get an emergency doctor on the phone. I remember Tina staying with Bez and trying to hold his arm together while everyone else tried not to freak out. Tina was a steady presence no matter what was happening. His arm looked really, really bad. Eventually, an ambulance arrived and took Bez to the hospital. When he returned later that evening his arm was held together with some contraption resembling the Brooklyn Bridge. Of course, Shaun wanted Bez's painkillers.

Next thing we found out was that the band had not prepared any songs. Well, that was not great news, but we had been in a similar situation with Talking Heads for *Remain in Light* and the first Tom Tom Club album so we were not overly concerned. Songs would be composed in the studio. These guys had written hits before, right? Shaun was nowhere to be found, but the rest of the band—Paul Ryder, Gary "Gaz" Whelan, Paul "PD" Davis, Mark "Moose" Day—were getting their gear sorted out. There was also a tech man, a white guy with impressive dreadlocks named Simon. Simon had some programmed beats and keyboard parts, which was a start, but he had a tough time getting them to play back because his digital gear did not love the surging power signal in Barbados.

Things were off to a bumpy start, but no one in the band seemed particularly concerned. I, however, was concerned about the fact that when I asked him what he wanted to hear in his headphones, Gary the drummer said, "Nothing. Don't want to hear the rest of the band." We found out why soon enough: Not only was the band without any prepared songs, they were seemingly unable to remember any arrangements. They would just jam endlessly without any song structure. Tina eventually devised a method of directing the band by holding up cue cards that indicated it was time to play the chorus or the bridge or return to the verse section. Mark the guitarist had a book of all the guitar chords known to man and he created guitar parts and riffs that the rest of the band used as a catalyst to create their parts.

While we were in the studio with the band, Shaun made a discovery. While there was no heroin available in Barbados, there was loads of crack cocaine. He was supposed to be writing lyrics but Shaun managed to find

a dealer and he began smoking rocks of crack instead. He tried to hide this from everybody else—as if we wouldn't notice.

Shaun and Paul's parents were more or less present in Barbados. Their mother was a sweet and charming schoolteacher who was seemingly not aware of Shaun's problems to the extent the rest of us were. Their father, who was known as Horse Man, was there at the studio to help with their gear like a roadie would. In the band's early days, he'd provided them with the musical gear that "fell off" the back of his delivery truck. He spent his down time at the studio reading *Wired*, the biography of John Belushi by Bob Woodward, as if he were preparing for the worst. He knew there was a big problem but for some reason felt powerless to do anything about it. The Mondays were from Salford, part of greater Manchester. According to the Mondays and their crew, Salford was one of the worst neighborhoods in the entire United Kingdom. It was rat-infested, and plagued with chronic poverty, unemployment, violent crime, and desperate slums. The Mondays' success was phenomenal and despite all of Shaun's bad habits, even those close to him were hard pressed to question his druggy lifestyle. After all, there was more money to be made. It was interesting to see that the band considered their label, Factory Records, to be their boss and therefore would try to spend as much money as possible before the boss told them to stop. They never understood or cared that every cent would be recouped from the band's royalties. I think their street sense told them that between the spending habits of Happy Mondays and label mate and fellow Mancunian band New Order, the Factory Records balloon was about to burst. There was also the idea that rock stars, like black sheep aristocracy, are supposed to be debauched and drug fueled, and don't worry about it because nobody gives a fuck. I had noticed this attitude particularly among British musicians, although it was really becoming a worldwide cliché.

While trying to get Shaun to write lyrics to go with the musical tracks that the band was creating without him, Tina found that he wrote best when lying on his stomach on the floor. While Shaun might have had dyslexia and ADHD, since he was unable to read and had great difficulty staying focused, somehow he was able to concentrate this way if Tina found him before his first hit of crack. After that first hit, though, it was hopeless. The band was recording very well now, but Shaun was unable or unwilling to keep up.

One evening the percussionist, Bruce Martin, found Shaun loading furniture from the guesthouse at Blue Wave Studios into the back of his car—to trade for crack. Bruce had to physically restrain Shaun from doing so. Shaun drove off without the furniture and no one had any idea where he had gone until the following day, when he called for someone to come and get him. He had driven his rental car right though a plate-glass window into the living room of some poor lady's home. In only a few weeks, the Mondays had managed to wreck five cars.

Not long after this, while in the control room of the studio, I received a call from the Barbados police force. They told me that they knew what "my boys" were up to and if they didn't behave themselves they would find themselves in jail the same way Jerry Hall did when she came down here with a suitcase full of marijuana. Barbados had zero tolerance for such things. As if Tina and I were not under enough pressure already. (As it turns out, Jerry Hall was not the right poster child for this threat, since while she had faced pot possession charges in Barbados, the charges turned out to be without basis.)

I spoke to the Mondays' manager, Nathan McGough. Nathan, who bore a strong resemblance to Paul McCartney, had told me that his mother was Thelma Pickles, who had dated three of the Beatles in their young Liverpool days. Nathan wasted no time in getting the one person that Shaun would obey, a guy named Muzza, down to Barbados. Muzza was able to keep Shaun more or less in line, but still no lyrics or vocals were forthcoming. One day we managed to get Shaun into the studio but he just wasn't able to perform. He couldn't even speak properly, never mind sing, and he kept trying to sing into the wrong side of the microphone. It was really heartbreaking.

Elektra Records sent the charming A&R executive Howard Thompson and their publicist down to see what was happening. We played him the tracks without vocals and I explained the situation. He could see the state that Shaun was in with his own eyes and it wasn't pretty. In order to blow off steam, Tina and I took Howard to see a great outdoor performance by the Mighty Sparrow that night, while the female publicist stayed behind and got loaded with Shaun on another all-night binge.

I managed to get Tony Wilson and Phil Saxe at Factory on the phone and explained to them that this record would never be finished unless they got

Shaun to dry out. We were out of time in Barbados. Their attitude was typically British rock star enabling: "Oh, that's just Shaun being Shaun." But after several more calls, including one from Gary Kurfirst's office, they finally saw the seriousness of the problem. We all went home and Shaun agreed to get treatment at the Priory in London. We would record vocals when the doctors said Shaun was okay.

When Shaun was finally clean, Tina and I flew to England and we recorded vocals at a residential studio called Comfort's Farm in Sussex. Shaun was a new man. The rest of the band was forbidden to come to the studio on his doctor's advice. Rowetta Idah, the Mondays' background vocalist, was the only exception, and she was exceptional. She added a lot of power to the tracks. Tina worked with Shaun on his lyrics when he got stuck. It was the month of May, and on the eighth, Jerry Harrison sent a stripper to the studio to celebrate my birthday with me. She put on a little show for a few minutes and then whispered in my ear that she was available for private partying. I told her I was married and sent her off with a nice tip despite some protestation from Shaun.

Shaun kept it together and delivered his vocals with great panache. He was still drinking—in this case, Boddingtons Pub Ale—but there was no other substance abuse that we could see. Within ten days the album was ready for mixing.

We brought Steven Stanley up to New York from Jamaica to mix the album, titled *Yes Please!*, at Axis Studios, upstairs from where Studio 54 once was. Everyone was pleased with the mixes and there was great relief all around. When it was released in September 1992, Tina and I felt it was a miracle that any record had been made at all.

STRANGERS IN PARADISE

I had done some sailing while I was at boarding school in Virginia on the Rappahannock River, but I had never cruised on a boat overnight. After Robin was born, Tina's father chartered a small sailboat out of Nassau and took us on a cruise of the Exumas. Even baby Robin came along. Staying out on the water for two weeks, we had an absolute ball. Tina and I learned that sailing was a great way to clear our heads and decompress from the music business. Sailing was not only a good time, it was healthy.

We decided to buy a sailboat of our own. Tina and her father contacted a good broker on the east coast and started looking at boats for sale. The broker knew that we didn't want just any boat. We told him we wanted a boat with classic lines that was good for cruising with a family, not some floating cocktail-party boat. He told Tina, there is this boat and that boat and then there is *Katrinka*. *Katrinka* was owned by a Connecticut family named Winder who had commissioned the great nautical architect Bill Tripp to design her. She had been built in Bristol, Rhode Island, and had the classic lines that real sailors dream about. She was a forty-eight-foot-long sloop with a center cockpit. The steering wheel was mounted on a pivoting podium. She had a diesel engine, a neat galley, and two heads, and could sleep a party of eight. She was yar and we bought her.

Our first cruise on *Katrinka* was traveling from New England to the

Katrinka undersail in the Exumas, Bahamas.

Bahamas on the Intercoastal Waterway. We chose to make this trip slowly, stopping to enjoy the sights and regional cuisine along the way. Also, I had to fly back to New York once a week to an outpatient clinic, where I was learning to straighten myself out. Let's just say that even I realized that I had developed a bad problem with cocaine. I was in a special program for successful people with drug problems. Tina was concerned that I might die, and I don't blame her. I had been bingeing for years, but mostly keeping it under control. Being in the music business, I could always tell myself that some other guy I knew was in much worse shape than I was. Tina took baby Robin to France for the summer of '84 and asked me not to come. After she left I found myself buying an ounce of coke and not stopping until it was gone. I was up for nine days. Nine days wandering from party to party, club to club, without sleep and not going home except to take a shower and change my clothes. I was not all right. In retrospect, I realize that I was in mourning for the Talking Heads dream I'd had. I could see what was happening to us after so many years of hard work and dedication. I was sad and

depressed, but of course cocaine and alcohol were not going to help. What helped me, finally, was Tina. She demanded that I get treatment or our marriage was over.

Sailing was a way to renew myself and learn self-reliance. Tina's father, Ralph, was a great skipper who had a very kind and patient way of teaching us how to handle such a big boat. *Katrinka* had a centerboard that, when raised, enabled us to get into the shallow anchorages of the Bahamas with ease. We did run aground every once in a while, but they say if you haven't gone aground, you haven't really sailed the Bahamas. For weeks and then months we cruised the islands of the Bahamas, visiting the Abacos, Eleuthera, the Exumas, Long Island, Cat Island, New Providence, and all sorts of beautiful tiny cays in between.

One time we found ourselves in Governor's Harbour, Eleuthera. We were at anchor in the harbor on an early Saturday morning and the kids wanted us to make French toast, but we were out of bread. So I rowed the dinghy ashore and sat on the steps of the only small grocery store in town and waited for it to open. It was a warm, sunny morning and there was not a soul around. Governor's Harbour is a very tiny out-island town and although there was a family-style Club Med across the harbor, at 7:00 A.M. the town was completely deserted and quiet.

As I was waiting and sitting in the shade and the temperature got hotter and hotter, I noticed what appeared to be a huge white balloon floating down the beach, brightly reflecting the sun.

As this big white thing in the distance came closer I began to see that it was, in fact, a person wearing a huge white cotton caftan and gliding slowly in my direction. As the apparition got closer I began to recognize who it was, but thought it couldn't be. It couldn't be Divine, the actor I had once met at Phebe's on the Bowery some years ago, the transvestite star of *Pink Flamingos* and *Female Trouble*. But, it was! Divine, sporting a bleach-blond crew cut, came up from the beach and glided past me while giving me a beatific smile and a little wave. I said, "Hi, Divine" and Divine said, "Oh, hiiiiiiiiii!" and then kept walking on though the dreamy calm Bahamian town. The store opened shortly after that and I bought some bread and eggs and rowed back to the boat.

Once at Staniel Cay in the Exumas, where James Bond's Thunderball Grotto is, I again rowed ashore to buy some groceries at a tiny general store.

While getting back in the dingy a gentleman on the dock looking out over the harbor asked me, "Isn't that *Katrinka*?" I said, "Yes, sir. That's her." He introduced himself as Thomas Hoving, the director of the Metropolitan Museum of Art. He had sailed a Bermuda Race aboard her with the previous owners. He said, "I love that boat. You know, most people have only seen her from behind."

Another time I took Tina and the boys to a beach not far from Nassau that was accessible only by boat unless you owned a home there. We took our secondhand Mako 25 called *Cool Runnings*. When we arrived at the spot, I secured the anchor and swam the short distance to shore with the boys. Tina stayed on board to catch some rays and take a rest. It was a gorgeous day. The water was lovely and warm. We were swimming and playing on the beach when I spied a single, solitary figure dressed all in black walking slowly our way. As the figure came closer I thought, *No, it can't be*, but there she was: Patti Smith, the High Priestess of Punk. I said, "Hi, Patti." She looked at me with surprise or paranoia or perhaps both. I said, "It's me, Chris

Frantz from Talking Heads. Good to see you." She still seemed extremely uncomfortable to be recognized in such beautiful surroundings. She said, "I'm only here for my boyfriend's sister's wedding." I said, "Oh, that's nice." She looked at me like I was crazy and said, "I've gotta go," and turned and walked away in the direction she had come from. She was probably the only person on the entire island dressed in black in such warm weather. Then again, if she hadn't been, I might not have recognized her.

We sailed back and forth from Nassau to Maine many times over the years. I can tell you that sailing north on the outside in the deep ocean can be one ass-kicking ride, particularly

Robin and Egan aboard Katrinka *in Maine.* around Cape Hatteras. In fact, it was

there in the "graveyard of the Atlantic" that we drank a toast to one of Tina's great-grandfathers, a sea captain who had gone down with the ship. In our case, we lived to tell the tale. You could say we'd been sailing for years through the uncharted world of art and rock and roll, weathering storms, rolling water, and changing tides. But it was much more romantic to do it in a boat.

WITHOUT ADVENTURES WE WON'T HAVE STORIES

Tina said to me, "Without adventures we won't have stories."

In 1991 David sneaked out of Talking Heads. We got a call from the *Los Angeles Times* to confirm something that David had told one of their writers. He told them, "Talking Heads has broken up or whatever you want to call it." We never had a meeting to decide we were breaking up. We'd never even discussed it. In the last meeting we had with David, in his SoHo loft, David shouted at me, Tina, Jerry, and Gary, "You should be calling me an asshole!" He was upset with us for keeping our cool in the face of his saying that he no longer wished to work with us. This was after keeping us on hold for several years. He had told other people this same thing so many times before and then come back to the band that we assumed he would change his mind. Evidently, a guy at Warner named Tim Carr—who later was murdered with a sword in his own apartment in Thailand—had told him that nobody at Warner would take his solo career seriously as long as Talking Heads was still in action. We believed just the opposite, that he could have his solo career *and* Talking Heads. After all, we'd done just that with Tom Tom Club. In fact, Gary had worked out a deal with Mo Ostin at Warner in which David would receive a million dollars per solo album for ten albums as long as he continued to make Talking Heads albums every two or three

years. Unfortunately for us and our fans, when Mo sat down with David to discuss the deal, he said nothing to David about Talking Heads' future. He gave David his solo deal with no obligation to continue with Talking Heads. Mo must have thought that David was the goose that laid the golden egg when, in fact, Talking Heads was the goose and David was the golden egg.

David stopped taking our phone calls and all communication from him ceased. Tina tried calling his office and his secretary said he was out of town even though we knew he wasn't and Tina could plainly hear his voice in the background. This was a sad time for us and our fans. As sometimes happens in a divorce, people take sides, even though they don't really know the whole story. I asked Gary Kurfirst if there was anything we had done to cause this divide with David and he said no, that we were the best friends David ever had. Then a few days later David fired Gary after insisting that he should manage only him and drop the rest of us. Gary told him that, as a manager, it was his job to keep the band together. David reneged on paying Gary his commission for his solo deal, too. Our lawyers asked, "Why does David treat you like he hates you? What did you do to him?" Then they were fired, too. David was cleaning house of all the people who had done right by him.

EMI sued Talking Heads because David told them we never intended to honor our contract. Warner did not sue because they knew better. David even signed a deal with EMI giving them full ownership of our back catalog. Why? Tina said no way she was signing that and so did Jerry and I. It was a very terrible time.

Tina and I had to do something. So, you know what we did? We built a great recording studio of our own and started making and producing records again. We spent more time with our family and friends. We became more active in our community. In 1990, as Tom Tom Club we toured with Jerry Harrison, Debbie Harry, and the Ramones on the Escape from New York tour all over North America. Perry Farrell of Jane's Addiction saw the tour at the Greek Theater in LA and later told Gary it gave him the idea to create Lollapalooza.

We've had a number of different Tom Tom Club lineups until we finally arrived at a great one. Victoria Clamp Palagy is our most loyal and beloved vocalist who stuck with us for thirty years. She received a degree in psychology after studying and writing papers in the back of a tour bus. Bruce Martin on percussion and keyboards has also been a real champion. We

originally hired him in 1990 as a percussionist and he was superb. Then one day he said, "You know, I can play keyboards, too." We gave him a shot and found out that he was a fantastic keyboard player who understood and appreciated our deceptively simple musical approach. Robby Aceto, Fuzz Sangiovanni, and Pablo Martin have each in turn rocked the guitar for us with uniquely impressive skills. All are wonderful guys. We were very fortunate to have Steve Scales and Abdou M'Boup on percussion. They both knew how to make each show a funky celebration. Mystic Bowie, a real Maroon tribesman from the Blue Mountains of Jamaica, sang additional vocals for us with tremendous *joie de vivre*. Together we have toured the world playing every type of venue, from tiny clubs to enormous festivals.

In the autumn of 2001, Tina and I got a call from Gary that Talking Heads was to be inducted into the Rock and Roll Hall of Fame along with our old friends the Ramones. Both bands were being inducted in their first year of eligibility. You can say what you will about the legitimacy of the organization and the people who run it, but I can tell you as a musician, when you get the call that you're being inducted into the Rock and Roll Hall of Fame, it is good news. In other good news, David Byrne and Jerry Harrison had agreed to perform with us at the induction ceremony. Talking Heads, at least for one performance, were reuniting after not performing live together for eighteen years.

We rehearsed at a small rehearsal studio in midtown Manhattan. It felt a little weird to be in the same room with David. He had not spoken to us for ages—all of our business was conducted with intermediaries—but things went well. Tina and I had been touring the world with Tom Tom Club so we were in good performing shape. Likewise, Jerry and David were on point. We asked Steve Scales and Bernie Worrell to join us, too. They never failed to rock the party.

We decided we would play "Psycho Killer," "Life During Wartime," and "Burning Down the House." Then we would play in an All-Star Jam of "Take Me to the River" with Steve Cropper of Booker T. and the M.G.'s and Sam Moore of Sam & Dave. We rehearsed for three afternoons and it was almost like old times. Everyone got along fine and we had fun together. Our faithful accountant, Bert Padell, brought us a bottle of Dom Perignon

and we toasted one another as bandmates. I said, "We should do this more often!"

On the day of our induction at the Waldorf Astoria Ballroom we set up our gear, sound checked and went to our rooms to get dressed for the evening. I did my best to remain calm. I was sporting some fine black leather trousers I bought for the occasion at The Leather Man on Christopher Street. Tina looked fabulous in a sheer black-silk T-shirt and a pair of pants she'd bought in New York when she was eighteen years old. Her jacket was a hand-me-down her sister-in-law Lally Weymouth had given her in 1969. We were ready to party.

We had two tables. David and Jerry sat at one table with their wives, Bonnie and Carol, Jerry's children, and David's manager at the time. Tina and I sat with our longtime manager, Gary Kurfirst, and his wife Phyllis, along with Bernie and Steve, Dee Dee Ramone, and our sons Robin and Egan. Robin and Egan were thrilled to sit with Dee Dee, who leaned over to Robin and said, "Ya know, your father is a real man."

Isaac Hayes kicked off the night with a tremendous version of his "Theme from *Shaft*" and then he was inducted. Brenda Lee, Gene Pitney, Chet Atkins and Tom Petty and the Heartbreakers were also inducted that night.

Because Joey had recently died of cancer, the Ramones could not perform but Green Day played some pitch-perfect versions of Ramones' songs. Robin and Egan ran to the front of the stage to pogo, pump their fists, and sing along. Tina and I felt very proud of our friends the Ramones. Eddie Vedder inducted them and pointed out that while the Ramones had never had a top ten record, their copycats had sold in the millions.

Then finally it was our turn. It was not our choice to be inducted by Anthony Kiedis of the Red Hot Chili Peppers, but he did a good job of it. His speech was hilarious. He said, "Talking Heads made me feel smart. Then I wanted to have sex with a lot of librarians." When we marched up to the stage, in order to show our gratitude, we brought Hilly Kristal with us. This was Tina's idea and it was a good one. Without Hilly and his bar CBGB, where we could play our original songs and learn our craft, there may not have been any Talking Heads. Everybody made a short acceptance speech. Mine was the shortest. I said, "I'd like to thank the Rock and Roll Hall of Fame for giving this band a happy ending."

We made our way over to our instruments and played the first song we had ever written. If you think it's easy to rock a crowd of music business executives dressed up in tuxedos, think again. But we got them going with "Psycho Killer." By the end of the song, I looked out at the smiling faces of Gary Kurfirst, Seymour Stein, Chris Blackwell, and our longtime agent Frank Barsalona. There was a wonderful feeling in the room.

We didn't know it but some unwitting stagehand had pulled the plug on our analog synthesizers after the sound check, so when Jerry and Bernie launched into "Burning Down the House," the keyboards were wildly out of tune and they had to tune them on the fly. There's always something, even when you're being inducted into the Rock and Roll Hall Of Fame, but what was really fantastic is that our children finally got to see us perform together live.

After we took our bows, we were ushered into a press conference. We posed together for some photos and answered a few questions, and then it was time for the real party to begin. Upstairs in the Waldorf Astoria all the record companies had big parties going on. Being on Sire, which was owned by Warner, we went to the Warner's party. There was champagne, and ice sculptures chilling caviar, shrimp, and lobster. There was a beautiful array of decadent sweets and cognacs. The Ramones, Tom Petty and the Heart-breakers, and Talking Heads were finally enjoying the fruits of our labors. Yes, we were a long way from CBGB. As I was reflecting on the evening, Bonnie Byrne came up to me and asked, "Chris, have you seen David?" I told her, "I'm sure he's around here somewhere. We were just doing a press conference together. He'll be here soon."

Dee Dee Ramone, looking fit and well in his purple silk suit, gave his award statue to Gary in appreciation. He also gave the black tie he wore that night to our son Egan. Two months later, Dee Dee was found dead of a heroin overdose alone in his Los Angeles apartment. Johnny Ramone died of cancer not long after that. Finally, Tommy Ramone, one of my favorite drummers of all time, perished from cancer as well. I wrote a tribute to him in *Rolling Stone*. I'm so glad they had this night of recognition before they died. I wish Joey had been there, too, but surely he was there in spirit.

Tina and I mingled, arm in arm, sipping champagne and basking in the afterglow of a very long week when Bonnie Byrne came up to us again. She said, "I still can't find David anywhere. He isn't answering his phone." I tried

Tina remains in love.

to call him on my phone, but it went straight to voicemail. I left a message that Bonnie was worried about him. Bonnie decided to leave so I walked her downstairs and put her into a cab. I told her I was sure he'd turn up, but this was a puzzling situation.

When I finally reached David the following afternoon, I told him that Bonnie was terribly worried about him. Was he at home? He said he would not be going home. He said he was leaving her. He had chosen the night we were inducted into the Hall of Fame to leave his wife. When I asked him why, he told me, "It's time to move on."

Tina and I continue to have a wonderfully romantic life together. We've been married for forty-two years. We treat each other with real love and we have many good friends who have shown us their love, too. Both of our sons have made us proud and have become artists in their own right—Robin in music production and Egan as a painter and sculptor. Both of them are really good at what they do and have developed hard-earned followings of their own. Tina and I have taught them to be honest, loving,

and kind. Tina told them the opposite of love is not hate. The opposite of love is selfishness.

We are devoted to our two beagles, Poppy and Kiki, and we take them with us to Tina's family home in France. Each year we stay a little bit longer. Poppy has crossed the Atlantic twenty-two times and Kiki is right behind her. They love Paris and the French countryside—who doesn't? They adore a friendly French café. If only they were allowed in museums.

Tina and I have had so many good adventures together and for that I am ever thankful. When people say, "It's time to move on," I am not down with that. When speaking about my family, my friends, and my band, I am not a person who "moves on." I remain—and I remain in love.

PHOTO CREDITS

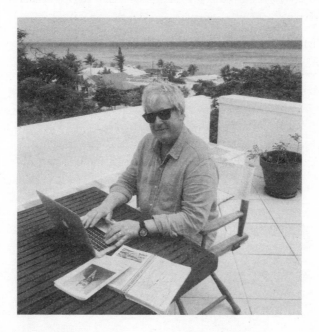

INDEX